Nietzsche and Emerson

Nietzsche and Emerson
An Elective Affinity

George J. Stack

OHIO UNIVERSITY PRESS   ATHENS

B 3317
S 654
1992

Printed in the United States of America
All rights reserved

Ohio University Press books are printed on acid-free paper ∞

Library of Congress Cataloging-in-Publication Data

Stack, George J.
    Nietzsche and Emerson : an elective affinity / George J.
Stack.
        p.   cm.
    Includes bibliographical references and index.
    ISBN 0-8214-1037-7
    1. Nietzsche, Friedrich Wilhelm, 1844-1900.
  2. Emerson, Ralph Waldo, 1803-1882—Philosophy.
  3. Emerson, Ralph Waldo, 1803-1882—Influence.
    I. Title.
B3317.S654   1992
193—dc20
                                                92-27599
                                                    CIP

Contents

Preface

For almost eight decades now there have been rumors about the affiliation between the writings of the quintessential American essayist and poet, Ralph Waldo Emerson, and the philosophy of Friedrich Nietzsche. In recent years the veracity of these rumors has been supported by bits and pieces of evidence presented by literary critics and a few philosophers. However, despite two works on the Emerson-Nietzsche connection by German scholars, the extent and depth of the relation between these literary philosophers has not been explored. The burden of this study is the exploration of this question.

By a happy coincidence, a reanimation of interest in the thought of Emerson and the philosophy of Nietzsche has come about during the same time period. Up to this point the reappraisal of their thought and writings has run on parallel tracks. But it is time that the intersection of these tracks be examined more carefully. Tracing the profound influence of Emerson on Nietzsche may engender surprise in some, perhaps many. I know it surprised me.

There has been much talk lately about the "new Nietzsche." But the tracking of the host of ideas, insights, and philosophical themes that are transmitted from Emerson to Nietzsche reveals, I believe, a new Emerson. Previously one heard that there is a parallel between Emerson's philosophy of self-reliant individuality and the existential philosophical movement in Europe. Emerson does not merely occupy the same intellectual and psychological space as the European existentialists; rather, his surprisingly radical thought entered directly into the bloodstream of this philosophical movement by way of Nietzsche. For more than two-and-a-half decades Nietzsche read and reread Emerson with great enjoyment and, as we shall see, with even greater profit. With uncharacteristic zeal Nietzsche praises the *Amerikaner* almost without reservation. True, he tells a friend in a letter from 1876 that the Emerson of the Second Series of *Essays* seems to have "grown old," that these later essays lack the luster and richness of *Nature* and his earlier writings. But then he ingenuously adds that Emerson has grown "too much enamored of life." He knew, as I shall attempt to show, that this wasn't true. He knew this because one of the centerpieces of his philosophy, the tragic optimism of his "Dionysian pessimism," was modeled on the insights of the American thinker. He knew this because he saw, as many American critics of the time did not, that Emerson was a hard-headed thinker who was quite aware of the tragic dimension of human existence, of what Emerson in his youth called "the ghastly reality of things." In fact, Nietzsche understood more of what Emerson was saying, as I shall seek to illustrate, than any of his contemporaries. As the numerous Emersonian themes in his own philosophical works amply show, Nietzsche was probably the most thorough and accurate interpreter of the thought of Emerson extant.

Nietzsche greatly admired Emerson's literary style and on quite a few occasions paid it the highest compliment: he imitated it. He not only admired his style, but he admired the man to the point of idealization, to the point of adopting him as an *alter ego*. A surprising number of things he says about himself and his own writings are extracted from the writings of Emerson. Even some of his self-descriptions or self-references in his letters echo comments or observations of the American poet and essayist!

The literary approach to philosophy that Nietzsche adopts, even in regard to the most serious issues, has bothered some commentators on his thought. His philosophy, admittedly with some justification, is thought to be "dangerous." But such flirtations with dangerous ideas and principles are not alien to Emerson in an antinomic mood. In fact, it is Emerson who tempts him to be a dangerous thinker, to write dangerously. In popular misinterpretations of the philosophy of Nietzsche he is often taken to be a spokesman for Mephistopheles. But in this regard, as in others, he is adopting the boldness of Emerson, a man who, by his own admission, serves, at times, as the "devil's attorney." The problem is that, as in the case of Nietzsche, there are many Emersons. It is not so much, as some literary critics have said, that both Emerson and Nietzsche have a number of "voices," as it is that their individual voices have an enormous range. Or, to change the metaphor, they are always, like serpents, shedding their psychic and intellectual skins. In "Montaigne" Emerson tells us that "The philosophy we want is one of fluxions and mobility." And that is the one he gives us, the one Nietzsche gives us. In the case of these two elusive thinkers we are not offered a philosophy, but, as Nietzsche once said of his own writings, "philosophies."

Emerson and Nietzsche are frequently criticized for the same reason: they are contradictory, self-contradictory. They continually seem to be engaged in arguments with themselves, adopting a standpoint and then, somewhere, criticizing it. But what critics consider a vice could be seen as a virtue. They are many-sided; they see many sides of an issue, a philosophical question. They are both restless thinkers, seekers, searchers, *Versucher*—"attempters." On this score Nietzsche says what Emerson thinks and displays: "The will to a system is a lack of integrity." But this is not the only reason for the paradoxes in the writings of both thinkers. For both Emerson and Nietzsche see man, life, and the world as riddled with ontological paradoxes. Existence for both is dialectical, oppositional, antagonistic. Polarities abound in their thought, in their writings, within pages, even within paragraphs. The dialectic of a Hegel seeks out mediations and syntheses: thesis, antithesis, synthesis. But for Emerson and Nietzsche there is no facile mediation; they let the antitheses stand because that is what actuality shows them; this is what they experience; this is what they feel. Joy and suffering, fate and freedom, good and evil, time and eternity, spirit and nature, the ordinary and the extraordinary are intertwined, ensnarled. The thought of Emerson and Nietzsche reflects this dynamic interplay. Reality for both is a "slippery Proteus."

It goes without saying that the American and the German thinker are passionate literary philosophers. What both seem to want to express—to couch in poetic, metaphorical language—is the *pathos* of existence. Despite the power of their rhetoric, the strong aesthetic component in their writings, both Emerson and Nietzsche seem to want to transcend language, to experience life fully, to immerse themselves in the stream of life. Philosophy is not an end in itself. It ought, ideally, to enhance life. Beyond reflection, beyond ratiocination, beyond theories, beyond interpretations lies a goal that can be discerned in the interstices of the texts of Emerson and Nietzsche: *ekstasis*.

Those who look for closure and completion, a theoretical tying of the knot, in the texts of Emerson and Nietzsche will be disappointed. Despite the forcefulness with which they present their insights, ideas, and values, neither wants to complete the circle of thought. Both offer reflective guesses at the riddle of the Sphinx. They are repelled by a dogmatic summing up. Although he is speaking of Montaigne, what Emerson says is applicable to himself, as well as to his unknown German friend: "An angular dogmatic house would be rent to chips and splinters in this storm of many elements."

In what follows, the "many elements" that Emerson unknowingly transmitted to a German philologist-turned-philosopher will be examined. I will show that Nietzsche's indebtedness to Emerson has been underestimated. This is especially so, surprisingly enough, in regard to theories and conceptions that have been, for almost a century now, attributed to Nietzsche's creative imagination. Through Nietzsche's assimilation of the thought of Emerson, the American thinker *par excellence,* it entered European thought and subsequently influenced more writers, poets, and philosophers than has previously been imagined.

Richard Rorty has said that Emerson introduced a "new genre" of philosophical writing. He is right about this. But we can see this new genre "writ large"—to a surprising extent—in the dramatic and intense philosophy of Nietzsche. In the case of these two thinkers we can see clearly that the line between literature and philosophy that has been the focus of so much recent discussion is often erased. But it must be said that neither Emerson nor Nietzsche, despite their rhetorical and poetic skills, can be contained within the aesthetic circle of literature. Both seem to desire to communicate to their readers Rilke's admonition: "It is necessary to change one's life." And not only to change one's life, but to change one's life-orientation, one's way of experiencing life and the world, one's feelings. Emerson and Nietzsche wrote for themselves and for ideal readers who would not only respond to their coruscating style, respond intellectually and impersonally to what they said, but who would respond to their sentiments and passions, to their culture and humanity. Without the existential reference of their language the panache and power of their writings would remain, but the value of their thought would be impoverished.

The echoes of Emerson's stylish insights and remarks *en passant* reverberate through the labyrinth of Nietzsche's discourse. I have not traced all of the threads of relation that connect the two, but have concentrated on the major themes that first appear in Emerson's prose and then reappear thinly disguised, but enhanced, embellished, raised to a higher power, in Nietzsche's writings.

Although it is not explicitly stated in this study of an elective affinity, an overriding theme is one which was expressed succinctly by Maurice Maeterlinck in *On Emerson and Other Essays.* Though it is said of Emerson, it applies to Nietzsche as well. "He has given an . . . acceptable meaning to this life which no longer has its traditional horizons, and . . . he has been able to show us that it is strange enough, profound enough, and great enough to have need of no other than itself."

Abbreviations

Nietzsche's Works

A *Der Antichrist (The Anti-Christ/The Antichristian)*
AsZ *Also sprach Zarathustra (Thus Spoke Zarathustra)*
EH *Ecce Homo*
FW *Die fröhliche Wissenschaft (Joyful Wisdom/The Gay Science)*
G *Die Götzen-Dämmerung (Twilight of the Idols)*
GM *Zur Genealogie der Moral (The Genealogy of Morals)*
GOA *Nietzsches Werke. Grossoktavausgabe.*
GT *Die Geburt der Tragödie (The Birth of Tragedy)*
HKG *Historisch-Kritische Gesamtausgabe.*
JGB *Jenseits von Gut und Böse (Beyond Good and Evil)*
M *Morgenröte (Dawn/Daybreak)*
MAM *Menschliches, Allzumenschliches (Human, All-Too-Human)*
SW *Sämtliche Werke (Complete Works)*
UB *Unzeitgemässe Betrachtungen I-IV (Untimely Meditations)*

Emerson's Essays

COL *The Conduct of Life. The Complete Works of Ralph Waldo Emerson*, vol. VI. Boston and New York: Houghton Mifflin, 1860.
EE *Emerson's Essays.* New York: Dutton, 1906. Reprint, 1980.
PE *The Portable Emerson.* Ed. Carl Bode. New York: Viking Penguin, 1946. Reprint, 1981.
RMNAL *Representative Men, Nature, Addresses and Lectures.* Boston and New York: Houghton Mifflin, 1876.

Chapter 1

From Emerson to Nietzsche

> *There are persons who are not actors, not speakers, but influences.*
>
> *[Ralph Waldo Emerson, "Divinity School Address"]*
>
> *. . . of the six or seven teachers whom each man wants among his contemporaries, it often happens that one or two of them live on the other side of the world.*
>
> *[Ralph Waldo Emerson, "Culture"]*

In recent years there has been a parallel resurgence of interest in the writings and thought of Ralph Waldo Emerson and in the philosophy of Friedrich Nietzsche. In spite of a general awareness of an association between these seemingly quite different literary philosophers, very few commentators or interpreters have focused on the direct relationship between Emerson and Nietzsche. Until early in the twentieth century the primary relationship between American thought and German philosophy during the period of the American literary renaissance was seen in terms of the impact that German idealism in general and Immanuel Kant in particular had on the transcendental movement and on Emerson. Over two decades ago, René Wellek covered this ground thoroughly in *Confrontations.*[1]

The direct and quite specific influence of Emerson's philosophical reflections on Nietzsche's thought was known in France over

seventy years ago,[2] even though the intellectual affiliation between
the American poet and essayist and the German iconoclastic philosopher was treated then, as since then, rather superficially in
terms of a few selected ideas and valuations that were shared in
common. In an early, sympathetic study—William Salter's *Nietzsche the Thinker*—there was a recognition of the parallels between
central ideas in Emerson's essays and those of Nietzsche. Ironically, Salter was completely unaware of the direct impact that Nietzsche's reading of Emerson had on his thought, even though he
often elucidated a remark, observation, or insight of Nietzsche's
by quoting from Emerson!

For some time now German historians of literature and some
commentators on Nietzsche have known about the relation between "the sage of Concord" and the German thinker who seems
the antithesis of the "optimistic," "cheerful," and "genteel"
Emerson.[3] A number of American literary critics have, from time
to time, called attention to the linkage between Emerson and
Nietzsche, but they have not delved into the detailed nature of this
curious association.[4] Ironically, the American deconstructionist
critics who have probed and dismantled Nietzsche's texts seem to
be uninterested in or unaware of his relationship to Emerson.
Even though a few American philosophers—notably Stanley Cavell—[5] are cognizant of the connection between the central figure of
literary transcendentalism and the philosopher of "the will to
power" and "the transvaluation of values," they have not pursued
this rich and revealing clue to some of the major and many of the
minor themes in Nietzsche's philosophy. Those European and
American philosophers who have discovered a "new Nietzsche"
or who are busy reinterpreting the "old Nietzsche" occasionally
spy a thread of relation between Emerson and Nietzsche, but they
approach this association gingerly.

Despite the work of German scholars, French commentators on
Nietzsche, American literary critics, and a coterie of American
philosophers on the theme that is at the center of my concern,
there has been no serious effort made to display in detail the philosophical and valuational lines of influence that closely link the
American poet and essayist who is deemed the quintessential
American writer and thinker (or, as Harold Bloom has said, "our
central man") and the iconoclastic nineteenth-century German
philosopher.

In the case of the profound and long-lasting influence of Ralph
Waldo Emerson on Nietzsche the thinker and Nietzsche the man,

we are dealing with a deep one-way relationship between a polished essayist, an original poet, an admired teacher in the art of wisdom and literary style and an unknown philologist-turned-philosopher who became the former's ardent and unsuspected admirer. We are dealing with an intellectual and spiritual relationship that is so profound and pervasive that the word *influence* doesn't do justice to it. For Nietzsche absorbed as much as he could from Emerson and developed and expanded a compressed, economically expressed philosophy of nature, life, and culture that is dispersed throughout Emerson's insightful writings.

Friedrich Nietzsche was born in 1844 and died in 1900. Emerson lived from 1803 to 1882. They never met. They never corresponded. And, of course, Emerson never heard of the German philosopher who lived in virtual obscurity and whose writings only became known, in any significant way, after his death at the age of fifty-six. Moreover, Nietzsche was mentally ill for the last eleven years of his life. Although there is controversy concerning the nature of his illness (even speculation, in some quarters, that he may have feigned mental illness), the consensus seems to be that his illness was a consequence of the contraction of syphilis in his youth during one of his extremely rare sexual encounters, probably with a prostitute. So Emerson had an unknown quasi-disciple in Germany who read him avidly in his youth and who returned to his writings for enjoyment, inspiration, or stimulus of his own thought over a long period of time. Nietzsche rarely travelled without his Emerson. And Emerson's *Essays* were quite literally treasured by him: the works of Emerson, in German translation, were the most frequently read books in his library. Over a twenty-six year period allusions to, or references to, Emerson cropped up in Nietzsche's notes or letters. His affinity with this man he knew only through his translated writings was so strong that he often referred to him as if he were a personal friend. In his published and unpublished writings Nietzsche made over a hundred direct or indirect references to Emerson. He often paraphrased him, adopted his tone or imagery, and appropriated his phrases.

Nietzsche's copies of Emerson's essays (the first and second series, as well as those comprising *The Conduct of Life*) are filled with heavy underlinings and occasional marginalia. Here and there in the margins of Emerson's works he wrote: *"Ja!"*, *"Das ist recht!"*, *"Das ist wahr!"*, *"Gut!"*, *"Sehr Gut!"* Without exception, he was enthusiastic about what Emerson wrote. He expressed no

critical comments, remarks, or asides. This reaction to a thinker
was atypical of a philosopher who was notoriously critical of so
many other writers and thinkers. It coincided with the general favorable remarks he made about Emerson in his published and unpublished writings and in his letters.

The first encounter Nietzsche had with the writings of Emerson was in 1862 when he was seventeen years old. He was immediately entranced by his literary style, as well as by his thoughtful
and insightful philosophical wisdom. The assertoric and rhetorical
form of Emerson's discourse, its grand manner, its lack of technicalities, suited Nietzsche perfectly in the earliest stages of his
philosophical development. The *Versuche* or *Essays* of Emerson
probably appealed to him not only because of the richness of the
ideas he found in them, but because of their polished, aphoristic
style, their similarity to the fragmentary writings of the pre-
Socratic philosophers with which he was familiar in his classical
philological studies. Emerson's assured conclusions have the ring
of authority about them. He persuades because of the obvious sin-
cerity of his opinions, the thoughtfulness they reveal, and the panache with which he presents them. The confident, sermonlike
pronouncements of Emerson are value-laden judgments, com-
pacted theories condensed to paragraphs, to sentences. The compressed insight suggesting long and hard reflections that led up to
it is Emerson's *forte.*

Although Nietzsche was quite capable of writing treatises, as
The Birth of Tragedy and *On the Genealogy of Morals* illustrate, he
preferred to express himself in an aphoristic form. Although this
aphoristic style was shaped by La Rochefoucauld, Chamfort, Lichtenberg and others, it was also surely suggested to him by
Emerson's taut, chiseled paragraphs and sentences. Carefully
crafted sentences in Emerson's essays jump out of their paragraphs
and threaten to cut short the continuity of his thought. Thus, in
the section on "Language" in his first book, *Nature,* we are told
that "the corruption of man is followed by the corruption of language." We are hardly tempted to finish the paragraph. We already know what is going to be said. The aphoristic sentence has
epitomized the thought of the entire paragraph. Nietzsche seems
to have responded to such compressed insights since he underlined
such sentences in his copy of Emerson's essays and, in his notes,
he never quoted long passages from his writings.

If the association between the sage of Concord and Nietzsche
were only a matter of analogies of literary style, tone, or form, it

would be interesting enough, but a rather minor link between two thinkers who might otherwise be thought to have nothing in common. That Nietzsche was impressed by and influenced by Emerson as a polished stylist is simply a fact. That he greatly admired the man is well known. What is less known in English-speaking countries than in Germany is that a great deal of the core of Nietzsche's philosophy was profoundly influenced by numerous aspects of Emerson's reflections. Many ideas that are closely identified with Nietzsche—ideas concerning nature, life, man, power, society, and the individual—as well as some of his central, positive, and visionary conceptions, were originally suggested to him by his deeply sympathetic reading of Emerson. His ingenuity in relation to Emerson is that he was able to build so much out of the materials he found in Emerson's insightful observations, his almost casual asides. Given that Nietzsche worked up a sentence, a paragraph, a short essay in Emerson into a theory, a philosophical doctrine, it would not be too much to say that Emerson served as Socrates to Nietzsche's Plato.

What is discernible in what Nietzsche called his "philosophies" forms an intricate, syncretistic tapestry. The list of writers, scientists, poets, and philosophers to whom he responded in a positive or negative way is a rather long one. Very few philosophers, despite their technical prowess, their logical and analytical skills, have been as responsive as Nietzsche to such a variety of cultural resources. His learning encompassed Greco-Roman literature, music, poetry from Anacreon to Baudelaire, representative eighteenth- and nineteenth-century scientists, history (specifically, Thucydides, Gibbon, Lecky, Buckle, Treitschke), oriental scriptures and philosophy, and a raft of contemporary German thinkers. His familiarity with Western literature extended from Petronius to Mark Twain. If we sifted through the bewildering variety of poets, novelists, essayists, historians, scientists, and philosophers with whom he was acquainted through his voracious reading habits throughout his productive years, we would be able to identify those who, positively or negatively, most stimulated his thinking and would come to see why he was essentially a philosopher of culture. In one case there is a deep personal influence that is not primarily based upon a study of a series of works alone: the close personal relationship, in friendship at first and then later in alienation and hostility, with the composer, Richard Wagner.

At first, Nietzsche was an admirer of Wagner and his Schopenhauerian music-dramas, a champion of his project to rejuvenate

German culture. Later, he turned against the man, his music, and his aesthetic ideal of tragic resignation. Although Nietzsche was initially attracted to the image of "the man of the future" extolled in Wagner's *Siegfried,* he soon began to look upon Wagner's portrait of a cultural hero as limited and negativistic. His conception of the *Übermensch* was, at least in part, intended as an anti-Wagnerian image of the man of the future.

In spite of his reputation for originality, his frequent proclamations of his own originality, as well as his genuinely original form of expression and thought, Nietzsche was surprisingly susceptible to intellectual influence. A great deal of his energy was expended in fierce polemical encounters with the ideas, theories, and values of the squadron of thinkers and writers with which he was familiar. If he was not attacking other thinkers, he quite often sifted through their writings for ore that he converted to steel in the furnace of his mind.[6] And of all those to whom Nietzsche was indebted, to a lesser or greater degree, Ralph Waldo Emerson was, as I shall attempt to show, one of his most prominent creditors.

Moving as he did from a sympathetic reading of Emerson to a study of Schopenhauer, Nietzsche would have noticed quite similar elitist cultural values and attitudes, as well as a sympathy with oriental thought. Many able commentators on Nietzsche's thought have believed that it was from Schopenhauer that he derived his idolization of creative geniuses and his contempt for mediocrity. However, in terms of the temporal sequence of his intellectual development this is not the case. For Nietzsche, before he discovered the philosophy of Schopenhauer, had already found, in Emerson's essays, a praise of genius and a disdain for the majority equal to that of Schopenhauer. Moreover, the idea of a will acting through nature—one associated with Schopenhauer—could already be found in the writings of the American poet and essayist. In fact, Emerson was already familiar with the central theme of Schopenhauer's thought and was not as startled by it as Nietzsche was. In his *Journals* (1864) he quotes Schopenhauer's epitome of his philosophy: "My great discovery is to show, how at the bottom of all things, there is only one force, always equal, and ever the same, which slumbers in plants, awakens in animals, but finds its consciousness only in man—the Will." And then he adds: "But it seems, Schopenhauer, in his youth, learned Sanskrit, and learned the secret of the Buddhists." Emerson was unsurprised by Schopenhauer's "discovery" because before he had heard his name he, too, had explored oriental philosophy and had come to believe that a "Will" pervades all reality. No doubt he would have sighed when he discovered that Schopenhauer had concluded that this cosmic "Will" in the form of the "will to live" had to be stilled, denied. For what Schopenhauer condemned, he praised; what Schopenhauer thought should be denied, he affirmed. Needless to say, this is a theme to which we shall have to return.

In Germany in the 1860s there were many eyes looking to the future. Although Richard Wagner had been sympathetic to radical socialist causes in his youth (even to the point of having collaborated with Bakunin in the Dresden revolt of 1849), he later proposed new cultural tasks to the coming creators or artistic 'heroes' who would revitalize German culture. A contemporary of his, F. A. Lange (whose *History of Materialism* Nietzsche studied assiduously), was also a supporter of socialist causes. In fact, he proposed a new cultural ideal that was to be brought about not by artists, but by powerful emergent leaders of the rising army of workers who would serve as the culture-bearers of the future.[7] The theme of a new, superior culture of one form or another, in coordination with the historical orientation that Arnold Toynbee called "futurism," was very much in the air in nineteenth-century Europe. With the notable exception of the pessimistic Schopenhauer, many of the thinkers Nietzsche respected were visionary about what culture and man might yet become, even as they disagreed about the form that this new culture and new man would take. By the time he wrote his first major work, *The Birth of Tragedy*, Nietzsche had already received what amounted to an education in futuristic ideals and elitist cultural values. What is less known is that some of these ideals and values were imported from America.

Despite sporadic glimpses of the affinity between the thought of Emerson and that of Nietzsche in the past, and aside from the recognition of "Emerson's influence on Nietzsche" in Gay Wilson Allen's biographical study, *Waldo Emerson,* there may still be some who are surprised that the optimistic transcendentalist, the ostensible champion of democracy and the common man, is closely linked to the elitist philosopher of the "beyond-man," of the "transvaluation of values," of "the will to power," the critic of every social and political leveling tendency of the modern world.

As serious students of his writings know, Emerson was a radical thinker. And a great deal of this radicalism was transmitted to, and perpetuated by, Nietzsche in a hyperbolic way in his positive doctrines. The nature and extent of the influence of Emerson on the German thinker who preferred to be called European is far more profound and much more extensive than has hitherto been suspected even by the few who have recognized and discussed this relationship.

The Beyond-Man

Nietzsche's aesthetically embellished image of the *Übermenschen* or the "beyond-men" of the future, the exemplary human types who were to serve as the justification of man, owes more to Emerson's poetic-philosophical sketches of "transcendent" human beings than it does to any other single cultural or intellectual source with which Nietzsche was familiar. The idea of the beyond-man did not evolve in Nietzsche's thought and suddenly burst forth in *Thus Spoke Zarathustra,* because long before, he was familiar with Emerson's repeated attempts to sculpt his image of "synthetic men" who would represent man perfected. Ironically, even after he introduced the conception of the beyond-man, Nietzsche was still working out the details of the characteristics of his version of Emerson's "sovereign individuals" in notes from the late 1880s.

More than what G. W. Allen called Emerson's idea of "the central man" is involved in this relation to the image of the *Übermensch.* The similarity between Emerson's supreme "bellwethers" of the future and Nietzsche's ideal of what man may yet become is far more than a family resemblance. By relating Emerson's writings on this specific theme to those of Nietzsche, we may come to see Nietzsche's conception in a new light. And, by the same token, Emerson's reflections concerning the possibility of the emergence of man perfected are illuminated, retrospectively, from a surprising angle of vision. Although it may be the case that the importance of Emerson's influence on Nietzsche provides a "clue to the nature of Emerson's poetry,"[8] it is a far more significant clue to the nature of and meaning of some of Nietzsche's central conceptions and valuations.

A great deal that has been attributed to Nietzsche's arrogance, his uncompromising elitism, is, in point of fact, derived from the tone, the content, and the valuations of the *soi-disant* "genteel" Emerson. It will be shown that Nietzsche not only adopted the Olympian aristocratic tone of Emerson, but consciously molded and embellished his imaginative construct of the *Übermensch* out of materials he found dispersed in Emerson's fertile and seminal reflections on those he called "exceptions."

When Nietzsche was in the process of composing *Thus Spoke Zarathustra,* he immersed himself once again in Emerson's stylistic and intellectual *ambiance.* His encomiastic descriptions in his most poetic work of the being of the future who will transcend man as he has been owe a great deal to Emerson's overlapping portraits of the ideal human being whose time is not yet. Although the suggestion of the idea of the beyond-man has been attributed to the ancient writer, Lucian, to J. G. Herder, to Jean Paul, to Goethe and others, there is much stronger evidence that Emerson was the primary source of this aesthetically imbued conception of the paradigmatic man. The template for the image of a man-beyond-man was originally manufactured in America by Emerson.

The influence of Emerson's experimental reflections on man perfected upon the centerpiece of Nietzsche's cultural ideal goes far beyond a superficial resemblance between the term "Oversoul" (*Überseele*) and the term "overman" (*Übermensch*). As we shall see, the connection between Emerson and Nietzsche is not, as one German commentator suggests,[9] a matter of related passages or phrases in their writings, similarities of style and tone, or family resemblances between some of Nietzsche's aphorisms and some passages in Emerson's essays. It is far deeper than that.

The American Existentialist

There is an unconscious irony in the commonly made observation that a substantial portion of Emerson's ethics of self-reliance, self-trust, integrity, and independence has been surpassed by the philosophy of existentialism. The irony, of course, is that the strong strand of existentialism or a philosophy of *Existenz* that runs through Nietzsche's writings, even though it is not the terminal emphasis of his thought, is indebted to Emerson's assertive and demanding morality of sovereign individuality. By virtue of his ethics of individuality Emerson entered the stream of existential thought *via* Nietzsche. This raises the question of whether it is Emerson or his Danish contemporary, Søren Kierkegaard, who is entitled to be called "the first existentialist."

The existential dimension of Nietzsche's thought makes its appearance in a discernible Emersonian guise in the *Untimely Meditations* of the 1870s. A curiosity about this set of four essays is that three of them deal with representative figures in German culture. In this sense they bear a resemblance to Emerson's *Representative Men* with the exception, of course, of "On the Uses and Disadvantages of History for Life." Although the essay on history is not centered on a cultural personality, it is not at all outside the perimeter of Emerson's pervasive influence. The emphasis on nonconformity, honesty, integrity, and the referral of the meaning of history to individual life, as well as the allusions to, and quotations from, Emerson's writings in Nietzsche's quartet of essays attest to the presence of Emersonian sentiments, attitudes, and values in them. But it is, as in other instances in which Nietzsche responds to the American poet and essayist, Emerson raised to the second power.

From the beginning of his life as a lecturer and essayist, Emerson was very much preoccupied with exceptional individuals who distinguish themselves by their strength of character and independence of mind. His earliest formulation of such a human type is found in his religiously tinged portrait of "the genuine man." He continued to work on this conception of an authentic individual, to enhance it, to place it in a secular, ethical framework. As he added self-reliance, self-trust, self-existence, and honesty to his depiction of the "true man," Emerson clearly anticipated the image of the existential hero. The emphasis on the importance of the trait of honesty was not lost on Nietzsche since, as *Redlichkeit,* it became the chief virtue, one he frequently claimed for himself and prescribed for others. Another feature of Emerson's genuine individual emerged during his middle period. Such an individual, he said, ought to cultivate a strong sense of realism about existence and a natural world that is often the reverse of friendly. As he increased the requirements for authenticity while denouncing conformity and the low standards of ordinary social being, Emerson began, in Kierkegaard's phrase, "to jack up the price of existence." What is uncanny is that virtually at the same time that Kierkegaard was writing in his journals that "an authentic existence" is not possible without appropriating what he called "the ethical requirement" Emerson was saying, in a different way, precisely the same thing. Just as Kierkegaard was lambasting "the crowd," condemning it as "in untruth," and urging his readers to avoid falling into it, Emerson was attacking the same phenomenon. It is not the case, then, that Emerson was overshadowed by the continental movement of existentialism or that his conception of the genuine person is "similar" to that of the authentic human being. For he was, in actuality, a contributor, by virtue of his influence on the band of a philosophy of *Existenz* that runs through Nietzsche's writings, to the existential concept of man.

Before 1860, America had already produced its own domestic brand of existential thinker, even though he has hitherto received little or no recognition for his original contribution to what is considered a purely European mode of philosophy. At the same time as a then-obscure Danish writer, Kierkegaard, was insisting on the discipline of a self-transforming ethics that required "the intensification of subjectivity," Emerson was forming his ideal of the man who has faith in himself, who values above all the integrity of the self, who is willing to stand alone, who strives to think, act, and live truth. While Kierkegaard was proclaiming "the intrinsic value" of the reflective ethical individual, Emerson, thousands of miles away, was preaching the same doctrine in sermonlike essays.

What is interesting about Emerson, particularly in regard to his association with Nietzsche, is that rather than calling, as Kierkegaard did, for a return to "New Testament Christianity," he moved further and further away from the traditional Christian dispensation that he had served, before his break with the church, as a Unitarian minister. Whereas Kierkegaard reached back to Jesus Christ as "the model," "the prototype," and even, in his notes, as "the overman," Emerson looked forward to the promise of the perfected man who will embody beauty, goodness, and strength. Since the secular idea of an exemplary man who possessed "genuineness" found its place in Nietzsche's thought and was retained in a less poetic and restrained form as the centerpiece of Martin Heidegger's conception of the genuine or authentic human being (*Dasein*), Emerson is a hidden presence in the development of existential thought.

An astonishing number of Emerson's insights and asides infiltrated Nietzsche's writings. And the recognizable Emersonian themes and elements that can be found in Nietzsche's works are not merely incidental or occasional, superficial or inconsequential. They are discernible at the very core of his philosophy. Many of the theories, ideas, and insights that are usually thought of as the original coinage of Nietzsche are enlarged, embossed, and enhanced replicas of Emerson's mintage.

Fate

That fate pervades nature and conditions man's being is a leading conception that Nietzsche absorbed from the American he admired. The constant wrestling with fate, the struggle with the meaning of fate in human existence, that Nietzsche frequently displayed in his coruscating writings was a recapitulation of Emerson's earlier attempts to come to terms with the power of fate. He understood fatalism, as Nietzsche did after him, as the force of unknown factors that condition the circumstances of man's concrete and spiritual existence. Fate is not construed as a cosmic power or force that acts upon man *ab extra,* as something apart from his being or nature that externally determines his destiny. In his copy of Emerson's *Versuche,* Nietzsche underlined a sentence in the essay "Fate" that is pregnant with meaning: "The book of Nature is the book of Fate." It is a "book" that Nietzsche brooded over, read, and interpreted throughout his philosophically productive life. He inherited the problem of fate from Emerson and found in his writings a dramatic resolution of it.

From the time when a young Nietzsche, in 1862, copied down Emerson's provocative observations on the freedom of our thinking and the fatality of our being-in-nature, to the time when he wrote his somewhat eccentric, but generally lucid, autobiography, *Ecce Homo,* Nietzsche grappled with a belief in the power of fate and the consequences of that belief. The reality and power of fate that he accepted *in toto* was directly appropriated, without modification, from the writings of the American poet and essayist whose sagacity he rarely questioned. Not only was Emerson's theme of the centrality of fate in human existence adopted by Nietzsche, but even the paradoxical exhortations to decisiveness, action, and self-transcendence in the face of the tyrannical "circumstance" of natural necessities were transferred from Emerson's writings to those of Nietzsche. The paradox of embracing a universal fatalism and then emitting a barrage of imperatives that imply freedom was first found in the essays of Emerson before it was projected on the large, colorful screen of the philosophy of Nietzsche.

In his earliest and unpublished essay, *"Fatum und Geschichte,"* a seventeen-year-old Nietzsche combined the titles of two of Emerson's essays, "Fate" and "History." More than that, as Karl Jaspers and others have noticed, he presented a brief overture that sounded many of the themes of his later philosophical symphony. He quoted Emerson in "Fate" and raised questions about the tension between free action and a "fatalism" that seems to pervade existence. He questioned the viability of traditional Christianity (as Emerson did in the "Divinity School Address" and elsewhere) and wondered about the "more than human" man who will have the courage to embrace fate and yet strive to guide and direct his powers. In this bit of juvenilia Emerson was quoted and mentioned by name; what was not mentioned was that the entire brief essay was, to put it mildly, in the spirit of Emerson.

Power/Reality

The overriding importance of power in the natural world, the significance of the role of power and its pursuit in human life, the omnipresence of a variety of forms of power in actuality are not conceptions that were originally discovered or articulated by Nietzsche. In terms of his intellectual development, it was in Emerson that Nietzsche first encountered the general theory that power is a fundamental reality in the cosmos and in the microcosmos of man's collective and individual existence. Later, this theory of power was reinforced by Nietzsche's familiarity with Richard Wagner's themes of the pursuit of power, and the loss and renunciation of power in his music-dramas. And, in the unlikely setting of a work he called a "treasure-house"—F. A. Lange's *History of Materialism*—he found a critical commentary on the religious and economic manifestations of man's "lust for power."[10]

That Emerson's transcendental idealism, his world-view formed out of a synthesis of German idealist metaphysics of the late eighteenth and early nineteenth century and aspects of Hindu idealism, bears any relationship to Nietzsche's interpretation of reality may seem, on the surface, implausible. This seems especially the case if we focus on Nietzsche's positivistic stage of thought or his apparent commitment to a form of physicalism. As a matter of fact, there is no real incongruity between the underdeveloped general philosophical views of Emerson and those of the German philosopher.

Emerson had been a Unitarian minister and, virtually from the start of his ministry, had rather liberal views of a theology that was itself one of the most liberal in Christendom. In point of fact, as David Robinson has shown,[11] many of the elements that emerged in Emerson's secular humanism were foreshadowed by ideas prevalent in Unitarianism during the period of his ministry—that is, the goal of "self-culture," the aim "to ennoble human nature," the value of "self-trust," and the belief in the perfectibility of human nature. In the wake of the untimely death of his first wife, Ellen (*née* Tucker), Emerson renounced his ministry and left the Unitarian church. But even before this his views were becoming increasingly unorthodox. In a sermon presented in Boston he was already speaking of the "holier work of forming *men, true and entire men.*"[12] In his theology, he was more concerned with "the God within" than with a remote divinity that harshly judges mankind. Emerson conceived of God as "the supreme Power" that manifested itself in the millionfold forms of life and was actively present in nature and man. The power of divinity was immanently present in the diverse forms of actuality and was expressed in innumerable modes of being and value. Traditionally characterized a transcendentalist, Emerson, in actuality, propounded a theory of immanence—that is, a belief, as he put it, that there is a spiritual force in nature that "seeks" material embodiment. For the most part, his emphasis fell on the being of man, on morality and culture, rather than on a transcendental being or reality.

There is a decidedly this-worldly emphasis in Emerson's writings and an emphasis upon redemption in the here and now. His humanism was sometimes expressed in terms of radical, defiant subjectivity. Even though he referred in his early sermons to God-reliance, his thinking turned more and more towards self-reliance and the prescription to try to attain contact with the immanent presence of divinity in nature, a divinity conceived of as a primordial power.

Only if Nietzsche's "hypothesis" of an immanent will to power pervading the cosmos is misinterpreted as a form of physicalism or materialism could one fail to see that his imaginative, experimental conception of the world "seen from within" postulated a spiritual *nisus* or *Tendenz* acting through all phenomena. The will to power is predominantly a creative tendency towards form, expression, and life that is analogous to Emerson's conception of an underlying spiritual "power" pervading nature and man, a power that endeavors to express itself in material form.

The will to power, for Nietzsche, was not a material force, even though it is assumed to be that which is actively present in the interior dynamics of matter. Nietzsche considered the theory that matter is the ultimate constituent of reality an "error," and he celebrated the conclusion of the eighteenth-century mathematical physicist, Ruggerio Boscovich, that matter is reducible to nonextended "point-centers" or "centers of force." "We have got rid of *materiality!*"[13] he exclaimed. What is curious about Nietzsche's exploration of scientific knowledge (which was surprisingly extensive) in order in find a key to the ultimate nature of reality is that it was a recapitulation of the intellectual habits of Emerson. For he, too, absorbed as much as he could from "the naturalists" not so much as an end in itself, but in order to accumulate ideas that he then incorporated into his guess at "the secret of nature." Like Nietzsche, Emerson also had what may be called 'positivistic' phases of development. However, they never led him to embrace scientism or the metaphysical theory that scientific knowledge is the only true knowledge and that this knowledge alone will give us an authentic interpretation of reality. In an early lecture, "The Naturalist," Emerson made his position plain: "The necessity of nomenclature, of minute physiological research, of the retort, the scalpel, and the scales, is incontestable. But there is no danger of its being underestimated. We only wish to insist upon their being considered as *Means*.¹⁴"

Nietzsche's admiration for and appreciation of the sciences and their methods of discovery also had limits. Emerson in a mild way and Nietzsche in a more intense way worried over the burgeoning culture of science. Both sought, again at different levels of intensity, to develop an aesthetically imbued philosophical interpretation of reality that would acknowledge the value and power of scientific knowledge, but not surrender to its domination of culture. For Emerson, as for Nietzsche, matter is not the ultimate reality; rather, it is a phenomenon, a manifestation of a spiritual reality the essence of which is a living power. Both embraced a dynamic, spiritual interpretation of reality.

In his *Nachlass* Nietzsche, at one point, described the will to power as a *pathos* that is analogous to man and his creative drive for more. The theory of the will to power is a self-consciously anthropomorphic experimental "hypothesis," a "reduced formula" that is modeled on what is posited as man's central characteristic: a striving for, a willing toward, power. It is a psychological theory of human nature that owes a great deal to Emerson's understanding of the springs of human conduct.

Despite his atheistic denial of the existence of a moral God as stern judge of pitiful human beings, as a being wholly transcendent to this world of becoming and constant change, Nietzsche did not exclude, in some of his reflections, the possibility of God as the epochal peak of the creative ascension of the will to power. In fact, in a note from 1887, Nietzsche, with no apparent irony, remarked: "Let us remove the highest goodness from God. . . . Let us also remove the highest wisdom. . . . God *the highest power*— that suffices! From it follows everything, from it follows—'the world' "[15] In notes from the same period Nietzsche referred to the irony of the occasional outbreak of religious sentiments in him. But he should not have been surprised at this since he had already proclaimed his Dionysian religion, a religion that embraces the world, as it is, as sacred, as pervaded by a spiritual dynamism.[16] By encompassing his interpretation of the will to power in this Dionysian interpretation of reality Nietzsche did not move further away from Emerson. Rather, he moved closer to the psychic and intellectual space that Emerson, as the Orphic poet who ecstatically celebrated the god "Bacchus" (=Dionysus), occupied earlier. Perhaps these two Dionysian thinkers[17] were not as far removed in their interpretations of reality as many may think.

Circular Philosophers

Many of the themes, as well as reverberations of meaning and tone, in Emerson's "Circles" have a way of appearing, in one form or another, in Nietzsche's writings. The central idea of the predominance of circularity throughout nature, in life, in human existence easily suggests Nietzsche's paean to "the eternal ring of becoming" and even the possibility, given the circular pattern of all things, of the eternal return of all things. There is, too, the celebration of flux, process, and change that points backwards to Heraclitus and forward to Nietzsche. Rather than bewailing the transitory nature of life, ideas, values, and institutions, Emerson, as Nietzsche after him, embraced it with passion. In nature "there is no sleep, no pause, no preservation." But, Emerson told us, foreshadowing the language of *Thus Spoke Zarathustra,* "all things renew, germinate and spring." Although Emerson admitted a degree of "permanence" in the world, he abjured a philosophy of Being or permanence and urged us to adopt a philosophy of "time and becoming," as Nietzsche had Zarathustra call it. Although Nietzsche was quite familiar with Heraclitus' theory of universal flux, there is no doubt that Emerson reinforced this conception in Nietzsche's mind. For what Emerson did in "Circles" was to draw out the implications of this way of viewing the world and the self. All that seems permanent is subject to change, the impertinence of the new. And what is new "destroys the old." Theories, generalizations, values, beliefs, and ideals that seemed at their birth to be eternal prove victims of the relentless power of temporality. Years later Nietzsche celebrated the endless becoming of all things with Emersonian enthusiasm and charged thinkers like Plato with "chronophobia," a fear of temporality, change, and passing away.

Aside from reinforcing in Nietzsche's thought the centrality of temporal becoming, "Circles" also spun out a number of ideas that lodged in Nietzsche's consciousness and eventually appeared in his writings. The image of the thinker as dangerous and the possibility of a revolution of the entire system of culture made their imprint and were quoted in "Schopenhauer as Educator." Even more important than this, especially for his critique of previous morality, were the flashes of Emerson's antinomic sentiments.

With typical sangfroid Emerson dealt with serious matters with an air of detachment. Justice and injustice are often matters of perception: "One man's justice is another's injustice." And as far as virtues go, there is not one that is final. "The virtues of society," Emerson tells us, "are vices of the saint." If man is truly to reform, he must learn to throw his virtues into the same pit into which he hurled his "grosser vices." A principle of good runs through everything and even penetrates evil and sin. For there is no evil that is pure evil. As we shall see in the discussion of the paradox of evil and good, Emerson often criss-crosses the same potentially dangerous terrain that Nietzsche later stakes out as his own. Aware that he has lapsed into antinomianism (as he does from time to time) in this context, Emerson reacts in a way that the young philologist-turned-philosopher never seems to have forgotten. Emerson reminds the reader "that I am only an experimenter. Do not set the least value on what I do, or the last discredit on what I do not, as if I pretended to settle any thing as true or false. I unsettle all things. No facts are to me sacred; none are profane; I simply experiment, an endless seeker with no Past at my back."

Although some literary critics find this evasion questionable or disingenuous, Nietzsche seemed to think of it as refreshingly anti-dogmatic or an indication that Emerson presented his ideas as "thought-experiments." For Emerson reveals himself as a *Versucher* (essayist, experimenter, attempter, tempter) in more ways than one, a role that Nietzsche adopted, after Emerson, with relish.

As we shall see, Nietzsche's use of Emerson's ideas and insights is somewhat complex. Thus, sometimes he responds to his observations impressionistically—adopting the image of reality as circular or becoming the "circular philosopher" Emerson ironically calls himself. In other instances, he conjoins conceptions that Emerson treats separately, creating theories out of his dispersed ideas. Sometimes he seems to superimpose in his mind two or more of Emerson's essays—say, "Circles" and "Fate," thereby relating a circular pattern of becoming to a fatalistic sequence of events that is affirmed. In the case of the paradox of evil and good, Nietzsche combines elements from numerous essays in ways that Emerson never does, and creates a set of interrelated notions concerning the value of 'wicked' or 'evil' drives for a morality of strength and the breakdown of the radical duality of good and evil. Even though the influence of Emerson on Nietzsche is not total, it is certainly polymorphous.

Janus-Faced Nature

In his youth Nietzsche wholeheartedly shared the nature-mysticism that Emerson espoused in *Nature*. The beauty, power, and grandeur of the natural world are reflected in the mirror of human consciousness. Although *Nature* owes quite a bit to Romanticism, it also is pervaded by the pithy insights and visionary thoughts that are Emerson's trademark. The natural world is described as existing for us or, at one point, as perhaps having no independent existence at all. In this brief book Emerson earns his reputation as a transcendental idealist insofar as the natural world is a conglomeration of phenomena that are shaped and formed by the mind. It is an understanding of the world that is an amalgam of Kant minus technicalities and Berkeley without arguments.

What is curious about the idealism in *Nature* is that it moves back and forth from a personal, subjective consciousness to an impersonal transcendental consciousness. The beautiful and stirring phenomena we perceive are alternately in the mind or a mind. Natural objects are sometimes referred to as if they were real, independent entities, and sometimes they are considered as appearances to the mind. In a way, Emerson's Orphic poet resolves these oppositions: the world truly exists for us; the world is suffused with the spirit of man. We are counseled to build our own world, to claim the "kingdom" that is ours, an intoxicating idea uttered by an intoxicated poet.

There is a deep subjectivity in *Nature* that has a liberating effect on the reader. In a spiritual sense, we are not in nature; we are transcendent to the natural world. What we call nature is suffused with anthropomorphic projections. Our language, shot through with metaphors, humanizes the phenomena of the natural world. "Nature is so pervaded with human life that there is something of humanity in all and in every particular." Here, no doubt, Nietzsche received the first imprint of two fundamental conceptions that recur in his philosophy: the metaphorical nature of language and the inevitability of the "humanization of nature."

Up to about the midpoint of his productive life Emerson reiterated his radical subjectivism. The "I" begins to replace the "transparent eye" of *Nature,* the depersonalized pure consciousness. The self is in the foreground, nature in the background. There is such a strong emphasis on subjectivity that a student of Kierkegaard's works would have a *déjà-vu* experience. The saying that "I am" in "Self-Reliance" seems, as Stanley Cavell suggests, reminiscent of Descartes' saying and thinking "I exist."[18] Unfortunately, he elides this into the existential emphasis on subjective existence in Kierkegaard's thought. This is unfortunate because Kierkegaard mocks Descartes' formula, "I think therefore I am," by offering his own: *Sum ergo cogito*—"I am therefore I think." Kierkegaard's conception of subjective existence is not essentially related to cognitive thinking, but to moods, subjective passion, to *pathos.* And any reader of Emerson can see that his approach to the self is *not* intellectual. Therefore, he is closer in spirit to Kierkegaard than to the rationalist Descartes. Despite the defiant subjectivity of "Self-Reliance," Emerson returns to a consideration of the "not-I" of the natural world in the ebb of three terrible losses in a period of five years: his wife Ellen and his two brothers. This second picture of nature bears almost no relation to the etherealized one in *Nature.*

In the essays comprising *The Conduct of Life* Emerson seems to have executed a *volte-face.* This is evident particularly in regard to man's relation to nature. More than that is the tempering of the earlier buoyant optimism and the absence of the poetic dematerialism of what is ugly and dangerous in the natural world that one found in *Nature.* The harsh realities of a physical universe are now emphasized. The powerful forces that limit and circumscribe existence are given prominence. He shows us that the other aspect of nature is not pleasing, that "Nature is no sentimentalist." In "Fate," in particular, Emerson dips his pen in black ink. The liberated spiritual consciousness of *Nature* is now pictured as surrounded by bands of necessity.

What we find in *The Conduct of Life* is a surprisingly hardheaded naturalism that continually seems to grate against his

underlying philosophical idealism. As we track Emerson's changing standpoint and begin to see a toughness that is, at times, startling, we begin to realize, as the late A. B. Giamatti saw, that
Emerson was about "as sweet as barbed wire."[19]

Emerson displays in "Fate" another face of nature, one which is
indifferent to its effects on human beings, one that is dangerous,
powerful, and destructive. And this realistic understanding of the
natural world runs through most of the essays comprising *The
Conduct of Life*. What has this to do with Nietzsche? A great deal.
For he, too, begins with a positive, uplifting conception of nature
as tending towards perfection, as a source of inspiration. He considers his first published work, *The Birth of Tragedy,* an "artist's
metaphysics" which he rather quickly repudiates. Skepticism is
then followed by a naturalistic orientation that puts in question religious and moral sentiments and probes beneath the surface of human motivation. Nietzsche recapitulates Emerson's spiritual
orientation to the ultimate nature of reality and his visionary conception of ideal human beings of the future combined with a realistic, even harsh, understanding of actuality. In regard to Emerson
and Nietzsche, William James' separate categorization of the
"tender-minded" and the "tough-minded" does not hold up. For
in their thought one finds an intermingling of visionary idealism
and biting realism, tender-mindedness and tough-mindedness intertwined. Every time Nietzsche forces himself to practice self-
overcoming by adopting a hard-headed realist's perspective on
nature, man, or life, he follows directly in the footsteps of Emerson, according to *his* prescription for *Selbstüberwindung*. And the
"idealism" of Emerson and Nietzsche is not otherworldly, but an
immanent idealism of valuation. Nietzsche characterizes his philosophical stance as "inverted Platonism." Presumably this means
that 'the ideal' does not reside, as in traditional Platonism, in a
pure, unchanging, perfect, transcendental realm of Being, but in
this Protean world of becoming in which life is the ultimate value.
In spite of his admiration for Plato and his early flirtations with
Platonism and neo-Platonism, Emerson had already moved more
and more towards an inversion of the hierarchy of Plato's value-
system.

Temperament

Having already mentioned the relationship between temperament
and thought in James' version, it may be pointed out that Emerson

seems to have been the inspiration for James' classification of philosophical temperaments. And he also was the source of Nietzsche's belief in the intimate relationship between individual temperaments and thought, between a thinker's personality and his or her *Weltanschauung*. Nietzsche's belief in the basically autobiographical nature of a philosophy, as well as his assumption that there is an intimate relation between life-experiences, stages of life, and modes of thought and value, is closely linked to Emerson's quite similar observations on this same theme.

Emerson held that a thinker is not an impersonal, pure mind, but first and foremost a person of flesh and blood. Thus, for example, in his oration, "The American Scholar," he observes that the thinker is involved in a process of "transmuting life into truth," that the misfortunes of life sharpen the mind and are "instructors in eloquence and wisdom." In fact, they provide "the raw material out of which the intellect moulds her splendid products." It is, he continues, a "strange process," this means "by which experience is converted into thought."[20] Nietzsche, too, was a conscientious student of precisely this same strange process by which he sought to convert his personal experiences, his *pathos,* into a philosophy of life.

"Temperament is the iron wire on which the beads" of our life are strung, so Emerson insists. The medical doctors have shown us, he says, how much of our feelings, our attitudes, beliefs, and thoughts are conditioned by our inherited temperament. In his earliest philosophical effort, "Fate and History," Nietzsche paraphrases Emerson's remark about temperament as fate: "Ask gifted doctors, says Emerson, how much temperament decides and what, in general, it does not decide." And he puzzles over and grapples with the idea of physiological and psychological factors "tyrannizing over character." Unlike some contemporary thinkers who analyze the multiplicity of causal factors that condition individual existence and behavior and then go about their business with scientific calm, Emerson and Nietzsche felt deeply the profound negative consequences of the admission of deeply rooted factors that condition our nature. They tried to think through the effects of psychophysiological factors on thought, on the concept of the self, on social existence and culture, on the cherished belief in freedom of the will, on human limitations and potentialities.

Emerson broods, in his essays, about the question of the power of temperament, about the cruel mistakes of nature, the negative effects of heredity, the delusion that each of us perceives the world the same way despite our different temperaments and interests (what Nietzsche later christens the doctrine of "immaculate perception"), the illusion of pure thought unadulterated by the temperament of the thinker, the plight of each person ineluctably trapped in the prison of his or her limitations or capacities. Nature, Emerson believed, bequeaths to us the tyrannical circumstances of our existence. It is quite clear that Emerson unwittingly did quite a job of injecting Nietzsche's mind, at the earliest stages of its development, with strong doses of a fatalistic understanding of the being of man. And, in a sense, he never really got over the effects of this dosage of fatalism, for it had a lifelong effect on Nietzsche both personally and philosophically.

In his examination of the influence of temperament on the nature of individuals, on the springs of human action, on perception and thought, Emerson introduced a lively strain of irrationalism into his interpretation of the condition of man. By emphasizing how much temperament shapes our being, our moods, our perception of the world and others, our philosophies, our "theologies," Emerson tended to undermine the ability of human beings to achieve objectivity. Given all he tells us about temperament, "the tyranny of circumstances," the inheritances that condition us physically and psychologically, we may wonder what happens to rationality, moral responsibility, the idea of freedom of choice. What happens to our presumed capacity to transcend our past? How can one strive to be "self-reliant" unless one has the temperament, the capacity, to do so? Or, for that matter, how can one strive for self-transcendence, as Nietzsche so often counsels, unless one has the temperamental capacity to do so? Can we ever truly escape what Nietzsche calls, after Emerson, our "spiritual fate"? If fate, if temperament, decides so much in our lives, then belief in the power of reason, in rational choice, would seem to be a delusion.

If one adds to the power of temperament Emerson's emphasis on the role of "the unconscious" in life, its expression in dreams, and the priority of instinct over reason, we can see how subversive his thinking was in regard to the centrality of reason in thought and conduct. If we trace the influence of Emerson in this regard on Nietzsche to the impact that Schopenhauer's stress on the irrationality of the will (with special attention paid to sexuality) had on his thought, and if we add to this von Hartmann's discovery of the operation of the unconscious practically everywhere (in his *Philosophy of the Unconscious*), we need not wonder why Nietzsche elevated the irrational and the unconscious to such a prominent place in his thought. Freud's theory of the unconscious mind and the irrational motivations of much of human behavior was a rather late arrival on the philosophical-psychological scene of the nineteenth century. Commentators on Nietzsche are pleased to cite the passages in his writings in which he speculates about the nature of dreams and the expression of the unconscious in them as miniature anticipations of Freud's analysis of dreams. Emerson is never acknowledged as the teacher of the German philosopher in oneiric mysteries.

Dreams, Instinct, and the Unconscious

Aside from calling attention to the conditioning factors in nature that shape our being (our genealogy, the inheritances of man's "natural history," and the concrete "circumstances" of our existence), Emerson probed the unconscious and nonrational basis of our nature. Although there is no evidence that Nietzsche has access to Emerson's *Journals,* there are instances in his writings in which it appears that he did. As early as 1840, Emerson speculates about the role of the unconscious in our life. What is interesting is that he questions the belief that our virtue and genius are unconscious in the sense that they are "the influx of god." He contends that the unconscious is "relative to *us*" insofar as "we speak, we act from we know not what higher principle." We have no direct access to the unconscious; we cannot "see at all its channel into us." In fact, "we have no language subtle enough for distinctions in that inaccessible region."[21] Throughout his essays Emerson sporadically refers to the influence of the unconscious on our thought, our "affections" (feelings), and our action. And even though he does not explicitly connect the two, the unconscious and dreams are, by implication, associated.

Here and there in his *Journals* Emerson makes observations on dreams that, in altered form, find their way into his essays. He finds in dreams not only "real knowledge," but "alarming hints" as well. Dreams are a kind of "vaticination." But what he says about them indicates that the prophetic character of dreams pertains more to the spiritual dimensions of the self than to grandiose prophecies about the history of the future. The presentation in disguised form of desires or fantasies is already suggested by Emerson. For he tells us that the psyche in dreams "has a subtle synthetic power which it will not exert under the sharp eyes of day. It does not like to be watched or looked upon, & flies to real twilights. . . . If in dreams you see loose & luxurious pictures, an inevitable tie drags in the sequel of cruelty & malignity."[22]

Elsewhere in his *Journals* Emerson perceptibly sees in Dante's *Inferno* evidence of powerful dream-imagery, fierce, pitiless, and horrible details. These dream-images, which are raised "to the tenth power," are construed as signs of abnormality.[23] In other entries in his *Journals* Emerson refers to dreams as providing inspiration, as containing some lesson in their "farrago," as a strange kind of entertainment and conversation. In another place he offers a condensed interpretation of the dream of a decent gentleman who dreamed that he was "a drudge, a miser, and a footman." Emerson attributes this common form of humiliation-dream to a "civil war in our atoms, mutiny of the sub-daemons not yet subdued."[24] In a journal entry from 1844 Emerson records an insight that anticipates Nietzsche's later inversion of it. "The text of our life," he writes, "is accompanied all along by this commentary or gloss of dreams."[25] Decades later, Nietzsche wonders if our conscious life may not be "a more or less fantastic commentary on an unknown, and perhaps unknowable, but . . . felt text."[26]

While Nietzsche's access to Emerson's journals is a question that cannot be answered with any certainty, we do know that he read his essays often and with great attention to detail. In "Spiritual Laws" he would have found Emerson's observation that

> Our dreams are the sequel of our waking knowledge. The visions of the night bear some proportion to the visions of the day. Hideous dreams are exaggerations of the sins of the day. We see our evil affections embodied in bad physiognomies. . . . As in dreams, so in the scarcely less fluid events of the world every man sees himself in colossal, without knowing that it is himself.[27]

Emerson was quite aware that in dreams we often combine wish-fulfillment with an expression of the aesthetic dimension of the self. In "the use of opium," in dreams and drunkenness, Emerson remarks, the individual finds "the semblance and counterfeit of . . . oracular genius . . . hence their dangerous attraction for men."[28] In *Human, All-Too-Human,* Nietzsche tells us that in dreams we express a great deal of our "artistic capacity" and that "dreams . . . paraphrase our experiences or expectations or circumstances with poetic boldness and definiteness."[29] Aside from such an insight, Nietzsche has much of value to say about the physical and physiological basis of the content of our dreams and thereby he moves beyond Emerson's *obiter dicta* on dreams. But there is little doubt that it was Emerson who was the chief stimulant of his reflections on dreams.

Before Nietzsche was exposed to Schopenhauer's theory of the irrational will that acts through us and all beings, and before he had taught him that the intellect is a tool of our drives and instincts, Nietzsche already had been instructed in the power and importance of instinct by the man he referred to as "the sage." The problem of even sketching Emerson's conception of instinct in relation to life is that there is no single place in which he presents such a conception. More than that, this notion is often implicitly linked to other aspects of what may rightly be called Emerson's philosophical anthropology. It is Nietzsche who synthesizes ideas that Emerson expresses without explicitly conjoining them.

In a letter to his friend, Erwin Rohde, Nietzsche wrote that "science, art and philosophy are now growing into one another so much in me that I shall one day . . . give birth to a centaur."[30] The philosophy of Nietzsche is this centaurlike creation. Ironically, on a smaller scale, America had already given birth to a kind of centaurian way of thinking that sought to combine two things that seem incompatible: "poetry and natural history."[31] Emerson was deeply impressed by the discoveries of the "naturalists" and tried to find a place for them in his interpretation of the human condition. As early as 1837 he began working on a lecture on "The Natural History of the Intellect" that he eventually presented years later. Given his own rudimentary conception of evolutionary transformation, Emerson gave priority to instinct. It is that which is transformed into the intellect and expressed through willing. He believed, to use one of his striking images, that just as carbon is converted into diamond over thousands of years, so, too, are man's higher mental and moral faculties derived from the raw material of instinct. As he puts it in "The Natural History of the Intellect,"

> Instinct is a shapeless giant in the cave, massive, without hands or fingers, or articulating lips or teeth or tongue; Behemoth, disdaining speech, disdaining particulars, lurking, surly, invincible, disdaining thoughts. . . . The instinct begins at this low-point, at the surface of the earth, and works for the necessities of the human being; then ascends step by step to suggestions which are, when expressed, the intellectual and moral laws.

Although Emerson gives due measure to reason and the power of thought, his emphasis on a philosophy of life tended to lead his thinking back to the value of and the potential danger of man's fundamental instinctive being. Having apparently borrowed an "organic metaphor" for human development from William Ellery Channing's work of 1838, *Self-Culture*,[32] Emerson often refers to man as a "plant" that must be nourished by many natural elements, some of them poisons in minute proportions, in order to grow.

In his essays Emerson frequently praises the individuals who are "natural," whose actions are "spontaneous" and instinctive. In *Nature* he laments the "retrospective" preoccupations of his times, the repeated groping "among the dry bones of the past." This orientation is often linked to our separation from nature, from the instinctive stimuli of our own nature. He attacks his age as one of introspection in "The American Scholar," as Nietzsche will later attack the "morbid introspection" of the ascetic personality. Thinking is fine, Emerson says in many different ways, but living is better. "Thinking is the function. Living is the functionary." And living invariably means for Emerson getting in touch with our natural instincts. If we try to jettison them, they will return, in one form or another, more powerful than before. In "History" Emerson insists that what we admire in the ancient Greeks is their naturalness, their energy, their ability to unify their spiritual and bodily natures, their lack of reflective habits of mind, their spontaneity. Modern man, in contrast, has become alienated from nature, has lost vitality and drive, has lost the health of instinctive life.

This theme of restoring spontaneity and instinct, as we shall see, is one that is augmented in Emerson's essays and particularly those comprising *The Conduct of Life* to the point at which he seems to attack reason and the uses of the intellect. The valuation of healthy "animal spirits" becomes so strong that it often tends to eclipse traditional moral values.

Nietzsche's critique of the hypertrophy of the intellect and his defense of instinctive action and "naturalness" is an Emersonian theme that reverberates through his published and unpublished writings. In *The Genealogy of Morals* he maintains that as human beings were gradually tamed and lived within the confines of society and relative peace, they lost what formerly had guided them: "their regulating, unconscious and infallible drives."[33] In notes comprising the nonbook, *The Will to Power*, it is said that "genius resides in instinct," that "one acts perfectly only when one acts instinctively." In another place, man's instinctive being is said to be characterized by "naturalness."[34] Again and again, Nietzsche prescribes a "restoration of nature," a recovery of instincts that are essential for ascending life and a morality of strength. In "Fate and History" Nietzsche had transcribed Emerson's emphasis upon the conditioning factor of traits inherited from our ancestors and included it under the category of 'fate.' In a note from the late 1880s he combines a number of elements in Emerson's thought in a summary of his reflections on instinct. Instincts, he maintains, are stored and transmitted from generation to generation. Self-discipline, industry, repetition of tasks, and skills accumulate over generations. These "accumulated forces"—with the assistance of "happy accidents"—lead to the emergence of persons who are "a prodigy of force."[35]

Again and again in his essays Emerson criticizes the separation of learning and knowledge from life, from action, from a way of being. The gains that mankind has made in knowledge and "mechanical" skills are paid for by a loss of "vitality" and "energy," by the loss of healthy instincts. Accomplishment in life is not a matter of intelligence alone. Persistence, achievement, creativity, and action require "strength," passion, and instinctive responses. As is often the case, Nietzsche lucidly articulates Emerson's tendencies of thought: our aim should be "to incorporate knowledge in ourselves and make it instinctive."[36] There are other aspects of Nietzsche's theory of instinctive drives and affects that are also derived from Emerson's psychological observations, but they will be examined in the context of discussions of the relation between natural drives and culture.

Illusions in Life

One of the many illuminating conceptions with which Nietzsche is closely associated is the view that life requires and is endurable only by means of illusions. Unconscious illusions pervade the entire organic world. And "conscious illusions" are equally necessary for life. They are the means by which a veil is cast over harsh realities and the horrors of existence. Deception, self-deception, and the projection of idealized images of oneself, others, and the world are inextricably interwoven in the fabric of life. In a note from 1872, Nietzsche observed that "we live only by means of illusions; our consciousness skims over the surface."[37] Even though this notion is later considerably expanded and developed by Nietzsche (to the point of formulating a theory of fictionalism in regard to ordinary language, as well as philosophical and scientific discourse), the basic ingredients for such a conception were originally presented by the man who, in his address before the Phi Beta Kappa Society at Harvard in 1837, "The American Scholar," inaugurated what Oliver Wendel Holmes called America's "intellectual Declaration of Independence."

Not only did Emerson insist that illusions play a role in our perception of and judgments of others, in our affections and self-concept, in our responses to the natural world, but he maintained that man values beauty and art as antidotes to the pain, suffering, and terrors of finite existence. The latter idea is incorporated *simpliciter* into Nietzsche's first major work, *The Birth of Tragedy*.

The development of a doctrine of "conscious illusion" (including the role that fictions play in life, conceptual thought, and science) was first suggested to Nietzsche by what is a relatively minor theme in Emerson's writings. In *The Philosophy of 'As-If,'* Hans Vaihinger contends that the notion that illusions pervade our life and thought was conveyed to Nietzsche by F. A. Lange in his *History of Materialism*.[38] A persuasive case can be made for this view, one that has convinced some interpreters of Nietzsche's philosophy that Lange was the primary, if not the exclusive, source of the theory that "conscious illusion" plays a central role in human experience and thought.[39] If, however, we realize how carefully Nietzsche read Emerson and how enthusiastic he was about his insights, this view would have to be revised.

There is no doubt that it was Emerson who first suggested to Nietzsche the idea that life is shot through with illusions, that, as he says in "Illusions," we are surrounded by "as many pillows of illusion as flakes in a snow-storm." The multiplicity of illusions that stir our "affections" and spur our behavior are deceptions in the service of life, in the service of ecstatic life. They stimulate efforts of will, ambition, affections, and the pursuit of goals of all kinds.

Emerson reaches back to oriental thought for support of the thesis of the illusion-filled nature of our feelings, sentiments, desires, hopes, beliefs, values, and loves. In this regard, Emerson seems to have laid the groundwork for Nietzsche's sympathetic understanding of Schopenhauer's theory that the phenomenal world is a "veil of illusion" or is what Hinduism calls the veil of *Māyā*. What strengthens the belief that it was Emerson who already softened the terrain for Schopenhauer's successful landing on the shores of Nietzsche's consciousness is the fact that he, too, derived his emphasis upon the role of illusion in life on the same Hindu doctrine of *Māyā*. This is only one instance in which Nietzsche was open to the possibility of transferring conceptions in oriental thought into his own philosophy.

Like Schopenhauer, Emerson was receptive to the influence of oriental philosophy. In "Illusions" in particular, he comes close to an aspect of the former's thought by counseling a liberation from the "kingdom of illusions," a liberation from "fascination" with the alluring deceptions of the world. Although Schopenhauer is a more structured, a more thorough philosopher than Emerson, there are curious relations of similarity between the two on certain matters.

Despite his keen awareness of the power of the subjective illusions that influence so much of our life, Emerson does not take the Schopenhauerian turn. That is, he does not advise turning away from the deceptions of life entirely or silencing "the will to live." He has faith in life and its value despite its snares, delusions, and deceptions. In fact, *contra* Schopenhauer, he urges us to view life as a gift, as something "sacred." Moreover, he urges us to penetrate the veil of illusion that covers life and force ourselves to look unblinking into the heart of darkness of reality. In spite of his reputation as a buoyant optimist, Emerson, especially in *The Conduct of Life,* counsels us to stare the negative aspects of existence in the eye, but not despair because of them. If we are to be thinkers, he says, we must endeavor to see through the illusions of life and face the truly terrible aspects of reality. In "Illusions" he tells us that "whatever games are played with us, we must play no games with ourselves, but deal in our privacy with the last honesty and truth." The sense of the reality of experience, the value of life, and the depth of the self are to be retained in the midst of illusions.

The Good of 'Evil'

Probably the most startling and least recognized association between the thought of Emerson and that of Nietzsche is that concerning the value of evil, immoral, or wicked tendencies or impulses for life. A correlative concept—the breakdown of the absolute distinction between good and evil—that is intimately associated with Nietzsche's thought is, in fact, an extension of

Emerson's bold reflections on traditional conceptions of morality. In his essays Emerson iterates and reiterates these two themes, themes that later emerge at the heart of Nietzsche's critique of various moralities. The critique of morality for which Nietzsche has often been excoriated was originally presented, in fragmentary form, by a surprisingly radical former Unitarian minister.

Although Emerson's ultimate aim is to create a foundation for a "new Morality," along the way he lashes out, from time to time, at what could be called, in Nietzsche's phrase, "moral prejudices." Very much disturbed by "religious fanatics," as well as fanatics of all stripes, Emerson sometimes proclaims that much of what society calls "good" is not and much that convention calls "evil" is not absolutely so or is, in fact, "good." The experiential and conceptual intertwining of 'evil' and good that is typical of so much of Nietzsche's easily misunderstood writings on this volatile theme and that has come to be associated with his *soi-disant* "immoralism" had already been foreshadowed—specifically, in his tendencies toward antinomianism—by the "genial" contributor to the literary renaissance in America.

Quite often Emerson pulls at the fringes of the values embodied in conventional, public morality. And sometimes, impatient with that conformity to custom that passes for morality, he seems to step outside the boundary of what is conventionally called 'morality.' In his vitriolic attacks on the "morality of custom," Nietzsche replicates, in a more intense way, Emerson's disdain for the same social phenomenon. And before Nietzsche made it popular, Emerson promoted fullness of life, courage, robust health, and life-affirmation in the context of a positive morality which is a synthesis of strenuous self-discipline, spiritual strength, and natural self-expression.

There are times when Emerson's impatience with restrictive, cloying moralities of prohibition leads him into a domain of moral ambiguity that Nietzsche inherited and dramatized. Emerson's autonomous, self-reliant, independent, noble individual is sometimes depicted as outside the circle of cramped moralities. The tendency to link public morality with social conformity, which is typical of Nietzsche's understanding of what he generally calls "previous morality," permeates Emerson's writings. By the time this open-ended and assertive mode of being, after having been amplified by Nietzsche, appears in cryptic form in Martin Heidegger's *Being and Time* in the form of the authentic individual or "authentic *Dasein,*" it is a mode of being, an attitude, that has a moral aura about it, but is no longer subject to constraint, restrictions, or any moral principles. Ironically, the creator of the pattern for this 'morality' of being is neither a German philosopher nor a European thinker. Rather, it was a surprisingly radical American poet and essayist. Unwittingly, Emerson's sketch for a "new morality" served, *via* Nietzsche's elaborations on it, as a blueprint for the self-existent, authentic individual who resolutely projects himself forward into the contingency and uncertainty of the future.

The conception of the good of wickedness (*böse*), the valuation of drives, passions, and impulses towards immorality, is a notion that Nietzsche appropriated from Emerson. Even the image of man as analogous to a plant, an image that is closely associated with Nietzsche, is one that has its origins in Emerson's metaphor. Just as a plant needs crude fertilizers in order to grow, so, too, does man. In *Beyond Good and Evil* (sec. 44) it is contended that "the plant 'man' " has grown vigorously not by virtue of tender care, but under conditions of pressure and danger. Nietzsche's variations on this theme—the depiction of the tree as the most healthy form of life because as its branches reach up to the heavens its roots shoot more deeply into the earth (a notion later reiterated by James Joyce)—are all related to Emerson's reflections. "Man," he tells us, " is that noble endogenous plant which grows like the palm, from within outward."[40] Just as plants convert minerals into food, so, too, does man convert natural raw materials to "human use." More directly and plainly than Nietzsche, Emerson joins growth—the natural tendency of life—to what is "base" in nature. There is "no plant that is not fed from manures." And this natural fact is transfered to human growth in order to emphasize the value of man's 'evil' traits, his drives, passions, and primal impulses. What Nietzsche presents as his deep and dangerous insight into the importance of wickedness for growth, strength, and sharp virtue is an accurate and only more dramatic expression of an Emersonian insight. For Emerson insists that "there is no man who is not at some time indebted to his vices, as no plant that is not fed from manures. We only insist that the man meliorate, and that the plant grow upward and convert the base into the better nature."[41]

The plant/man metaphor is only an element that links, to one of Emerson's fundamental themes, Nietzsche's repeated emphasis on the need to preserve our naturally inherited, life-preserving 'immoral' traits and to transform them into growth and virtues of strength. Whereas Emerson expresses himself concerning the conversion of evil into good from that cool zone of indifference from which he believed hard truths should emanate, Nietzsche preferred to transmit such ideas in the tone of a dangerous thinker. Nonetheless, he does not distort or misconstrue what Emerson said and meant.

History and Life

Nietzsche does not agree with Emerson in all respects. He tends to ignore those occasions on which Emerson, checking his own tendencies towards aristocratic disdain which, nonetheless, recur, expresses respect for the common man and hope in the promise of an imperfect, but bustling, American democracy. The irony is that just as there is an identifiable "gentle" and "tough" Nietzsche so, too, is there a gentle and a tough-minded Emerson. Just as literary critics have discerned a number of "Emersons,"[42] so have others seen quite a few "Nietzsches." What is even stranger is that the shifts of perspective that characterize what Nietzsche called his "philosophies" parallel the shifting points of view in Emerson's essays.

When it comes to the significant issues in the philosophy of Nietzsche, it is instructive to look for the Emerson-connection. For in most cases, though certainly not all, it will be found. This is particularly so in regard to the appraisal of the meaning and value of history for life in what is the best of the essays comprising *Untimely Meditations*, "On the Uses and Disadvantages of History for Life." The understanding of the value of history for life that is defended in this essay is a clearly identifiable theme of Emerson's. The strong subjective perspective presented there is one that closely relates Nietzsche to the existential strain that appears and reappears in the first series of Emerson's *Essays*. For a long time Nietzsche continued and dramatized Emerson's philosophy of individuality. However, the intensification of subjectivity is not a terminus for either Emerson or Nietzsche. It is a rite of passage that leads away from the crowd and the force of public opinion. Ultimately, it leads first for Emerson and then for Nietzsche to a self-suppression of subjective individuality, a cosmic vision of a circular process of actuality that is construed as sacred. But in his essay on history Nietzsche has not yet come to "think cosmically." Rather, like the Emerson of the first set of essays, his focus is on "man, man, man."

The presence of Emersonian views and valuations in "On the Uses and Disadvantages of History for Life" is apparent both in the argument for the value of history, properly understood, for life and in the foreshadowing of the image of the *Übermensch* in the celebration of the importance of "great men." Although Nietzsche's period of genius-admiration was encouraged by Schopenhauer's apotheosis of geniuses and his praise of the saint, the artist, and the philosopher, he was already familiar with Emerson's frequent hymns of praise of "the great." With an eye on the possibility of a stirring new culture, Emerson was preoccupied with the centrality of "great men," "transcendent men," for the restoration of a meaningful culture, for the creation of a higher culture.

Virtually all of the important ingredients in what I've called an existential theory of history in Nietzsche's essay can be traced back to Emerson, to his observations on the meaning of history for the individual and for life, to ideas he presents in "Uses of Great Men" and in other essays. Although Emerson's essay "History" is the template for Nietzsche's treatment of the problem of history and its relevance for life, it is not the only source in Emerson's writings that he mines. Once again, we shall see how Nietzsche works with and upon Emersonian insights. For he interrelates conceptions and observations that Emerson presents separately in several different places. His ingenuity in joining together elements of Emerson's reflections on the relation of history to life and present existence, on the dangers of the "overinfluence" of the great creators of the past, on the nature of "greatness," on the nature of life and living, as well as those on incidental issues, cannot be faulted: it is remarkably faithful to the spirit and direction of Emerson's thinking. In fact, in his discussion of history Nietzsche not only puts Emerson's ideas to fruitful use, but also approximates his tone and style.

Philosophers of Culture

A great deal of Emerson's writings fall under the rubric 'philosophy of culture.' Emerson, like Nietzsche, was deeply concerned with cultural values and disvalues. Although other thinkers later reinforced Nietzsche's awareness of a coming crisis in Western culture in general and an emerging crisis in Christian culture in particular, it was Emerson who first conveyed to him the idea that Christendom was in decline, that the official doctrines of the

Christian religion were losing their hold on the minds and hearts of men. His allusions to the question of the status of the claims to truth in Christianity, as well as to changing attitudes toward them, in "Fate and History," were framed in the context of his recent reading of Emerson.

In his 1838 address to the Harvard Divinity School, Emerson, in a condensed form, expressed criticisms of official Christianity that were milder than, but similar to, those of Søren Kierkegaard in his *Attack on Christendom*. During his lifetime, Kierkegaard waged polemics against "Christendom" or the public, official version of Christianity for its staleness, its emphasis on dogma and theological speculation rather than practice, for its separation from "true Christianity." Before Emerson said virtually the same thing, he insisted that "Christianity no longer exists." Emerson criticizes the Christendom of his time and place more economically, but with equal fervor. It is no wonder that his address was assailed by conservative theologians and that it precluded further invitations to address the divinity school until decades later.

Even though Emerson, given his Unitarian orientation, eschews the idea of the divinity of Christ, and Kierkegaard places the God-Man at the center of his call to "New Testament Christianity" or "primitive Christianity," there are curious similarities in their critiques of "historical Christianity" and their emphases on radical subjectivity. Kierkegaard saw Hegel's placement of Christianity as an important "moment" (*Momente*) in the evolution of the Absolute Spirit in history as its burial, its negation. In the same spirit Emerson declares that the essentials of Christianity have become "ancient history," that "historical Christianity has fallen into the error that corrupts all attempts to communicate religion." As Kierkegaard already did in Denmark, Emerson laments the formalism of the preaching and teaching of Christian doctrines. Emerson tells us that the people need and want "a stern, high, stoical, Christian discipline," one that Kierkegaard prescribes in his reformation of Christianity. Both attack the veneration of "numbers" and equate general society with "the crowd." In "Worship" Emerson suggests that the conformity required by Christendom emasculates men. In *Attack on Christendom* and elsewhere Kierkegaard charges that the same system produces "geldings." Nietzsche later repeats this theme quite often.

From time to time, Emerson returns to the issue of the decline of historical Christianity. On the one hand, he criticizes the way Christianity is presented in Christendom and, on the other hand, he laments the loss of religious faith in a culture increasingly devoted to the pursuit of material, commercial success. In addition, he points out that the rising "culture" of natural science is eroding religious belief. In his neglected essay, "Worship," Emerson describes his age as a "transition period," one in which "infidelity" of all kinds is rampant. The traditional religious beliefs that were once the cement that held modern Western societies together seems to be crumbling. Mankind seems to be entering a period of crisis, a period in history that Nietzsche will later examine in an exhaustive way: the period of the emergence of nihilism.

What is needed, Emerson tells us, is a "new morality" and a "new religion." Many commentators on the thought of Emerson maintain that this new ethico-religious ideal is transcendentalism. On the surface, this may appear to be a valid judgment. However, the essential elements of this proposed ideal, which are scattered throughout numerous essays, suggests a conception of reality and embraces a cultural goal that is only tangentially related to philosophico-religious transcendentalism. In fact, as one traces the unfolding of Emerson's unorthodox faith it is clearly revealed as an affirmative religion of *immanence*.

As early as 1834, Emerson saw that we've "lost our God of tradition" and are no longer moved by "our God of rhetoric." But once having lost these, once we realize that the traditional idea of God is dead, we may yet come to discover the God who will "fire the heart with his presence," the god in the self.[43] What Emerson sought was a religion of life and affirmation, a religion of beauty and strength, that would replace the encrusted forms of "historical Christianity." This new religion will prescind morbidity and guilt-consciousness. It will celebrate beauty, knowledge (*gnosis*), power, strength, health, and the divinity in *this* world, in man. The "beyond," "the next world," "the other world" interests Emerson very little.

Even though he insists that man's being is dependent upon the immanent power of a spiritual being acting through nature, Emerson focuses his attention on the human use of the energy of spirituality, on man's use of spiritual power, on the immense value of the present, on the manifestations of divinity in the world of time and becoming. Although the intuitive power of the mind is the transcendental ground for our experience of nature, the world, and actuality, we are nonetheless immersed in the world, in nature, in an actuality in which we should strive "to be" and look towards the perfectibility of spiritual reality in living forms.

Like the ideal poet, we should seek "to enhance the great and constant fact of Life."

There is little pure Platonism in Emerson.[44] The world of forms or ideas, the ultimate 'Good', is not separated from this world of uncertainty, change, circumstances, and impermanence. Through the Protean forms of nature there acts a spiritual *nisus* towards perfection which reaches its peak in the possibilities of man. Although Emerson pays homage to the transcendental One, the 'Oversoul', he does not dwell on it; rather, he is far more concerned with what man does with his spiritual potentialities here and now, in this world. Insofar as Emerson has a philosophical religion, it is a religion of immanence.

Needless to say, Nietzsche's appraisal of the situation of the Christian religion and culture in Europe is tantamount to that of Emerson, even though he expresses himself in such a passionate, hyperbolic, and dramatic way that Emerson's relatively sober prose is completely overshadowed by his fiery rhetoric. The theme of a new religion which would be unlike previous religions is, of course, a red thread that runs through most of Nietzsche's writings. Even though he extensively augments and exaggerates Emerson's remarks on the state of traditional religion and the possibility of creating a new religion, he neither misunderstands nor distorts what Emerson actually says. He understood full well the significance of the decline of historical Christianity and the rise of a powerful, but problematic, "culture" of science. Before Nietzsche became acquainted with a variety of theories in physics, biology, and the social sciences, Emerson had already communicated to him the importance of the new powers that have been put in the hands of mankind by the rapidly emerging scientific culture. And he was also sensitive to the cultural-intellectual effects of this penetration of the natural world. It is, as he says in "Illusions," causing us to raise "terrible questions," and it is eroding earlier systems of belief. While our ancestors believed in magic, we are now "coming on the secret of a magic which sweeps out of men's minds all vestige of theism and beliefs which they and their fathers held and were framed upon." In "Worship" the culture of science is linked to the waning of religious faith, and a long and painful period of transition is seen as modern man's near-future.

Emerson was the first thinker to instill in Nietzsche's mind that Western man is at a promising, but dangerous, crossroad. Amplifying Emerson's occasional worries over the impact that man's power over nature through scientific knowledge might have on culture to the highest degree, Nietzsche predicted the coming of nihilism, a century of nihilism. Following Emerson's suggestions, he, too, saw the need for a "new morality," a "new religion," that would be the foundation of a new culture that would enhance human existence. As in the case of Emerson, this new "higher" culture would be informed by knowledge (as *gnosis*), a transformation of values, and propelled by a "Dionysian" affirmation of life and existence. Nietzsche took up the torch of a new cultural vision from the hands of the American "teacher of the ideal," carrying it forward, adding to its fire the fuel of his creative philosophical imagination.

The overriding importance of culture, the power of culture in shaping the ideals and lives of a people is a theme to which Emerson frequently returns. Aside from his concern with the loss of faith in American culture and with the emergent powers of a culture of science, he deplores the corruption and chicanery of American politics in harsh, but appropriate language. Quite often he attacks social institutions, freely knocking down the "house of cards" of which, he believes, they are made. Society is viewed as at war with individuals, as a leveling force that resents genuinely independent persons. Emerson lashes out at an economic system that is often "a system of selfishness" and deplores the "cynicism of the streets." He seems to reserve his sharpest language for critical forays against society and cultural deficiencies.

Emerson insists, as Nietzsche later does, that the State and politics must serve culture and provide the conditions for the perfectibility of man. His criticisms of the politics of his day and of the quality of American culture are virtually repeated by Nietzsche in his attacks on German culture and politics. The materialism of American culture, which has been exacerbated by time, is criticized by Emerson in language that later surfaces in Nietzsche's polemic against the same tendency he finds in the Germany of the 1870s. Despite his assaults on the business practices, politics, and social institutions of his time, Emerson does not want to push reform to the point of absurdity. "I do not wish," he tells us, "to push my criticism on the state of things around me to that extravagant mark that shall compel me to suicide, or to an absolute isolation from the advantages of civil society."[45]

Often enough, Nietzsche insisted upon establishing an "order of rank" in society that would frankly acknowledge human inequalities and recognize qualitative distinctions among persons. This aristocratic scale of values and powers is presumed to be one

derived from "the law of life" and nature. Such a conception of a
natural aristocracy has been characterized by critics of German
thought in general, and critics of Nietzsche in particular, as a typical form of Teutonic arrogance. Unfortunately, it is Emerson,
once again, who previously proposed the recognition of a "scale of
rank" in society and who insisted upon the need to make qualitative distinctions among persons. Even though he sometimes says
that he sides with the "common," and even though he has been
called a "philosopher of democracy," Emerson often supports a
conception of society based upon a "natural aristocracy."

The aristocracy of spirit that Nietzsche was passionately concerned with conserving and preserving in opposition to the incur-
sions of anarchy, socialism, communism, and the rise of "the
masses," is virtually identical to Emerson's predominant sentiments concerning this same valuation. In terms of strong and
harsh judgements about the majority, Emerson and Nietzsche
speak the same language. Or rather, the latter appropriates the language of Emerson. The "aristocratic radicalism" that was attributed to Nietzsche could just as well be attributed to an American
radical.

Insofar as Emerson, from time to time, expresses compassion
for the foolish, the ignorant, and the uncultured, he mitigates his
harshest judgments about what he called "the masses" or "the
herd." However, the fact that Emerson occasionally shows a pater-
nal concern for the majority does not differentiate his social attitudes from those of Nietzsche. For he, too, especially in his early
writings, occasionally preaches tolerance of the wayward majority.

In *Human, All-Too-Human* the "exploitation of the worker" is
criticized, and Nietzsche recommends social reform and a more
equitable distribution of wealth in society. In notes from the 1870s
he proposes the idea of a "physician of culture" who promotes geniuses and the conditions for the emergence of the genius for the
sake of the entire culture and its peoples. In his first essay on Richard Wagner in *Thoughts Out of Season,* he goes so far as to say that
no one can be truly free and creative until all human beings are
liberated from deprivation and suffering. Precisely in regard to
such opposing attitudes towards the majority does the influence of
Emerson on Nietzsche become apparent. For Nietzsche not only
adopts, amplifies, and organizes many of Emerson's conceptions
and insights, but he also absorbs and reflects the internal tensions
in Emerson's judgments. An aphorism in *Human, All-Too-Human*
could be said to allude to Nietzsche himself or to Emerson or,

more likely, to both: "Positive and Negative—This thinker needs no one to refute him—he is quite capable of doing that himself."[46]

Nexus

The son of a Unitarian minister, Ralph Waldo Emerson was born in Boston in 1803. His father died when he was eight years old, and he was raised, in semipoverty, by his aunt. He attended the Boston Public Latin School where he already began to display literary talents. He was later admitted to Harvard College at the age of fourteen, graduating in 1821. At about this time, he was forced to take an extended rest in order to recuperate from a debilitating lung ailment. Although he was relatively healthy throughout most his life, Emerson complained of a lack of energy and the need to husband his resources. There is some evidence that he suffered from a premature old age. Despite whatever physical limitations he may have had, he became a very effective lecturer and, of course, a productive and remarkable essayist and poet. His voluminous journals reveal a deep, critical, and vital inward life.

In 1829, Emerson became a Unitarian minister, serving at the Second Church in Boston. His conscientious preparation for sermons, as well as his habit of keeping a journal, paved the way for his successful career as a lecturer. In the same year in which he assumed his ministry, Emerson married Ellen Tucker. When she died of tuberculosis in February, 1831, he was profoundly grief-stricken. Shock followed on shock when, in 1834, his beloved brother Edward died, and then, two years later, his brother Charles—his admired friend, his "spheral" man—succumbed to the ravages of tuberculosis. All of this brought about a serious crisis in his life and, for a time, his despair was profound.

About a year after Ellen's death Emerson resigned his ministry. The reason he gave was that he was unwilling to administer communion because he could no longer accept its sacramental meaning. In addition, he felt that he could not commit himself fully to the religion he was supposed to serve. The confluence of deep, personal loss and religious and intellectual doubts produced a terrible period in his life.

In the winter of 1832, after receiving financial support from family and friends, Emerson traveled to Europe. In England, he met Coleridge, Wordsworth, and Carlyle. His meeting with

Thomas Carlyle developed into a lifelong friendship, and he and Carlyle corresponded with each other for a number of years.

Before he left for Europe, sometime in March, 1832, Emerson made the following disquieting entry in his notebook: "I visited Ellen's tomb & opened the coffin." Some have said that this was a reference to a dream, while others have contended that it had the symbolic meaning that he had to turn from his dead wife to life. Whatever this Poe-like entry may have meant for him, there is a poignant sadness in its tone. Within a two-year period the painful realities of the death of his brothers increased the dosage of his suffering.

After returning from his European journey, Emerson was awarded a modest income through the settlement of his wife's estate. Sometime in 1834, he permanently settled in Concord where, except for lecture tours and occasional trips, he was to remain for the rest of his life. Although he no longer had a ministry, Emerson accepted invitations, from time to time, to give guest sermons. During the 1830s throughout the Northeast and the Middle West, the "lyceum" movement took root, and Emerson became an active lecturer on the lyceum circuit. For about thirty years the lecture platform gave him a modest income and supported him and his family. For a period of two years Emerson served as editor of *The Dial,* a magazine which had been founded by a small group of transcendentalists in 1840.

A year after his second marriage, Emerson's first major work, *Nature,* was published. It launched his career as an author even though it did not receive a great deal of attention. Over time a handful of American intellectuals discovered Emerson, and his oration on the American Scholar, presented to the Phi Beta Kappa Society at Harvard, was well attended and enthusiastically received. The publication of two series of essays established his international reputation. The collection of essays under the title, *The Conduct of Life,* which many consider his best work, contains some of his most important essays. Collections of his poetry appeared in 1848, 1857, and 1876. His last collection of essays, *Solitude and Society,* published in 1870, was well received even though it reveals a decline in sharpness and a weakening of literary power. A general decline of intellectual acuity and memory loss marked his later years. He died in 1882 at the age of eighty.

A turning point in Emerson's intellectual life occurred shortly after the death of his son, Waldo, in 1842. Added to the earlier losses within an eleven-year period, this last blow gave him a permanent acquaintance with the dark side of life. Some of his contemporaries and some recent literary critics resent his survival of these disasters as a person and as a productive writer. A more charitable account of this is that Emerson had great powers of endurance and an unusual spiritual strength. In his writings after this period his earlier idealistic optimism and his hymns to the unlimited possibilities of man give way to the recognition of the ineluctable limitation of circumstances, to the power of fate. It is quite clear, however, that even during the period of his optimistic faith, as some of his reflections and observations in his notebooks indicate, Emerson was never a naive or superficial optimist. His optimistic faith in life and man was a reflection of a deep, personal religious faith combined with an effort to overcome skeptical doubts and affirm the value of existence despite its obvious flaws and imperfections. Both his essays and his journal entries, to say nothing of his poetry, reveal a person determined to transcend, by an effort of will and strong faith, any temptation to fall into a defeatist pessimism.

The Conduct of Life includes some of Emerson's most insightful and powerful essays. In "Power," "Fate," "Culture," and the biting "Considerations By the Way" we see the emergence of the tough, hard-headed side of Emerson. *Representative Men,* a series of biographical sketches of various types of uncommon men, reveals Emerson's ability to present a sympathetic understanding of individuals quite unlike himself, as well as his capacity to stand back from his subject and view him with detachment. He illuminates his "representative men" from a number of perspectives and invariably offers balanced portraits of the individuals he depicts. Like the German philosopher Wilhelm Dilthey, he had a good eye for the ideal type.

A central figure in the American literary renaissance, a friend of Alcott, Hawthorne, and Thoreau, Emerson was an admired and respected figure whose writings were translated into over a dozen languages. His influence extended to an army of poets, writers, and thinkers, and he is undergoing, especially in the hands of several literary critics, a positive reappraisal today. His philosophy of self-reliant individualism, his humanistic cultural ideals, still have the power to inspire and edify. His emphasis on the inward life, which is analogous to Kierkegaard's stress on ethical and religious "inwardness," as well as his prescription of self-trust, integrity, and independence signify Emerson's obvious affinity with the spirit of the existential standpoint to which he, *via* Nietzsche, unknowingly contributed.

As early as 1857 Emerson's writings were available in German translation. In Nietzsche's library the following works of his were found: *R. W. Emerson's Essays,* Hannover, 1858 (translated by G. Fabricus); *Die Fuehrung des Lebens, Gedanken und Studien,* Leipzig, 1862 (translated by E. Sartorius); *Emerson: Neue Essays,* Leipzig, 1876 (translated by Julian Schmidt); and *Essay ueber Goethe und Shakespeare,* Leipzig, 1857 (translated by H. Grimm). In these books are found underlinings of many passages, as well as expressions of agreement or approbation in the margins. That Nietzsche read, studied, and responded positively to Emerson's writings is beyond dispute. In preparation for writing *Thus Spoke Zarathustra* he copied out in his notes numerous excerpts from Emerson's essays. And there is evidence that before writing his autobiography, *Ecce Homo,* he reread many passages in the *Versuche* or *Essays,* writing in the margins, here and there, the phrase "Ecce Homo."

In an apparent emulation of an Emersonian essay, in notes from 1862, Nietzsche, as previously mentioned, combines two titles of Emerson's essays in *"Fatum und Geschichte."* That he had just begun to pay serious attention to the American essayist is shown by a note to himself in which he reminds himself to read more of "Emmerson" [*sic*]. In a later entry from June, 1863, he once again urges himself to read Emerson over his vacation and suggests that he make "an outline of books for my friend." He randomly jots down the following: "His wise American reflections"; "On Wealth"; "Beauty"; "Summaries of all the 'Essays.' " In the same place he writes: "On philosophy in life." Nietzsche refers to a newly acquired book by Emerson that was probably *The Conduct of Life.* In journal entries from the same period are found abbreviated inscriptions of thoughts on "Nature" and some excerpts from "Beauty." During the 1860s, Nietzsche's journals are dotted with several direct quotations from the Sartorius German translation of *The Conduct of Life.*[47]

Some of the last direct references that Nietzsche made to Emerson are found in his correspondence with Franz Overbeck during 1883 and 1884. A few of his remarks about him show his habit of being condescending to those to whom he is most indebted. Closing a letter to Overbeck, he writes: "Tell your dear wife that I feel in Emerson a soul-brother (but the mind is badly formed)." A year later he asks Overbeck, "How goes it with Emerson and your wife." In December of 1884, he informs Overbeck that

> I'm having a long essay of Emerson's translated into German which cast some light on his own development. If you like, it is at your and

your dear wife's disposal. I can't tell you how much I would give to effect retroactively the strict disciplining, the genuine scholarly education of so great and splendid a nature, with its spiritual and intellectual wealth. As it is, we've lost a philosopher in Emerson.[48]

The presence of the pregnant phrase, "Ecce Homo," in the margins of a few of Emerson's essays indicates that as late as 1888 (when the autobiographical work, *Ecce Homo,* was written) Nietzsche was still returning to Emerson for inspiration. His appropriation of Emerson's observation, "to be great is to be misunderstood," is only one of a number of echoes of Emerson's voice in *Ecce Homo.* In an early draft of his autobiography there is a paragraph which was not used in the final version. In it Nietzsche once again praises Emerson in a typically personal way. "With his essays," he wrote, "Emerson has been a good friend and cheered me up even in black periods. He contains so much *skepsis,* so many possibilities, that even virtue attains *esprit* in his writings. A unique case! I enjoyed listening to him even as a youth."[49] This retrospective appraisal, however, is somewhat misleading insofar as Emersonian themes, conceptions, and phrases can be found in *Twilight of the Idols, On the Genealogy of Morals,* and, here and there, in his notes from the late 1880s.

From the moment that Nietzsche became acquainted with Emerson's life and works, he felt a strong affinity to him. Aside from his reaction to his literary style and thought, he may have felt a psychological bond with Emerson because they had quite a bit in common. For he, too, was the son of a pastor, and his father died when he was a child of four and a half. Nietzsche was precocious in literature and he, like Emerson, was steeped in classical literature and philosophy. Both were raised only by women. Both were strongly attracted to a solitary way of life. Emerson and Nietzsche suffered, at one time or another, from serious eye problems and debilitating illnesses. Both made heroic efforts to overcome physical limitations. Nietzsche suffered throughout his life from an array of complaints, and Emerson suffered first from a lung disease and, as has been said, seemed to be plagued by premature aging. In both men one can detect, in their expressed attitude towards life and their ideals about what human beings can become, a strong element of overcompensation.

Despite his literary and intellectual expression of optimism, Emerson was neither a particularly vital individual nor a perennially buoyant personality. In *Twilight of the Idols* Nietzsche calls attention to Emerson's "youthfulness" and seems to have emulated his manner of injecting into his writings a buoyant cheerfulness, a youthful tone. The contrast between the vivacious tone of Nietzsche's writings and his physical and mental sufferings is similar to the relationship between Emerson's writings and his actual states of being. Thus, at the age of thirty-two, in a journal entry of August, 1835, he wrote that "after thirty a man wakes up sad every morning excepting perhaps five or six until the day of his death." One finds in his essays and poetry not the slightest hint of such a depressed attitude or feeling. The same contrast can be found between Nietzsche's reports of illness and sadness in his letters and the sprightly, even exuberant, tone of his published writings.

In regard to a preference for solitude and an annoyance at sociability, Nietzsche definitely discovered in Emerson a temperamental affinity. His unusual psychic relationship to Emerson or to his image of him was not only one of admiration (at a considerable distance) or intellectual influence alone. He felt a strong bond with the American poet and essayist, a very personal identification with his image of Emerson the man. At times he refers to him as if he were a personal friend.

In his notes Nietzsche says that he always felt "at home" with Emerson. "Emerson—I have never in a book felt myself so much at home and in my home as—I dare not praise it, it is so close to me."[50] This close identification with Emerson as a person and as a thinker often led Nietzsche to adopt, intentionally or not, attitudes or judgments that were typical of Emerson. Thus, to cite one of many examples, he once proclaimed that "I write for myself." Only "in this way," he continues, "shall each one do his best for himself according to his kind."[51] Years before he made this observation, in the early 1860s, he had copied out in his notebook the following sentence from Emerson's "Spiritual Laws": "He that writes to himself writes to an eternal public."

Many of Nietzsche's heartfelt sentiments are, in actuality, paraphrases of, or unconscious echoes of, Emerson's writings. When, for example, he asserts that he writes with his "body and life" and claims that "all truths" are, for him, "bloody truths," he echoes Emerson's approbation of the works of Burns, Goldsmith, Cowper, Carlyle, Wordsworth, and Goethe in "The American Scholar"—"This writing is bloodwarm." Or, perhaps, he recalled Emerson's remark in "Montaigne"—"Cut these words and they would bleed; they are vascular and alive." There are so many instances of this phenomenon—that is, Nietzsche adopting Emerson not only as teacher and model, but as *alter ego*—that to speak of intellectual "influence" here is a considerable understatement.

Not only do we know that Nietzsche scrutinized Emerson's essays, but there is some evidence that he was familiar with the notes that his son appended to the essays. When in *On the Genealogy of Morals* Nietzsche refers to "my *unknown* friends,"[52] he seems to have borrowed the phrase from Edward Emerson's claim, in notes to "Friendship," that his father had many friends who were "unknown to him," but "had few close friends in all his life."[53]

There is no doubt that Nietzsche absorbed the language, thought, and sentiments of the American writer. And his praise of a man he seemed to consider as his "teacher of the ideal" was unusual considering his more typical blistering attacks on other writers and thinkers. In the *Nachlass* of 1881–82 he writes that "the author richest in ideas of this century has been an American (unfortunately clouded by German philosophy). Milky glass."[54] Here he snipes at Emerson's loose reliance on German idealism and characterizes the cloudiness of Emerson's thinking in terms of an image ("milky glass," *Milchglas*) that epitomizes his opinion about the murkiness of late eighteenth-and early nineteenth-century German thought. Ironically, Emerson implied this metaphor in his critical remarks on the British historian and essayist, Thomas Carlyle, in a journal entry: "O Carlyle, the merit of glass is not to be seen, but to be seen through, but every crystal and lamina of the Carlyle glass is visible."[55]

In *Human, All-Too-Human* there are numerous echoes of Emerson's style and tone, as well as allusions to the content of some of his essays. In an aphorism entitled "Forward," Nietzsche urges his readers to move "forward on the path of wisdom, with a firm step and good confidence!" He advises them to "throw off the displeasure at your nature, forgive yourself your own individuality, for, in any case, you have in yourself a ladder with a hundred steps upon which you can mount to knowledge."[56] In "Circles" Emerson had proclaimed that "Men walk as prophecies of the next age. Step by step we scale this mysterious ladder; the steps are actions, the new prospect is power."[57] In Nietzsche's aphorism there are references to Emerson's view of the correct perception of history, to the supreme value of the pursuit of knowledge, to the need to listen to the "voice of nature," to the consolation of a wisdom that is "joyful" even in the face of the "mists of death." What Nietzsche does in this aphorism is typical of his constructive use of, and amalgamation of, Emerson's dispersed insights. He combines various

assertions sprinkled throughout the essays in order to form a statement of principles, to express a point of view, to delineate an attitude or project a personal or cultural value. He often joins together
what Emerson presents asunder. René Wellek correctly identified
a feature of Emerson's thought that, in some instances, is replicated in the writings of Nietzsche. He "was . . . a fragmentary,
though not . . . inconsistent, thinker who disparaged all system,
all elaborate chains of reasoning . . . the whole method of discursive philosophy."[58] Emerson was the master of the *aperçu,* the
striking insight, the prophetic inscription.

Although there is a rough unity in his philosophy, Nietzsche
quite often presents his thought in an unsystematic way. He approaches philosophical theories intuitively, often building his
thought around an aphoristic insight. He synthesizes his own ka-
leidoscopic philosophical views almost in the way in which he as-
sembles the *disjecta membra* of Emerson's reflections. What is only
suggested in passing by Emerson is constructively developed, organized, expressed in the form of a recognizable "doctrine" or a
reasonably consistent interpretation of a significant human or cultural phenomenon. Insofar as he presents his thought unsystemat-
ically, Nietzsche was clearly encouraged in this tendency by
Emerson.

Virtually from the beginning of his reflective life Nietzsche
was impressed by, and attracted to, Emerson's literary style, his
flashing insights, his understanding of the positive and the negative in nature and human nature. Although the thought of Nietzsche contains many "philosophies," it is primarily in what may be
called his wisdom literature, as well as in his positive ideas, that
Emersonian themes are most prevalent. In some of his earlier essays and in his letters Nietzsche sometimes seems to be emulating
Emerson's style and tone. Thus, in a letter to his sister sent from
Bonn in 1865 he justifies his turning away from religious faith and
presents his own credo in terms that are reminiscent of some of
Emerson's basic sentiments. He asks his sister whether it is not
more difficult "to strike new paths, fighting the habitual, experiencing the insecurity of independence and the frequent wavering of
one's feelings and even one's conscience, proceeding often without
any consolation, but ever with the eternal goal of the true, the
beautiful, and the good?"[59]

Although it may be said that Emerson had no monopoly on
such sentiments and that Nietzsche is expressing feelings typical of
romanticism, it is also the case that in the early 1860s and up to the

1870s the imprint of Emerson's language acted powerfully on Nietzsche's consciousness. For a time he was under the spell of his romantic nature-mysticism and under the sway of the apotheosis of the "Truth, and goodness, and beauty" that Emerson declared to be "but different faces of the same All."[60] In a letter sent to his friend Carl von Gersdorff in the spring of 1866, Nietzsche writes that

> sometimes there comes those quiet meditative moments in which one stands above one's life with mixed feelings of joy and sadness, like those lovely summer days which spread themselves expansively and comfortably across the hills, as Emerson excellently describes them. Then nature becomes perfect, as he says, and we ourselves too; then we are set free from the spell of the ever-watchful will; then we are pure, contemplative, impartial eye.[61]

The last line is directly associated with a passage from *Nature* in which Emerson describes a pure, impartial relationship to the natural world: "Standing on the bare ground—my head bathed by the blithe air and uplifted into infinite space—all mean egotism vanishes. I become a transparent eyeball."[62] There are instances in which, when one compares the assertoric judgments of Nietzsche to those of Emerson, one has a subliminal sense of *déjà-vu*. At times, it is difficult to tell whether one is reading Emerson or Nietzsche if one looks at an isolated, unattributed passage. The following observation is Emerson's even though it sounds like a typical Nietzschean remark: "Beware when the great God lets loose a thinker on this planet. Then all things are at risk. It is as when a conflagration has broken out in a great city, and no man knows what is safe, or where it will end."[63]

Not surprisingly, Nietzsche underlined this passage in his copy of the *Essays*. And in his *Untimely Meditations* he quoted it with acknowledgment and enthusiasm. He felt as Emerson did about the power and influence of thinkers, and he aggressively adopted an attitude towards his own philosophy that may be said to have sought to justify Emerson's warning. In notes from 1872 there are references to the impact of the philosopher on history and culture. And there is one notation that seems to turn Emerson's warning around. "Philosophers appear," he writes, "during those times of great danger, when the wheel of time is turning faster and faster."[64] In his own philosophical stance he certainly wanted to convey the impression that his philosophy was dangerous, that his thinking was like "dynamite," that his "way" led to a "dangerous

perhaps." He seems to have wanted to live up to Emerson's prophetic warning about the effects of a great thinker on the world.

The presence of Emerson surfaces here and there in *Human, All-
Too-Human*. In an aphorism in this work Nietzsche seems to allude to, and respond to, Emerson's remarks on the difficulties of
friendship. In "Of Friends" there is a lamentation about the fragility of friendship, the many occasions for mutual misunderstanding. One can understand, Nietzsche writes, the bitter remark of
"the sage": "Friends, there are no friends!"[65] But, Nietzsche continues, with some sense of self-knowledge, with a sense of our
own faults, we may learn to bear with our friends and they with
us. Although "the sage" (Emerson) does not quite go so far as to
say that there are no friends (though he cites Napoleon's judgment
that "friendship is but a name"), he calls friendship a paradox of
nature, recognizes its rarity, sees the hypocrisy that threatens it,
and laments that "friends such as we desire are dreams and fables."
Nietzsche does not literally copy Emerson, but he adopts his tone,
his rhetorical style, and, in an eclectic manner, picks and chooses
what he wants to use from Emerson's *corpus*.

In "Schopenhauer as Educator" Nietzsche once again reveals the
influence of Emerson on his thought. Despite the title of this essay, it is not about Schopenhauer's philosophy *per se,* but it is concerned, among other things, with an idealized portrait of
Schopenhauer the man. The philosophical sentiments actually expressed in this essay are closer to those of Emerson than to the
thought of Schopenhauer. It is argued, at one point, that the aims
of culture and of nature are basically the same. Nature "wants" to
render man's life significant by virtue of the generation of the artist and the philosopher. There is a tendency towards perfection in
nature even though it is often thwarted. Here Nietzsche recognizes
design in the natural order, even though the ends of nature are not
efficiently realized. Commenting on such early descriptions of a
teleology in nature in Nietzsche's writings, Walter Kaufmann
worried over them and suspected a mystical concept of natural
purpose that goes against the grain of Nietzsche's later, more typical, denial of an objective teleology. However, there is nothing
strange about this interpretation of nature if we see that it is a reflection of Emerson's conception of the natural world in *Nature*.

There are, Emerson contended, spiritual tendencies in nature
that are analogous to those of human life. The aims of culture reflect the aims of nature. A "meliorating" tendency pervades nature
that reaches its apogee in the aspirations of man, of the "poet and

the philosopher." The striving for perfection in human life and in history is not antagonistic to the "impulses" of nature, but is a continuation of nature's purposes. The law of nature, we are told in "Compensation," is growth. The personification of nature that is typical of Emerson is, in his essay on "Schopenhauer," adopted by Nietzsche. The poetic, anthropomorphic personification of nature which appears in this essay attests to the hidden presence of Emerson in his thinking.

La gaya scienza

In Emerson's "Considerations By the Way" there are a number of notes sounded that are echoed later in the writings of his German admirer. One in particular is striking because it is considered as a distinctively Nietzschean notion. After expatiating on the importance of health for a full and creative life, a theme that Nietzsche will carry forward and amplify in his naturalistic ethics, Emerson announces that, in order for knowledge to be genuinely valuable, we must cultivate a "cheerfulness of wisdom." He quotes with approval a Latin proverb: *Aliis laetus, sapiens sibi*, "Be merry *and* wise."[66] In his lecture "Prospects" he had proclaimed himself a "professor of the Joyful Science," and elsewhere he characterized poetry as "the *gai science*."[67]

This juxtaposition of the valuation of knowledge and cheerful wisdom brings us into the cognitive and rhetorical *milieu* of Nietzsche's *The Gay Science*. In this coruscating work Nietzsche serves as a champion of Emerson's gospel of *"la gaia scienza"* in a direct way. For Emerson repeats this theme of a joyful wisdom in a few places and emphasizes the playful creativity of the person of knowledge as a life-ideal, one that would wipe away the "pale cast of thought" while retaining a personal knowledge that would enhance life. The link between such ideals of existence and those of Nietzsche is strengthened by the fact that Emerson thinks of the individual in whom joyfulness and knowledge are combined as extremely rare, as an exceptional type that has not yet come to full realization.

The sprightly and affirmative *The Gay Science* is imbued with the spirit of Emerson, as well as being surcharged with some of Nietzsche's most striking insights and images. The motto for the 1882 edition of this work is a slight variation on a passage from Emerson's "History." It is quoted in the following way: "To the poet and sage all things are friendly and sacred, all events profitable, all days holy, all men divine." Emerson's original proclaimed that "to the poet, to the philosopher, to the saint, all things are friendly and sacred, all events profitable, all days holy, all men divine." In his notes from 1882 Nietzsche accurately quotes Emerson from the German translation of the *Versuche*. In the motto he drops the reference to the saint, no doubt because his message is one of secular liberation.[68]

Although there is much in *The Gay Science* that is not traceable to Emerson, many of its most powerful themes are associated with a number of the philosophical views and valuations of Emerson. This does not only pertain to the prescription of a joyful knowledge joined with "great healthiness," for it includes Nietzsche's admonition to recognize "the necessary characters in things as the beautiful,"[69] an attitude towards existence that is vintage Emerson. In "Fate" he celebrated "beautiful necessity" and praised the insight into the necessity in things. Emerson proclaimed that the "ring of necessity" educates man and teaches him that "there are no contingencies."[70] Even one of the centerpieces of *The Gay Science, amor fati* or "love of fate," is indebted to the inspiration of Emerson, as are other themes as well.

A passage in *The Gay Science* that is often cited is the aphorism entitled "Differences in the Dangerousness of Life." In it Nietzsche avers that we do not know what we experience because we "run through life as if intoxicated." And we particularly do not recognize that *life* is our greatest danger.[71] Even though previous commentators have noticed that this aphorism is derived from Emerson, they minimize its importance for him and do not indicate where he expresses his view on how we experience life and how we ought to do so. First in "The Method of Nature," next in "Fate," and then in "Illusions" does Emerson assert that "Life is an ecstasy." We are, he says, moved by our own madness, pulled by the strings of our "constitution," our states of being, our needs, our desires, our moods. In "Illusions" we are said to live by our imaginations, by our likes and dislikes, by our sentiments, by the host of illusions that motivate most of our actions. We awaken, Emerson tells us, from one dream and enter another. The intoxicated "sot" is easily amused. But none are exempt from this condition: "everybody is drugged with his own frenzy."[72] Elsewhere we are told that "men live in their fancy, like drunkards whose hands are too soft and tremulous for successful labor."[73]

Our illusions, Emerson insists, bring us into a world of "hallucination" and "deception." The theme of the power of illusions in life, even the power of the "illusion of love," is a recurrent one in his writings. Emerson was the first to imprint on Nietzsche's mind the notion that, in order to endure life, illusions are necessary. And he was the first thinker who suggested to him the relativity of human experience, the subjective element in perception and thought, the power of what Nietzsche calls "perspectival knowing." As in regard to other conceptions, Nietzsche expands, develops, and dramatizes insights that Emerson presents in an almost causal way.

In regard to references to the role of danger in life found in Emerson's essays, it has been said that Nietzsche goes beyond him by making danger a principle of life.[74] The truth of the matter is that the paradigmatic Nietzschean imperative—"live dangerously"—is first suggested to him by Emerson. Although he does not coin this striking existential imperative, he often extols the value of danger for personal and moral growth, for the strengthening of character, for the attainment of excellence.

In "Worship" Emerson declares that man should face "danger" for the sake of the right. In "Considerations By the Way" it is said that no one should be overprotected or spoiled by ease, that facing dangers cultivates "broader wisdom and manly power." Daring and fearlessness enable an individual to live more deeply than others. Some men embrace "danger in fight" and, paradoxically, become more civil. Some individuals possess a "sacred courage" that enables them to face dangers and accept difficult tasks.[75] Emerson often urges his readers to face the dreadful realities of life in a courageous, "manly" way, to accept the insecurities and uncertainties of existence. In "Heroism" he advises those who aspire to wisdom "to look with bold eye into those rarer dangers which sometimes invade men."[76]

The step from many of Emerson's counsels on this point to the flamboyant imperative, "live dangerously," is a short one. Nietzsche prescribed danger as a principle of life after Emerson, even though neither advocated recklessness or risk-taking as an end in itself. Indeed, in *The Gay Science,* it is an "ideal" attitude or way of thinking that is said to be "full of danger"; that is, "the ideal of a humanly superhuman welfare and benevolence." In another place, Nietzsche speaks (in a voice more dramatic than that of Emerson, but in language he would have understood) of the thousandfold multiplication of the dangers that life entails when one seriously attempts to be an authentically "independent" individual.

Emerson understood only too well that independence, self-reliance, and nonconformity will cause the world to "whip you

with its displeasure."[77] But Nietzsche understood even better than
he the psychological dangers to which the truly independent person is exposed if "he loses his way, becomes lonely, and is torn
piecemeal by some minotaur of conscience." Uncannily anticipating the *pathos* of his later situation in life in *Beyond Good and Evil,*
Nietzsche says that when such an individual loses his way, it will
happen so far outside the comprehension of others that they will
neither sense it nor sympathize. And this hapless individual is unable to go back, unable even to receive "the pity of men."

Emerson was very much on Nietzsche's mind during the writing of *The Gay Science.* In an aphorism dealing with "Prose and
Poetry" he includes him, along with the nineteenth-century pessimistic Italian poet Giacomo Leopardi, the French writer Prosper
Mérimée, and the English author Walter Savage Landor, among
"masters of prose." In a later work, *Twilight of the Idols,* he again
praises Emerson, this time in a more personal way:

> *Emerson*—Much more enlightened, more daring, more multifarious,
> more refined than Carlyle; above all, happier. . . . Such a man as in-
> stinctively feeds on pure ambrosia and leaves alone the indigestible in
> things . . . a man of taste. . . . Emerson has that benevolent and intel-
> ligent cheerfulness that discourages all severity. He has no idea how old
> he is or how young he may become—he could say of himself, in the
> words of Lope de Vega: "I am my own successor." His spirit is always
> finding reasons for being tranquil and grateful; and sometimes he
> verges on . . . cheerful transcendence.[78]

Many subsidiary themes in *The Gay Science* suggest the influential presence of Emerson. There are, for example, attempts to
describe "nobility of character" that are associated with Emerson's
emphases upon the development of character. Related to the issue
of the development of character is a theme presented in "Considerations By the Way" and elsewhere, one that insinuated itself into
Nietzsche's reflections and is treated in *The Gay Science* without
alteration. It is held that the strongest and most wicked individuals, by awakening sleeping passions, have contributed greatly to
the advancement of mankind. It is further contended that man's
'evil' impulses are expedient and indispensable to the conservation
of the species.[79] Emerson's focus of concern in the essay included
in *The Conduct of Life* is precisely on these same points. For it is
said that "malfeasance" and rough passions have made great contributions to civilization, that "nature turns all malfeasance to
good."[80] As we shall see, what is often ascribed to Nietzsche's
self-styled "immoralism"—the belief that 'evil' or wickedness can

produce good—is basically a view originally presented by the "benign" and "genteel" Emerson. That this is not a superficial connection between Emerson and Nietzsche will be shown in a more detailed tracking of this seeming paradox as it is transmitted from the thought of the former to the philosophical discourse of the latter.

What may seem to be observations made *en passant* in *The Gay Science* that we would easily attribute to Nietzsche's perspicuity often have the mark of Emerson on them. At one point, it is said that the ability to contradict, to have a good conscience about criticizing hallowed, traditional ideas or values, is an astonishing trait of Western culture, a sign of intellectual emancipation.[81] This remark seems to replicate Emerson's stress upon the value of nonconformity, his valuation of the antagonism of the new, his account of the replacement of one set of cultural ideals by another, and his general experimental approach to ideas. And Nietzsche's comment also echoes, as previously mentioned, Emerson's awareness of the cultural effects of the emergent "magic" of science in "Illusions," a magic that contradicts earlier modalities of magic and causes us to raise "terrible questions" that threaten traditional ways of thinking.[82]

Liberation from stale, outworn traditions was one of Emerson's many preoccupations. He both encouraged and practiced a free, philosophical critique of culture. There are times, he urges, when we must let go of past forms and traditions. "When we have new perceptions, we shall gladly disburden the memory of its hoarded treasures as old rubbish."[83] Although a great deal of Nietzsche's iconoclasm had its roots in his temperament and polemical inclinations, it probably owes something, perhaps more than we can show, to Emerson's surprising radicalism. The following was specifically said about a central value of Nietzsche's, but it would be equally applicable to that of the sage of Concord: "Nonconformity is the necessary condition of self-realization."[84]

The essential ideas in Emerson's best known essay, "Self-Reliance," are very much in evidence in Nietzsche's promulgation of the ideals of becoming who we are, affirming our originality, asserting our uniqueness, exercising our self-legislating capacities. Emerson urges us "to be" and not seem; "to live"; to be "genuine", to be "natural"; to hold sacred the integrity of the self. Repeatedly, he opposes the genuine individual to the group, the majority, to society. Being different is a priority value for Emerson and Nietzsche.

The existential stage of, or dimension of, Nietzsche's thought reflects virtually every personal exhortation of Emerson's: cultivate "self-trust"; live "onward"; strive for the reality of "self-existence"; strive for honesty and integrity; act according to the law of our own constitution; "walk alone"; be independent; be a nonconformist—especially in the domain of thought; be open to new experiences; become an "endless seeker," an "experimenter" in the colorful laboratory of life.

The case for my view that virtually all of the significant aspects of Nietzsche's philosophy of existence are influenced by Emerson's proto-existential conception of self-becoming is overdetermined. So much so that it makes the common observation that Emerson's defense of autonomous self-existence has been "surpassed" or "overshadowed" by modern existential philosophy an ironic anachronism.

Nietzsche combines his philosophy of strenuous *Existenz* with a "new healthiness" that entails strength, endurance, boldness, and cheerfulness in practically the same way in which Emerson combined an ethics of self-reliance with the ideal of superabundant health. In "Experience" he tells us that "life is not intellectual or critical, but sturdy." The "energy of health" is considered more important in life than talent. Our "animal spirits" imbue the present with a sense of power and they are "the spontaneous product of health."[85] Natural health, a synthesis of physical and psychic health, was a priority valuation for Emerson as it later was for Nietzsche. What is especially interesting in this connection is that Emerson (and Nietzsche after him) seemed to make health, vitality, and cheerfulness not only life-enhancing personal attributes, but ethical values as well.

The specificity of the influence that Emerson had on Nietzsche is shown not only in evocative prescriptions of ideal ways of existing, but in minor ways as well. In a buoyant passage in *The Gay Science* it is said that we must discover the fool in ourselves, the fool "that is hidden in our passion for knowledge," so that we can be as joyful in our folly as in our wisdom.[86] Even though not much is made of it by Emerson, it is likely that a lynx-eyed Nietzsche spotted and then elaborated on the passing comment that "a man is a golden impossibility. The line he must walk is a hair's breadth. The wise through excess of wisdom is made a fool."[87] For Nietzsche deftly turns this remark on its axis and proclaims that "just because we are heavy and serious men in our ultimate depth . . . there is nothing that does us so much good as the *fool's cap and bells."* In this instance, as in others, we cannot fault Nietzsche for improving on Emerson . . . in the tone and style of Emerson!

Anti-Materialism

Even though it is part of a more general valuational perspective, there runs through Emerson's reflections on the human condition both a disdain for the overrefined, too comfortable members of the wealthy class and a disapproval of the busy bourgeois class that is too much preoccupied with what Wordsworth called "getting and spending." Although Emerson sometimes expresses admiration for the energy of the creators of new enterprises, he more typically condemns the relentless pursuit of money. Commerce is, at best, a necessary evil that the "wise man" will avoid, if he can. "Men, such as they are, very naturally seek money or power; and power because it is as good as money." They tend to seek the so-called "spoils" of office.[88] With his characteristic charity towards others (which, as we'll see, is sometimes roughly put aside), Emerson attributes this pursuit of money to a search for something "higher" that, in the "sleep-walking" of the average person, is taken for a greater good.

By the time he wrote "Politics," Emerson was convinced of the venality of the politician and the corruption of every state. He despised corrupt politicians. And he is well known for his antimaterialism, his criticism of a culture devoted to the accumulation of more and more possessions. He refuses to accept "the base estimate of the market" as the criterion of "what constitutes a manly success."[89] Success in life is defined in terms of excellence of character, not in terms of the accumulation of capital. In a statement as apt today as it was when it was first written, Emerson laments that "they measure their esteem of each other by what each has, and not by what each is."[90]

Emerson often worries, with good reason, about the effects on cultural values and the quality of culture of the peculiarly "American" busyness and immersion in commercial life. Anticipating the social history of America up to the present, he maintains that wealth without genuine culture is empty; that riches without "character" or "nobility" generates vulgar display; that vast accumulations of money without "good breeding" produces social and personal waste. In a moment of passion he proclaims that "I hate this shallow Americanism which hopes to get rich by credit, to get knowledge . . . or skill without study . . . or wealth by fraud."[91]

In an ancient cliché (except for those who experience its truth), Emerson declares that "the first wealth is health." Despite his animadversions concerning the growing commercialism of American society and the emergence of materialistic values, Emerson views this phenomenon in a different light and offers an interpretation of the meaning of the pursuit of material goods and wealth that dovetails with Nietzsche's similar observations. Even though he himself values health, even superabundant health, as a supreme good, he probes the psychology of the quest for material goods and wealth. This search for underlying motivations in his study of man's nature led Emerson into a speculative, theoretical domain that was, in a more dramatic way, highlighted in the philosophical and psychological analyses of Nietzsche. Although it will be discussed later, it may be said here that the primordial motivation of human behavior that Emerson uncovered is one that would be familiar to anyone acquainted with the thought of Nietzsche: a "search after power."

Like Emerson, Nietzsche was temperamentally and intellectually skeptical of, and strongly opposed to, the metastasizing materialistic values of the modern world. Nietzsche continues the critical stance of his "soul-brother" on this issue and he attacks the frenzy of the American pursuit of "gold," accurately observing that it is fast invading Europe. He envisions a time, a time he believes has already arrived, in which no one will be able to live a "contemplative life" without bad conscience or self-contempt.[92] In another place, he calls attention to the "culture" of "buying and selling" that he views, as Emerson did, as contrary to "nobility."[93] That Nietzsche specifically links busyness and commercial preoccupations to America in *The Gay Science* indicates, once again, the presence of Emerson in this work and his habit of appropriating Emerson's value judgments.

Nietzsche rarely misses an opportunity to speak disdainfully of money-counters and the emerging "merchant's culture." By implication, he champions the reflective, knowledgeable, and noble individuals who stand above the rising tide of marketplace values. Emerson sought to create a countervailing cultural ideal that would preserve neither an effete aristocratic class nor what Nietzsche later sarcastically called a "gold aristocracy," but a new aristocracy of spirit and character. Even though Nietzsche did not depend upon Emerson alone for the cultivation of this same aristocratic attitude of mind, his own promulgation of an aristocracy of spirit was inspired by and reinforced by his sympathetic study of Emerson. He welcomed Emerson's antimaterialism and discerned, beneath the surface of his democratic sentiments, the core of elitism that ran through the center of his thought and values.

Life as a Means to Gnosis

There is a specific conjunction between the conception of the "how" of existence espoused in Emerson's writings and a curious stance adopted by Nietzsche in *The Gay Science* that bears scrutiny precisely because it is an atypical position for him to take. It serves to confirm the close intellectual bond between him and the American thinker he admired so much. In an aphorism entitled *"In Media Vita"* he said that life has become more desirable and mysterious because of the liberating thought that it "may be an experiment of the thinker," that knowledge itself could be "a world of dangers and victories, in which even the heroic sentiments have their arena." Reversing his more typical view that knowledge is, and ought to be, in the service of life, Nietzsche, in this instance, enunciates a new principle: *"Life as a means to knowledge."* By virtue of embracing this liberating principle, one can be brave and *"live joyfully."*[94]

Although it would be natural to attribute this novel, existential "how" to Nietzsche's experience and reflections, it is not possible to do so in light of the special impact that Emerson had on his counsel concerning how one ought to live, on attitudes towards existence. Early in his creative life Emerson praised the life of the serious seeker of knowledge in terms normally associated with heroic self-discipline. Thought was not construed as idle musing, but as a mode of *action*. Emerson says it better: "The preamble of thought, the transition through which it passes from the unconscious to the conscious, is action."[95] An exemplary individual "will be strong to live, as well as strong to think."

Whoever pursues knowledge should be "self-relying and self-directed." An individual who strives to be an authentic scholar should be self-confident and never defer to popular sentiments. Self-trust, freedom, and bravery should be the traits of such an individual. Emerson praises the dedication, the steadiness, the ability to contemplate "severe abstractions," the patience of neglect and of reproach of the genuine seeker of knowledge. Addressing himself to the Phi Beta Kappa Society at Cambridge in 1837, Emerson told its members that "in yourself slumbers the whole of Reason; it is for you to know all; it is for you to dare all."[96] Against the background of his religious sentiments, he offered the assembled scholars a credo that anticipates that of "Self-Reliance": "We will walk on our own feet; we will work with our own hands; we will speak with our own minds."[97] The message is clear and simple. The life of the mind, the pursuit of knowledge, can be, ought to be, a heroic one that has its proper disciplines and its own subjective tensions.

In his address to the divinity college at Harvard in the year after his earlier oration, Emerson continued the same theme of dedicated independence and self-discipline. He admonished his listeners "to go alone," to imitate no models, to adopt a standard of moral goodness above that of a flaccid public morality, to cultivate independence (even of one's friends), to acquire courage and endurance, to show that the ought of duty is one with "science" (= knowledge), and compatible with beauty and joy.[98]

The concept of intellectual heroism, independence, and integrity that is so closely associated with Nietzsche was already laid out as an ideal way of life by Emerson. This orientation, in coordination with the previously noted stress on experimentation in thought and life, brings Nietzsche's existential and philosophical principles in line with those of Emerson, for he had proclaimed that "I unsettle all things. No facts are to me sacred, none are profane; I simply experiment, an endless seeker with no Past at my back."[99] In *The Gay Science* Nietzsche advocates an experimental approach to ideas: "Let us try it." He commits himself to an open attitude towards thought and conceptual proposals and is no longer interested in any questions that do not allow for experiment.[100]

In *Beyond Good and Evil* a new species of philosophers is anticipated, a type that will be "attempters" *(Versucher)* or experimental thinkers.[101] This very designation seems to allude to Emerson *(Versucher* or "essayist", "experimenter") and his avowal of experimental thinking, as well as to a secondary meaning of *Versucher,* "tempter." What is significant about this projected ideal of experimental thought is that it is closely related to a way of existing. There is little doubt that Nietzsche's celebration of life as a means to knowledge, his valuation of experimental thinking in relation to life (what may be called his existential pragmatism), as well as his idea of a joyful wisdom, are derived from Emerson's evocative proposals for a new mode of existence.

Even though Emerson lamented the loss of faith in the world, he did not, as one might have expected, propose a Kierkegaardian "leap of faith." Rather, he encouraged an experimental approach to thought and prized the accumulation of knowledge—knowledge of nature, of the world, of the human condition, and of the self. Only in passing does he hint why he values cognitive insight over "faith alone," why he insists upon the need to cultivate a joyful wisdom. This view emerges in connection with the Hindu notion that true liberation requires *vidya,* knowledge as 'seeing' or insight *(vid).* Wisdom, in this context, is insight into the illusions of existence and the overcoming of them. In "Illusions" Emerson not only counsels seeing through the deceptions of existence, but claims that the thoughts and theories that were once finalities yield, in time, to a "larger generalization." Seeing through deceptions and renouncing our former beliefs is what Nietzsche later calls "self-overcoming." That is, deliberately overcoming one's own cherished ideals, one's consoling illusions. That Emerson may have suggested this process to Nietzsche is indicated not only in his prescriptions to relinquish previous modes of thought and values, but in the advice he offers in "Montaigne": "Let a man learn . . . to bear the disappearance of things he was wont to reverence without losing his reverence."[102]

Under the rubric "Orientalist" in his notes Emerson reveals the original stimulus of his reflections on the importance of insight or knowledge *(gnosis)* for the attainment of a liberating wisdom. He remarks that there is nothing so important in the "history of the intellect" as the Hindu teaching that the highest good "is to be obtained through science" or knowledge. By virtue of a clear perception of the real and the unreal, by bracketing qualities, affections, and matter, by seeing through "*Maias* or illusions," we may arrive at a contemplation of eternal life.

As we shall see in subsequent discussions of this theme, Emerson moves back and forth between an emphasis upon individualistic self-reliance and self-existence to a concern with a sense of sympathetic identification with the divine unity of the cosmos. What is distinctive about what may be called his mystical tendencies is that they never entirely sacrifice the self-reflective individual. There is a tension in his thought between a tendency to let go of the personal self and immerse it in the circular flow of life and existence and a strong tendency to affirm the inexpungeable reality of the self. Insofar as he may be said to have a mystical 'doctrine', it is a paradoxical existential mysticism, an orientation that is not at all foreign to the experiential dimension of Nietzsche's philosophy. For he too emphasizes the attainment of meaning and liberation in an intensified state of *Existenz,* as well as prescribing the need to "think cosmically."

Despite the originality of his mode of expression, the power of his polemical writings, and his original and relentless analysis of the problem of nihilism, Nietzsche responded in a positive or negative way to a variety of thinkers both in his published works and in voluminous notes. Along the way, he mined a surprising number of Emerson's scattered treasures. There are a number of instances in which he definitely appropriated specific observations and insights of Emerson's and presented them as his own. At other times, he seems to have duplicated unconsciously the assertions and judgments of Emerson, sometimes adapting them to his own style and sometimes preserving Emerson's tone and style. Charles Andler was on target when he remarked that "Emerson was one of those beloved authors whose thought Nietzsche absorbed until he could no longer distinguish it from his own."[103]

Nietzsche revealed the intimate psychological and intellectual affinity he had with the American poet and essayist when he told Franz Overbeck in a letter (December 14, 1883) that ". . . *ich Emerson wie eine Bruder-Seele empfinde . . .*". Although he sometimes adopted a condescending attitude towards his "soul-brother," Nietzsche never denied his creative power or his genius as a literary philosopher. And his admiration for the man or his image of the man was unstinting.

As we examine the correspondence between the thought of Emerson and the philosophical ideas and themes of Nietzsche, we shall see that even though there may not be a neat, uniform correlation between Emerson's and Nietzsche's thinking in all respects, we are not dealing with a casual or superficial case of intellectual influence, but with a profound and intimate philosophical and valuational relationship of thought. Emerson's insights often serve as sparks to Nietzsche's philosophical flames.

In histories of American philosophy Emerson is often given short shrift. And he is sometimes treated with an air of condescension. This attitude towards him, where it exists, is unjustified. Through Emerson American thought passed, by way of Nietzsche, into the stream of European philosophy in a general form that has previously been noticed, but that has not been examined in detail. The profound influence of Emerson's thought and character on the radical German thinker who seems far removed from the "genteel" tradition in American literature with which Emerson is associated is far deeper, far more pervasive than has been recognized or shown previously. Having sketched the strong lines of intellectual, stylistic, attitudinal, and valuational influence that can be traced from Emerson to Nietzsche, we'll now turn our attention to a larger screen on which significant, overlapping doctrines and themes in the writings of both thinkers are projected. Perhaps we will come to discern how Nietzsche fulfilled what were suggested, inchoate patterns of thought dispersed throughout Emerson's poetic and literary gold mines.

Chapter 1 Notes

1. René Wellek, *Confrontations: Studies in the Intellectual and Literary Relations between Germany, England, and the United States during the Nineteenth Century* (Princeton, N.J.: Princeton University Press, 1965). Wellek refers to the fragmentary nature of Emerson's writings, his nonsystematic thought, and notes that Emerson had a confused and superficial understanding of Kant's philosophy. Although I would not agree with his view that Jacobi, a defender of intuitive faith with antinomian sentiments, hardly enters Emerson's horizon, Wellek's remarks on the influence of German idealism on Emerson are sound and insightful.

2. Cf. Charles Andler, *Nietzsche, sa vie et sa pensée*. Andler lists Emerson as one of fourteen of Nietzsche's *précurseurs*. He devotes thirty-five pages to Emerson and makes some valid judgments, but misses the mark here and there. Andler claims that Nietzsche found "German reminiscences" in Emerson which led him to overestimate Emerson's intellectual powers. This is not the case since Nietzsche viewed some of Emerson's thinking as "clouded by German philosophy." There is some truth in his judgment that Emerson served as "one of the prototypes of Zarathustra." Andler superimposes Nietzsche on Emerson by calling him "an immoralist" even though, as we shall see, this is not entirely without reason. In general, Andler's treatment of the relation between Emerson and Nietzsche is neither sustained nor substantial.

3. The earliest mention of this association seemed to have been in: Richard M. Meyer, *Nietzsche*. Eduard Baumgarten's *Das Vorbild Emersons im Werk und Leben Nietzsches* is more complete than others dealing with this topic. It stresses comparisons of various texts in Emerson with some of Nietzsche's aphorisms, but it does not probe any serious philosophical themes. Baumgarten's study is useful because it points the reader in the direction of discovering the philosophical observations which Nietzsche

appropriates from Emerson and because it includes the first publication of a series of excerpts from Nietzsche's copy of the *Essays*. The latter are found in the *Nachlass* of Nietzsche in notes from the beginning of 1882. See: *Friedrich Nietzsche. Saṁtliche Werke,* 9: 666–72. These excerpts indicate Nietzsche's continuous study of, and rereading of Emerson and only scratch the surface of the deep relationship between his thought and Emerson. Stanley Hubbard's *Nietzsche und Emerson* is primarily comprised of quotations from Nietzsche's German translation of the *Essays* (First and Second Series). The remainder is commentary on various similarities of thought between the two. Hubbard does not develop any one theme at any length. What he did was illustrate Nietzsche's thorough attention to the writings of Emerson.

4. In Erik I. Thurin's *Emerson As Priest of Pan* there are a number of apposite references to the relation between Emerson and Nietzsche. Gay Wilson Allen, in *Waldo Emerson: A Biography* makes a number of references to Nietzsche, some of which will be mentioned in another context. In his review of this biography Alfred Kazin remarks that "Allen sees the connection with Nietzsche only in relation to the phrase 'gay science', and the way the 'science' somehow appears in poetry" (Alfred Kazin, review of Gay Wilson Allen's *Waldo Emerson: A Biography* in *The New York Review of Books,* XXVIII, Nos. 21–22 (January 21, 1982) p. 6. In *Fate and Freedom: An Inner Life of Ralph Waldo Emerson* Stephen Whicher made a few references to Nietzsche which will be cited subsequently. In these works, as well as in occasional articles, there are sporadic mentions of the connection between Emerson and Nietzsche, but there is really no attempt to analyze this important relationship in detail or in terms of philosophical themes.

5. In a number of his articles and essays Stanley Cavell has touched upon the association between Emerson and Nietzsche in a perceptive way. Cf. "Being Odd/Getting Even," *Salmagundi.* Cf. also: "Thinking of Emerson," *New Literary History,* and "Emerson, Coleridge, Kant," in *Post-Analytic Philosophy.* Cavell has attempted to rejuvenate an interest in Emerson as philosopher and to overcome the "repression" of Emerson in American philosophy. In "Emerson, Coleridge, Kant" Cavell offers insightful comments on Emerson's essay "Fate." He correctly remarks that Emerson has been misunderstood as a "genteel" thinker and that "Fate" is a turning point in his development. What is not mentioned in this context is that "Fate" had a significant influence on Nietzsche, both in regard to his espousal of fatalism and some of his central ideas. There is no doubt that Cavell is one American philosopher who sees beneath the veneer of the surface Emerson and appreciates his radical and innovative thought. He has done a great deal to rejuvenate Emerson as a thinker who ought to be taken seriously. In his recent study of Emerson, *Conditions Handsome and Unhandsome,* Cavell continues his defense of Emerson as philosopher against his detractors. He has insightful things to say about a theme that runs through this study: the perfectibility of man. Cavell correctly re-

cognizes the elitist strain in Emerson's ideal of perfectionism, but he construes it as "compatible with democracy" (Ibid., p. 28). Cavell emphasizes that, for Emerson, freedom is autonomy. This *is* his ideal, but it cannot be separated from his strong stress on the limitations of the concrete "circumstances." Since Cavell's treatment of the idea of fate in Emerson's thought will be presented in another venue, I cannot comment on how he would deal with this tension in the reflections of Emerson. My own interpretation of this issue is found in the chapter on "Fate and Existence." The most relevant of Cavell's essays to the theme of this work is his discussion in "Aversive Thinking: Emersonism Representations in Heidegger and Nietzsche." His discovery of the presence of Emerson in the philosophy of Heidegger is something that I cannot dispute since this association was noted (and restated here) in the first draft of my study in 1985. Cavell perceptibly spys the presence of Emerson's conception of "man thinking" in Heidegger's *What is Called Thinking?* (translated by Fred D. Wreck and J. Glenn Gray, New York: Harper and Row, 1968.) From my point of view, whatever aspects of Emerson's thought that are found in Heidegger's philosophy are accountable in terms of his incorporation of Nietzsche's insights in his writings. The discernment of Emersonian themes in the unlikely place of Nietzsche's "Schopenhauer as Educator" by Cavell is on target and parallels my own independent perception of the same phenomenon. Finally, Cavell zeroes in on the same issue that is dealt with in my chapter on "The Paradox of Evil and Good." He avers that "moral perfectionism" is an unwelcomed ideal in modern philosophy. The disapproval of moral perfectionism in the works of Emerson and Nietzsche is attributed to the following: "A hatred of moralism—of what Emerson calls "conformity"—so passionate and careless as to seem sometimes to amount to a hatred of morality altogether (Nietzsche calls himself the first antimoralist; Emerson knows that he will seem antinomian, a refuser of any law, including the moral law). . . . An expression of disgust with or a disdain for the present state of things so complete as to require not merely reform, but a call for a transformation of things, and before all a transformation of the self—a call that seems so self-absorbed and obscure as to make morality impossible" (*Ibid.*, p. 46). This is an accurate and concise account of common oppositions to the views of both Emerson and Nietzsche. It parallels my own presentation of the most volatile aspect of the Emerson-Nietzsche call for a "transvaluation of values." One difference between Cavell and me on this issue is that I'm more sympathetic with the ideal of what I consider spiritual aristocracy than he is. In addition, as I indicate elsewhere, both Emerson and Nietzsche are concerned with carving out a "new morality" that is opposed to a "morality of custom," a morality of pity or sympathy, and to all forms of negative moralities of prohibition. As I mention in the chapter on "The Paradox of Evil and Good," the flirtations with antinomianism are potentially dangerous in the wrong hands or if they are misconstrued (in a way Emerson and Nietzsche never intended) as active antinomianism or immoralist acting out. Correcting some perceptions of his standpoint, Emerson remarks, in "Self-Reliance," that "The populace think that your rejection of popular standards is a rejection of all standards and mere antinomianism." Would that Nietzsche had made his own orientation towards this issue as plain.

6. In chronological sequence we can trace the dominant influences on Nietzsche's thought: the classical Greek poets, dramatists, and philosophers; the writings of Emerson; the works of Schopenhauer; the writings of F. A. Lange, especially his *History of Materialism;* and, finally, the music-dramas, biographical and aesthetic writings of Richard Wagner. In addition, a contemporary of his who was quite popular in his day, Eugen Dühring, should be included. For even though Nietzsche was critical of virtually every philosophical position he advocated, Nietzsche's positive philosophy of life was, to some extent, influenced by Dühring's *Der Werth des Lebens (The Value of Life)*. Nietzsche was particularly offended by Dühring's anti-Semitism, his socialitarian political thought (which, being a form of national socialism, anticipated Nazism), his theory that justice is based upon resentment, and his rancorous attitudes. Marx and Engels wrote a book called *Anti-Dühring,* but Nietzsche was actually more anti-Dühring than they. Of scientists with whose work he was familiar, the following were the most important: Ruggero Boscovich, the eighteenth-century mathematician and theoretical physicist; Robert Mayer, the nineteenth-century contributor to the theory of thermodynamics; the German astronomer and physicist, Johann Zöllner; the eighteenth-century natural scientist, Georg Lichtenberg; Charles Darwin, and the neo-Darwinian anatomist and physiologist, Wilhelm Roux. Nietzsche's earliest introduction to the ideas of a variety of scientists was in the form of his detailed study of F. A. Lange's *History of Materialism,* a work he first read in September, 1865. In a letter to a friend he characterized this rich work as "the most significant philosophical work that has appeared during the last ten years" (*Nietzsche Briefwechsel, Kritische Gesamtausgabe,* 1 2, p. 184) Cf. Jörg Salaquarda, "Nietzsche und Lange," *Nietzsche-Studien* 7 (1978): 237–40.

7. In a work of 1865, *Die Arbeiterfrage,* F. A. Lange predicated a coming social Darwinian struggle for survival and argued that the demanding tasks of the rising working classes would produce strong leaders who would form a powerful, new, superior class of human beings. Cf. Jörg Salaquarda, "Der Standpunkt des Ideals bei Lange and Nietzsche," *Studi Tedeschi* 22 (1979): 27–28.

8. Allen, *Waldo Emerson,* p. 470.

9. Cf. Eduard Baumgarten, *Das Vorbild Emersons im Werk und Leben Nietzsches,* 16–24.

10. Cf. George J. Stack, *Lange and Nietzsche,* Chapter X.

11. Cf. David Robinson, *Apostle of Culture*.

12. Ibid., p. 9.

13. *Sämtliche Werke,* 12: 384. (Subsequently cited as *SW* followed by volume and page numbers. For major works German titles will be abbre-

viated [e.g., *Geburt der Tragödie*, *GT; Morgenröte*, *M.*, etc.] Volume number, section number, and page number will follow. Sections will be indicated by §).

14. *The Early Lectures of Ralph Waldo Emerson, 1833–1842*, 1:80. In notes from the 1870s Nietzsche says virtually the same thing about science in general. His aim, he tells us, is not to seek to destroy science, but "to subordinate science" (*Nietzsches Werke* [GOA], X:114). Elsewhere in his notes he avers that science provides the basic "presuppositions" with which a new philosophical "goal" ought to agree (*Werke* [GOA], XII:357).

15. *SW* 12:507.

16. *SW* 7:421.

17. Cf. Rudolf Schottlaender, "Two Dionysians: Emerson and Nietzsche," *South Atlantic Quarterly*. Before Nietzsche, Emerson celebrated Dionysian ecstasy in his poetry, as well as in "Poetry and Imagination." "O celestial Bacchus! [Dionysus] drive them mad,—this multitude of vagabonds, hungry for eloquence, hungry for poetry, starving for symbols, perishing for want of *electricity to vitalize this too much pasture*" *The Complete Works of Ralph Waldo Emerson*, VIII:70.

18. Stanley Cavell, "Being Odd, Getting Even," *Salmagundi*.

19. A. Bartlett Giamatti, *The University and the Public*, p. 174.

20. *The Portable Emerson*, pp. 59–60 (hereafter cited as *PE* followed by page number or numbers).

21. *Journals* (April 27–29, 1840).

22. *Journals* (Fall–Winter 1857).

23. *Journals* (July–August 1867).

24. *Journals* (October 1848).

25. *Journals* (January–March 1844).

26. *SW* 3, *M* §119.

27. *PE*, p. 197.

28. "Circles," *PE*, p. 240.

29. *SW* 2, *MAM* 2, ii, §194.

30. *Sämtliche Briefe*, 3:95.

31. R. A. Yoder, *Emerson and the Orphic Poet in America*, p. 74.

32. Robinson, *Apostle of Culture*, p. 10.

33. *SW* 5, *GM* II §16.

34. *The Will to Power*, §387.

35. *Werke* (GOA), XVI:358. In another place Nietzsche says that the strong individual is one who, through "precision and clarity of direction," develops urges around a central "dominating instinct" (*Werke* [GOA] XV:172).

36. *SW* 3, *FW* §11.

37. *SW* 7:434.

38. Cf. Hans Vaihinger, *The Philosophy of 'As-If'*.

39. Prior to initiating my study of the influence of Emerson on Nietzsche some years ago, I more or less accepted Vaihinger's view that the idea of conscious illusion in the thought of Nietzsche was derived from F. A. Lange's references to this notion in his *History of Materialism*. Ironically, it

seems, Lange reinforced the conception that illusion is necessary for life which Nietzsche first found in the writings of Emerson. Cf. Geo. J. Stack, *Lange and Nietzsche*, 303–329.

40. "Uses of Great Men," in *Representative Men, Nature, Addresses and Lectures*, p. 12.

41. "Considerations By the Way," in *The Conduct of Life*, p. 259.

42. Leonard Neufeldt, *The House of Emerson*, p. 11.

43. Joel Porte, ed., *Emerson in His Journals*, p. 129.

44. Woodbridge Riley appears to have disagreed with such a judgment insofar as he claimed that the inspiration for Emerson's transcendentalism "was the philosophy of the Academy." He cites a passage from *Representative Men* in which Emerson remarks that "transcendental truths have a kind of filial retrospect to Plato and the Greeks." This does not, however, seem to commit him to Platonism and it's a slight piece of evidence for the influence of Plato on Emerson's transcendentalism. In fact, Riley is not consistent on this point. Earlier in his study he said that "Emerson's philosophy" includes an "immanence in respect of nature." Furthermore, he claims that this means "the unity of the intelligent principle in the world." Moreover, "immanence implies that all that exists, exists in God." Riley then correctly points out that Emerson repudiated both "Calvinistic transcendence" and transcendental "deism." That the emphasis of Emerson's metaphysics falls on immanence is made clear by Riley's cogent observation that, in Emerson's considered view, "The doctrine of a deity separate from his world, absolute, arbitrary, inscrutable in his ways, is . . . supplanted by the doctrine of the deification of the world" (Woodbridge Riley, *American Thought: From Puritanism to Pragmatism and Beyond*, pp. 161–62; 146–47). Octavius Frothingham succinctly summarized transcendentalism in the following way: "Practically it was an assertion of the inalienable worth of man; theoretically it was an assertion of the immanence of divinity in instinct, the transference of supernatural attributes to the natural constitution of mankind" (Octavius Frothingham, *Transcendentalism in New England*, p. 136).

45. Larzer Ziff, ed., *Ralph Waldo Emerson: Selected Essays*, p. 141.

46. *SW* 2, *MAM* 2, §249, p. 662.

47. Cf. *Historisch-Kritische Gesamtausgabe Werke*, Vols. II and III (Hereafter cited as *HKG* followed by volume and page or pages.) Aside from these early journal references to Emerson and occasional references to him in published works, in notations from 1882 a series of excerpts from the *Essays* are copied out. References to, or citations from, the first and second series of Emerson's *Versuche* or *Essays* are dispersed throughout Nietzsche's *Nachgelassene Fragmente* over a twenty-six year period.

48. *Sämtliche Briefe*, 6:573.

49. Erich Podach, *Friedrich Nietzsches Werke der Zusammenbruchs*, p. 236.

50. *Werke* (GOA), XII:179.

51. *Friedrich Nietzsches Gesammelte Briefe*, II:567. In a letter to Erwin Rohde (July 1882) he says that he has written for himself—"thereby it en-

dures" (*Sämtliche Briefe*, 6:226). In notes from 1867–68 he copied down Emerson's assertion from the G. Fabricus translation of the *Versuche* (114): "Der der für sich selbst schreibt, schreibt für ein unsterbliches Publikum." The translation is from "Spiritual Laws": "He that writes to himself writes to an eternal public" (*PE*, p. 200). Cp. *HKG* III:370.

52. *SW* 5, *GM* 27:410.

53. *Essays* (First Series), Boston and New York, 1865, 411n.

54. *SW* 9:602.

55. John Burroughs, *Emerson and His Journals*, p. 81. Cf. Hermann Hummel, "Emerson and Nietzsche," *The New England Quarterly*, p. 66.

56. *SW* 2, *MAM* 1, §292, pp. 235–36.

57. "Circles," *PE*, p. 231.

58. Wellek, *Confrontations* p. 187.

59. *Sämtliche Briefe*, 2:60.

60. "Nature," *PE*, p. 11.

61. *Sämtliche Briefe*, 2:119–20.

62. "Nature," *PE*, p. 11.

63. "Circles," *PE*, p. 212.

64. *SW* 7:421.

65. *SW* 2, *MAM* 1, §376, p. 263. Cp. "Napoleon; or the Man of the World," *PE*, p. 343. Cp. also: "Friendship," in *Emerson's Essays*, p. 123. (Hereafter cited as *EE*, preceded by essay title and followed by page number or numbers.)

66. "Considerations By the Way," in *The Conduct of Life*, p. 264. (Hereafter cited as *COL*, preceded by the essay title and followed by page number or numbers.)

67. *The Complete Works of Ralph Waldo Emerson*, VII:37. Cf. Gay Wilson Allen, *Waldo Emerson: A Biography*, pp. 469–70.

68. In his biography of Emerson, Allen refers to this "epigraph" taken from Emerson's essay "History" and quotes Nietzsche's German version. That Nietzsche drops the reference to "the saint" is not noticed even though the epigraph is translated as if it were included in the German sentence (*Waldo Emerson*, p. 469). In *Thus Spoke Zarathustra* this Emersonian reference is reduced to Zarathustra saying that "All days shall be holy to me." And Zarathustra refers this to the "joyful wisdom" of his youth (*SW* 4, *AsZ* II:143).

69. *SW* 3, *FW* §276, p. 522.

70. "Fate," *PE*, 346–74.

71. *SW* 3, *FW* §154, p. 496.

72. "Illusions," *PE*, p. 379.

73. "Experience," *PE*, p. 237.

74. Stanley Hubbard, *Nietzsche und Emerson*, p. 82.

75. "Courage," in *Society and Solitude*, p. 259.

76. "Heroism," *EE*, p. 147.

77. "Self-Reliance," *PE*, p. 144. Commenting on the meaning of Nietzsche's admonition to "live dangerously," Walter Kaufmann noted

that "Nietzsche is not thinking of big-game hunting but of not clinging to
the life, the views, the world that are familiar to us and spell security"
(Walter Kaufmann, *Existentialism, Religion, and Death*, p. 231). This is certainly a judicious assessment of Nietzsche's prescription to live dangerously. It points back to Emerson's original advice to the individual who
strives to be independent and self-directed. Kaufmann went on to say that
the theme of living dangerously was "inspired by Goethe's great example." Although it is true that Nietzsche was a great admirer of Goethe,
this claim is questionable given the fact that Emerson clearly and specifically anticipated what became an existential imperative for Nietzsche. For
Emerson, living dangerously pertained to a wide range of human behaviors and attitudes, including physical risk-taking. Living dangerously is
linked to overcoming a fear, to creative and intellectual daring, to the acceptance of fate, to facing the terrible and the ugly in life, and much more.
As Emerson puts it, "There are many forms of courage")"Courage," in
Society and Solitude, p. 252).

78. *SW* 6, *G* §13, p. 120. Cp. *SW* 13, *Nachgelassene Fragmente* 1887–
89, p. 21.

79. *SW* 3, *FW* §4, p. 376.

80. "Considerations By the Way," *COL*, p. 252.

81. *SW* 3, *FW* §297, p. 537.

82. "Illusions," *PE*, p. 382.

83. "Self-Reliance," *PE*, p. 152.

84. Walter Kaufmann, *Nietzsche: Philosopher, Psychologist, Antichrist*, p.
176. Kaufmann mentioned Emerson once in this work and denied that he
(among other putative precursors) was "important for Nietzsche's
thought" (Ibid., 306n).

85. "Society and Solitude," *PE*, p. 392–93. In "Power" a "*plus* health"
is said to be valued because "all difficulties vanish before it." It is characterized as an "affirmative force," a "vital force" that is needed for action
and achievements of all kinds ("Power," *COL*, pp. 56–57, 61).

86. *SW* 3, *FW* §107, pp. 464–65. In a note from the Zarathustra period
Nietzsche cites Emerson after writing: "Oh you wise ones, have you
learned to rejoice over your foolishness!" (*SW* 11, p. 378).

87. "Experience," *PE*, p. 279.

88. "The American Scholar," *PE*, p. 66. Cp. Nietzsche's remark in
Thus Spoke Zarathustra: "Look at the superfluous ones! They accumulate
riches and become poorer. They desire power . . . and the lever of power,
much money—these impotent ones" (*SW* 4, *AsZ*, p. 63).

89. "Compensation," *PE*, p. 167.

90. "Self-Reliance," *PE*, p. 163.

91. "Success," in *Society and Solitude*, pp. 173–74.

92. *SW* 3, *FW* §329, p. 557.

93. Ibid., §31, pp. 402–3.

94. Ibid., §324, pp. 552–53.

95. "The American Scholar," *PE*, p. 59.

96. Ibid., p. 70.

97. Ibid, p. 71.

98. "Divinity School Address," *PE*, pp. 72–91.

99. "Circles," *PE*, p. 238. Emerson also asserts in the same essay that "No truth so sublime but it may be trivial tomorrow in the light of new thoughts." This is a feature of Emerson's thought that disturbs some literary critics and delights others. In "Intellect" Emerson relates his experimental orientation to truth in a proto-Nietzschean way. He avers that "if a man fasten his attention on a single aspect of truth, and apply himself to that alone for a long time, the truth becomes distorted, and not itself, but falsehood." As in the case of Nietzsche, the search for truth requires an antidogmatic attitude of mind. "He in whom the love of truth predominates will keep himself aloof from all moorings and afloat. He will abstain from dogmatism, and recognize all the opposite negations . . ." ("Intellect," *EE*, pp. 187, 189). In John Michael's *Emerson and Skepticism: The Cipher of the World,* this skeptical aspect of Emerson's thought is effectively examined. Michael accurately notes that "in Emerson, it is never the resolution of the conflict that signifies, but the interplay of the opposed views that create conflict" (Ibid, p. 154). B. L. Packer sees this experimental feature of Emerson's thinking as valuable. "The agility of Emerson's mind—its endless willingness to revise its previous interpretation under the pressure of new facts, new thoughts, new experiences—is what makes it perennially interesting" (B. L. Packer, *Emerson's Fall,* p. 32). Insightfully, she relates the various "voices" of Emerson to Nietzsche's advice to thinkers to disguise themselves with "masks and subtlety" (Ibid, p. 19). Aside from this apt analogy, I think Emerson's approach to knowledge provided the rudiments for Nietzsche's development of a perspectival theory of knowledge, as well as the model for the presentations of what he calls his "philosophies."

100. *SW* 3, *FW* §51, pp. 415–16. Some commentators on Nietzsche have suggested that he is referring to scientific experiments in this context. This probably results from the fact that a fair number of passages in *The Gay Science* refer to science, scientific theory, and the scientific interpretation of nature. It is more likely that, after Emerson and others who proposed similar ways of trying to understand various phenomena, Nietzsche is advocating thought-experiments, as well as valuational experiments. Even though Nietzsche seeks to go beyond a pragmatic orientation towards ideas and knowledge, there is a strong anticipation of pragmatism in certain phases of his philosophy. Emerson was the first to suggest this to him, but not the last. F. A. Lange and a number of scientists who adopted a conventionalistic orientation towards scientific concepts and theories reinforced the experimental approach towards ideas and theories that Emerson had suggested to him. There is little doubt that Emerson paved the way for the emergence of pragmatism in American thought.

101. *SW* 5, *JGB* §42, p. 59. Nietzsche's image of the "new philosophers" seems but an amplification of, and extension of, what Emerson had already practiced in a literary way. This is particularly evident in

"Montaigne." For there Emerson states that "the philosophy we want is one of fluxions and mobility." In regard to truth-claims, he says, "I neither affirm nor deny. I stand here to try the case. I am here to consider. . . ." He wants "to consider how it is." (A Greek word appears in the text that is meant to be *skopein*—" to look at," "to consider"— but which, through a printer's error or Emerson's, would have to be transliterated as *schopxin*!) In "Montaigne" we see clearly Emerson's antiorthodox, antidogmatic stance. We shall see, in another context, that he links this standpoint to personal and intellectual strength, as Nietzsche later does.

102. In an oblique way, the idea of seeking to overcome one's previous beliefs or ideals may be suggested in the motto to "Illusions": "The hero is not fed on sweets,/ Daily his own heart he eats." In regard to Emerson's advice to have reverence for ideals which may no longer be live options for us, Nietzsche seems to have taken it to heart in some strange way. After blistering criticisms of Christianity and some of its leading figures in *Daybreak* and *Human, All-Too-Human*, Nietzsche responds to his friend's comments on his "argument with *Christianity*" in a surprising way. He tells his friend that he thinks that Christianity offers the best kind of "ideal life" with which he is acquainted and that ". . . from childhood days I have pursued it into many corners and I believe I have never in my heart been grossly disrespectful towards it" (Letter to Heinrich Köselitz ["Peter Gast"], July 21, 1881. *Sämtliche Briefe*, 6:108–9).

103. "*Emerson fut un des auteurs aimés, dont Nietzsche a absorbé la pensée jusqu'à ne plus toujours la distinguer de la sienne*" (Charles Andler, *Nietzsche, sa vie et sa pensée*, 1:340).

Chapter 2

Nature: The Riddle of the Sphinx

*Nature transcends all our moods of thought
and its secret we do not yet find.*

[Ralph Waldo Emerson, "Art"]

The particular essays of Emerson that Nietzsche first read,
"Nature" and "History," left an indelible imprint on his philosophical consciousness. In the second of his *Untimely Meditations* he
conceived of nature as imperfectly striving for perfection and,
hence, as imbued with purpose. In addition, he thought of culture
as a continuation of a natural *nisus* toward perfection. He maintained that man ought to assist nature in achieving its posited goal
by redeeming it by virtue of his own striving for self-perfection.
Although this notion of a human responsibility for the redemption
of nature may seem to be a peculiarly Nietzschean idea, it was
probably suggested to him by some of Emerson's occasional remarks on precisely this subject. For a time, he accepted Emerson's
vision of the natural world, his early romantic and mystical image
of a beautiful order that conspires with spiritual reality to emancipate man.

Nature, in Emerson's earliest interpretation, is pictured in idealized images and perceived through the medium of a metaphysical
idealism. It encompasses the physical being of men, others, art,
and what Emerson calls external nature proper. Art is not in con-
tradistinction to nature because nature itself is emblematic, pervaded by poetic figures and images. The predominant tendency of
nature is creative. Its aim is growth. There is an overpowering

beauty and grace in whatever is natural. In every event there appears what seems to us to be effects of an "exercise of the Will." A creative, cosmic will seems to act through all things. There is a general perfection in the totality of nature that is manifested, albeit imperfectly, in all its microcosmic parts. Despite all that man has come to know about the natural world, Emerson insists, there is a mystery in nature, a riddle posed by an inscrutable Sphinx.

Whatever man knows about the natural world is filtered through his reason, perception, imagination, feelings, moods, and sentiments. Hence, the natural world is construed as pervaded by "human life" or is, as Nietzsche will later say, embellished by our "aesthetic humanities." In effect, the nature we come to know is invariably "humanized." Not only does man "spiritualize" nature by means of the symbols of his thought, but there appears to be a spiritual tendency immanent in nature. This idea caught Nietzsche's eye. It is one of many underlined passages in his German translation of *Nature*. "*Es scheint eine Geiste innewohnende Notwendigkeit zu sein, sich in materiellen Formen zu manifestieren.*"[1] This statement, that "there seems to be a necessity in spirit to manifest itself in material form," is one that Nietzsche thought through for some time, one that eventually found a place in his attempt to disclose the immanent presence of "spirit" (*Geist*) in "nature" (*Natur*).

Given Nietzsche's critical attitude towards German idealism, it is ironic that Emerson, who was already familiar with eighteenth- and nineteenth-century German idealist thought, as well as influenced by it, reinforced in Nietzsche's thinking a concern inherited from the idealist tradition in German philosophy. That is, the search for the answer to the question, "What is the relationship between *Geist* and *Natur?*"

In light of the above, we may wonder how the idea of the need for a redemption of nature could be tied to Emerson's thoughts on the metaphysical question of the relation between spirit and nature.

What seems to have happened is that Emerson, as he does at various stages of his intellectual development, adjusts and modifies his original position. In his oration, "The American Scholar," he introduces a conception of a rhythmic undulation in the course of nature that is manifested in the inspiration and expiration of breath, day and night, heat and cold, the ebb and flow of the sea, the *polarity* that is even found in the internal structure of the atom.[2] This theory of polarity, which is similar to doctrines found in ancient Chinese thought, in pre-Socratic Greek philosophy, and in the writings of Goethe, is Emerson's revised perspective on nature. In *Nature* the unity, beauty, integration, harmony, and order of the totality of things was emphasized. Now Emerson points to the fact that nature is not a seamless web of permanent Being, but a process of becoming. It is composed of oppositions, antagonisms, or, as Nietzsche will later say, *antitheses.*

In his essay on the American scholar, Emerson maintains that "a man is related to all nature." This notion that each individual is part of a complex system of relations, that nothing exists in perfect isolation from other entities or events, is one that, after it is buttressed by Nietzsche's study of Lange's rudimentary philosophy of science in his *History of Materialism,* becomes central to his conception of the place of man in nature, to his theory of a dynamic world of relations in which everything is interconnected. This is not so much a theory of a universal determinism as it is a conception of the dialectical interaction of all individual beings and events. Man is no exception: he, too, is subject to this universal, dialectical process of relational interaction.

Not only does Emerson claim that there are polarities in the natural order, but he holds that there are imperfections in what, from a global perspective, has the appearance of an overall perfection. In regard to the microcosm that each person is considered to be, "every piece has a crack."[3] What Emerson has become aware of since writing *Nature* is man's (and especially *his*) "double consciousness." In certain ebullient moods, and when viewed from an edifying perspective, the cosmos seems not only beautiful, but perfect. However, at other times, looking at the natural world with a cold eye, we may quickly find ourselves in an "Iceland of negations." It requires an Olympian view of, and love of, nature to find in the order of things compensation for "the violated order and grace of man."

Towards the conclusion of his meditations on the human condition in "The Transcendentalist," Emerson sounds a note that carries us up to the point of spying glimpses of the ideal of "superior chronometers" who are "rare and gifted men," an ideal that had a powerful effect on Nietzsche's conception of a possible, superior culture of the future. Having observed the real imperfections of nature even in relatively capable specimens of men, Emerson wants to shoot the arrow of nature higher, up towards a perfection that he can imagine, but that he believes has not yet been present in the world of man. If, he seems to say, the general, natural tendency towards perfection were consciously cultivated, promoted, encouraged in the cultural world, it is possible that this natural tendency could be brought to fulfillment in certain types of human beings.

The postulated polarities and dualities in nature indicate struggle and conflict. And they suggest to Emerson's mind different levels of, or modalities of, a single, but Protean, nature. This is especially obvious in the case of *human nature*. Thus, in "Self-Reliance," it is argued that "a true man" manifests the presence of nature in a paradigmatic way. Here the term "nature" is being used as a positive attribute of a genuine person and is not used merely as a general term. Later, in the same essay, strength is equated with living "with nature in the present." The positive tendency of nature is in the direction of "conservation and growth." This tendency also means that, as Emerson starkly reports, "Nature suffers nothing to remain in her kingdom which cannot help itself."[4]

Given his reputation in literary criticism and in histories of American thought as an optimistic, starry-eyed idealist, it is not surprising that many who have read Emerson under this dispensation have been blind to his frequent flashes of hardheaded, not to say harsh, realism. Needless to say, Nietzsche was quite aware of this tough side of Emerson's reflections and observations. And he fully understood him to be espousing a courageous optimism that overcomes skeptical doubts, faces and accepts the negative aspects of the natural world and existence. In this regard, Emerson cannot be called a typical philosophical or popular idealist insofar as his actual standpoint is a paradoxical *realistic idealism*.

Nietzsche did not find in Emerson's writings a neatly delineated 'doctrine' of man's need to redeem nature or to carry forward its constructive tendency by means of a striving for human perfection. But he found much in his sometimes romantic, sometimes radically unsentimental conception of nature that provided the raw materials for a doctrine quite similar to the one he himself later forcefully proposed.

Before the emergence of his *soi-disant* 'positivistic' period, in which he interpreted religious and moral ideas from a psychological and sociological perspective and promoted the strict methodological approaches to phenomena of the "exact sciences," Nietzsche, by his own admission, had embraced a romantic-artistic metaphysics that uncritically accepted Schopenhauer's conception of a "primal Will" pervading all beings. This cosmic will is manifested in man primarily in a "will to live" that, Schopenhauer insisted, ought to be denied in order to attain liberation. Nietzsche, for a time, became an ardent convert to Schopenhauer's pessimism just as he had earlier become a follower of Emerson's romantic nature-mysticism.[5]

This intermixture of philosophical views accounts, to some extent, for the fact that, in "Schopenhauer as Educator," Emersonian ideas are prevalent even though the essay advocates, on the surface, the thought and existence of Arthur Schopenhauer. Ironically, Emerson had suggested, and Schopenhauer had strenuously argued, that nature is an objectification of a spiritual force, will, even though Schopenhauer was a past master at disclosing the negativities generated by this posited metaphysical power. In his early letters Nietzsche shared Emerson's glorification of the beauties of, and beneficial effects of, the natural world.

Some of the features of Emerson's cursorily drawn philosophy that are conspicuous by their absence from most accounts of his thought are two ideas that, coincidentally, he shared with Schopenhauer. There is, first of all, the above-mentioned interpretation of the natural world as an objectification of a spiritual volitional process. Secondly, there is the elevation of the genius as an ideal human type. Despite his protestations of loving the "common," Emerson is often elitist in his sentiments, and he praises the genius with an enthusiasm rivaled by that of Schopenhauer. This enthusiasm is also lavished on heroic historical figures and eventually bestowed upon ideal human types who, Emerson believes, are yet possible. Further discussion of this aspect of Emerson's thought will have to put off until our attention is focused on the influence that Emerson's vision of "complete" men had on Nietzsche's conception of supreme human beings who would represent man perfected. At this point, we are more concerned with Emerson's changing perspective on nature.

In spite of his early idealization of the natural world, Emerson was not at all impervious to the negativities of nature. Although he announces that his "philosophy is affirmative," he quickly adds that it "readily accepts the testimony of negative facts."[6] The gradually evolving conception of nature, which Emerson presents *seriatim* in his essays, shows that he was sensitive to the chiaroscuros of the natural world. There is light and darkness in nature, and there are imperfections in everything produced by the divine will or the "supreme Power" that pervades all beings. In his own, less dramatic way, Emerson was as aware of the horrors of nature as Schopenhauer was.

As Nietzsche jettisons his earlier romantic-artistic metaphysics and deliberately puts metaphysical questions out of action or, as he says, "on ice," his approach to the world becomes more and more naturalistic and closer to a scientific understanding of nature. The "psychological observations" of *Daybreak,* for example, are clearly naturalistic insofar as moral, spiritual, and idealized states of being, attitudes, feelings, and behaviors are interpreted in a protopsychoanalytical way. Sociological and physicalist analyses make their appearance in his critical works. Ironically, even in this new positivistic philosophical orientation, Nietzsche has not entirely escaped the circle of Emerson's equally 'naturalistic' sphere of thought.

In "Compensation" the idea of polarity as being at the heart of nature is again emphasized. But it is now applied to the "dualism" in human nature, to the paradoxes of human personality. Every excess in a person, Emerson says, generates a defect; every defect an excess. Every positive aspect of life or of an individual has its negative, "every evil its good."[7]

Gradually, over a relatively brief period of time, Emerson's thinking moves from a global interpretation of nature as a whole to an interpretation of the nature of man, of man conceived of as a self-reflective microcosm. The natural world is presumed to be engaged in a putative compensatory process and it cannot be "deceived." Human life, too, is permeated by "inevitable conditions."[8] These conditions, in turn, tend to produce living paradoxes. Thus, for example, it is said that our "strength grows out of our weakness."[9] In the manner of Kierkegaard, Emerson emphasizes the paradoxical nature of human existence and goes on to describe man as "that middle-point whereof every thing may be affirmed and denied with equal reason."[10]

In addition to insights concerning the paradoxical features of human existence, Emerson also places emphasis on the virtues of truthfulness, integrity, and honesty in a way in which Nietzsche later does. At times, one senses that, as in the case of Nietzsche, Emerson turns his intellectual honesty *against* beliefs and ideals that he had once cherished. In "Experience," in particular, he offers what may be called a psychology of spirit that probes the naturalistic basis of our perceptions, our attitudes, and our experiences.

So much of our behavior, Emerson suggests, is unthinking, unspontaneous, and customary. We are governed by our moods far more than we like to admit. We have great difficulty in getting in touch with reality. Things seem to slip through our fingers. In the final analysis, we seem to be prisoners of our particular temperaments. What may be called Emerson's conception of the psychological determination of experience comes to full blossom when he avers that "temperament . . . enters fully into the system of illusions, and shuts us in a prison of glass which we cannot see. There is an optical illusion about every person we meet."[11]

If temperament is a powerful conditioning factor in our experiences, in our values, and in our theoretical commitments, then perception, valuation, and knowledge are not processes that give us access to an objective order or independent reality. Our perceptions of persons, events, and things, our knowledge, our metaphysical beliefs are rooted in a powerful subjective ground. As Nietzsche later argues, the psychology of a culture, a group, or of individuals enters into interpretations of reality.

In his critical theory of knowledge, Nietzsche seems to elaborate on some of Emerson's passing observations concerning the subjective element in human experience, perception, and knowledge. In *Beyond Good and Evil,* he attributes our belief in *necessary* truths to "the perspectival optics of life."[12] And in *Daybreak* we are pictured as being "in prison" because of the deceptions of our senses and the effect of these on our 'knowledge'.[13] Although Nietzsche's skepticism about the possibility of objective knowledge develops under the influence of diverse critical philosophical standpoints, there is a thread of Emerson's thought in the multicolored quilt of his skeptical epistemology.

Although it would be false to say that every aspect of Nietzsche's critique of traditional concepts of knowledge and truth is derived from Emerson's rudimentary conception of human knowledge, a few of his observations seem to infiltrate Nietzsche's epistemic views. The following notions found in Emerson's writings have their analogues in Nietzsche's theory of knowledge: the anthropomorphic character of man's understanding of nature; the selectivity of our perceptions; the experimental approach to conceptions and the concern with the effects of beliefs, concepts, and values on future experience (later amplified and developed in pragmatism); the influence of temperament and moods on our thinking; the illusions that condition our experience; the metaphorical nature of language; the use of analogical reasoning to induce insight; the critique of abstractions; the reliance on intuitive insight; and the emphasis upon the subjective, perspectival nature of knowing.

Nietzsche seems to follow Emerson in accepting a general Kantian view that what we know is conditioned by our concepts, percepts, and intuitions of space and time. And, like Emerson, he pushes Kant's thought one step further by stressing the physiological and psychological determinations of our understanding of, and experience of, the world of Protean forms. The problem here is that Nietzsche was also powerfully influenced in his skeptical theory of knowledge by many nineteenth-century scientists who adopted an agnosticism about our understanding of the nature of reality, as well as by the skeptical standpoint of people like F. A. Lange. And, of course, he probes the questions of knowledge and truth with a subtlety and sophistication that goes far beyond the passing suggestions and insights of Emerson on this complex issue.

There is a stronger case for the relationship between Emerson's *obiter dicta* on the problem of morality and Nietzsche's critique of traditional ethical ideas. When he aims to speak frankly, Emerson is even willing to bypass his own moral prejudices. In "Experience," for example, he says that he would like to be "moral and keep due metes and bounds," but, he continues, "I have set my heart on honesty."[4] He sees nothing in genuine success or failure other than the presence or absence of "vital force." Emerson frequently expresses discontent with what passes for the conventional, public, socially approved 'morality'. In his praise of self-reliance he opposes his new ethic of individuality to the debilitating and leveling values of society. Like Kierkegaard, in another context, he points out that men no longer dare to say "I think" or "I am." Expressing a sentiment that is a central feature of existential philosophy, he asserts that "conformity" is the chief social virtue, that "society everywhere is in conspiracy against the manhood of every one of its members."[5]

In his search for a new, more demanding, more vital, morality, one which recognizes the values of naturalness, of "vital force," of "joy," Emerson is guided by his admiration of the great person, the genius, the exception. Such individuals, he believes, display the overflowing energy, the creativity, and the power of nature in its most fully realized form.

It is obvious that Nietzsche took to heart Emerson's praise of nonconformity and the ideals of self-trust and self-reliance. More than that, his unrelenting attacks on the "morality of custom" (which is basically a morality of coercive social conformity), his remarks on the people's hostility to new ideas and to innovators, even his critique of negative morality, especially in *Daybreak,* are certainly reminiscent of points forcefully made by Emerson. In his preface to *Daybreak* Nietzsche tells us that he is attacking morality "out of morality." He even explicates what he seems to have found in Emerson *in re* a critique of a flaccid, conformist 'morality' in such a way as to articulate what Emerson only hinted at.

The virtues promoted by centuries of Christian morality—honesty, integrity, forthrightness—are, Nietzsche argues, turned back upon a culture that is ostensibly Christian. Although Emerson does not put forward such a notion, he implies it in his critique of negative moral attitudes, in his emphasis on honesty and integrity and his condemnation of the customary 'morality' of a putative Christian community. More specifically, Emerson, in his portrait of the skeptical Montaigne, comes close to expressing what later becomes Nietzsche's orientation toward previous moralities and ideals of virtue: "Now shall we, because a good nature inclines us to virtue's side, say, There are no doubts—and lie for the right? Is life to be led in a brave or in a cowardly manner? and is not the satisfaction of the doubts essential to all manliness? Is the name of virtue to be a barrier to that which is virtue?"[16]

The virtue that Emerson wants to promote is repeatedly related to nature, to naturalness, to "instinct," to "spontaneity." He sought to promote a conception of "tart cathartic virtue" that will raise the level of human existence above that of the common 'virtues' of passive weakness. Basically, what Emerson sought to encourage was a morality of natural strength, a positive, affirmative morality of "health." Observing those around him, he finds many who are weak, dependent, self-pitying, many who are barely able to function at all. As Nietzsche later will, in a hyperbolic way, and with constant emphasis upon inherited or acquired "decadence," Emerson attributes many of the deficiencies of modern man to previous abrogations of the natural order: "The violations of the laws of nature by our predecessors and our contemporaries are punished in us also. The disease and deformity around us certify that infraction of natural, intellectual, and moral laws, and often violation on violation to breed such compound misery."[17]

Emerson, before Darwin, sketched a general theory of man's evolutionary development out of lower forms of life. However, he did not view civilization as displaying a progressive development of the human species. Much is gained in the growth of civilized techniques and the spread of civilizing influences like the Judeo-Christian system of values, but much is lost along the way. Nietzsche will later amplify statements such as the following in his criticism of modern, domesticated man: "If we dilate in beholding the Greek energy, the Roman pride," Emerson tells us, "it is that we are already domesticating the same sentiment."[18]

A vital, healthy culture will make room for such natural virtues. The natural, well-turned-out man is the truly successful person. But the emergence of this ideal, natural being is a rare event. For, man is a "stupendous antagonism," an unstable synthesis of polarities that are derived from his entire developmental history. The "new powers" that man acquires in civilized life are paid for by the loss of old powers. If, Emerson points out, we compared the health of an aboriginal New Zealander with that of a white man, we would have to admit that the latter "has lost his aboriginal strength."[19] The civilized, domesticated man loses a rough, primitive vitality and becomes alienated from his *natural* powers.

The difficulty in becoming a complete, natural human being lies in the problem of living with and coordinating the opposing traits in the individual that compete with each other for dominance.[20] It takes a strong will, Emerson claims, to master and to control the antithetical characteristics that are in conflict in the self. And this mastering will is itself derived from nature. In fact, "The one serious and formidable thing in nature is a will."[21] Needless to say, this was one of the chiseled sentences that Nietzsche had heavily underlined in the *Versuche*.

In Emerson's works Nietzsche found the basic ingredients that he incorporated in his idea of a natural morality of growth. He, too, expresses the apotheosis of "naturalness" as a virtue, projects the goal of an idealized natural perfection in man, and describes man as a dynamic combination of antithetical traits and propensities. In *Ecce Homo* he tells us that "my theory" is that "everything decisive arises as the result of opposition."[22] More specifically, he claims that for his task of "transvaluing values" he himself had to be possessed of opposing abilities and capacities that are not mutually destructive, that he had to be a multiplicity of contrasts that does not become a chaos. This was a requirement for his "long, secret labor."[23] This self-portrait is not theoretically anomalous insofar as he had previously described man as a complex of contrasts, a microcosm reflecting the characteristics of nature itself.

In his *Nachlass,* Nietzsche refers to the greater complexity of the higher type of person, the presence of multiple, *antithetical* drives, the dynamic, paradoxical tensions of a complex self. The highest type of human being would be an individual in whom "*the antithetical character of existence*" would be present in an exemplary way.[24] When he declares that nature must be construed on the basis of human analogy, as subject to error, engaged in experimentation, good and evil, imbued with struggle and antitheses,[25] Nietzsche seems to complete the circle of his kinship with Emerson on this central point.

In *Nature* Emerson contended that "man is an analogist" who "studies relations in all objects," that natural facts are represented by spiritual facts and spiritual facts by natural facts. Nietzsche fully understood what Emerson meant by this, and he adopted it as his general interpretation of nature and of man-in-nature. That is, he held that we ineluctably interpret natural phenomena in terms of our perceptions, conceptions, and our psychological nature. And, conversely, we often seek to comprehend our nature in terms of what Emerson called "natural symbols." The main point here is that the anthropomorphic interpretation of nature was impressed upon Nietzsche's mind, at the very earliest stages of his intellectual development, by Emerson, even though it was a notion that was later reinforced by subsequent study and thought. Despite his criticism of anthropomorphism in scientific thought and his ironic attitude towards the "anthropocentric idiosyncrasy" by which we distort reality, Nietzsche's own symbolic interpretation of nature as pervaded by a "will to power" was a deliberately anthropomorphic one.

A voluntaristic, anthropomorphic interpretation of the universe was espoused by Emerson in *Nature*. There he held that every particular in the natural world has something of "humanity" in it, that there is an "exercise of . . . Will" in each event, and that the world may be construed as a "realized will," as "the double of man." The transference of the language by which we describe nature to man and the ascription of human traits to nature suggested by Emerson is continued by Nietzsche. In his notes, however, he reverts to Emerson's portrait of man-in-nature in "Fate" and articulates a fundamental principle: "the dehumanization of nature and then the naturalization of man; after this, the pure concept 'Nature' has been attained."[26]

Although Nietzsche came to interpret the natural world, largely under the influence of scientific theories of nature, as comprised of an infinitely complex process of interacting centers of force, as a "chaos," his earlier conception of nature, as well as his positive morality of growth, health, and naturalness, was indebted to Emerson's presentation of an anthropomorphically conceived nature. The young German philologist who turned to philosophy was quite impressed by Emerson's curious blend of idealism and naturalism, by the way in which he located man at the heart of the natural world and saw, before Darwin, that man was the product of a very long, very difficult, process of evolutionary development. In an early unpublished essay, "Homer's Contest," Nietzsche seems to express Emerson's view of man as immersed in nature:

> When we speak of *humanity*, the idea is fundamental that this is something which separates and distinguishes man from nature. In reality . . . there is no such separation: "natural" qualities and those called truly "human" are inseparably grown together. Man, in his highest and noblest capacities, is wholly nature and embodies its uncanny dual character.[27]

As man seeks to probe more deeply into the detailed structure of the natural world, it recedes from view and retains its "secret." Emerson is found of paraphrasing Heraclitus' dictum that "Nature loves to hide." He often hints at the mystery that he believes lies at the heart of the natural world. Using an image that Nietzsche will later adopt, he pictures "the Sphinx" at a roadside as prophets from age after age try their hand at "reading her riddle." Nature, as well as *homo natura* and the meaning of human existence in nature, is the fundamental riddle of life. What Emerson sought to divine, and Nietzsche after him, was the underlying "secret" of nature, a secret that both suspected was essentially *spiritual* in form.

Even though Emerson points beyond the natural world and beyond man to a transcendental 'One' or 'God' or 'Oversoul,' he is far more concerned with the human condition and with man's potentialities in *this* world. Despite all the ink that has been spilled in discussions of Emerson's transcendentalism, his predominant concern was with the immanent realization of meaning, purpose, and value, with a new ethics and a new religion that he hoped would enhance human life in *this* world. In his oration of 1837, "The American Scholar," he maintained that "the first in time and the first in importance of the influences upon the mind is that of nature." And he insisted that the serious thinker or the "scholar" must, at some point, finally settle the question, "What is nature to him?"[28]

Nature meant different things to Emerson depending on the perspective from which he viewed it. If we look at the grandeur and sweep of a landscape, the quiet drama of a setting sun, the gracefulness of a deer, the renewal of a sparkling dawn, we see the astonishing beauty of the natural world. If we attend to the physiological development of a vital individual, we see the miracle of growth, the subtle and intricate stages of maturation. Emerson's early celebration of these aspects of nature have long since passed into poetry and common lore and language. He expressed a romantic mysticism in which truth, goodness, and beauty are synthesized in the totality of nature. This idealization of the natural world continues in his tracing creative development to the complete man who would embody the form, beauty, power, intelligence, and energy of a concentrated, personified nature.

Becoming

Emerson is not a naive or sentimental optimist, even though he exalts the "optimism of nature." In "Circles," he looks at another aspect of the natural world and stresses the impermanence of civilizations, cultures, institutions, arts, and of men. The cosmos appears permanent, but is actually "fluid and volatile." At best, permanence is a matter of degree. Although Heraclitus is not mentioned, his principle of the everlasting flux is present in Emerson's reflections on the impermanence in nature.

The dynamic process of nature continues in cultures: new visions, new thoughts, and new theories have the power to "upheave" all creeds. Historical and cultural changes have a special significance: "A new degree of culture would instantly revolutionize the entire system of human pursuits." Nature has no regard for the old, for conservation, for inertia, for rest. In its endless processes "there is no sleep, no pause, no preservation, but all things renew, germinate and spring." Only what is *becoming* is "sacred" to nature. The "way of life" is a letting go of the past, of painful memories, of recollected calamities. To be able to live with and within the flow of life without torment or debilitating dread is already a sign of a higher nature. The movement of nature, the movement of life, is "onward," onward to the open possibilities of the future. Out of this perspective on the natural world Emerson carves a subjective imperative: "Let me live onward."

It is strange, in a way, that this emphasis upon the universality of impermanence avoids its inevitable corollary: all things are destructible, nothing lasts, every living being is carried forward by the momentum of natural processes towards death. The circular process of nature that Emerson embraces points to apparent new beginnings, but it also entails an indefinite series of endings. The Buddhists proclaimed the same insight as that of Emerson and of Heraclitus before him—"All component beings are subject to destruction"—but they responded by urging us to "Work out your salvation with diligence." Rather than seeking a way out of the 'circle' of nature or seeking escape from what the Buddhists call "the wheel of birth and death," Emerson (and later Nietzsche) tries to focus on the sacredness of the circular process of natural, living *becoming*. Rather than seeking a permanent liberation from time and becoming, both Emerson and Nietzsche affirm the circular process of nature and seek redemption within the world of impermanence. Although Nietzsche is referring to Heraclitus in the following passage from *Philosophy in the Tragic Age of the Greeks*, what he says is equally applicable to Emerson's reflections on the impermanence of actuality:

> The eternal and exclusive becoming, the complete impermanence of everything actual, that constantly . . . becomes but never is . . . is a terrible and paralyzing thought. Its impact on us may be compared to the feeling in an earthquake when one loses confidence in a firmly grounded earth. It takes amazing strength to transform this effect into its opposite: sublimity and blessed astonishment.[29]

Between the appearance of *Nature* and the completion of "Circles" some four years later, Emerson turned from a poetic portrait of the unitary Being of nature to a picture of the natural world as pervaded by impermanence. This is not a contradiction in his thinking, even though Emerson *is* prone to embrace paradoxical truth-claims. It is basically a change in perspective. A holistic image of nature leads us to look at its stability and permanence. From the perspective of the particular, Protean, multiple forms in nature, however, we see its variety, its plurality, as well as its process character. There is unity in nature and plurality; relative permanence and radical impermanence; universality and specificity; cooperation and antagonism; interrelatedness and unique individuality.

In his general theory of *compensation* Emerson took into account the play of opposites in actuality, the "action and reaction" in every dimension of the natural world. The ebb and flow of waters, the systole and diastole of the functioning of the heart, centrifugal and centripetal forces, all suggest a rhythmic process of action and reaction in the natural order.[30] There is more truth than mysticism in his belief that the entire system of things is represented in every particle, especially if we think of the immense complexity found within the atom, the symmetry that is produced by a polarity of electric charges of sub-atoms. Or we could turn to structuralism to discover the binary oppositions that are the basis for the formation of meaningful structures. What Emerson was seeking was a general explanation for the interaction of things, events, and persons. He saw the negative within the positive; the positive within the negative; the rebound of thoughts, speech-acts, and actions in the world; the actions and reactions of human behavior and life. It is a poetic-philosophical view that relies upon analogical thinking, a mode of thinking at which both Emerson and Nietzsche excel.

As in the case of Nietzsche's variation on Emerson's theme, there is no facile Hegelian mediation of the antitheses of actuality. True, for Emerson, there is compensation or a kind of balance of forces and values in the active and reactive forces in nature and in human life. But the dynamic natural process continues on in temporality. "There is never a beginning, there is never an end," Emerson oracularly tells us in "The American Scholar," "to the inexplicable continuity of the web of God [nature] but always a circular power returning into itself."

At this point, Emerson's transcendental idealism *seems* to separate his metaphysics from Nietzsche's experimental pantheistic tendencies. However, what Emerson is suggesting is that in *this* world the happy synthesis of antagonism is possible only in the form of the possible realization of wholeness in an exemplary human existence. In temporality, there is, as in Nietzsche's thought, no ultimate reconciliation of polarities, antagonisms, or antitheses. Or, to be precise, there are only *peak experiences* during which one may attain a liberation from the flux of becoming and from the restrictive limitations of particular circumstances. But this leads us prematurely to the difficult question of the meaning of the appropriation of the thought of the endless, circular, cosmic process in the philosophy of Nietzsche and its possible relation to certain fertile suggestions he found in Emerson's essays.

Realism

It is clear that, in the essays comprising *The Conduct of Life,* Emerson has changed his mind about a lot of things. His experiences and reflections have led him to admit the power and tyranny of circumstances, the force of destiny, the conditioning factors that shape events and human life for better or worse. His early optimism has become restrained. The shadow of fate falls upon his otherwise brightly lit intellectual landscape. A insurgent realism begins to clash with Emerson's philosophical idealism. However, by virtue of his judiciousness and his eye for paradoxical tensions, he tries to retain an idealistic perspective within the context of a growing sense of the brute reality of nature.

Nature is beautiful and powerful, but not benign. Whoever looks upon the panorama of nature with clarity will soon enough see "hints of ferocity in the interior of nature."[31] The natural world is not sentimental and does not "pamper" us. In fact, the world is "rough and surly" and the forces of nature will wipe away individuals, scores of individuals, as if they were nothing. Natural forces, diseases, gravity, lightning, poisonous insects and snakes, ferocious animals, "the crackle of the bone of his prey in the coil of the anaconda," are all part of the system of nature. With ironic understatement, Emerson remarks that "the way of Providence is a little rude."[32] If we remove our rose-tinted glasses, we will see "race living at the expense of race," we will see "expensive races," such as our own, that are deadly for other species.

Given Nietzsche's early attraction to Emerson's tuition, it is probably from him, and not from Darwin (whose theory of natural selection he encountered about four years after he had discovered Emerson), that he acquired the habit of emphasizing the conflict, struggle, and violence in the natural world. In his *Nachlass,* he practically paraphrases Emerson when he writes that "Life always lives at the expense of other life."[33] Neither Emerson nor Nietzsche relished this simple, "ugly" truth. It is simply a sad and poignant fact that man, like all other organic beings, lives by doing violence to other species. Given the assumption that culture evolves out of nature, Nietzsche honestly and accurately observes that "culture rests upon a horrible foundation."[34]

If one is to deify life and culture, then honesty requires that the negativities underlying life and culture be admitted and faced. Nietzsche, in this regard, is only following the advice of Emerson. If we would aspire to a "manly courage," we *must* face harsh realities. And one of the harshest of these realities, as Emerson knew, was, as Nietzsche later put it, that living entails growth, that growth requires the assimilation of external "forces" and beings. Emerson understood, as well as Tennyson did, that nature is "red in tooth and claw." And Nietzsche appropriated his reluctant realization that culture is an extension of nature and is not possible without some "exploitation," in the broadest sense of the word, of environments and of the resources, inorganic and organic, upon which man's continued existence depends. [35]

When Nietzsche chides the socialists and the communists for believing that exploitation can be eliminated, he does so in an Emersonian spirit. For, life is not possible without *some* form of exploitation. This is not a malevolent prescription. It is intended as a brutally frank description of the conditions for human life, the conditions for culture.

Aside from the unveiling of the dangerous features of the natural world and the dependence of life on life, Emerson returns to the theme of the tyranny of temperament over the individual and over the species. In a passage that Nietzsche paraphrased in his notebooks of the early 1860s, he says: "Ask Spurzheim, ask the doctors, ask Quetelet if temperaments decide nothing?—or if there be anything they do not decide?" [36]

Spurzheim, an associate of Gall, the founder of the outmoded "science" of phrenology, which claimed that the shapes of the skull determined different character and personality traits, had lectured in Boston, where Emerson heard him, in 1832. Quetelet was a Belgian statistician who made the first major contributions to social and behavioral statistics in the 1840s. Whatever the scientific merit of the work of these thinkers may be, their studies contributed to the general theory of the physical and sociological determinism of human behavior, a theory that has recently been resuscitated in the far more sophisticated scientific form of sociobiology. Given the influence of this orientation towards human behavior on Emerson, it is not surprising that Oliver W. Holmes, in his *Autobiography,* believed that Emerson, especially in "Fate," was espousing a form of physiological determinism. There is no doubt that Emerson, at one stage of his development, was profoundly impressed by the host of physiological and psychological factors that condition human behavior, perception, valuation, and thought. And it is precisely this kind of physiological and psychic determinism, this kind of naturalistic interpretation of human behavior, that was adopted by Nietzsche in his analysis of *homo natura.*

Man, the self-conscious microcosm in whom nature has come to an awareness of itself, is exempt from no natural factors or circumstances. The single, most powerful circumstance limiting human nature is the "fatality" of nature itself. In a memorable line that Nietzsche certainly did not fail to see and to ponder, he declares that "the book of Nature is the book of Fate." The cosmic forces of the natural world are so overpowering that man is but an insignificant fragment in a vast process, an inhabitant of a small planet. There is nothing for it, Emerson says, in effect, we must accept this reality of our condition and, hence, accept many "odious facts." We must especially accept the painful fact that human life is circumscribed by "necessity."[37] The cement of the universe is not only causation, but a fatality that runs through matter, mind, morals, through all of the strata of thought and character.

As his concessions to the naturalistic facts of man's being-in-nature increase, Emerson generates an antagonism in his thought between a unitary philosophical idealism coupled with a radical subjectivism and a deterministic, naturalistic standpoint. In *Nature* he had proclaimed that "the world exists for you." The panorama of nature exists for human consciousness and its structure is projected by the mind. On this point, it has been said that Emerson follows Kant by assuming "the hypotheses of the permanence of nature" insofar as he thinks that the permanence, stability, and unity of nature are not descriptive of reality, but are a reflection of the structure of the mind. Cognition enters into our experience of relative permanence. Hence, we tend to experience the world as persisting through time rather than "short-lived," relatively stable rather than "mutable."[38] However, Emerson probes behind the Kantian understanding (*Verstand*) by disclosing the influence of our moods on our experience, by calling attention to the way in which our sentiments and feelings are projected into reality. By stressing the psychic factors that condition our experience and thought about the world, Emerson's epistemology clearly becomes a form of psychologism.

On the one hand, Emerson argues for an idealist conception of the subjective, cognitive-affective understanding of nature and, on the other hand, he insists upon the reality of natural entities, forces, and circumstances that act upon man. By joining *Nature* with "Fate" we see that Emerson's philosophical position is clearly paradoxical: it could be characterized as a naturalistic idealism or as an idealistic naturalism. This is a consequence of Emerson's propensity to interpret various phenomena (in this case, the being of man or the condition of man in relation to the natural world) from different perspectives. It is a general philosophical method or orientation that is paralleled in Nietzsche's interpretations of the natural world and man's relation to it. Though we are aware only of the phenomena we have constituted by our perception, our categories, our psychology, and our "conditions of existence," we believe that the "forces" of nature act upon us, are beneficial and useful or dangerous and destructive, and are ontologically real. However, our understanding of the world is conditioned by our concepts or categories, our selective perceptions, and our "psychology." Hence, our representations of natural phenomena, facts, and events are not strictly objective insofar as we "humanize" what we come to know. Even in the exact sciences, Nietzsche avers, we attain only a useful "symbolization of nature." Although Kant and neo-Kantian philosophers of science contribute to this *interpretation* of the external world that Nietzsche proposes, Emerson may be said to have laid the groundwork, in an impressionistic, intuitive, and nonsystematic way, for the development of such a theory in the philosophy of Nietzsche.

Evolution

There is yet another *nexus* between Emerson and Nietzsche, one associated with the idea of the developmental character of nature. Some twenty years before the appearance of Darwin's *The Origin of Species* Emerson celebrated in his prose and poetry the ascent of forms of life from primitive modes of being up towards man. In his anticipation of the concept of transformational evolution, Emerson, like Jean Baptiste de Lamarck, emphasized the role of *effort* in the developmental process and viewed the survival and prosperity of species and of individuals as a triumph over adverse circumstances.

In the motto to *Nature* he spoke of "the worm" that strives to be man and mounts "through all the spires of form." He seems to have assumed that there were scales of organic being that led to man, a unique being who uses his ingenuity and the powers inherited through natural processes to rise above his physical limitations. This viewpoint slides easily, in Emerson's thought, into a consideration of man's striving for increments of *power* that is the initial point from which he develops his general conception of power, a conception that will be treated in detail in another place. The point, at any rate, is that nature reveals scales of being, progressive developments of form, and an immanent "effort" to overcome limitations. All of this dovetails with Emerson's discovery of processes and actions in nature that testify to what he considers as signs of will in nature. This apparent volitional *conatus* is construed as a constant process of 'striving' to overcome obstacles, resistances, and limitations, a 'striving' towards more, towards more perfect forms of being.

In *Nature* it is said that the history of nature, insofar as we know it, seems to involve the building of greater and more all-encompassing worlds. The elaborate cultural world of man is seen as the apogee of the evolutionary process thus far. But it is predicted that "the kingdom of man over nature" will become "a dominion such as now is beyond his dream of God."[39]

Although he is not enamored of the emergent scientific culture, Emerson views man's increasing mastery of the natural world and its forces as a means to further cultural development. Nietzsche, too, called attention to the enormous power that the mastery of nature will bring to man, a power the likes of which has never been seen before. He maintained that "when power is won over nature, then one can use this power" to stimulate the enhancement of life, especially the life of the highest types of human beings.[40]

At the same time, Nietzsche feared that the scientific worldview, if used for purely utilitarian ends, and if allied with the leveling social and political tendencies of modern times, would accelerate the appearance of nihilism. Scientific knowledge and the scientific mastery of nature ought to serve a higher culture and not be used to suppress an artistic culture that could cultivate exemplary human types. Despite their respect for the achievements of the scientific interpretation of the world, neither Emerson nor Nietzsche conceived of the ideal culture in terms of the dominance of scientific or technological values. Both conceived of scientific knowledge and techniques as *means* to the creation of a higher cultural ideal and not as ends in themselves.

Emerson contended that as soon as living beings appear there is a "self-direction and absorbing and using of material."[41] A similar notion is presented by Nietzsche in the form of the view that "assimilation" and "exploitation" continue apace in the development of organisms. In the case of man, this process takes on an additional intellectual or spiritual form: the assimilation of information, knowl edge, and experiences is a cultural transformation of the more basic assimilation of food. In "Swedenborg; or, the Mystic" Emerson said virtually the same thing when he described the mind as a finer, ethereal "body" that continues "the process of alimentation" by "acquiring, comparing, digesting and assimilating experience."

Throughout his evolutionary sojourn, man, according to Emerson, has acquired accumulated capacities and has in his nature the most constructive and most negative capacities found in the natural world. The cunning of the most cunning animal, the cruelty of the cruelest creature, lies coiled within the complex nature of man. What is *natural* is, in Emerson's considered view, beautiful, vital, healthy, creative *and* terrible. It need hardly be said that this dual perspective on nature is replicated in the philosophy of Nietzsche.

Just as man has had a long natural history so, too, does he have a cultural history that carries forward the tensions, antagonisms, and negativities of the former. The Protean character of nature is duplicated in the Protean nature of man. Historical periods manifest the various aspects of man's complex, microcosmic nature. And there are periods when the ameliorating tendency of nature (which, invariably, comes in conflict with "retardations" or regressive tendencies) seems to reach a peak. Reflecting on this point, Emerson tries to explain the almost universal attraction that the ancient Greeks hold for mankind.

Grecian Nature

The remarkable achievements of the ancient Greeks fascinate us because every person passes through a grecian stage of existence. Ancient Greek culture represents a perfection of the senses, of bodily existence, a culture in which the spiritual nature of man is in union with the body. The manners of the ancient Greeks are, to our eyes, both simple and fierce. These people exhibit exuberance, have a code of honor, but are lacking in discipline. They are, Emerson believes, like young men, even boys. What we admire in the figures of Greek history, art, and literature is their common sense, their unreflective habits of mind, their quick wit, their free speech, their spontaneous energy. In effect, we admire their *naturalness*. What they managed to combine is "the energy of manhood" with the attractive "unconsciousness of childhood." The ancient Greeks were spontaneous, unreflective, gifted with sharp senses, healthy adults possessed with the "grace of children." Anyone who could become an individual with such dynamic energy and "childlike genius" would, Emerson believes, be a Greek.[42]

This idealization of the ancient Greeks, this valuation of their "naturalness" and their youthful spontaneity, was a common theme in the eighteenth and nineteenth century, one that is traceable in the poetry of Hölderlin, in some of the writings of Goethe.

It is present in Johann Winckelmann's eighteenth-century study, *History of the Art of Antiquity.* However, the specific nature of Emerson's characterization of the ancient Greeks seems to recur in Nietzsche's first major work. In *The Birth of Tragedy* Nietzsche agreed with Emerson that the "Greeks are eternal children." And he also agreed with him that they prized personal qualities such as courage, a sense of justice, self-command, strength, and dexterity. He especially emphasized their valuation of individuality. The turning of this ideal of cultivating individuals into a goal for his age is reminiscent of Emerson's ethical individualism.

Nietzsche's image of the ancient Greeks was, at least in part, shaped by the judgments of Emerson. Of course, he went beyond him and beyond his contemporaries in disclosing the pessimistic undercurrent of Greek culture that stimulated the creation of the illusions of art. But he is at one with Emerson in contrasting the youthful energy and buoyant individuality of the ancient Greeks with modern men who are "as alike as peas." As Emerson tries to form his ideal of the authentically natural, healthy and vital individual, he incorporates, as Nietzsche later will, many of the traits of the ancient Greeks, as he perceived them, into his depiction of such human types.

The valuation of culture over the political State, the retention, in a superior culture, of instinctive, spontaneous capacities, the conception of the role of culture as providing the conditions necessary for the emergence of "great men" who are unique individuals, all of these notions are first put forward by Emerson. A broadly conceived naturalness that retains "manly" virtues, that expresses the energy of nature without its cruelty and violence, is first included in Emerson's ethical ideal before Nietzsche expounded it.

For Emerson, the exemplary person is one who acts with the precision and solidity of a "natural agent." The creative or "crescive self" must be rooted in "absolute nature."[43] A natural morality, a morality of growth that overcomes resistances and promotes spontaneity and health, is typically and correctly associated with the philosophy of Nietzsche. However, the blueprint for a morality of creative and spontaneous naturalness is, in point of fact, outlined in the essays of Emerson. Even Nietzsche's alarming antinomian tendencies are foreshadowed by Emerson's suggestion of a freedom, in unusual circumstances, to breach the consensual moral principles of society. Charles Andler goes too far when he contends that we must call Emerson "an immoralist." But he has touched a nerve. For he has discerned his tendency to admire the audacious, courageous "hero" to such an extent that he exempts him from the norms and moral prohibitions that pertain to lesser mortals. Insofar as he does so, it is for the sake of a higher good, a higher value. The *anti-nomos* attitude Emerson sometimes prescribes has religious origins in the sense that he opposes ecclesiastical subscription and orthodox legalism.

There is an obvious synonymy between Emerson's portrait of the "beautiful," "strong," and "natural" individual and Nietzsche's various attempts to depict a "synthetic" man. And he follows Emerson closely in the contrast between the genuine "natural" human being and the timid and cowed modern man.

In the course of mitigating Nietzsche's rare praise of the bold and guiltless "blond beast" of man's earlier history, a commentator on Nietzsche compares this image to Emerson's remark that "bruisers and pirates" are more promising in trade and politics than are "talkers and clerks." And the following observation of Emerson's is presented as if it were merely a coincidental analogue to some of Nietzsche's sentiments and not the original template of them: "In a good lord there must first be a good animal, at least to the extent of yielding the incomparable advantage of animal spirits."[44]

Contra Darwin

Although Nietzsche accepts the Darwinian notion of a struggle for existence in the natural world, he does not accept the optimistic belief that the natural evolutionary process favors the superior types of a species. In the remote past, when the environment was extremely harsh and human existence was crude and extremely dangerous, the most cunning, the most brutal, the physically strongest of human beings survived and reproduced themselves. These forceful and cruel beings are the "blond beasts" of Nietzsche's speculative anthropology. They are considered as superior to modern man in the sense that they are construed as stronger, more daring, less impeded by guilt and "bad conscience," more energetic, more spontaneous and instinctive than "domesticated" modern man. But (and this is an important but) Nietzsche *does not* propose a return to the way of life and mode of behavior of such healthy, brutal animals. He, like Emerson before him, wants to recapture the positive, *natural* traits of earlier breeds of men in order to rejuvenate civilized or overcivilized modern man.

What Emerson sometimes calls "Corinthian" overrefinement tends to weaken men, to make them too passive, too timid, too sensitive, too much susceptible to moral corruption. Nietzsche agrees, but goes further. He condemns as "decadent" the tendency to want peace, quiet, and rest above all; to desire security, ease, and comfort as essential values; to desire to live without tension, antagonism, or conflict; to want to withdraw from the struggle for existence; to desire a pleasing, conflict-free gregarious *Gemütlichkeit*.

Against the optimism of the evolutionary cheerleaders of his day who saw only progressive intellectual, moral and spiritual developmental tendencies in the modern world, and in agreement with Emerson, Nietzsche pointed to signs of regression, of devolution, evidence that the class of the mediocre was becoming more and more prevalent, was, in fact, by sheer force of numbers, gaining more and more ground in the modern world. The "masses," as Emerson called them, were threatening to level the goals, aims, standards, and values of culture. They were becoming a negative force in relation to all higher values. The presumed selective process of evolution seemed to be more and more unselective, seemed, in point of fact, to favor the growth of the average of the species. Almost in the words of the Danish thinker, Kierkegaard, Emerson lamented "our slavish respect for numbers."[45] He worried, with good reason, that we may be becoming "a mob," that genuine individuals were becoming an endangered species.

Paradoxically, man's technological progress has outrun his moral and spiritual development. Applied science changes the face of the earth; but man is not improved. The collective power of the social group has been progessively developed at the expense of individuality. "Man does not stand in awe of man" in the sense that a collective consciousness has arisen that views everyone as, more or less, "the same."[46] Self-trust has yielded to mass consciousness. People devalue themselves by calling themselves, in Emerson's words, "the mass," "the herd."[47] Culture is being turned upside down, and the virtues comprising "nobility of character" are either ignored and unrewarded or devalued. The implications of such social changes are that evolutionary advance has halted in modern times or that the conditions of existence in the nineteenth century favor the prosperity of the average man. The typical human being has one trump card: he has numbers on his side.[48]

There is little doubt that these suggestions of Emerson's provided the basis for one of Nietzsche's criticisms of Darwinism. He argues that "the weaker dominate the strong again and again" because they "are more numerous and more *clever*." They are clever in dissimulation, patience, and foresight. They have "spirit" in the sense of cunning and the power of "mimicry."[49]

The social form of the biological defense mechanism of mimicry is the ability to blend in with crowds, to adopt the manners and mores of social groups, to mimic conventional moral or social values. Such cleverness obviously has a high degree of survival value. Sometimes Nietzsche has been thought to contradict himself by arguing that the weaker or the unfit survive and reproduce while the fit and the stronger tend to perish. But there is no contradiction here at all. Independent, self-directed, intelligent, perceptive, creative, and solitary individuals who are able to go against the grain of the majority are stronger, fitter types of human beings *individually*. But they are no match for cooperative, dependent, uncreative, sociable majorities. Exceptional individuals who are, in the strict sense of the word, "unpopular" have "the majority against them."[50] This is more or less the point that Emerson made when he quoted with approval de Boufflers' observation that the majority "have the advantage of number. . . . It is of no use for us to make war with them; we shall not weaken them; they will always be the masters."[51] Of course, a cultural world in which the majority are masters is looked upon by Emerson, to say nothing of Nietzsche, as a deplorable state of affairs.

Natural evolution does not necessarily generate progressively better, fitter members of a species *en masse*. It tends to favor the growth of the typical members of a species. The majority, according to Emerson, are "unripe" and have no *individual* values or opinions. With them, "the quadruped interest is very prone to prevail."[52] A collective social force is very powerful in a natural environment and it continues to be powerful, perhaps more powerful, in civilized societies. It is a strong conditioning factor in psychosocial evolution.

The entire approach to the dissimilarities between the majority population and those both Emerson and Nietzsche called "exceptions," the general understanding of the practical, long-range effects of evolutionary transformation and related ideas are interpretations that are traceable regressively from Nietzsche to

Emerson. Many of the value-judgments about the differentiation between exceptional individuals and the majority that are considered vintage Nietzsche were originally expressed by Emerson.

Genius

To indicate how close this relationship of thought and attitude is in Emerson and Nietzsche, we can point to the specific view of Nietzsche's that exceptional human beings are, in fact, vulnerable to destruction, disability, and madness because their nature is complex and involves a delicate balance of paradoxical tendencies. The higher type of individual, Nietzsche tells us, presents, in comparison with the average person, a greater totality of coordinated elements: "therefore, disintegration, too, becomes incomparably more probable. The "genius" is the sublimest machine there is— hence, the most fragile."[53]

The similarities among the typical members of the species serve as a bond or kinship that augments their survival powers insofar as they have a basic, surface understanding of one another, can assist each other more easily, and are able to cooperate for their mutual survival or prosperity. The "genius" is vulnerable precisely because he or she is different, because he or she does not respond readily to common signs or stimuli. The special talents, skills or abilities of the "genius" separate him or her from the *ethos* of the social group, from the use of common survival mechanisms.[54]

Such interesting and plausible insights parallel, point by point, those of Emerson. Genius is, like life itself, a delicate balance of antagonistic tendencies, especially a balance of "form and power."[55] The independence and nonconformity of the exceptional individual, Emerson believes, makes such a person vulnerable to criticism and to social isolation. Whoever casts off the ordinary motivations of mankind and cultivates self-trust must have "something godlike in him" in order to swim against the common current and survive.[56] Genius is, as Nietzsche will remember when writing *Ecce Homo,* prone to being "misunderstood."[57] For independence of mind and aloofness from ordinary sociability, society will retaliate against the exception. Aside from the indifference or hostility of the majority, the genius must be able to cope with the negative effects of the accomplishments of past geniuses, the feeling of being overshadowed by the "overinfluence" of great talents and superior character.[58]

The private life of a creative individual is often spoiled by the time and energy that is put into his or her work. In the broadest sense of the term, "art is a jealous mistress."[59] The genius is a very delicate balance indeed. As Emerson puts it, "your man of genius pays dear for his distinction. His head runs up into a spire, and, instead of a healthy man, merry and wise, he is some mad dominie. Nature is reckless of the individual."[60]

The lack of prudence in the "man of genius" can easily lead to reckless self-indulgence, to querulousness, to dissipation. There have been many unfortunate cases of "the tragedy of imprudent genius." The exhaustion and despair experienced after years of struggle, of poverty or near-poverty, leaves the creative genius depleted, "like a giant slaughtered by pins."[61]

There is no need to pile citation on top of citation from Emerson's writings in order to show that Nietzsche has, in this instance, as well as in many others, followed Emerson's reflections on the dangers and travails of genius as closely as one could imagine. He only extends Emerson's thought slightly when he contends that the "stronger" (in the sense of having superior creative power and energy), exceptional individual is "weaker" than the majority that acts as a negative force against him and is subject to internal destruction or self-destruction because he is a sublime, but "fragile," mechanism.[62] For both Emerson and Nietzsche, the perfectability of nature in the form of exceptional individuals who can master the inherited and acquired antithetical characteristics of their nature is a very rare phenomenon.

Nature in Culture

The immanent, if sometimes disguised, presence of nature in culture that is one of the bases of social Darwinism and sociobiology is one of Nietzsche's fundamental conceptions. He is a past master at disclosing the mailed fist beneath the velvet glove; the malice underlying excessive kindness; the contempt concealed by obsequious affability; the moral and psychological blackmail that is sometimes employed by the physically or psychologically weak. He uncovers the subtle cruelty that is sublimated in drama and tragedy, exposes the "savage animal" that still lives in the most civilized person. Nietzsche anticipated psychoanalytical theory by unmasking the unsavory, potentially dangerous and savage drives that are concealed by the masks of language, manners, morals, culture, and civilized existence. But it was the "genteel" Emerson who planted the seed of such ideas that Nietzsche later cultivated or, some might say, overcultivated.

Before he read Charles Darwin, Nietzsche was familiar with the general theory of evolutionary transformation and the idea of the continuity of nature in culture from his conscientious reading of the American thinker he admired so much. In his second essay on nature, Emerson observed that "we talk of deviations from natural life, as if artificial life were not also natural. The smoothest curled courtier in the boudoirs of a palace has an animal nature, rude and aboriginal . . . omnipotent to its ends."[63]

Natural tendencies cannot be driven out of culture or out of the cultivated individual. There is, Emerson argues, a vital "impulse" in nature that can neither be denied nor eliminated. In man, nature has come to self-consciousness or "self-explication." A culture that seeks to suppress or deny the natural in human nature produces truncated, distorted men, or worse. The roots of man's being run back into the primordial impulses of natural life. In man is found traces of primitive forms of life and energy that are not deleted by civilization.

The natural origin of man, Nietzsche held, must be recognized and understood again in order "to translate man back into nature; to become master over the many vain and overly enthusiastic interpretations and connotations that have so far been scrawled and painted over that . . . basic text of *homo natura*."[64] This recovery of nature, however, either in the case of Emerson or Nietzsche, is *not* intended as the conversion of civilized man into a "beast," blond or otherwise. For the raw natural drives, passions, or "instincts" of man are, if unchecked, extremely dangerous. The control and creative expression of natural, "crescive" propensities is fundamental to Nietzsche's conception of a rejuvenated human existence. The primitive drives of man must be "sublimated" or "spiritualized" if a meaningful life and a meaningful culture is to be possible. This creative transformation of natural, vital energy was expressed by Emerson before it was promulgated by his disciple in this domain of thought.

Emerson traced the roots of human nature to their source in the fertility and energy of nature. He tried to follow their course to the point at which they became entangled in the web of fatalism. Ultimately, he believed that everything emerged out of the ground of an aboriginal, "supreme Power" that was conceived as the spiritual unity from which the multiplicity of phenomenal beings came forth and still comes forth. The natural world, despite all that is known of it, is not transparent to reason. In fact, the underlying reality of the world, the springs of its perpetual, creative becoming, was seen by Emerson as an enigma, a riddle. The ultimate facts of nature, the "capital facts of human life," are hidden from our view.[65] Even at the heart of the atom man is confronted with the mystery of being. As man seeks to penetrate this mystery, he brings with him the "deception of the senses," "illusions of sentiment and of the intellect," and thereby the objectivity of nature eludes him.

Emerson, like Nietzsche after him, is alert to the limits of man's knowledge of the natural world. He held that "our thoughts are not finalities . . . the incessant flowing and ascension reach there also, and each thought which yesterday was a finality, today is yielding to a larger generalization."[66] In regard to absolute knowledge of the natural world, we are precluded from attaining any such thing. This is not only because of the presumed "mystery" of nature, but because of our own psychophysical makeup, because of the deceptions and illusions to which we are prone. Our "senses interfere everywhere" and our "organization" (as Nietzsche will also say) conditions even our most immediate experiences. Our imagination, our feelings and sentiments, our temperaments infiltrate all of our ostensibly objective judgments. Even the natural facts cherished by the rising scientific culture have a "symbolic character." In the final analysis, Emerson confesses that "all is riddle, and the key to a riddle is another riddle."[67] For Nietzsche, too, nature has a Sphinx-like visage. It is like an obscure text that is subject to a variety of interpretations.

When Nietzsche later chooses to enter a "new domain of dangerous insights" and seeks to guess the secret of nature, to offer his answer to the riddle of the Sphinx, to interpret nature in terms of man and man in terms of nature, he does not proceed unaided or unarmed. He uses and improves upon the tools originally supplied by Emerson's radical, homemade insights. What Charles Andler has said of the relation between Emerson and Nietzsche is generally correct and is particularly relevant to the conception of nature, the valuation of naturalness, and to the related notions we've discussed in this context. "Emerson," he wrote, "a very convinced mystic, has not anticipated all the theories of Nietzsche, but he obliged Nietzsche to establish them."[68]

Chapter 2 Notes

1. *Werke* (GOA), XIII:64.
    2. "The American Scholar," *PE*, p. 61.
    3. "The Transcendentalist," *PE*, p. 101.
    4. "Self-Reliance," *PE*, p. 153.
    5. Nature mysticism has been described as a feeling of unity with the whole of nature or, occasionally, as the sense of being one with nature construed as a manifestation of a spiritual being or power (R. C. Zaehner, *Mysticism Sacred and Profane*, pp. 95–118).
    6. "Spiritual Laws," *PE*, pp. 201–2.
    7. "Compensation," *PE*, p. 169.
    8. Ibid., p. 173.
    9. Ibid., p. 180.
    10. "Spiritual Laws," *PE*, p. 191.
    11. "Experience," *PE*, p. 232. The emphasis in this essay on the coloration and distorting effect of our "subject-lenses" on our experience of the world and others prefigures Nietzsche's idea of "the perspectival optics of life," as well as his general perspectival conception of experience and knowledge. So, too, does Emerson's observation in "Spiritual Laws" that "a man is a method, a progressive arrangement, a selecting principle. . . . He takes only his own, out of the multiplicity that sweeps and circles round him. He is like one of the booms which are set out from the shore on rivers to catch driftwood, or like the lodestone amongst splinters of steel." *PE*, p. 195.
    12. *SW* 5, *JGB* §11, p. 26.
    13. *SW* 3, *M* 2, §117, p. 110. In the course of discussing the deficiencies of man's prescientific beliefs, Emerson avers that "we know nothing rightly, for want of perspective" ("Nature" [Second Series], *EE*, p. 300). Even though he never explicitly says it, Emerson's conception of the power of individual perspectives, as well as his use of various perspectives in his writings, suggest that this is a means of augmenting human knowledge. Once again, Nietzsche brings his suggestions to completion by arguing that "there is *only* a perspectival seeing, *only* a perspectival knowing." And the more "eyes" and "affects" we bring to bear on a phenomenon, the more complete our concept of it, our 'objectivity,' is (*SW* 5, *GM* III, §13, p. 365).
    14. "Experience," *PE*, p. 280.
    15. "Self-Reliance," *PE*, p. 141.
    16. "Montaigne," in *Ralph Waldo Emerson: Selected Essays*, ed. L. Ziff, p. 332.

17. "Heroism," *EE*, p. 140. In "On the Uses and Disadvantages of History for Life" Nietzsche seems to echo Emerson's remark. "Since we are . . . the outcome of prior generations, we are also the consequence of their aberrations, passions, and errors, even of their crimes. It is impossible entirely to be free of this chain. If we condemn these aberrations and think we have escaped them, we cannot escape the fact that we spring from them" (*SW* 1, *UB* II, §3).

18. Ibid., p. 144.

19. "Self-Reliance," *PE*, p. 161.

20. "Fate," *PE*, p. 358.

21. Ibid., p. 362.

22. *SW* 6, *EH*, pp. 336–37. Emerson, as we've seen, also interpreted the natural world in terms of polarities and oppositions. "Nature," he says, "is upheld by antagonism" ("Considerations By the Way," *COL*, p. 254).

23. Ibid., p. 294.

24. *Werke* (GOA), 16:296.

25. *Werke* (GOA), 12:240.

26. *SW* 9, p. 525. *"Meine Aufgabe: die Entmenschung der Natur und dann die Vernatürlichung des Menschen, nachdem er den reinen Begriff 'Natur' gewonnen hat."*

27. *SW* 1, p. 783.

28. "The American Scholar," *PE*, p. 53.

29. *SW* 1, pp. 824–25. In "Circles" Emerson describes the impermanence and fluidity of the "becoming" of nature, and in "The Method of Nature" he cites with approval Heraclitus' idea of universal flux and asserts that "total nature is growing . . . is becoming . . . is in rapid metamorphosis" (*Representative Men, Nature, Addresses and Lectures*, p. 194).

30. Sherman Paul places the idea of correspondence at the center of Emerson's angle of vision. It is construed as a metaphysical principle of "faith" that joins the spiritual and natural aspects of actuality. Although Paul overstates his thesis somewhat, he correctly sees the importance of Emerson's dialectical approach to significant issues, his technique of viewing a central question or phenomenon from different vantage points. This is especially apparent in regard to his various interpretations of nature and the being of man. Cf. Sherman Paul, *Emerson's Angle of Vision*, Cambridge, Harvard University Press, 1952.

31. "Fate," *COL*, p. 8.

32. Ibid., p. 7.

33. *Werke* (GOA), 15:407. In *Beyond Good and Evil* life is described as "exploitation" and the desire to eliminate all modes of exploitation is said to be a false promise of a "life in which there will be no organic functions" (*SW* 6, p. 208). This remark echoes Emerson's observation that man continuously exploits plant and animal life in order to satisfy his basic organic needs, but does so in a manner and in a context in which it could easily be misconstrued.

34. *Werke* (GOA), IX:151.

35. *Werke* (GOA), XVI:179.

36. "Fate," *COL*, pp. 8–9.

37. Ibid., p. 19.

38. David Van Veer, *Emerson's Epistemology*, p. 31. Although Van Veer has much of value to say about Emerson's epistemic notions (which are more often implied than made explicit), the central lacuna in his study is the absence of a treatment of the most important aspect of Emerson's un-systematic discussion of human knowledge: the perspectival nature of knowledge and the consequent elusiveness of pure, objective knowledge. In addition, even though Van Veer deals with Emerson's skepticism (especially in "Montaigne"), he minimizes it. This leads to an obscuring of Emerson's *experimental*, antidogmatic approach to the problem of knowledge. For a thorough account of Emerson's skeptical orientation, see: John Michael, *Emerson and Skepticism*.

39. "Nature," *PE*, p. 50.

40. *Werke* (GOA), XV:232.

41. "Fate," *COL*, p. 38.

42. "History," *PE*, pp. 127–29.

43. "Experience," *PE*, p. 285.

44. "Manners," *EE*, p. 271. Cf. William Salter, *Nietzsche the Thinker*, p. 369.

45. "Self-Reliance," *PE*, p. 163. In his published works and in his journals Kierkegaard rails against the modern veneration of "numbers," "the crowd," and "the mass." In his journals alone there are some eighty-six critical or satirical remarks made concerning the modern obsession with "numbers" and the overvaluation of "the public." Cf. *Soren Kierkegaard's Journals and Papers*, ed. and trans., H. V. Hong and E. H. Hong, 7 vols., Bloomington and London, Indiana University Press 1967–1978.

46. "Self-Reliance," *PE*, p. 154.

47. "The American Scholar," *PE*, p. 66.

48. "Considerations By the Way," *COL*, pp. 250–53.

49. *SW* 6, *G* §14, p. 120.

50. *Werke* (GOA), XVI:149.

51. "Considerations By the Way," *COL*, p. 253.

52. Ibid., p. 252.

53. *Werke* (GOA), XVI:148.

54. Ibid., 146–48.

55. "Circles," *PE*, p. 236.

56. "Self-Reliance," *PE*, p. 156.

57. Ibid., p. 146. Cp. "The Transcendentalist," *PE*, p. 100.

58. "The American Scholar," *PE*, p. 57.

59. "Wealth," *COL*, p. 114.

60. "Culture," *COL*, pp. 138–39.

61. "Prudence," *EE*, pp. 132–33.

62. *Werke* (GOA), XVI:148.

63. "Nature" (Second Series), *EE*, p. 302.

64. *SW* 5, *JGB* §230, p. 169.

65. "Illusions," *PE*, p. 321.

66. Ibid., p. 320.

67. Ibid., p. 313.

68. Charles Andler, *Nietzsche, sa vie et sa pensée*, 1:342. "*Emerson, mystique très convaincu n'a pas prévu toutes les théories de Nietzsche, mais il à obligé Nietzsche à les éstablir.*"

Chapter 3

History and Existence

> History no longer shall be a dull book. It
> shall walk incarnate in every just and wise
> man.
>
> [Ralph Waldo Emerson, "History"]

During the period in which he wrote the four essays comprising his *Untimely Meditations,* the philosophical ideas of Emerson were very much on Nietzsche's mind. To be sure, his own thinking was percolating and he was responding to other intellectual stimuli. From the time he had jotted down notes on Emerson's essays in the 1860s to the time at which he wrote *Ecce Homo,* Nietzsche had returned to Emerson's writings for both personal and intellectual inspiration. However, in the middle of the 1860s he had come under the spell of Arthur Schopenhauer and Richard Wagner. Through his friendship with Wagner he became intimately acquainted with the composer's music-dramas, even to the point of having access to librettos when they were works in progress.

Having recently discovered Schopenhauer's *The World as Will and Idea,* Nietzsche was very pleased to find that Wagner was not only a follower of Schopenhauer's but incorporated themes from his pessimistic philosophy into his music-dramas. Aside from his own original thoughts, the *Untimely Meditations* are pervaded by the ideals, conceptions, and idealized images of the personalities of an unusual troika of aesthetically sensitive thinkers: Emerson, Schopenhauer, and Wagner.

The fourth of Nietzsche's untimely observations, "Richard Wagner in Bayreuth," is basically a hymn of praise to the creative artist as "hero" and spearhead of a higher, artistic culture. Wagner is described as overcoming resistance and obstacles to his "greatness." His supreme desire for "power" is transmuted into artistic form and expression. Nietzsche's paean to the composer includes the belief that in his music-dramas Wagner presented a dreamlike recollection of the great man's (Wagner's) "heroic existence." Much of this apotheosis of the artistic-philosophical hero is presented in terms reminiscent of the evocative portrait of the new, "great" man whose vision rises above the values of the typical social world, a portrait that can be clearly discerned in Emerson's essays and poems. However, when Nietzsche, in this same meditation, describes the presumed effect that Wagner's work will have on "the people," he clearly echoes Schopenhauer's philosophy. He claims that the art of Wagner will unite people in a communal need and suffering that will (ostensibly) ennoble their lives. Art, especially the art of Wagner, would also serve as a protection from the painful recognition that life is suffering. Under the spell of Schopenhauer's idea of renunciation of the "will to live" and his praise of the redemptive power of art and aesthetic experience, at this stage of his thinking, Nietzsche has obviously not yet seen the light of Emerson's joyful acceptance of life in face of "negative facts" and the realities of existence.

In the third of his unseasonable meditations, "Schopenhauer as Educator," there are many interwoven themes. The first section of the essay, in which we are urged to "be your self," is close in spirit and tone to Emerson's "Self-Reliance." It also contains a quotation from Oliver Cromwell—"a man never rises higher than when he does not know whither his path can still lead him"—which is a slightly modified version of Emerson's quotation of Cromwell in the last paragraph of "Circles." This third meditation ends with a long quotation from "Circles" that refers to the effects that a philosopher can have on a culture or a civilization. In effect, "Schopenhauer as Educator" begins and ends with allusions to Emerson.

Schopenhauer is depicted as "the great man" who defies his age and its values. His courage and tragi-heroic call for a renunciation of life, as well as his admiration for the philosopher, the saint, and the artist as higher human types, is unstintingly praised. Of special interest is the assumption of a continuity between nature and culture. To this Emersonian theme is added Nietzsche's lamentation about the waste in nature that seems to be required to produce the genius. In response to this, Nietzsche simply resigns himself to this tragic reality.

In the course of defending Schopenhauer the man and thinker, Nietzsche lashes out at "academic" philosophy and its lack of vitality and integrity. He deplores the separation of philosophy from life and contrasts the formal, professional teaching of philosophy to Schopenhauer's philosophy of life. Although Nietzsche here appropriates Schopenhauer's praise of genius and his contempt for academic philosophy and then applies it to Schopenhauer himself, there is a similarity between his idealized delineation of the 'heroic' philosophy of Schopenhauer and Emerson's championing of a "brave" and courageous "philosophy of life." In "Schopenhauer as Educator" it would seem that the intermixture of Schopenhauer's pessimism and Emerson's optimism had a synergetic effect on Nietzsche's thinking. But this effect is not entirely beneficial.

On the one hand, German culture of the 1870s is criticized, in "Schopenhauer as Educator," for squelching genius; for promoting the "teaching" of philosophy while ignoring its practice; for submitting higher culture to the needs of the State; for training students for business careers and professions while undermining genuine education for culture and life; for serving "greed" and jingoism; and, finally, for promoting a rising tide of mediocrity. On the other hand, a philosophy advocating the *renunciation* of life is offered as a cure for these cultural ills! Why, one may ask, should the 'heroic' philosopher who faces the realities of life, who chooses to deny in himself the "will to live" after having seen into the insatiable will that acts through all beings, be concerned with the fallen, defective, and inadequate nature of German culture? Nietzsche's critique of German culture of the 1870s and his vision of a genuine, superior culture is at odds with his defense of Schopenhauer's philosophy of withdrawal, renunciation, and denial. Why would someone seriously committed to a philosophy, largely modeled on Buddhism, that teaches the cessation of desire, attachment, and the clinging to the illusions of existence be concerned with the state of a particular national culture? Wouldn't the denial of the will to live entail the denial of a will to culture? Furthermore, what little Nietzsche does say about the cultural ideal he is promoting indicates that it is definitely not a Buddhistic culture.

What irritates Nietzsche, as it should anyone who recognizes the value of, and uses of, philosophy, is the contempt of, and indifference towards, philosophy shown by the "culture philistine."

Anticipating aspects of his later thought, Nietzsche proclaims that genuine philosophy should be "fearsome," and he advises that "men called to the search for power ought to know what a source of the heroic wells within it."[1] At this point, he should have realized that if he was looking for a philosophical 'hero' upon which to build a higher, more demanding, and more vital culture, Schopenhauer was an unfortunate choice.

Obviously following Emerson's suggestions, Nietzsche is looking for a "dangerous thinker" who will radically change the direction and meaning of culture, who will create a new table of values. It is at this point in "Schopenhauer as Educator" that he quotes Emerson's provocative warning: "Beware . . . when the great God lets loose a thinker on this planet." After quoting the entire paragraph following this sentence, he then emphasizes an assertion that is not directly connected with it, but which is accurately treated as if it were. Thus, he quotes the following sentence and links it with Emerson's warning about dangerous thinkers: "A new degree of culture would instantly revolutionize the entire system of human pursuits."[2] Finally, in the penultimate sentence of this impassioned essay, Nietzsche asserts, in Emersonian tones and language, that philosophers should demonstrate "by their deeds that love of truth is something fearsome and mighty."[3]

In "Schopenhauer as Educator" Nietzsche lashes out at many aspects of German culture of the 1870s. He attacks it because it lacks respect for "greatness"; because it is excessively practical and utilitarian; because its teachers of philosophy rummage through antiquarian history and do not relate philosophy to life; because it encourages mediocrity; because it has forgotten that learning and knowledge are not ends in themselves, but means to the enrichment of life, perhaps even means to the 'heroic' life of a "great man." Although much of the content in this essay pertains to Schopenhauer the man and the philosopher, there are many sentiments expressed in it that are reminiscent of the "*Amerikaner*" who is quoted with enthusiastic approval. In point of fact, a considerable number of Nietzsche's criticisms of German culture in the 1870s are quite similar to Emerson's earlier criticisms of the American culture of his day. Emerson attacks the quality of American life quite frequently. He criticizes the greed and materialism of its commercial class, the corruption of its politics, its fanatical worship of financial success. "Americans," he writes, "are tainted" with an insane pursuit of success, "as our bankruptcies and our reckless politics . . . show. We are great by exclusion, grasping, and egotism."[4] Emerson despises "shallow American-ism." Americans, he believes, live by "show, puffing advertise-ment, and manufacture of public opinion; and excellence is lost sight of in the hunger for sudden performance and praise."[5]

The possibility that when Nietzsche criticizes German culture for its excessive practical, utilitarian, and commercial concerns, for its materialism, he is applying Emerson's criticisms of American culture to the Germany of the 1870s is supported by the fact that, especially in *The Gay Science,* America is attacked for its commer-cial values. Nietzsche, in the spirit of Emerson, lashes out at the savage "manner in which Americans strive after gold;" at the "breathless hurry of their work;" at their "strange lack of intellec-tuality." He charges that, in America, thinking is done "with a stopwatch" and "dining is done with the eyes fixed on the finan-cial newspaper." A life devoted to such a passionate pursuit of fi-nancial gain "continually compels a person to consume his intellect, even to exhaustion, in constant dissimulation, overreach-ing, or forestalling."[6]

History and Life

In what is unquestionably the most theoretically interesting of the four *Untimely Meditations,* "On the Uses and Disadvantages of History for Life," we are presented with a conception of the essen-tial meaning of history that is clearly derived from Emerson's ideas concerning the use and value of history. The central thrust of this second meditation is directed against the deification of history, especially in the form of Hegel's theory that reason (*Vernunft*) per-vades history and that there is a progressive, rational, dialectical movement immanent in history. The excessive veneration of his-tory, as well as the ideology of historicism, has led, Nietzsche ar-gues, to a kind of "historical illness" that is debilitating. Although he admits that his age is entitled to be proud of its "historical cul-ture," he also believes that if historical consciousness is divorced from life, if it is used as an argument *against* the present and the future, it can have a negative, depressive, and demoralizing effect on vital existence and inhibit action altogether. How man *uses* his historical knowledge is important because of its effect upon cul-ture and on the value and meaning of individual existence.

Not only is the central contention of this discussion of history directly related to Emerson's reflections on history, but it is satu-rated with insights, observations, and value-judgments that are recognizably of Emersonian coinage. Emerson called attention to the fluidity and volatility of nature and directly applied the notion of impermanence to individuals, generations, societies, cultures, ideas, values, and theories. Nature and history plow under the old, and every fresh moment is new. Life is essentially transition. And, as Emerson put it, "the past is always swallowed and forgotten, the coming only is sacred."[7] As much as we may desire stability and permanence, neither nature nor history provide it.

Although he later praises the acceptance of the process of becoming, Nietzsche, in the context of analyzing the uses and abuses of history for life, sees its negative aspects and describes its impact on a man who is unable to "forget": "The extreme case would be the man who, without the power to forget, is condemned to see "becoming" everywhere. Such a man no longer believes either in himself or his own existence; he sees everything fly past in an unending succession and loses himself in the stream of becoming."[8]

Having recognized the insights of Emerson, Nietzsche encourages a forgetfulness of the past in history and in our personal lives which, nonetheless, is not absolute. Emerson, too, had encouraged forgetfulness of the past even though he added that "the new position of the advancing man has all the powers of the old, yet has them all new."[9] We must not let the past, he tells us, lie like a dead weight on our backs. We should live "onward," letting go of whatever in our own past (or in the historical past) fetters our forward momentum. In "Compensation" he urges that the biography of temporal man should involve "a putting off of dead circumstances day by day," as the individual "renews his raiment day by day."[10] We should absorb from history, from the history of man and our own life-history, what we can use, what enhances, rather than overshadows, the present.

The affinities with the past that we experience are not the recognition of dead facts. "When," Emerson writes, "a thought of Plato becomes a thought to me—when a truth that fired the soul of Pindar fires mine," the distance between past and present is demolished.[11] History is not an alien record of deeds and sayings because a human mind wrote it and a human mind must comprehend it. The meaning of history is not found in a catena of facts or in a narration of events; rather, it is discovered in the individual's relation to it, his response to it, his affinity to the humanity in it.

Collecting together the scattered observations of Emerson on history and filtering them through the system of his own mind, Nietzsche expresses clearly what Emerson obscurely tried to articulate. That is, that there is a time to forget the past and a time to remember it; a time to feel historically and a time to feel "unhistorically." He calls attention to the "plastic power" of an individual and a culture that enables both to grow beyond themselves or, as he will later say, attain "self-overcoming." This notion corresponds to Emerson's claim that man and his culture are "plastic and permeable to principles" and refuse to be "imprisoned" by the past.[12] The tendency of man is to move outward to new "immense and innumerable expansions."[13]

Having argued that one who is unable to forget the past would have an intensified sense of the evanescence of things that would be negative, Nietzsche then turns this around, as Emerson had already done, and claims that the deeper the inner nature of an individual, the better able he would be to appropriate the past. Only "the greatest and most powerful nature" could have a profound "historical sense" without it generating negative effects.[14]

One of the curious features of Nietzsche's discussion of the effects of the historical sense is the way in which he shifts back and forth between referring to history proper and to the life-history of *the individual*. This way of thinking exactly parallels Emerson's approach to this same issue. History, in his view, is ultimately to be "explained from individual experience."[15] This extreme position is mitigated, to some extent, by the fact that he goes on to say that, in order to understand history, we must "become" the peoples and individuals in it. Although this may seem an exotic idea, what Emerson is suggesting is a very rudimentary form of Wilhelm Dilthey's conception of historical understanding (*Verstehen*) as involving "reliving," in imagination, past events and attaining a sympathetic understanding of historical agents. Of course, Emerson does not develop anything like such a *theory* of the nature of historical understanding. But he insists upon the importance of our subjective response to history in order to grasp, as far as this is possible, its vital meaning. That Emerson is assuming a continuity of man's lived-experience from the past to the present is clear when he states that "each new law and political movement has a meaning for you. Stand before each of its tablets and say, 'Under this mask did my Proteus nature hide itself.' "[16]

Reflecting on the unhistorical attitude of mind, Nietzsche admits that man would not have become man without some sense of history. But as man acquires an *excess* of historical consciousness, he tends to become inhibited in regard to action. So, looked at from a favorable point of view, being unhistorical is allied with strong passion, is often the basis of bold and daring actions. The man of action, Goethe says, is without conscience. But Nietzsche adds that such a man is also often *without knowledge* insofar as he leaves the past behind and strives "to be." Engrossed in the ecstasy of an ideal, a value, a goal, such an individual is capable of producing just and justifiable actions and results. Great historical events are, then, often accomplished by individuals who are "unhistorical" or whose historical sense has, for a time, been put out of action. In a roundabout way, Nietzsche seems to be elaborating on Hegel's dictum: "*nothing great in the world* has been accomplished without *passion.*"

It is certainly not a coincidence that, in "Circles," Emerson described this same "unhistorical" attitude without calling it so. He observed that the "aspiring" impulse in man is a striving "to be" that has priority over "to know." The advancing individual, in the thrall of action, casts away in the "new movement" the intellectual baggage of the past. Whoever follows a "new road to new and better goals" also sees the possibility and excellence of what has been unthought and untried; the "great man" is neither convulsed by nor tormented by events. The calamities of the past do not immobilize him. Such a person exemplifies the truth of the statement that "nothing great was ever achieved without enthusiasm." Whether Emerson is citing Mme. De Staël or paraphrasing Hegel here is not particularly relevant. What is relevant is that this description of an individual immersed in aspiration to action is paralleled in Nietzsche's discussion of precisely such a state of being.

Emerson concludes his account of the making of history by quoting with approval Oliver Cromwell's observation that "a man never rises so high as when he knows not whither he is going."[17] There is an abandonment of the weight of the past in the performance of history-creating actions. Even though Emerson commonly advises solitude, reflection, and the calm pursuit of wisdom, a craving for action periodically emerges in his writings. In his prescriptions he elevates instinct and spontaneity to virtues. The man of action, he believes, projects himself forward, in forgetfulness of the past, towards the impermanence and uncertainty of the future.

When Emerson avers that the aspiring history-maker must forget past history and enthusiastically devote himself to the new idea, the new ideal, the new aim, he transfers to Nietzsche a central theme in his treatment of the proper use of history. Curiously enough, both Emerson and Nietzsche assume, in their analysis of the "unhistorical" man of action, that the outcome, the effects, of such passionate and enthusiastic action will be valuable, constructive, and beneficial to mankind. Unfortunately, as the history of this century has illustrated so lucidly and so tragically, the unreflective man of action can be a curse rather than a blessing. And it is not usually "love" (as Emerson and Nietzsche say) that motivates the enthusiastic and uninhibited actions of one who desires to change the world. The unhistorical man of action has sometimes produced chaotic destruction.

In the course of examining various ways of construing history and of relating ourselves to it, Nietzsche considers the "suprahistorical" standpoint that views history from above, recognizing its blindness and injustice, seeing that evolution is not leading to any redeeming peak, discerning the sameness in the apparent diversity of the contingent forms of history. From such a standpoint, past and present fuse in an image of imperishable, eternally present, types that have immutable significance. History is then looked upon either with calm wisdom or loathing.

Nietzsche rejects this suprahistorical standpoint primarily because it does not enhance life or provide a perspective that encourages active individuals to strive for "more life." This early rejection of a suprahistorical stance does not prevent him from later seeking, often in tortuous ways, a means of attaining not only a suprahistorical vision of history, but a suprahistorical, liberating state of being. This brings us prematurely into the tricky waters of the meaning that the thought of "the eternal recurrence of all things" had for Nietzsche, something we shall have to contend with later.

If history is construed as a species of venerable, pure, objective knowledge, Nietzsche argues, it would become a dominant, deadening force that would put a seal on life. In effect, it would become what it was for James Joyce's Stephen in *Ulysses*—"a nightmare from which I am trying to awake."[18] If history is to be useful to man rather than harmful, it must have a life-giving, life-enhancing influence. Rather than always glancing backward, we should look forward to a new "system of culture." At this point, he discusses three distinguishable uses of history: "the monumental, the antiquarian, and the critical."

Three Modes of History

Monumental history pertains to the conception of history as an education for government, leadership, and action. This modality of history serves a belief in humanity, serves as a source of counsel for the maker of history. Models of greatness in history also console us by showing us what man is capable of, by showing us what deeds he can accomplish through actions careless of life. The essence of monumental history is the record of a greatness that once was, and still is, possible. The history of the Renaissance, for example, stands as a reminder of the greatness that men, even a minority of men, can achieve. However, this perception of past greatness can also lead to fictional idealization, to a mythology of the past. The idealization of figures in the past may produce beneficial or destructive effects. In the hands of an egoistic and tyrannical individual, monumental history would be the reverse of harmless. An appropriate illustration of Nietzsche's point here is the use which Hitler made of the legend of the Holy Roman Emperor, Friedrich Barbarossa, even to the point of personally designating his Russian campaign "Barbarossa."

One aspect of Nietzsche's critique of monumental history is specifically related to some of Emerson's insightful comments on history. He saw, as Nietzsche did, the importance of idealized historical personalities for the inspiration of the man of action. However, he also saw that a "fatal disservice" is done when the heroes or geniuses of a romanticized past are raised so far above present humanity and its capacities for action and creativity that this "overinfluence" is discouraging and paralyzing. Overestimated "greatness" can easily serve to undermine a striving for personal achievement or the projection of new cultural ideals.[19] The elevation of the accomplishments of men and women of the past can also serve as a means to nip aspirations to greatness in the bud. Nietzsche accurately characterizes those he calls the secret haters of "greatness" as being only too pleased to remind the aspiring artist (or, as is implied, any creative individual) that: "See, the great thing is already here!" Thus, in this case, monumental history is used as a weapon *against* creativity and innovation, used as a weapon against the *living*.[20]

As is often the case in Nietzsche's formulations of the insights and suggestions of Emerson, *both* perspectives on past "greatness" or "genius," the positive as well as the negative effects of "monumental history," are extracted from Emerson's reflections on history. In the final analysis, however, Emerson is interested in the value of history for the future, to the individual, for its constructive effects on the living, for the rejuvenation of present and future culture. As much as he admires the "great men," the heroes, and the geniuses of the past, he does not want the unique individuality of living persons, or the uniqueness of the new, to be stymied by, or suffocated by, the glories of the past. At one point, resenting too much time spent reading about the exploits of historical personalities, Emerson snaps: "My time should be as good as their time—my facts, my net of relations, as good as theirs."[21] The overestimation of historical figures is an excessive attitude that undermines our self-confidence, self-trust, and growth.

Antiquarian history collects and venerates everything from the past. Like the fanatical antique collector, the antiquarian historian values something, no matter how trivial and inconsequential it may be, *because* it is old. The problem with this approach to history is that it is blind to the fact that "values and perspectives change" in relation to the person or nation that looks backwards to the past. It also tends to become a kind of archaism that loses touch with the vitality of existence and ends by mummifying life. Antiquarian history preserves and venerates the past at the expense of the present and hinders "the mighty impulse to a new deed."

Although Emerson, as much as anyone, valued the records and annals of the past deeds and wisdom of men and had a certain reverence for history, he also insisted that, in the final analysis, "genius looks forward." Admiration of past institutions and superlative individuals is fine as long as the creations of geniuses of the past do not become "the enemy of genius." When the study of the past becomes wearisome, when artistic inspiration flags, when thinking reaches an impasse, Emerson observes, the individual has one final recourse: "to live."

The student of history will conscientiously preserve and communicate the noble and heroic actions of historical individuals, the oracles of human sentiment, the literature and thought of the past. But he or she will leave room for the subjective living of truths, for the genuine "total act" of existing.[22] The "single person," the genuine individual, has a value that must be preserved in relation to the grandeur, the heroic deeds, the knowledge and art, of the past. In fact, the value of the true individual must be upheld in relation to the entire world. For, as Emerson declares, "the world exists for the education of man."[23]

The last of this troika of ways of understanding and approaching history, the critical way, can serve life by bringing the past to judgment, by questioning it and even condemning it. What condemns the past is the insatiable life-impulse itself. Recalling a comment of Emerson's that we mentioned earlier, Nietzsche alludes to the "injustice" of life in the sense that man exploits other beings for the sake of his own life and in the sense that there are numerous victims of history. Synthesizing a few of Emerson's insights, he remarks that "it requires great strength to be able to live and forget how far life and injustice are one."[24]

The critical process of analyzing and negating the past is a dangerous one because we tend to cut ourselves off from our ancestors and their errors and thereby falsely assume that their mistakes have nothing to do with us. Like Emerson, Nietzsche adopts the view that the mistakes or defects of our ancestors are, in some way, transmitted to us. The cutting edge of critical history is too sharp and cuts too deeply. It serves life at the cost of separating the present too radically from the past that infiltrates it.

Although life, in some measure, is served, albeit in an imperfect way, by monumental, antiquarian, and critical history, the excessive accumulation of historical knowledge, as well as its veneration, has generated not a genuine culture, but a culture *about* culture. This knowledge-culture is contrasted to the unhistorical sense of the ancient Greeks. As if criticizing someone like Kierkegaard, Nietzsche laments the excessive "inwardness" of modern man. He undoubtedly remembered that Emerson had raised the question whether the modern age is not an "age of Introversion" that suffers from the unhappiness of Hamlet, who was "sicklied o'er with the pale cast of thought."[25] And Emerson, too, had pointed to the spirit, energy, and childlike unreflectiveness of the ancient Greeks in implied opposition to modern man. He regretted that history had become a large and dull book of knowledge that is examined by "the dissector or the antiquary."[26]

Hypertrophy of the Historical Sense

Historical knowledge has, in Nietzsche's considered opinion, stunted feeling, spontaneity, and instinct. And it has disunited culture. In this context, he describes the separation of the creative individual from the general population and regrets the loss of the sympathy of the people. We should call attention to Nietzsche's concern here with communicating with a larger audience, as well as to his distress at no longer being met halfway by "the instinct of the people." His uncharacteristic dismay at speaking only to a relatively small segment of the total population should also be noted. Such concerns were present in some of his other early writings.

They seem to indicate the influence of Emerson insofar as he typically takes the sting out of his social criticisms and occasional "overweening" stances by charitably (and often inconsistently) including the people or the "common man" under his cultural umbrella.

Taken at his word, Emerson is actually a very confusing teacher. At times, he adopts standpoints or attitudes that are arrogant and elitist. At other times, he is supremely charitable to the humblest individuals and a teacher of humility to the proud. Sometimes he combines these opposing attitudes in the very same essay. In "Considerations By the Way," for example, we are presented with harsh criticisms of "the masses" and an expression of contempt for them that is as vitriolic as anything Nietzsche, taking up Emerson's crusade for the recrudescence of a noble culture, ever wrote. And, in this same work, we are told that "nothing is so indicative of deepest culture as a tender consideration of the ignorant."[27] The "gentle Nietzsche" was also capable of such generous attitudes even though he, like Emerson, but far more passionately and persistently, was typically a severe critic of ignorance, mediocrity, and mass sentiments.

During the 1870s especially, Nietzsche thought of the philosopher-artist as a physician of culture whose knowledge and wisdom would benefit *all* men; whose new cultural ideal would serve *all* men. At one time, he said, in an Emersonian spirit he seems to have adopted, that "hatred against mediocrity is unworthy of a philosopher . . . precisely because he is an exception, he has to take the rule under his protection; he has to hold all the mediocre in good heart."[28]

Nietzsche's absorption of so many of Emerson's insights, ideas, and values was probably not a conscious and deliberate appropriation of the thought of another, but an unconscious process of assimilation stimulated by a profound feeling of recognition of his own inner thoughts. Emerson would have understood this kind of experience because he believed that "in every work of genius we recognize our own rejected thoughts; they come back to us with a certain alienated majesty."

The excess of historical knowledge and a hyperbolic sense of history are dangerous to the life and spirit of the period in which they appear. A threatening condition arises when an age adopts an ironic attitude towards itself. There is also the danger of the spread of a cynical egotism that grows and gnaws away at the vital strength of such an age and corrupts or demoralizes the populace.

The former threat is tantamount to Kierkegaard's description of an ironic mode of existence that undermines and negates everything and represents, for this reason, an essentially "nihilistic standpoint."[29]

The second danger that Nietzsche sees as a consequence of an excessive historical sense is a cynical egotism that is negative in its sociocultural effects. These negative consequences of an excess of historical consciousness tend to extirpate man's reliance on his "instinct" and undermine confidence in the value of individuality. The elimination of instinctive life converts human beings into "abstractions." No one, under such circumstances, any longer displays a genuine personality; but, instead, everyone wears the mask of the "man of culture."

If Nietzsche seems to contradict himself by condemning cynical egotism and praising personal, self-assertive individuality, this is not actually the case. The egoist who is cynical knows, as Oscar Wilde once said, the "price of everything and the value of nothing." The egoist desires only selfish ends and will wear any convenient mask available to attain a self-seeking goal. An egoist preserves the selfish "I" by any means and often lacks a developed or integrated self. An egoist is certainly a personality; but he or she is not a *person* who strives to deepen individuality, who seeks to *become* a genuine, integrated self. The self-seeking, self-protecting egoist dissipates the true self in the satisfaction of constantly renewed desires. The egoist usually lacks discipline and self-control whereas the person striving to become a genuine individual seeks a honing and disciplining of the self. Whoever seeks a deeper individuation is self-critical and capable of commitment. The cynical egoist, on the other hand, is interested in preserving the practical, cunning actuality of an undeveloped self. Such an individual values nothing beyond the efficiency of a functional social mask. A person, Nietzsche says, must be *sincere* towards himself and towards others in word and deed. But the cynical egoist must never be sincere to anyone, least of all himself. What is called the "hypocrisy of convention" is the common mask that Nietzsche believes is worn in his time, an age that is one of "outward conformity."[30]

The polemic waged by Nietzsche against an excess of historical consciousness and against the types of people it ostensibly produces seems to owe a debt to Emerson's passionate outcries against conformity, public opinion, popular ideas, and the "mediocrity" of his age. In what is put in opposition to the age he lashes out at, Nietzsche also seems to echo Emerson, even though the latter does not put the decline of social and personal existence solely at the doorstep of an excess of historical sense and historical knowledge.

Emerson proposed the sacredness of integrity, nonconformity, honesty, genuineness, independence, and strong character. And he identifies spontaneity and instinct as the essence of life, genius, and virtue. Some of his exhortations are clearly proto-Nietzschean in tone. "Let us," he urges, "affront and reprimand the smooth mediocrity and squalid contentment of the times." Even the martial, saber-rattling language that frequents and often mars Nietzsche's prose is anticipated by Emerson. At one point, for example, he urges his readers that they should resist the temptation to pusillanimity: "let us enter into the state of war and wake Thor and Woden, courage and constancy, in our Saxon breasts. This is to be done in our smooth times by speaking the truth."[31]

One can imagine someone with sinister motives lopping off the last sentence in such a passage as the above and making Emerson sound like a champion of barbaric militarism.[32] Although there is no such intention on Emerson's part, his hostility towards the mediocrity, conformity, and lack of courage he perceived in modern society led him to emphasize spontaneity, instinct, "animal spirit," feeling, and life-impulses to such an extent that he could easily be understood, without distortion, as a defender of *irrationalism*.

On one point especially, Nietzsche agreed completely with Emerson: that life in general, and life exemplified in the "essential man," the individual of spontaneity and instinct, has priority over reason and knowledge. The value of history, the value of an understanding of nature, the value of practically everything Emerson speaks of, is "to enhance the great and constant fact of life."[33] This valuation of life and its highest and strongest expression plays a central role in *his* philosophy of existence. And it shapes his cultural ideal of outstanding types of human beings whose existence is possible and who, as Nietzsche also believed, will enhance the quality of a culture and raise the consciousness of the people.

Returning to the question of the most fruitful attitude towards history and its traditions, it is to be noted that Nietzsche, despite all that he's said on the matter, does *not* counsel a forgetfulness of history. In fact, he maintains that it is only the strongest persons who can endure an unsentimental understanding of history. What is to be avoided is a purely objective, impersonal attitude towards history. One must neither be neutral in relation to history nor neutered by its impressive pyramid of facts and knowledge or its heroic personalities.

The historical training of individuals should be such that they can exert some "influence on life and action." In seeking a proper understanding of the past, we should be guided by a sense of justice supplemented by the ability to make sharp judgments. The combination of a sense of justice and the power to pass sound judgments on the past should be brought under the organizing control of an aesthetic interpretation of history that incorporates relevant historical facts, but makes no claim to a detached objectivity. The character, wisdom, and experience of the historian is profoundly relevant to the quality of historical understanding. Just as in one aspect of Dilthey's theory of historical understanding, Nietzsche claims that the historian should have the ability to project himself back into the historical situation and "relive," in imagination, the experience of the historical agent. Given all that Nietzsche says against an impersonal, objective attitude towards history, its events and its personalities, this reliving of the situation of an historical actor would not necessarily entail sympathy for his or her choices, decisions, and actions.

If an unrestrained historical sense is brought to fruition, Nietzsche believes, it will negate illusions and have a deleterious effect on the future. Even if an historical sense of justice is brought to the comprehension of historical events, it, too, if it is not directed towards a living future, can produce a negative effect.

A destructive or embalming history that has no constructive impulse at all destroys illusions and either undermines historical values or preserves the past by first killing it. Nietzsche specifically refers, in this context, to the destructive effects of the Hegelian rationalization of, and historical devitalization of, Christianity whereby a religion that was vital to millions is negated *as* religion and preserved as "knowledge." Here Nietzsche unknowingly reproduces a point that Kierkegaard had made: that the Hegelian treatment of Christianity as a stage in the evolution of the "Absolute Spirit," as a demystified object of historical knowledge, was a kiss of death to a living religious faith, which, *via* theoretical cooptation, is explained away and effectively destroyed in the process. As soon as historical dissection begins, we are, of course, dealing with something that is being treated as a corpse. History, like life itself, needs illusions in order to survive and remain vital, creative, and meaningful.

If life is made subservient to knowledge, then this will not be life in its typical form, the form of life that requires illusions and instinctive values. Under the aegis of historical consciousness, and by means of the consequent labor in the knowledge factory, the product created is usually "successful mediocrity." The learned class either become narrow specialists whose labor is more and more divided into fragmentary knowledge or they become popularizers who write for the "general public."[34]

As previously mentioned, those who are trained in historical objectivity and are bombarded by masses of facts tend to cultivate an ironic existence. An overdevelopment of the historical sense encourages "ironic self-consciousness" because it is fundamentally an education in *skepticism*. The study of past cultures, of historical figures of the past, of the life and death of empires, from the standpoint of a detached objectivity, not only generates skepticism, Nietzsche argues, but it becomes a colossal reminder of death. What is needed, by individuals, as well as by cultures, are reminders of life.

In order for man to be liberated from the long shadow of history, he must, ironically, understand the historical process by which historical consciousness became a problem for a proper grasp of the meaning of history. Nietzsche, from this perspective, would not disagree with Emerson's remark that "man is explicable by nothing less than all his history."[35] The one proviso would be that the condition of *modern man,* especially under the impact of an intensification of historical consciousness, the growth of knowledge, and the spread of skepticism, is itself explicable in terms of the historical development of man. What this proviso seems to anticipate is Nietzsche's analysis of the historical emergence of nihilism and his prediction that the twentieth century would be an age of nihilism.

A solution to the problem of a detrimental veneration of universal history is to transcend this cultural condition by virtue of a recovery of the ancient Greek spirit. The ancient Greeks should be our models because they were, as Emerson had previously said, unhistorical and because everything, in their age, was "great, natural and human."[36] This unhistorical spirit could serve as an antidote to the Hegelian idolatry of success, to the acceptance of historical actuality as an ordained good, to the belief in the rationality of the actual. The presumption that there is a "rational necessity" in history means that we ought to accept and venerate "what is" in an attitude of complete submission. No virtuous, independent human being would voluntarily be such a slavish worshipper of "the actual." Rather, such an individual would rail against "the tyranny of the actual." Here, in an ironic way, historical knowledge protects itself from a theory of the progressive, necessary, dialectical, rational evolution of history by offering models of those who opposed, criticized, or fought against the historical actuality of their times.[37]

The apotheosis, in Hegel's theory of history, of the world-process makes man an insignificant fragment that is carried forward by a powerful, dominating dialectical process. But there is an irony in this perception of history. Men of the past who did not have the advantage of a 'higher' historical consciousness, who could not look down from the enormous pyramid of the "world-process," were naturally the pawns of "the cunning of reason" (as Hegel called it) in the unfolding of historical actuality. The learned *epigoni*, however, believe that they and their culture are the epitome of the perfection of nature. This is the delusion that the latest human beings are the best or are better than their ancestors, a delusion that is not uncommon today. So we have the skeptic, the cynic, and the proud product of the world-process—all produced, supposedly, by an excess of historical consciousness. Add to this the pessimism of Eduard von Hartmann's *Philosophy of the Unconscious,* which oddly combines world-and-life negation with philistine values, and you have what Nietzsche characterizes as a 'culture' of mediocrity and "disgust at all existence." This is where the worship of the historical world-process ends. The oft-cited "becoming" of world-history terminates, in the hands of von Hartmann, in a becoming-unto-death!

Exaggerating to drive home his point, Nietzsche sees the rise of a hyperbolic sense of history as the primary cause of the apocalyptic visions of his day. Against what are described as the absurdities of philosophies such as that of von Hartmann, Nietzsche says that a time will come when "we shall no more look at masses but at individuals who form a sort of bridge over the . . . stream of becoming."[38] The aim of history is not to bring history to an end, to be made irrelevant by history, or to provide "bread and circuses" for the "masses." The aim of history is to create the conditions for the possibility of "great men." Nietzsche insists that, "the goal of humanity lies, in the final analysis, only in its highest exemplars." He calls for combat against the absurd notion of an evolution towards nothingness, against the excesses of the historical sense at the expense of existence and of life itself.

If, in addition to the corrosive power of an outlandish historical sense, the Darwinian idea of a continuity between beast and man continues to infiltrate the mind of man, then people will soon become self-seeking egoists, and there will no longer be a unified people upon which to build a meaningful culture. To interpret history solely from the standpoint of "the masses" is to lower the level of general 'culture' to a point at which we are no longer entitled to speak of a higher genuine culture at all. At best, Nietzsche tells us, the masses may be seen as "copies of great men, printed on poor paper from worn-out plates," as contrasts to great men, or as instruments of culture. For the rest, he remarks, let the devil or "statistics take them." And what statistics will tell us is that there is a uniformity and commonality of "masses," a predictable averageness in their behavior.[39]

The unfortunate conflation of mass values, mass consciousness, and private egotism and selfishness is positively deadly. If this social trend continues, Nietzsche predicts, the egotism of masses will seek the State as protector of its self-seeking. The soul of individuality will be sold to the State for the sake of selfish, short-term, narrowly conceived, ends. This is the cynics' bargain with the "powers that be."

The outcome of this dialectical analysis of the apotheosis of the historical sense is that "man must learn to live, above all, and use history solely in the service of the life he has learned to live."[40] The authentic culture of a people grows out of life and not out of knowledge, especially not out of a 'culture' comprised of a "knowledge of culture." Modern education has perpetuated this dependence on historical knowledge, this knowledge about past cultures, to such an extent that it is *contra* nature.

The true teacher is life, experience, immediate contact with existence or, in a word, "Nature." An education centered on "words, words, words," and words about words, leads to "the malady of words." Nietzsche would substitute for the intellectualistic Cartesian motto, *cogito ergo sum,* a new dictum: *vivo ergo cogito,* "I live, therefore, I think." In effect, he wanted to give a new sense to the Latin proverb, *primum vivere, deinde philosophari,* "first live, then philosophize."

Nietzsche is not, of course, suggesting that knowledge *per se* is detrimental to human development. Nor is he proposing the complete priority of practical or physical education over intellectual development or training. And, as we learn from "Schopenhauer as Educator," he is not advancing, as many contemporary academic administrators are, the idea that specific, "technical" training for purely utilitarian, *ad hoc,* practical occupations that serve the temporary needs of the State should be the chief aim of education. What he is proposing is simple to state, but exceedingly difficult to carry off successfully. That is, the integration of life-experiences and education, the synthesis of spontaneous instinct and knowledge, the marriage of buoyant, healthy energy and balanced, judicious, cultural knowledge.

An excess of historical awareness is an illness, one that has as its primary symptom the inability "to use the past as a means of strength and nourishment."[41] The antidotes to a bloated historical sense are the cultivation of an unhistorical attitude in which one exercises the art of forgetting and the development of a superhistorical standpoint that turns away from the stream of transitory becoming and looks to art and religion for stability and a sense of eternity.

In the debate between the priority of life or of knowledge, Nietzsche's position is crystal-clear; life is a higher value than knowledge simply because there would be no pyramid of knowledge without forms of life; because knowledge serves life, or ought to serve life, insofar as it is rooted in the striving for self-preservation found in all natural beings. The tendencies of youth would normally lead to a valuation of strength, health, and of a naturalness that is derived from the vital powers of "Nature."

Returning to his earlier theme, Nietzsche argues that a rejuvenated attitude towards history would enable new generations to study history in a monumental, antiquarian, and critical way without drowning in a sea of historical consciousness. This new attitude would view culture as a refined nature, a transformation of nature, in which there is "a unity among life, thought, appearance and will."[42]

In this rich meditation Nietzsche is concerned with attacking the belief that the aim of learning is the accumulation of (historical) knowledge as an end in itself. He does not argue that history should be forgotten or ignored *in toto*. Nor is he dismissing the relative value, in different contexts, of monumental, antiquarian, or critical modes of historical understanding. What he is presenting is a corrective to the hyperbolic development of the historical sense, to the excessive veneration of a postulated "world-process," to the devaluation of the individual, the present, and life itself. The negation of the influence of the past through "forgetfulness" or an "unhistorical" orientation is not intended as an end-in-itself or an absolute standpoint. Rather, it is intended as an antidote to the worship of "History" and as a means of renewing the sense of the value of life in general, and individual life in particular.

Although Nietzsche's understanding of the proper relation that one should have to the historical past leaves the door open, unintentionally, to a reconstruction of the past or a temporal suspension of knowledge of the past that is subject to abuse by cynical "leaders," it is meant as a medication to relieve the symptoms of the "malady of history." It was intended to serve the intelligensia, to proffer a fresh, uncluttered, proportioned sense of history. What Nietzsche wanted was to make history a living force that invigorates rather than intimidates, stimulates rather than depresses, the then–present and future generations that study it.

Against Hegel and the Hegelians, Nietzsche maintains that an obsequious "worship of success" is dangerous to the individual, society, and culture. He offers an alternative to this cult of the actual in the form of a just appraisal of the past that does *not* withhold value-judgments combined with a critical stance towards the actuality of the present. In addition, he is concerned with attacking the pretention, associated with Hegelianism, that the present, because it is a consequence of a long process of historical development, necessarily marks the peak of morality, wisdom, and knowledge. The present, like the past, has a potential for "greatness," for the creation of a higher culture. This is the optimistic stance of Nietzsche at this stage of his intellectual development. He refuses to condemn the present in the name of the past and desires to open the door to the possibilities of the future.

Before Martin Heidegger, Nietzsche was a laudator of "the silent power of the possible." With all of his cutting negations, he did not deny the potentialities of man, his capacity to create a new and envigorating culture. His eyes, as always, look forward to the open sea of the future. Superior human beings *are* possible now and in the future if the conditions for their cultivation, their discipline, and growth are ripe. Against all that he later says about the necessity and fatality in existence, Nietzsche's position, at least in "On the Uses and Disadvantages of History for Life," is that there is hope because there is *contingency* in history, because new cultures with different value-systems are possible. "What actually happened" in the past was not absolutely necessary; and what will happen is not construed as subject to an "iron necessity" either. Put simply, Nietzsche's understanding of the proper "use" of history takes the side of the optimism of youth against the position of the wise old men, the "greybeards" who sigh in face of what they accept as "historical inevitability."

Despite the value of all that Nietzsche has said so far, it must be admitted that his overemphasis on the subjective value of history for life, for more life, his praise of instinct over reason, his willingness to forget the past if it is convenient to do so, his admiration for unhistorical "action," are all potentially lethal weapons in the hands of tyrannical fanatics. There is an uncomfortable similarity between such stimulating, unexamined values and the praise of sudden action and instinctive behavior one finds in the writings and speeches of the Italian and German fascists. This century knows only too well what happens when "leaders" brag that they "think with their blood." The Nazis, for a time, claimed to be creating a "new culture" based on instinctive vitality, military virtues, physical health and an activistic life. It is the bane of Nietzsche's entire philosophy that he was misunderstood by the philistines and the "new barbarians" and understood only by a minority of the reasonably civilized. By admitting the potential for misuse of *some* of his thoughts on history no concession is made to the belief that this is what he intended. His tendencies of thought in this meditation are liberating and colored with an aristocratic humanism. Nietzsche intended to influence the creation of a dynamic, *creative* culture in which there would be real individuals, not political actors who play with the world like a toy and manipulate and annihilate millions of people at whim. Politics is specifically *excluded* from his picture of a healthy, unified, positive culture that is built out of constructive, creative deeds.

Nietzsche intended to liberate individuals from the dialectical machinery of the "world-process," to create a blueprint (which is admittedly vague at crucial points) for a higher, creative culture in which exceptional individuals would be possible, promoted, and prized. It is a blueprint for a culture that, in large measure, most sane and ascending civilizations would find attractive and acceptable.

What Nietzsche put forward as his understanding of the correct uses of the historical past could legitimately be called an *existential theory of history*. The primary aim of history ought to be the enhancement of the life of genuine individuals and the building of a foundation for a culture in which "greatness" would be possible. He values, as all sensible human beings do, health, vitality, strength, and the energy to move "onward" with confidence. He wants to lift the often oppressive burden of the past from the shoulders of those who have the ability to shape a fresh future. What has not previously been recognized is that a surprising number of the central ideas in this understanding of the appropriate use, meaning, and value of history, as well as the proposed open-ended cultural ideals and the idea of liberation from the tyranny of the past, are specifically derived from the reflections of Emerson.

Virtually throughout all of his essays Emerson repeats a common theme: we should recognize and value the history of courageous, bold, and inventive "great men," but we must also remind ourselves of the value and meaning of "the present" and hope for, and dream of, the "great men" who will be possible *in futuro*. The German poet Goethe is often cited by Nietzsche in such a context just as he had been cited by Emerson. Great men of the past are exemplars for people of the present and offer models of what man can become. Like Carlyle, Emerson believes that history is often simply "biography." But, for Emerson, these impressive biographies of outstanding individuals should not dwarf the value of men of the present. To understand the "great men" of the historical past, we must relive their history. The facts of history are not dead facts. Rather, they are "symbols," symbols that should be presented in such a way as to stimulate "the range of our affinities." The value we find in impressive personalities in the panorama of history is the recognition of the fulfillment of, or virtual fulfillment of, "universal nature" in their being and acts. The meaning of history in general, and of the historical biographies of superlative individuals in particular, in the last analysis, is its meaning *for us*. We only truly understand the narrated historical fact when it corresponds to something in our own experiences or thoughts. Only then can the fact "be credible or intelligible." It is quite apparent that Emerson proposed a subjective conception of the use and meaning of history that is, if anything, even more radical than that put forward by Nietzsche.

Since we will deal with Emerson's speculative proposals for the possibility of a new breed of cultural exemplars in the future in another context, we will focus here on other striking similarities of thought between Nietzsche and Emerson, specifically in regard to the use, meaning, and value of history. Referring to "great moments of history," Emerson avers that we sympathize with these events, these accomplishments, these "great resistances," because we feel that a deed was done, a blow was struck, "*for us*." We respond to the historical sage in his Protean forms because what is held up to us is the ideal of our "unattained but attainable self." We comprehend history because of a cognitive-affective affinity we have with the *dramatis personae* of history.

Through thought and sympathetic imagination, we can relive "all history" in ourselves. If we turn our attention from history towards our own existence, we may transfer the point of view from which history is commonly understood to ourselves since we have as much value as the human drama of history itself. Whether we realize it or not, we judge the historical past in terms of our "private experience." An aesthetic element, too, enters into our response to historical greatness. In the study of history, "a profound nature awakens in us by its actions and words, by its looks and manners, the same power and beauty that a gallery of sculpture or of pictures addresses."[43] And this aesthetic aspect of historical understanding is also rooted in our memories, our experiences, our sensibilities, our subjectivity.

As we've seen earlier, Emerson, like Nietzsche after him, appreciates the youthful vitality of the ancient Greeks and applauds their "inborn energy," their "health," their paradoxical "childlike" manliness. What we respond to in ancient Greek culture, Emerson explains, is the presence of "the natural" in the behavior and actions of its impressive figures. The attractiveness of the ancient Greeks pertains to our affinity with them insofar as we are still youthful and capable of combining the strength and vitality of adults with the "engaging unconsciousness of childhood." Although he does not speak specifically of their "unhistorical" attitudes, everything he does say about the ancient Greeks points in the direction of an unconsciousness of the historical past. Once again, we see how skillfully Nietzsche consolidates and works up Emerson's insightful asides and puts them to theoretical use.

When Emerson declares that the genuine meaning of history is its relevance to living individuals, that history should "walk incarnate in every just and wise man," when he affirms that "all history becomes subjective," it is obvious that he is proposing, albeit in a nonsystematic, rhetorical way, the rudiments of an existential conception of history that stimulated Nietzsche's thinking along precisely these same lines.

According to Emerson's considered view, we invariably interpret the past in terms of the present, and our subjective experiences and our imagination enter into a sympathetic understanding of the nature of, and deeds of, historical personalities. By implication, he alludes to the value of historical exemplars whose past lives enliven the present in what Nietzsche later calls monumental history. But, like Nietzsche after him, he insists that, in the final analysis, "Greatness appeals to the future."[44] Just as our understanding of the natural world is conditioned by our perceptions, our psychology, and our values, so, too, is our appreciation of, and comprehension of, history infiltrated by our subjectivity. More subjectivistic than the early Nietzsche, Emerson asserts that "history is an impertinence and an injury if it be any thing more than a cheerful apologue or parable of my being and becoming."[45]

There is little doubt that Emerson would have heartily agreed with Kierkegaard when he said, thinking of Hegel's conception of history, that he would not want to be "a paragraph in the biography of the Absolute." One has the impression, despite his reverence for the Oversoul, that Emerson would not want to be a paragraph in anyone's biography, not even that of the Oversoul. He does not want his individuality wiped away by an Absolute, by society, or by history. What especially exercises him, as it later does Nietzsche, is that "man . . . does not live in the present." We demean the trivialities of daily life and timidly remain buried in the crowd because we see grandeur only in the remote and glorious past. However, we ought to be concerned with our own existence. Self-existence is the attribute of the divine, and it ought to be our chief characteristic as well.[46]

The genuine person is cowed neither by history nor the opinions of "the mob." Such an individual does not put off his life; he lives it in the present. The aim of each person is "to live," to be a self-directed, self-reliant, self-existing individual. If we can "live truly, we shall see truly." The person who is genuine, no matter what the circumstances, will endeavor "to speak and write sincerely."[47] All of Emerson's maxims or counsels of attitudinal orientation ultimately focus on the true or genuine individual who expresses an honest and independent individuality. In the process, the rudiments of an existential conception of man is anticipated.

In regard to the historical process as such, Emerson adopts the position that societies never, in any strict sense, advance. For every gain that is made there is a loss. In the continual changes in history, the movement from barbarism to civilization, from Christianity to wealth, and on to scientific practice, there is no discernible "amelioration." If a society acquires new arts, it loses "old instincts." Gains in civilized comfort are mitigated by losses of robust "health."[48] Men pride themselves on the "improvement of society," but they do not notice that "no man improves." The conformity, timidity, and concern for numbers on the part of modern man not only do not indicate progressive development, but are, in fact, signs of decline and regression.

In democratic countries, Emerson tells us, the gross tendency is material and sensuous. Using the most various means to a common end, rich with "mechanical powers," modern, democratic man subordinates all of his intellectual and spiritual energies to "material success." The Western world has become dedicated to "the spirit of commerce, of money and material power."[49] Both the conservative and the democratic classes of American society are motivated by self-seeking even though labor is "entombed in money stocks, or in land and buildings owned by idle capitalists."[50] Inevitable amelioration in history? Emerson sees no signs of it. And he certainly does not venerate the vaunted culture of "material success." A commercial, materialistic culture characterized by conformity and timidity, a culture more and more influenced by the rising tide of "the masses," is not the culmination of human history and is certainly not its goal.

Sensitive, intelligent, scholarly, poetic, and solitary, Emerson admires, as Nietzsche with a similar temperament would after him, men of action. In his early oration, "The American Scholar," he remarked that action and scholarship are often antipodal. But action is essential for life, and whoever is without it is "not yet man." Reflection cannot ripen into truth without a relation to life and action. The intellect derives its power from life-experiences. These are the raw materials out of which the mind creates new products. It is our "private history" that provides us with the materials which are given form by intelligence. Therefore, whoever puts his strength into appropriate and constructive actions receives a rich return in wisdom. If we would be a scholar of the world and not of books only, then life must be our "dictionary." There is, Emerson insists, something that is higher than historical knowledge and higher than the intellect. That something is *character*.

Modern man, Emerson maintains, has lost touch with nature, has lost the capacity for self-trust, has lost self-confidence; he has, in effect, lost sight of his own unique value as a person. In an excessively commercialized, complaisant, conformist atmosphere, the most promising young people who begin with great hopes are quickly discouraged. Like Nietzsche, Emerson often claimed for himself the ability to look into the heart and the mind of youth. He believes that promising young people "are hindered by the disgust which the principles on which business is managed inspire, and turn drudges, or die of disgust, some of them suicides."[51]

The cure for this malaise, a malaise that Nietzsche later attributes, in part, to the egoistic greed prevalent in German society in "Schopenhauer as Educator," is to rely on one's instincts, to have patience, to retain one's admiration for greatness, to communicate ideal principles, and to seek "the conversation of the world." Aside from assigning such an ambitious task to the budding

scholar, Emerson urges him to become a "university of knowl-
edges," a person who will "dare all." He charges Americans, as
Nietzsche later charges Germans, with having become "timid, im-
itative, tame." The life that Emerson proposes for the American
scholar is described practically in military terms: he must be
brave, fearless, willing to face danger, strong, bold, manly.[52] Is it
too much to say, given Nietzsche's intimate knowledge of Emerson's reflections, that in this oration, delivered before the Phi Beta
Kappa Society at Harvard in 1837, we find the prototype for the
type that Nietzsche will later call "the warrior of knowledge"?

The popular literary image of Emerson as a genteel idealist who
loved all things humble and common is severely strained, if it is
not shattered, by a careful study of his stern and bluntly realistic
perceptions of the social world around him. Again, in "The American Scholar," we find him lamenting the sad state of the men of
his day in tones and in language that, if the author of the passage
were not indicated, could easily be attributed to Nietzsche: "Men
are become of no account. Men in history, men in the world of today, are bugs, are spawn, and are called "the mass" and "the
herd." In a century, in a millenium, one or two men, that is to say,
one or two approximations to the right state of every man."[53]

Earlier we mentioned Nietzsche's comment that the "masses"
should be relegated to the concern of the statistician. This apparently insouciant observation seems to be directly derived from a
reference to the views of the Belgian statistician Quetelet on human temperament found in a note to an allusion (in the essay
"Fate") that was included in the German translation of *The Conduct
of Life*. In this note, Quetelet is quoted as saying that whatever
pertains to the human species *en masse* is of the order of physical,
statistical facts. The larger the number of individuals studied, the
more does the "individual disappear." What remains is a series of
general facts that pertain to large-scale, predictable conditions, behaviors, and actions.[54] What is now a sociological commonplace
was a novelty in the mid-nineteenth century. And it was surely a
notion picked up by Nietzsche in his careful and repeated readings
of Emerson's works. A minor point perhaps, but one that is so
minute and specific that it secures the bond of influence connect-
ing these surprisingly compatible thinkers.

There are other incidental points of affinity linking Nietzsche's
essay on the uses and abuses of history to Emerson's thoughts on
the subject that may be mentioned *en passant*. The reference to the
need for illusion in life and history is too close to the content of

Emerson's essay, "Illusions," to be merely coincidental. And, of course, the same relationship of similarity holds for Nietzsche's general notion that conscious illusion is essential for life. Even Nietzsche's correlative notion that the dissectors of history and those who demythologize historical figures or events tamper with life-preserving illusions about history and historical personages is briefly touched upon, in a slightly different context, by Emerson in the aforementioned essay. Since we live, Emerson accurately observes, by our admirations, feelings, sentiments, and our subjective imagination, we rightly "accuse the critic who destroys too many illusions" and we do not love our "unmaskers." The "carnival," the "masquerade," of life (or, for the matter, of history) requires disguises, masks, deceptions, and illusions. Although he is speaking of women in particular, the following observation of Emerson's pertains, with equal force, to men and historical luminaries as well: "how dare any one . . . pluck away the *coulisses,* stage effects and ceremonies by which they live?"[55] There is little doubt that the *initial* stimulus to the idea that illusion is necessary for life and for an appreciation of history owes a great deal to *Emerson's* reflections of the powerful role of illusions in life.[56]

It may even be the case that Nietzsche's paradoxical, self-assigned task of being an "unmasker" of the disguised underlying *nisus* of life, of primal human motivations, of *homo natura,* of virtually every illusion that he, from another perspective, thought necessary for life, was probably subliminally suggested to him by Emerson's *obiter dicta* on this theme. Thus, Nietzsche proclaims that illusions are necessary in order to endure the terrible realities of life while, at the same time, he seeks to undermine these illusions and force us to face unpleasant realities and see actuality as it is. That Emerson is a significant influence here is supported by the fact that this paradoxical project is a replication of *his* dual tendencies of thought. For he, too, urges us to face the harsh realities of nature and life even though he also encourages our dependence on the *coulisses* that enhance life and existence.

The subjective meaning and value of history, its necessary connection with the living present, and its relevance to the future—in effect, the existential value and meaning of history—is indebted to Emerson's radically personalistic ideas about the "use" of history. He was very much attuned to "the new importance given to the single person," to the potentialities of genuine, self-reliant individuals.[57] The annals of history, he insisted, must be written from the position of "ethical reformation, from an influx of the ever-new, ever-sanative conscience."[58] The writing of history and the understanding of history must be undertaken from the perspective of the present with a view to tomorrow. In the last analysis, history, like nature and literature, is a "subjective" phenomenon.[59] The self-existent person is the center of actuality and has priority over the world and history. Although we have inherited a world and have a long, evolutionary, natural history, we nonetheless have an obligation to build *our own* world.[60] Man does not exist either *for* the world or *for* history. Nature and history exist *for* man, for his "upbuilding," his edification, his education.

In his analysis of the use and disadvantages of history for life, Nietzsche clearly echoes many of Emerson's reflections on history. No more so than when he asserts that we have, under the Hegelian dispensation, heard enough about "world, world, world" and now need to speak decently about "man, man, man."[61] Life has priority over intellection; vitality over reflection; instinctive wisdom over knowledge. History has a utility that is advantageous to life if it raises the level of human culture; if it enhances, rather than depresses, life; if it instills confidence in humanity and leads man forward to the uncharted, open seas of an uncertain, challenging future.

Emerson, with good reason, laments the "cynicism of the streets," the "spirit of cowardly compromise," the "frightful skepticism" that he finds in the America of his day. The conformity of the times seems to cry out for a new faith, a faith that, first and foremost, must be placed in man's potential for reform and rejuvenation, a faith that will make greatness possible again. Man perfected, man as he ought to be, is not only found in the remote, misty past despite the many exemplary individuals who have acted on the stage of history. We must learn, Emerson affirmed, to look for the perfectibility of man in the promise of the future. He proclaimed (in *Representative Men*), and Nietzsche remembered that he proclaimed, that "It is natural to believe in great men." For they represent the fulfillment of nature in its cultural expression. History possesses great value if it makes such human beings possible or if it generates an attitude and a spirit that creates the conditions for the possibility of their emergence . . . out of history.

Synthesizing Emerson's dispersed observations out of season, we may say that he conceives of culture as the spiritual refinement of the primitive energies of nature and sees history as the developmental process through which this transformation occurs. He recognizes that a functioning, growing society needs people with diverse skills and abilities, needs people with strong backs. But he also believes that there must also be individuals who serve as "meters of character" in order for a culture to avoid a sedimentation of values and aspirations.

The hygiene of culture calls for "the exciters and monitors, collectors of the heavenly spark, with power to convey the electricity to others." A culture lacking such individuals is one in which there is no admiration, one in which man comes to count for nothing. Like Kierkegaard, Emerson is in revolt against the levelling of aspirations, goals, and values in the modern world, against the spiritual devolution of man. The morale of authentic culture requires that "we should now and then encounter rare and gifted men, to compare the points of our spiritual compass, and verify our bearings from superior chronometers."[62]

It is hardly surprising that Nietzsche ends his study of the uses and disadvantages of history for life with a plea for a new kind of education for the development of a vivifying higher culture. For Emerson often calls for a new "teacher" of a cultural ideal who will show us that moral obligation is one with knowledge, that both are one with beauty and joy. And he saw clearly that this grand process of cultural and educational conversion required a "new ethic" and a new religion that is, in his hands, no longer recognizable as a Christian religion.[63] The vivification and rejuvenation of culture could be achieved, he believed, by means of a new, aesthetically conceived morality and an inspiring cultural ideal; by something that could be designated a 'religion of life.' In his reflections on history and in his later thought, Nietzsche's project could be construed as an attempt to flesh out, perpetuate, and fulfill Emerson's impressionistic philosophy of culture.[64]

Chapter 3 Notes

1. *SW* 1, *UB* 3, §8, p. 426.

2. Ibid. This structural detail is mentioned in order to illustrate how carefully Nietzsche read Emerson and how well he understood his hortatory messages and imperatives. Cf. "Circles," *PE*, pp. 232–33.

3. Ibid., p. 427.

4. "Success," in *Society and Solitude*, p. 270.

5. Ibid., pp. 273–74.

6. *SW* 3, *FW* §329, p. 556.

7. "Circles," *PE*, p. 219.

8. *SW* I, *UB* 2, §1, p. 250.

9. "Circles," *PE*, p. 239.

10. "Compensation," *PE*, p. 185.

11. "History," *PE*, p. 129.

12. "Self-Reliance," *PE*, p. 153.

13. "Circles," *PE*, p. 230.

14. *SW* I, *UB* 2, §1, p. 251.

15. "History," *PE*, p. 116.

16. Ibid.

17. "Circles," *PE*, 239–40. In his copy of the *Essays*, Nietzsche heavily underlined the last paragraph in "Circles." In notes from 1883, at the time he was writing *Thus Spoke Zarathustra*, Nietzsche refers to this passage in "Circles" in regard to "*das Selbst vergessen*," "forgetting the self" (*SW* 10:486).

18. For an interesting account of the relation between Nietzsche's analysis of history and similar views expressed in James Joyce's fiction, see: J. A. Buttigieg's "Struggle Against Meta (Phantasm)-physics: Nietzsche, Joyce and the 'excess of history'," in *Why Nietzsche Now?*, ed. D. O'Hara, pp. 187–207.

19. "The American Scholar," *PE*, p. 37. In "Uses of Great Men" Emerson expresses the same sentiment. For "a new danger appears in the excess of influence of the great man. His attractions warp us from our place. We have become underlings and intellectual suicides" (*Representative Men, Nature, Addresses*, p. 31).

20. *SW* I, *UB* 2, §2, pp. 262–64.

21. "Spiritual Laws," *PE*, p. 207.

22. "The American Scholar," *PE*, pp. 62–71.

23. "History," *PE*, p. 118.

24. *SW* I, *UB* 2, §3, p. 269.

25. "The American Scholar," *PE*, p. 68.

26. "History," *PE*, p. 137.

27. "Considerations By the Way," *COL*, p. 260.

28. *SW* 12:559–60.

29. Cf. George J. Stack, *Kierkegaard's Existential Ethics*, Chapter 1.

30. *SW* I, *UB* 2, §5, pp. 279–82.

31. "Self-Reliance," *PE*, p. 154.

32. Nietzsche carries this penchant for militant language much further than Emerson did and, hence, his meaning has often been misconstrued and distorted. The eulogies of 'war' in *Thus Spoke Zarathustra* and elsewhere have frequently been used to condemn Nietzsche of literal militancy. But occasionally he makes quite clear that he champions intellectual and valuational warfare. In a note from 1883 he writes: "Krieg (aber ohne Pulver!) zwischen verschiedenen Gedanken! und deren Heeren!" "War (but without gunpowder!) between different thoughts! and their armies!" *SW* 10:515.

33. "The Poet," *PE*, p. 251.

34. *SW* I, *UB* 2, §§5–7.
35. "History," *PE*, p. 115.
36. *SW* I, *UB* 2, §8.
37. Ibid.
38. *SW* I, *UB* 2, §9.
39. Ibid.
40. Ibid., §10.
41. Ibid.
42. Ibid., p. 334.
43. "History," *PE*, p. 123.
44. "Self-Reliance," *PE*, p. 147.
45. Ibid., p. 151.
46. Ibid., p. 153.
47. "Spiritual Laws," *PE*, p. 200.
48. "Self-Reliance," *PE*, p. 161.
49. "Napoleon; or, The Man of the World," *PE*, p. 236.
50. Ibid., p. 325.
51. "The American Scholar," *PE*, p. 71.
52. Ibid., pp. 64–65.
53. Ibid., p. 66.
54. "Notes," *COL*, pp. 341–42.
55. "Illusions," *PE*, p. 380. That Emerson specifically refers to women in this regard suggests Nietzsche's elaborations on this theme in *Beyond Good and Evil* and elsewhere. Derrida emphasized Nietzsche's observations on women's need for illusions and accurately summarizes his view that a woman "plays at dissimulation, at ornamentation, deceit, artifice, at an artist's philosophy" (Jacques Derrida, *Spurs: Nietzsche's Styles/Éperons: Les Styles de Nietzsche*, p. 67). Perhaps Derrida could have reminded Nietzsche that his attribution of artifice and illusion-creation to women could only be a matter of degree since he claims that with the appearance of "organic life" deception enters the world. Moreover, one can find Nietzsche proclaiming that "dissimulation" is the natural tendency of *all* human beings. Cf. "On Truth and Lying in a Non-Moral Sense," in *Philosophy and Truth*, ed. and trans. Daniel Breazeale.
56. A basic theme of Nietzsche's is that the emergence of organic life (e.g., plant life) reveals modes of illusion and "deception." In human life illusions play an even more important role. Imaginary beliefs enter into knowledge-claims and infiltrate the intellectual and cultural world. Such illusions are indispensable for the aesthetic embellishment of existence, for the endurance of suffering, for the beautiful deceptions of art that enable mankind to withstand the terrors of life. Our thoughts, intentions, and actions are "veiled in illusion." We live, for the most part, in a "network of illusions." Everyday life is a "surface" affair characterized by superficial perceptions and judgments. The language by which we describe and understand the world around us is shot through with "metaphors." Each organic being, Nietzsche contends, necessarily views the world and other

beings from the standpoint of "the perspectival optics of life." Ineluctably, then, this means that there are illusions that make a specific form of life possible, endurable, and selective in relation to the experience of the environment or "the world." What pertains to each organic individual also pertains to species, civilizations, societies, and cultures. That is, each has its own perspectives, ideals, illusions, and myths.

The fact that Nietzsche, in *Human, All-Too-Human,* quotes the same line from Voltaire's writings as Emerson did—"*Croyez-moi, mon ami, l'erreur aussi a son mérite*"—and then applies it to the idea of the necessity of illusory beliefs, of "errors," for life, suggests a direct connection between Emerson's views and those of Nietzsche on precisely the same point. However, Nietzsche goes far beyond Emerson in developing a theory of knowledge and a conventionalistic theory of scientific theories and concepts that emphasize the role of "useful fictions" in the interpretation of the world, nature, and the self. Even so, there is good reason to believe that it was in Emerson's essay, "Illusions," that Nietzsche first encountered the notion of the intimate association among life, values, beliefs, and illusions. Emerson claims that we are all "victims of illusion in all parts of life," that "everybody is drugged with his own frenzy." Most of the time, he believed, we "live amid hallucinations." What we perceive around us is often comprised of "radiations" from ourselves. There are, Emerson maintains, illusions of the senses, of the passions, of the intellect, of time, etc. He also suggested, following Immanuel Kant, that our intuitions of space and time may also be subjective illusions. Such illusory beliefs or subjective intuitions enter into our conception of nature and of the properties of matter. Cf. "Illusions," *PE,* pp. 375–86.

Ironically, the idea of the influence of illusions on existence, specifically in the form of the Hindu doctrine of *Māyā* or "the veil of illusion" that coats our experiences, was initially conveyed to Nietzsche through his reading of Emerson. Later, it was reinforced by his enthusiastic study of the philosophy of Arthur Schopenhauer. In addition, Nietzsche's one-time close friend, the composer Richard Wagner, had developed, as part of an aesthetic theory, the conception of the artistic creation of "hallucination" and had adopted Schopenhauer's Buddhistic and Hindu ideas. Finally, the social scientist and historian of philosophy, F. A. Lange, whose *History of Materialism* Nietzsche had thoroughly studied, stressed the need for "ideals" for the enhancement of life. Poetic ideals are, he said, essential for their edifying effects, and they serve as a way of going beyond the "fragmentary truths" of the exact sciences. Lange called the projection of speculative, poetic, and imaginative general conceptions the adoption of "the standpoint of the ideal." Lange also guided Nietzsche's thinking in regard to the development of a theory of *useful fictions* in philosophy and in the sciences. Despite these later, diverse influences on the philosophical thought of Nietzsche, it was Emerson who first insinuated the conception of the necessity of conscious and unconscious illusions for the continuance of, the endurance of, human life in Nietzsche's mind. As far as I know, this specific and distinctive relationship of thought between Emerson and Nietzsche has not previously been noticed. For a succinct account of Nietzsche's "Doctrine of Conscious Illusion," see; Hans Vaihinger, *The Philosophy of 'As-If'*, pp. 341–62.

57. "The American Scholar," *PE*, p. 70.

58. "History," *PE*, p. 137.

59. "The Transcendentalist," *PE*, p. 94.

60. "Nature," *PE*, p. 50.

61. *SW* 1, UB 2, §9.

62. "The Transcendentalist," *PE*, p. 109.

63. Harold Bloom construes this as a literary religion which involves endless self-experimentation. This religion entails a critical and philosophical self-reliance and breaks with tradition. He also sees this literary religion as a mythology of America itself. Cf. Harold Bloom, *Agon*, pp. 19–20.

64. If, as has been said, Heidegger was influenced by Nietzsche's conception of history in "On the Uses and Disadvantages of History for Life" (and incorporated it into *Being and Time*), and if what I've called his existential theory of history was, as I've argued, derived from Emerson's writings on history, then Emerson is a hidden presence in Heidegger's major work. Cf. Jeffrey A. Barash, *Martin Heidegger and the Problem of Historical Meaning*, Dordrecht: 1988, Martinus Nijhoff, p. 154.

Chapter 4

Power in Nature
and the Search after Power

> *Life is a search after power.*
> *[Ralph Waldo Emerson, "Power"]*

In his preface to the third edition of his work, *Nietzsche: Philosopher, Psychologist, Antichrist,* the late Walter Kaufmann tended to deprecate studies that were "Nietzsche and . . ." titles. He claimed that "any attempt to define his significance and meaning . . . in terms of one such juxtaposition is bound to be misleading."[1] And any attempt to find a significant clue to his thought in this way is "simple-minded." At the risk of being placed in the category of the "simple-minded," I beg to differ with such understandable, but hasty and overstated, judgments.

In order to gain a full understanding of a philosopher we need to know what basic problems, questions, and issues exercised him or her. We would like to know why a problem was stated in a particular way. And we would like to know what means or "methods" were used to resolve or deal with crucial issues. We want to discern the interpretative perspective from which a thinker approaches the questions and issues that stimulate inquiry. There is also a certain fascination in exploring the intricate archaeology of thought of a significant thinker. One insight is worth a thousand words. This is especially the case when we are dealing with a thinker whose works are imaginative, syncretistic creations and one who was in the habit of looking at theories, conceptions, and values from many perspectives.

In Kaufmann's otherwise judicious interpretation of Nietzsche, it is not necessary to wonder how or when Nietzsche "discovered" the conception of "the will to power." If he had sought to trace discernible influences on his thought, he would have found out why he was right in saying that the conception of the will to power was *not* a variation on Schopenhauer's theory of a universal "will to live" and why his observation that this notion "did not spring from Nietzsche's head full grown"[2] is quite accurate. Moreover, there is a comparative study ensconced in Kaufmann's bibliography—Hubbard's *Nietzsche und Emerson*—that would have demonstrated to him that Nietzsche had studied Emerson's essays with microscopic care. He would have seen that he had underlined numerous, especially striking, passages. Although Hubbard only scratches the surface of the deep and abiding influence that Emerson exerted on Nietzsche, he does provide irrefutable evidence that the *first,* though by no means the last, "discovery" of the notion that "life is a search after power," that power in nature is manifested in human culture, was made between the covers of what Nietzsche read as the *Versuche* (or *Essays*) of Ralph Waldo Emerson.

It has already been shown that Emersonian *aperçus* are very much in evidence during the period of the *Untimely Meditations,* and they are especially noticeable in "On the Uses and Disadvantages of History for Life" and "Schopenhauer as Educator."

Modes of Power

Very early in his tortuous journey of discovery Nietzsche was concerned with the psychology of motivation. In "Schopenhauer as Educator" he asks why people hide themselves behind customs and popular opinions. There are, he believes, two basic reasons for this: fear of one's neighbor (who typically demands and expects conventional behavior and relaxed laziness) and a conformity and uniformity that is reinforced by modesty. This fear of, and desire for the approval of, others makes cowards of us all. Nietzsche finds it strange that even though each of us is a "unique" individual, we "act and think like a member of a herd." It is primarily laziness and secondarily timidity and fear that prevent us from practicing "unconditional honesty." Ruled by conformity and public opinion, every "unique miracle" of humanity lazily disappears in the anonymity of the crowd. Whoever does not want to belong to the "mass" need only follow the dictates of his conscience. And the call of conscience is "Be your self!"

In earlier notes Nietzsche had said that fear was the negative factor affecting our excessive regard for the opinions of others, and "will to power" the positive factor.[3] The specific will to power mentioned in this context seems to refer to overt success in the social world. A desire for success in the world is associated with the conformity that is frequently required in order to attain it. The striving for power, which is ascribed to Richard Wagner in "Richard Wagner in Bayreuth," is equated with a passionate craving for public success and is considered as an essentially negative characteristic.

Power is sometimes construed by Nietzsche as an evil, but, at the same time, as Kaufmann has pointed out, he also saw that a strong desire for social power or public success could be channeled into productive artistic creativity.[4] The case of the composer, Richard Wagner, was an instructive one. His passion for success or power was a very deep motivation in his life. But, as Nietzsche believes, Wagner managed to translate this "desire for supreme power" into artistic creativity.[5] He expresses himself, through the medium of his art, to himself. He no longer addresses himself to a public that he once hoped would grant him great success. In this way, he achieved and expressed a creative "power" through a renunciation of a previous passionate drive for success *via* conformity to a public's perceived values, beliefs, and needs.

Nietzsche's psychological observations are often expressed in the form of disconnected insights that seek to uncover the primitive desires, drives, and motives of individuals that are normally hidden beneath the masks of social conventions and common opinions. Before he ever spoke of his "hypothesis" of an immanent, universal will to power, he made occasional observations on the various modalities of power without any further theoretical generalization. In *Human, All-Too-Human*, for example, he understands the socialist movement in Europe not simply as a "problem of right." For, if it is a matter of an oppressed group rising against oppressors who have kept the former downtrodden for centuries, then the central problem is actually one of "power."[6]

The socialist movement is compared by Nietzsche to a "natural force" such as steam. It may be pressed into human service or, if it is misused or not controlled properly, may be dangerous. Basically, the question concerning the increasing force of socialism is how best to turn it into an instrument of constructive human purpose. Even though this is pretty standard fare, what is interesting is the analogy that is used in this context. A political movement is a social force which, in turn, may be compared to a *natural* source of power that may be beneficial to a society or positively dangerous to it.

It is curious that in the "Notes" appended to *The Conduct of Life* which pertain to the essay, "Power," reference is made to a line that Emerson intended to use in another place. "It was Watt who told King George III that he dealt in an article of which kings were said to be fond—Power."[7] James Watt, inventor of the steam engine, wittily compares the power that his invention produces to political power. Not much could be made of this apparent coincidence (i.e., the fact that Nietzsche also uses "steam" to illustrate a "natural power" and then compares it to political power) except for the passing reference to the dangers of such powers and the further similarities of the analogy. In "Fate" Emerson refers to the godlike power of natural forces such as steam and then links them with "higher kinds of steam" or political forces. He pictures the "Fultons and Watts of politics" as controlling the dangerous social and political forces that threaten to topple governments or turn societies upside down. Social and political powers are like natural powers. If they are carefully used, controlled, and channelled, they can be constructive and creative; if misused or abused, they can be explosively dangerous.

This specific association between Nietzsche's remarks on the nature of, and forms of, power and Emerson's comments on this same issue is only the tip of a shared cognitive iceberg. If we try to bring together all of Emerson's numerous observations concerning power in nature, in society, and in the individual, we shall see that an early stimulus to the conception of a universally active will to power in nature and in man-in-nature was emitted by Emerson. Although the seventeenth-century English philosopher Hobbes had attributed to man "a desire for power after power, that ceaseth only in death," he conceived of this desire as motivated by a need for security. And Nietzsche certainly was familiar with Emerson's discussion of the modalities of power before he knew anything about Hobbes.

Emerson discerns the "search for power" in protean forms: in the desire for conquest, the desire for preeminence, the quest for worldly success. The pursuit of power is found in the political conservative's preservation of the *status quo* and in the radical's desire for revolutionary change; in the energetic pursuit of money; in the effort to master the forces of nature; in the corrupting quest of State-power; in the coercive force of numbers and "public opinion"; in the excessive ambition of the military-political leader; in the ambitions of thinkers; in the behavior of religious leaders; in the individual's striving for independence and self-reliance.

In *Human, All-Too-Human,* Nietzsche ascribes to man an "ineradicable trait," the desire for preeminence. It is a trait he considers as deeper and more primitive than any "joy in equality."[8] It is obvious that he is thinking of the pursuit of power. In *Daybreak* he argues that a long period of fear and impotence in man's development stimulated a craving for a feeling of power. This desire for power has become man's "strongest propensity," one that has been cultivated to a high degree of "subtlety."[9] Even though Emerson rarely speculated about the origin of the desire for power, he, too, saw it as a deep-rooted human trait—a propensity that has been inherited from man's long natural history.

Emerson refers, as Nietzsche later will, to many modalities of power, many levels of power, and even to natural "scales of power." He discusses the idea of power as a metaphysical conception of nature, as a psychological basis of human motivation, as a social phenomenon, and as a spiritual phenomenon. Although neither a theory of will to power nor a theory of power as such is presented by Emerson, he provides, in his reflections on power and in his metaphysical belief in the immanence of "will" in the world, the rudimentary materials out of which such a general theory could be constructed.

In his occasionally obscure early work, *Nature,* Emerson conceived of the natural world as imbued with a spiritual tendency towards embodiment and form. A natural fact, he maintained, should be understood as the terminus of a manifestation of spirit. He even suggests a necessary process by which spiritual force assumes material forms. What is presented in *Nature* is a metaphysical belief that spirit underlies matter and has a propensity to express itself in natural forms.

When Emerson describes God as the "supreme power" and emphasizes the association between power and nature, his general conception of reality is not far removed from *some* of Nietzsche's later attempts to develop the "hypothesis" of the will to power. Many of Nietzsche's arguments for the "interpretation" of the world as an immanent manifestation of a will to power lead to a dynamic, "spiritual" conception of actuality that is far removed from the materialism that is sometimes falsely ascribed to him. For he rejoices in the notion that matter, in the sense of solid atoms, does not exist. And he provisionally adopts Roger Boscovich's theory of force-centers largely because it entails what Norwood Hanson has called the theoretical "dematerialization" of matter. The will to power is a "formula" for the notion of an immanent "energy" *(Energie)* pervading all entities. Like Emerson, Nietzsche postulates various levels of, manifestations of, spirit, from the grossest to the most sublime. Despite the dramatic and unconventional way in which Nietzsche presents his imaginative interpretation of reality, his experimental answer to the "riddle of existence," it is recognizable as a form of voluntaristic *idealism.*

According to what has been called Emerson's "mystical" conception of the natural world, the study of, and understanding of, the universe shows us that an "exercise of Will" or a "lesson of power" is taught in every physical event. Nature may be construed anthropomorphically as "the double" of man insofar as it is a "realized will." The universe may be comprehended as suffused with "a breath of Will that blows through it eternally."[10]

The unity of the natural world is, in fact, a "unity in variety." And the individual forms of being are each microcosms that faithfully reflect the essential voluntaristic character of the macrocosm. The multiplicity of natural forms represents an enormous scale of powers. From the atom to the stars, Emerson sees the symbols of nature as expressions of spirit, as pervaded by will and power.

In our attempt to understand the natural world we naturally use language. But language or words are inadequate to describe the immensity and complexity of "what is." At best, words "break, chop, and impoverish" the richness of actuality.[11] Despite this limitation, language-use, and action as well, signify the emergence of the "human form," the highest degree of "organization" in the natural world. With man, the hints of reason in nature are fulfilled and matured. And natural processes conspire with spirit to lead man to liberation. There is a spiral tendency in nature that moves towards higher modalities of form. Here Emerson expresses poetically his idea of an evolutionary development that emphasizes the spiritual gap between man and the "worm" that strives to be man. In this regard, it is understandable that Lewis Mumford saw Emerson as a Darwinian before Darwin because of his doctrine of development and transformation. But, in a strict sense, Emerson was not "Darwinian" in any classic sense of biological theory.[12] For he maintained that transformations of physical or biological form were external manifestations of what he construed as a spiritual evolution. Moreover, he suggests that species are not absolutely separated insofar as he conceives of the transmission, through the evolutionary process, of earlier, more primitive forms of life. In the human body, for example, he found remnants of numerous, more primitive, forms of life. Although he refers to his ideas on evolution in poetic, literary ways, his thinking was informed by scientific theories of his day concerned with the structural evolution of forms of life or morphogenesis.

It is, in all probability, this Emersonian conception of development that is reflected in Nietzsche's evolutionary concepts insofar as he is typically critical of Darwinian notions (such as that adaptation for survival is central to organic life) even though he espouses a "morphology" and expresses an interest in a "theory of the evolution of the will to power." Just as Emerson did, he looks for a spiritual *nisus,* an underlying striving for power, as the basis for all living beings. Even though Nietzsche does accept the Darwinian (actually, the Spencerian and, before that, the Malthusian) conception of a "struggle for existence," he also wants to preserve Emerson's notion of a spiritual hierarchy, a "scale of rank," in the natural order. From Nietzsche's point of view, Darwin forgot the "spirit" in man that can be put to creative or destructive uses. His biological theory of "natural selection" gives sanction to species survival at the expense of "exceptions," of unique individuals. Darwin's theory of natural selection tends to favor the assumption of a "selection" of the majority, the typical members of a species, those who reproduce themselves most frequently. What may be called a process of spiritual "selection" would be a diametrically opposed process.[13] We shall have to return to this issue in the course of examining Emerson's strong and sometimes harsh views concerning a desirable "natural aristocracy."

Nietzsche was raised, as a thinker, on a pre-Darwinian conception of evolution or transformation and this, in part, explains what has sometimes been seen as his incongruent criticisms of central theses in Darwin's theory of evolution by means of natural selection, a theory that *seems* to be reflected, to some extent, in his own views. The suspicion that Nietzsche was an evolutionist is well founded even though he did not adopt many of the central ideas of Darwin's theory of evolution.

Emerson proclaims an openly anthropomorphic conception of the natural world. Man is present, in a sense, in all the "particulars" of nature. The reason why he puts forward such a view is that he holds that we know nature by means of "spiritual," symbolic facts. We are construed as continuously projecting our feelings, sentiments, and emotions into our understanding of natural phenomena and "natural facts." As is the case for Nietzsche, we are said to comprehend nature by virtue of a symbolization of it. In consonance with Emerson, he stresses that our "aesthetic humanities" infiltrate our comprehension of the entire natural world both in everyday observations and in scientific interpretation.[14]

Although Nietzsche spills a lot of ink laying bare our "anthropomorphic" understanding of the world around us, he returns to an interpretation of actuality in terms of "human analogy" in his conception of a spiritual *Tendenz* or propensity pervading the world: "the will to power." The idea of a universal will to power is derived from what he believes to be the chief factor motivating human behavior: the organic individual's striving for, or "search for," power. The rationale for this is tantamount to the Emersonian belief that macrocosmic nature is comprehended through man's intellect, imagination, feelings, sentiments, and metaphorical language *and* that man is himself a microcosm, a concentrated, self-conscious reflection of the underlying dynamics of the natural world.

Metaphoric Transference

Man, in Emerson's considered view, is a natural analogist; he intuitively sees relations among all things. He uses images derived from nature to describe mental states. A lamb signifies innocence; a snake, cunning and spite. Indo-European languages use light and darkness to refer to knowledge and ignorance. A river suggests flux. Natural facts symbolize spiritual facts and spiritual facts are represented by natural symbols. There is, Emerson observes, a store of similar symbols in language-families. We find in this seminal work, *Nature,* a remarkably original, succinct analysis of language that anticipates later semiotic theory. In combination with other sources, Emerson's compressed treatment of language had its effect on Nietzsche's early analysis of language in his unpublished essay, "On Truth and Lying in a Non-Moral Sense."

Words, for Emerson, are signs of natural facts, and these signs are used as symbols of "spiritual facts." Many of the words we use to express a moral or intellectual factor can be traced to their derivation from some material appearance. Something is "right" if it is "straight." The "wrong" is "twisted." The word "spirit" is derived from "wind," "air," "breath." "Supercilious" refers to "raising" one's eyebrows. Words derived from descriptions of physical appearances are transformed into "spiritual" or mental phenomena. Emerson's insights in the segment in *Nature* under the rubric "Language" even touch upon the structuralist notion of an unconsciously derived set of basic concepts. For he maintains that "the process by which this transformation [of words used to describe things into words used to denote spiritual phenomena] is made, is hidden from us in the remote time when language was framed; but the same tendency may be daily observed in children . . . and savages."

Words symbolize things and natural phenomena symbolize cognitive "facts." What is stressed, in this rudimentary notion of semiotics, is the *metaphorical* nature of language. By means of language "outward phenemona" are converted into something in human life. The world we perceive and know is "emblematic" or symbolic. In fact, nature may be conceived of as "a metaphor of the human mind." Even technical statements have a certain meaning borrowed from human life and judgments. Language translates experience of external phenomena into metaphorical, symbolic word-images that have an anthropomorphic significance.

Language is a system of signs that is shot through with anthropomorphically colored metaphors. Since we express our knowledge of the external world by means of language, it is symbolically and metaphorically represented and, in the process, it is "humanized." The world that may be said to be "pictured" by our symbolic, metaphorical, linguistic signs is ineluctably an anthropomorphic world.

In Nietzsche's unpublished essay on language there are echoes of Emerson's rudimentary theory of signs, as well as additional features that seem to have been derived from then-current physiological theories of sensation. The intellect is described as emerging out of man's relation to nature, as a tool used to the end of preservation. Deception and illusion are linked with the constructive nature of the intellect and the structure of language. Even truth itself is valued for its life-preserving uses and social utility.

Language is comprised of arbitrary significations. We assign genders to natural entities, and we use words to designate only certain features of natural beings. Thus, a snake *(Schlange)* is an animal that twists or winds *(schlingen)*. We use the word "leaf" with casual familiarity, having forgotten that we have arbitrarily discarded a host of individual differences and aspects we observe in our experience of each unique "leaf." The hypothetical creators of language that Nietzsche imagines designate "things" in their relation to man and human experience and employ the "boldest metaphors." We believe that we have genuine knowledge of things, but "we possess nothing but metaphors for things—metaphors which correspond in no way to the original entities."

Nietzsche goes beyond Emerson's linguistic views by holding that terms such as "leaf" are used symbolically. Such terms do not refer to any concrete, perceived entities. A conception deletes individuating characteristics of particulars and gives the false impression that there are abstract entities in the natural world. Claims to truth in the commonsense, everyday, social world are actually symbolizations of things, persons, qualities, and acts. Conventional truth is a "moving host of metaphors, metonymies, and anthropomorphisms." A totality of "human relations . . . have been poetically and rhetorically intensified, transferred and embellished." Over a long period of time these "truths" are assumed to be "fixed, canonical, and binding." This sedimentation of metaphors is considered to have occurred over a considerable span of time by virtue of an "unconscious" process of habit and assimilation. When we talk about our knowledge of the external world, Nietzsche contends, we are really referring to "the metamorphosis of the world into man."[5]

Although not everything in "On Truth and Lying in a Non-Moral Sense" is reminiscent of Emerson's discussions of language in *Nature,* the similarities between the two essays are striking. To be sure, Nietzsche presents a sketch of a theory of truth and thereby goes beyond the letter of Emerson's analysis. However, his references to the nature of truth could be seen as an extension of the latter's standpoint in regard to the symbolic form of "natural facts." The idea of truth as pertaining to the "sum of human relations" is similar to Emerson's assertion that man studies relations in all things and that "a ray of relation passes from every other being to him."

Nietzsche's construal of nature as symbolically/metaphorically represented in language is analogous to Emerson's insights concerning the metaphorical nature of language. Even though he is ironic towards the anthropomorphic interpretation of the natural world that Emerson celebrates, in the final analysis he doesn't deny the inevitable tendency we have to interpret nature in human terms.

Sarah Kofman's interpretation of Nietzsche's use of metaphorical language in his "hypothesis" of the will to power places emphasis on the wrong side of the language/interpretation equation. She claims that "the metaphorical style" signifies "fullness of life and life-affirmation" whereas conceptual-linguistic forms reveal a "will to nothingness" and a commitment to the "ascetic ideal."[16] But in his essay on truth and lying Nietzsche discloses the metaphorical nature of *ordinary language*. And he argues that concepts are denuded metaphors. It is Nietzsche's understanding of man as microcosm that leads him to transfer a "will to power" to actuality, not only its metaphorical nature. As anthropomorphic transference (as Emerson already suggested), metaphorical language is inescapable. The humanization of nature entails anthropomorphisms. Kofman is right about "will to power" being metaphorical, but she overinterprets Nietzsche's rationale for adopting this particular metaphor for actuality by assuming that it is its metaphorical character that prompts Nietzsche to employ it.

The idea of a will to power pervading all entities is based upon "human analogy." Man, the natural analogist, thinks, speaks, and writes about the world *via* anthropomorphisms. Following Emerson's hints (and those of others), Nietzsche adopts a methodological habit: to interpret nature in terms of man and man in terms of nature. The language derived from our description of our perception of and knowledge of nature is applied to *homo natura,* and the language by which we describe human nature is applied to nature. These habits of thought are reminiscent of Emerson's reflections on the relation among man, language, and the understanding of nature. If we add to this the obvious parallel between Emerson's and Nietzsche's conception of the metaphorical representation of actuality in language, the relation between the two, on this point, goes beyond a mere coincidence of independent insights.

This relation between Emerson's remarks on language and Nietzsche's conception of the metaphorical symbolization of the world is relevant to the development of the principle of a will to power in nature. Human experience may be reduced to two basic modes of acquaintance. Through perception we encounter the not-I, the otherness of entities, phenomena, and events. Through thought, reflection, and conceptualization we "experience" internal phenomena (psychic or mental events, cognitive states, etc.). The natural language by which we describe both domains of phenomena is, as Emerson saw and Nietzsche later claims, infiltrated by a host of analogies. Nietzsche contends, practically in the language of

Emerson, that analogies between physical phenomena and movements and mental states (what Emerson calls "spiritual facts") lead
us to see that we can speak metaphorically of each class of phenomena in the language of the other.[17] We tend to transfer symbols
used to refer to cognitive processes to the external, natural world
and we transfer terms used to describe physical phenomena to the
"inner world" of consciousness. These two domains are, Nietzsche argues, treated as "symptoms" of an underlying reality that
we cannot know directly.[18]

What Nietzsche expressed was the view that the external world
and the internal world are, because they are interpreted in terms of
our feelings and desires, our imagination, and our cognitive-
linguistic "signs," both symbolic or, as Emerson said, "emblematic." If both domains are elaborate systems of symbolization, then
it is natural for us to speculate about what it is that these symbolic
systems "stand for" or represent. It is at this point that Nietzsche
sought to go beyond phenomenal experience and "conditional
knowledge" in order to proffer *his* interpretation of reality "seen
from within," *his* answer to the "riddle of existence."

Given his metastasizing skepticism, we must look for the few
remaining articles of Nietzsche's philosophical faith in order to understand why he moves from a kind of skeptical phenomenalism to
an elaborate interpretation of the essential basis of all actuality.
The movement of his thinking, at this point, is more a subtle form
of subjectivism than that of Emerson, the poetic thinker who first
suggested this approach to the ontological question to him.

Nietzsche affirms the reality of nature as a fluctuating process
and affirms the reality of man-in-nature. But, in agreement with
Emerson, he contends that the form or structure of the natural
world, how it appears to us, is profoundly conditioned by our subjectivity, our physiology, our feelings, by our evolved epistemic
habits, and our metaphorical ways of describing the natural world.
However, it is also assumed that man is a self-reflective microcosm, the only such entity that we know to exist. This is a strong
point of affinity between Emerson and Nietzsche. For the former
referred to the increase of knowledge of nature as the unfolding of
the intelligibility of nature to a being who discovers the analogical
relation between his own mind and nature itself. Thus, as Emerson
expresses it, "the ancient precept, 'Know thyself,' and the modern
precept, 'Study nature,' become at last one maxim."[19] We are
again encouraged to see the analogical relation between macrocosmic nature and microcosmic man. And if we adopted Emerson's

analysis of language and subjectivity, we would be committed to a reflection on, or analysis of, the essence of human reality in order to speculate about the global, 'transhuman' nature of reality. But, of course, in our efforts to arrive at a viable interpretation of reality in terms of the most fundamental aspect of the human self, we are inevitably committed to a "humanization" of that reality. To be sure, Emerson himself does not tie together all of the pieces of his scattered, insightful reflections on this question in such a neat, philosophical way. It was left to his unknown German "soul-brother" to gather together and synthesize the random and dispersed observations and *aperçus* of the American thinker and poet.

In *Nature* Emerson fuses the mystery, beauty, order, power, and spiritual will in nature into a monistic vision of a cosmic emanation of divinity. A realistic portrait of the negativities in the natural world only began to emerge in his writings between 1844 and 1860. His earlier poetic description of nature gave way to more somber insights into the fatality in the world, the destructive forces of nature, the waste and failures that result from the play of fecund natural forces. But Emerson does not change his mind about the "power" that man acquires by means of a deeper study of the order of nature. The penetration of the intelligibility of nature converts what was previously "unconscious truth" into "a part of the domain of knowledge" through an interpretation of, and definition of, a multiplicity of objects and processes. This acquired knowledge becomes "a new weapon in the magazine of power."[20]

In the spirit of Francis Bacon, Emerson reiterates his idea that "knowledge is power." Carried away by the optimistic prospect of man's increasing control of natural forces, Emerson calls the coming "kingdom of man over nature" a triumph of spirit that will create "a dominion such as now is beyond his dream of God."[21] Later, Nietzsche sees this "power . . . won over nature" as a means to the enhancement and strengthening of human existence.[22] Typically, Emerson intermixes his visions of a glorious future with a highly subjective counsel. We are told that the world exists *for* us; that, in the proper spiritual attitude, it will appear as a perfect phenomenon. The revolution in the knowledge of nature and in the technological mastery of the world will correspond to a "spiritual" evolution of man. Thus, Emerson proposes his earliest and simplest imperative: Build . . . your own world."[23] Like some of Emerson's essays, *Nature* is stimulating, provocative, edifying, poetic, and evocative; but it is not exactly a logically consistent or crystal-clear philosophic exposition. In all likelihood, he would parry this kind of judgment and respond with a typical riposte: "A foolish consistency is the hobgoblin of little minds."

"Life," Emerson announces, "is not dialectics." There is a great need for strength of body and mind in order to withstand the storm and stress of life, to endure "the slings and arrows of outrageous fortune." Intellect alone is not enough, as important as it is. What is needed for the forward movement of life is strength of character and even "muscular activity." Culture, taken in excessive doses, "ends in a headache." The basic impulse of life is "not intellectual or critical, but sturdy." A person of "native forces," a strong individual with character, exemplifies the ascending nature of life, its careful "mixture of power and form."

Beneath the social and cultural forms of life, Emerson contends, there is "power"; it surges through "the subterranean and invisible tunnels and channels of life."[24] Through every natural entity, through every organism, a divine "vital force" moves. The ultimate "Power" that pervades all living beings waxes and wanes and is concentrated in no single place, in no singular entities. Although Emerson only vaguely refers the actuality of nature back to the ultimate divine power, he is fascinated by its millionfold manifestations in the natural world and in man. What is perpetually revealed in actuality, through countless changing forms, is a "spiritual" reality, a reality that we recognize in ourselves, in others, in nonhuman organic entities, in the dynamics of nature, as "power."

After the publication of "Experience" in his second series of essays (in 1844), Emerson begins to discern evidence of power and the striving for power practically everywhere. In his dual-perspective portrait of Napoleon in *Representative Men,* he understands him as a courageous and cunning political representative of the rising and spreading valuation of a pursuit of "power and wealth." Napoleon is a thoroughly "modern" man, a man in whom, because he thrives at the "lowest ground of politics," we can see the naked pursuit of power laid bare. He is described as a "prophet" of "the spirit of commerce, of money, and material power." In this epitome Emerson displays his ability to look beneath the glitter of fame to disclose the symbolic meaning of persons and events. Napoleon is a striking individual. But he is more than an individual; he is a sign of a shift in cultural values. The cunning and conscienceless pursuit of political and material power of Napoleon discloses the unrestrained ruthlessness of a "natural agent." He had at his center, Emerson contends, an iron will that pitilessly ploughed under whatever stood in its path. His aggressive military coups were necessary to him. "My power," Emerson quotes him as saying, "would fall were I not to support it by new achievements. Conquest has made me what I am, and conquest must maintain me." Exuding "the good-nature of strength," Napoleon describes life as a "fortress," the powers of which we little understand.

Emerson sees Napoleon's virtues, his courage, his daring, his cutting intellect, his energy, and his animal cunning. But he also sees that he achieved power, like his twentieth-century counterparts, at the expense of the well-being and lives of many; that his selfishness and egotism soiled and corrupted his actions and power. Emerson does not literally say that Napoleon was consumed by a strong and crude "will to power," but he says everything that would be included in such a characterization of the man.[25]

Previously I've alluded to Emerson's depiction of the raw power of nature and its destructive impact on human life. Attention has also been called to the constraints and restraints that are imposed upon our existence by the necessities of nature. The forces of the natural world are so awesome, so overpowering, that individuals, groups, entire societies and cultures are occasionally obliterated by them. The destructive powers of nature seem to be at war with the creative, vital power that is immanent in living beings.

Negative/Positive Power

In "Fate" Emerson changes his earlier emphasis on the "positive power" of nature and begins to stress its sinister "negative power." Human potentialities or powers are circumscribed by the fatalities that act upon man through the dynamic processes of nature. And yet, Emerson sees some light at the end of the metaphysical tunnel. The power of nature is indeed immense; but positive, creative power is also immense. It is antagonistic to the force of "fate." Man's roots run deep and back into his own "natural history" and he betrays, in his physical form, his phylogenic relation to primitive forms of life. But his reflective nature and his power of intellect generate an impulse towards choosing, towards initiated action, towards "freedom." Here we encroach upon the paradoxical juxtaposition of fate and freedom that Nietzsche inherited, as a lifelong preoccupation, from his sustained study of Emerson, something that requires separate treatment.

In the course of uncovering the determinism that shapes the chief characteristics of each individual, that forms temperaments, Emerson also insists that "spiritual chemistry" cannot be analyzed or reduced to simple components. Feeling or "affection" is essential to will, and a "strong will" can make a considerable difference in the quality of a person's life. Strong motivation, deep determination, can make the difference between genius and an intelligent, unmotivated do-nothing. The "power" of a strong will is deeply rooted. For "when a strong will appears, it usually results from a certain unity of organization, as if the whole energy of body and mind flowed in one direction. All great force is real and elemental."[26]

Fate is "limitation," restriction, a circle drawn around each individual. But "power" is equally as real and is a countervailing natural force in the person, the group, the society. Although Emerson does not make this precise connection, he might easily have said that power in man is "possibility," the "power to be" *(po-esse)*. What he *does* say on this point certainly made an imprint on Nietzsche's philosophical consciousness: "The one serious and formidable thing in nature is a will."[27]

About four years after discovering Emerson, Nietzsche accidentally came upon Arthur Schopenhauer's *The World as Will and Representation*. There he found a similar, but stronger, recognition of the power of will in nature and man. But this fierce will was presented as something to be stilled, to be overcome, and, finally, as something to be *denied*. Schopenhauer reverses Emerson on this point. The will to life is, for Schopenhauer, the ultimate cause of discord, suffering, and pain. Therefore, he preaches that "liberation" is attained through the surrender of this will to existence (which is an emanation, acting through nature and man, of a "primal will"). The composer and dramatist, Richard Wagner, reinforces this Schopenhauerian idea and presents it at the heart of many of his music-dramas. For Schopenhauer and Wagner, the Buddhistic ideal of the renunciation of desire and hence of the craving for more life becomes an article of faith.

Emerson's *positive* conceptions of power, his emphasis upon a healthy affirmation of the will, his optimistic understanding of the creative uses of will-power, are temporarily eclipsed, in Nietzsche's mind, by the strong influence of the Schopenhauerian and

Wagnerian resignation of will, power, and life. But it is obvious, especially in *Thus Spoke Zarathustra,* that Nietzsche reached back to Emerson for support for his attempt to overcome what he later perceived as a *nihilistic* attitude towards life and existence.

The priority of willing, as well as its association with power and the "accumulation of power," is one of Emerson's most forceful philosophical views. He laments, as Nietzsche later will, the fact that many "worthy people" (for Nietzsche, read: "the good") are, to put it mildly, not notorious for their courage, boldness, or dynamic volition. They may have "insight" or they may have "affection" (i.e., feeling or passion), but they rarely have both. What Emerson calls the "energy of will" requires a fusion of both. In fact, "there can be no driving force except through the conversion of the man into his will, making him the will, and the will him."[28]

Although it has been said that what Emerson means by power is simply the "power of interpretation,"[29] this is not a defensible view. For, Emerson examines power from *many* diverse perspectives, and he conceives of it as having numerous modes of expression and form. He refers, for example, to the "aboriginal Power,"[30] the divine power, which acts through all natural events, processes, and beings. And he proclaims that the human power of will is derived from "aboriginal Nature." Even though this power is assumed to have a transcendental origin, it is recognized primarily in its Protean manifestations in nature, in nonhuman organic beings, and in man's physical and spiritual capacities. In the natural world, Emerson insists, nothing is dead. Everything is alive and imbued with varying degrees of power. This power flows persistently through the multiform underground pathways of organic being.[31]

The primordial power that Emerson refers to is, like Nietzsche's will to power, immanent in the dynamics of actuality. What is emphasized is that the "spiritual" undercurrent of actuality manifests what appears to be a voluntaristic tendency to "seek" expression, embodiment, and form. Underlying the phenomenal appearances of all entities is a posited spiritual *nisus* towards actualization, towards a synthesis of "form and power."

Psychology of Power

Considering the polarities of actuality, we must also look at the other aspect of Emerson's voluntaristic metaphysics: the power of the negative, the recognition, that is, of imperfections in the natural order, in the social world, in individuals. Destruction, imperfection, failure, weakness, dissolution, and a host of cultural, social, and individual negations are also elements in the panorama of existence. Perfection and imperfection, concord and discord, order and disorder, coherence and chaos intermingle in the cosmic process. Civilizations, cultures, societies, and individuals have their peaks of existence and their troughs. Emerson speaks, for example, of the "unconscious strength" of the ancient Greeks and generalizes to moments in history when the "perceptive powers" of a people are ripe. At these peak historical moments these people have not yet come to see the world with critical, scientific eyes: they do not scrutinize reality or life with a "microscope." There are glorious cultural peaks in human history when there is a "culmination of power." Cultural history reflects the ascending and descending patterns that are already present in organic existence and in the dynamic processes of the natural world.[32]

The conception of the centrality of power in nature and in man comes to maturity in the essay "Power." Before turning our attention to this insightful discourse on the place of power in human existence and the "search after power" in cultural life, we may first reach back to a previous assertion of Emerson's that seems to have found its way into Nietzsche's early, typically (though not universally) negative judgments about power and its pursuit. In *Daybreak*, Nietzsche speculates about the growing impatience to accumulate money in modern times, the criminality in society which generates, then as now, fraud after fraud. What, he asks, is driving these people to lie, cheat, and steal in order to increase their wealth and possessions? Directly, he attributes this drive to an ancient fanaticism, a *"lust for power."* The means used by this craving for power are different in modern times than in the past. What was formerly done "for the sake of God" is now done "for the sake of money . . . for the sake of what now gives the highest feeling of power."[33] What is now a *cliché* of popular novels, dramas, motion pictures, and television was once an original insight. But before Nietzsche penned these accurate observations of modern man, we know that he read, in Emerson's "The American Scholar," that "men, such as they are, very naturally seek money or power, and power because it is as good as money . . . they aspire to the highest, and this, in their sleep-walking, they dream is higher."[34]

Elsewhere, Emerson attributes the emerging passionate commercial spirit, the "capitalists' " desire for more and more wealth not, as Marx often did, to greed, but to a "search after power."

If he could, Plato would stamp Platonism on the world, would claim "copyright on the world." The philosopher is more than a philosopher. He, too, seeks, by indirection to be sure, to impose his will on the world. Alexander the Great's intense desire for military conquest is mild compared to Plato's intellectual "ambition."[35] A new mind imposes a new classification on the world. An intelligence of unusual power imposes the imprint of "its classification on other men . . . a new system."[36] Nietzsche only completes Emerson's thoughts concerning Plato in particular and philosophers in general when he declares that "philosophy . . . is the most spiritual will to power."[37]

Even though Richard Wagner and F. A. Lange will underscore the importance of the "lust for power" in human behavior (and thereby deepen Nietzsche's concern with this phenomenon), it was, without doubt, Emerson who was his earliest mentor in regard to the Protean forms that the pursuit of power takes and to its centrality in human existence and motivation. Although others had spoken of the power-motive in human nature (e.g., Callikles in Plato's *Gorgias* and, in modern times, Thomas Hobbes), it is not too much to say that Emerson was the first thinker to examine not only the human desire for power, but he was the first to disclose its multiple forms and its presence in *all* existence.

In a journal entry from 1852, Emerson speculates about the force of natural laws in relation to human desires and wishes. He notes that they impose a limitation on man, a limitation of "power." "We exert power. The very discovery that there is Fate, and that we are thwarted, equally discloses Power." The exertions of the will in face of restrictions, constraints, limitations and obstacles "makes the strong will."[38] The determinism affecting life, as real as it is, does not necessarily render us impotent.

In "Fate," Emerson makes a point of saying that his conception of the "circumstances" that limit human life is *not* tantamount to the fatalism of "the Turk" who firmly "believes his doom is written on the iron leaf in the moment when he entered the world" and, hence, he "rushes on the enemy's sabre with undivided will."[39] Even this distinction that Emerson makes *en passant* apparently did not escape Nietzsche's perceptive eye. For he explicitly distinguishes *his* conception of fate from that of "Turkish fatalism" or the belief that fate and man are separate and opposite each other; that there is an overpowering fatality above man that renders him totally impotent and bereft of meaningful individual action.[40]

It is because man is part of the natural world and inextricably involved in its total system of relations that he is subject to fate. As is the case with Emerson, man-in-nature cannot "be disentangled from the fatality of that which has been and will be."[41] Neither Emerson nor Nietzsche, despite their mutual acceptance of the conditions impinging on human existence, exclude human potency, capacity, effort, or *power*. Just as man's fragility and subjugation to "circumstances" has a natural origin, so, too, does his power, as finite as it may be, represent a natural inheritance.

Emerson (and Nietzsche after him) moves freely from discussions of one modality of power to another, from an identification of one degree of power to that of another. He emphasizes the enormous power of nature to create and destroy, calls attention to the specific "powers" of nonhuman beings and natural forces. And he also stresses man's essential power (in the sense of potentiality or what Aristotle called *dynamis*) to organize, to control, to shape, to form, to master, and to act upon others and on his environment. In his motto for "Compensation," he poetically expresses his belief that there is "power to him who power exerts," thereby joining the idea of power as potency to that of "power" as something attained. In addition to the above, Emerson also refers to the tremendous instrumental power of the intellect, as well as to man's (or, specifically, the artist's or poet's) power to create the new, the beautiful, and the ideal. But he, and Nietzsche following his lead, posits a natural propensity in man to "search after power." Despite the awkwardness of the expression, one could call this the potentiality (or "power") to seek power; the capacity to augment one's power, to strive for *more* power.

The evolution of the intellect adds a significant dimension to man's "organic power." The intellect serves as a conscious means of continuing the unconscious organic tendency towards growth. Throughout all of nature there is an immanence of power *and* an immanent, "spiritual" *nisus* towards the attainment of power. Although he does not express it in precisely this way, it could be said that, for Emerson, in the evolution of consciousness in man this natural striving for power comes to self-consciousness.

Nietzsche's "doctrine" of a universal will to power in nature and, hence, *a fortiori,* in man, society, culture, and history is fundamentally a completion of impressionistic conceptions that were originally forged in his mind by Emerson. This is especially apparent in Emerson's treatment of, and understanding of, the striving for power in the social world. Of course, Nietzsche does not simply adopt all of Emerson's views uncritically. He absorbs some, adapts and transforms others, and inverts a few. In general, however, he tends to synthesize what are fragmentary and disjointed insights in Emerson's experimental thinking. In doing so, he is surprisingly faithful to the American poet and essayist, even to the point of duplicating his paradoxical assertions.

Emerson came to conceive of the world as "saturated" with power. Power has a magnetic attraction for men. It both attracts individuals and is, at the same time, the source of creativity and action. Although what is called an "affirmative force" is not equally distributed among all individuals, it is central to the constructive, active impulse in society. The power-motive is a fertilizing factor in the growth of civilization and it separates inventive and creative individuals from those who are neither. This "plus" factor derives from a constitutional power, a surplus energy, a robust health that lends "vivacity" to the actions of select individuals. Personal power, energetic natural resources, and vigor are desired by mankind generally; but they are possessed by few.

The basic form of power that man desires is *not* power over others, but a subjective sense of energy, strength, health, a feeling of overcoming "resistances." This "plus" factor in life is a good if it is directed towards constructive goals or if it is "in the right place." Individuals who possess this "vital force," those comprising the "affirmative class," have a monopoly on "the homage of mankind," for genuine success in life is usually associated with this "positive power."

Nietzsche, in the manner of Emerson, posits a propensity, a *Tendenz*, a *nisus (Wille zur Macht)* that *acts through* all entities. Whereas Emerson had previously referred, in his earlier essays, to the divine origin of the energy in the universe found in the "atom" and in the cosmos as a whole, in "Power" and, in general, in his other later essays, he no longer does so. Typically, he speaks simply of an immanent "vital force" in the universe and in man. The shift from his earlier transcendentalism (as tenuous as that actually was) to a philosophy of immanence is practically complete. The implication of this change of metaphysical emphasis for the purposes of my argument is obvious: the appropriation of, and considerable elaboration on, the core idea of a universal *Tendenz* towards power in nature and in man on the part of Nietzsche is facilitated or encouraged in this way though his recurring study of Emerson. To be sure, this does not mean that Nietzsche, as the creator and founder of his new "Dionysian" religion, had entirely abandoned the occasional tendency to speculate about the meaning of "God" in *his* philosophical vision.

God

The possibility of God as a supramoral being is not, despite his atheistic standpoint, absolutely excluded by Nietzsche. Even though he certainly denied the existence of God as moral judge, God as creator of a universe out of nothing, or God as construed in the Judeo-Christian tradition, he did not consistently exclude the idea of God from his thought. In his notes from the later 1880s, he posits God as a "moment of culmination," as "a high point of power" in the dialectical cosmic process of ascension and decline.[42] Elsewhere, he claims that if we bracket the idea of God as "the highest goodness" and as "the highest wisdom," we could still admit God as *the highest power*—that suffices! From it follows everything, from it follows—'the world.' "[43] In these fragmentary experiments in thought, he is seeking a deanthropomorphic conception of God, a conception of God as *beyond* morality, as an impersonal, creative immanent power. It is as if Emerson were to remove all of the attributes of his conception of God (which, in fact, he sometimes does) except one: God as the "supreme Power." Since Emerson insists that this divine power is not apart from this world but is in it, that there is God within man, his theology takes on the form of a conception of the immanence of the spiritual dynamics of power that is not far removed from some of Nietzsche's experimental reflections on the possibility of God.

Aboriginal Power

In the course of his discussion of what he variously calls "force," "vital force," "energy," or "spirit" in his essay, "Power," Emerson introduces a number of observations that seem to have left their imprint on Nietzsche's thought. He avers that strong peoples and individuals seem to be endowed with a surplus of "natural forces." Such forces are exemplified in the "savage" who, in Emerson's poetic image, "is still in reception of the milk from the teats of Nature." A crude "aboriginal might", in its raw state, is admirable because it exemplifies overflowing energy. The inhibiting, negative affects are not yet present in such individuals and they exude uninhibited energy and power. It is curious to note that Salter, in his interpretation of Nietzsche,[44] stumbles once again upon a similarity between Emerson's occasional admiration for savages with a surplus of "animal spirits" and Nietzsche's often-criticized, and often-misunderstood, celebration of the *soi-disant* "blond beasts" of the past without noticing that Nietzsche's admiration for the energetic, vital, and uninhibited "blond beasts" of his imagination is obviously *derived* from Emerson's writings.

Emerson expressed admiration for the strength and natural powers of the primitive savage especially in contrast to the relatively feeble, inhibited, timid, weak, uncourageous modern man. And it was he who encouraged Nietzsche, by indirection, to exaggerate this distinction between the two types of men. The contrast between the instinctive, and strong, primitive type of man and the overcivilized, inhibited, unhealthy, and introspective man of modern times runs through Emerson's writings.

Neither Emerson nor Nietzsche desire a return to primitive culture or even a "return to nature" *per se*. Neither elevates the "blond beast" or the "savage" into a model for modern man or for the men of the future. Both would have liked to have seen some of that (presumed) surplus energy and raw health, that bodily power of the "natural" man infused into a (presumably) declining, self-doubting, morbidly introspective, modern man. Both wanted to see primitive energy and overflowing vitality fused with the intelligence, knowledge, subtlety, and tensed self-control of the best types of civilized human beings. Nietzsche denied that he desired a Rousseauian "return to nature." This would be, in actuality, a return to mindless brutality and wanton bloodshed.[45] What he wanted to do was to "restore" nature to man, to recapture or recover what was best in the early men he imagined; he wanted man to transfigure his inherited "nature," not surrender to it. A true man ought to be an antagonism of opposing forces, each balancing and checking the excesses of the others. The ideal individual is neither a primitive "blond beast" nor an overcivilized, "decadent," neurasthenic. Even in regard to this notion, he seems to have followed a pathway that was first cleared by Emerson. Ironically, we may gain a more judicious understanding of what Nietzsche meant in regard to this issue by reading the original Emersonian text that he interpreted. The great moment in human history, Emerson argued,

> is when the savage is just ceasing to be a savage . . . you have Pericles and Phidias, not yet passed over into the Corinthian civility. Everything good in nature and the world is in that moment of transition, when the swarthy juices still flow plentifully from nature, but their astringency or acidity is got out by ethics and humanity.[46]

As Nietzsche later does, Emerson worries about the spread of an excess of "Corinthian civility," the cultivation of overrefinement, the growth of an overly delicate *psyche,* the emergence of "decadence" in thought, manners, and behavior in modern man. Both were convinced that man was losing his heartiness, his health, his natural toughness.

Both Emerson and Nietzsche were alert to man's tendency towards corruption by virtue of his estrangement from "nature" and a spontaneous naturalness. They lamented what they construed as a loss of elemental strength and power in modern man, as well as the growth of a debilitating sensitivity. They deplored the increasing numbers of hypersensitive and psychologically unstable individuals. In terms of literary images, Emerson and Nietzsche were critical of the type of men represented by Kierkegaard's aesthetic personality ("A") in *Either/Or,* by Huysmans' character des Esseintes in *Against the Grain (A Rebours),* by Oscar Wilde's Lord Henry in *The Picture of Dorian Gray,* by Thomas Mann's von Aschenbach in *Death in Venice.* Like Hemingway in the twentieth century, Emerson and Nietzsche were preoccupied with delineating, preserving, and depicting the domain of masculinity. Emerson and Nietzsche were repelled by what they perceived as effete, decadent, and psychologically weak personalities. And they are both motivated in this attitude by a concern to strive for a "self-overcoming" of their own sensitivities. Although both exhibit a nostalgia for heroic men of action, they reserve their considered praise for individuals who endure, who resist, who display spiritual courage.

Emerson and Nietzsche exalt courage, an inward, disciplined strength, a "manly" sense of reality, and power for the simple and obvious reason that they believed that an excess of tenderness, a hypercivilized way of life, an excess of sensitivity, and overrefined manners and tastes led to, and is leading to, what they consider a deplorable and dangerous emasculation of man.

Emerson sees in unruly, strong, unbridled impulses an "animal spirit" that modern man seems to have lost in the long process of civilization. And he says often enough that every gain in culture or quality of life (in a material sense) entails a loss. He admires the power and what he insightfully calls the *"sex of mind"* of the creative, innovative individual. Where there is a "great amount of life" there may be grossness, a "coarse energy," and vices enough. But those possessing these traits at least have "the good nature of strength and courage." Emerson is tolerant of the primitive nature of crude and energetic men because he believes that they contribute to the dynamics of, and growth of, society and culture. The externalization of subjective power or potency in the pursuit of power is a necessary ingredient of positive action and sociocultural development: "It is an esoteric doctrine of society that a little wickedness is good to make muscle . . . the world cannot move without rogues."[47]

Adventurers, explorers, innovators and risk-takers of all kinds have a surplus energy and are often the very opposite of saints. If this raw energy could be preserved, to some extent, in "the civil and moral man," he would be worth an island-full of "cannibals." If the raw materials in the nature of primitive man could be annealed by the values and restraints of civilization, then a new, healthier, more powerful type of man might be cultivated.

Many of the great triumphs of peace, Emerson proclaims, followed, ironically, in the wake of war. The habits and discipline of war or of warlike conditions of existence carry over into civilized life: "the compression and tension of these stern conditions is a training for the finest and softest arts."[48] Although Emerson does not praise the military or the militant life in itself, he does praise some of the virtues that he believes are brought forth in the individual under stress. The preservation and conservation of such virtues, when transferred to civilized conditions of life, contributes to an energetic and creative life.

Unfortunately, the plus-factor that is the basis for human accomplishments is rarely found in a proper balance in individuals who are vital, but coarse. Hence, this drive for *more* is frequently an "excess which makes it dangerous and destructive."[49] Emerson is making precisely the distinction that Nietzsche later makes in regard to this theme: the recognition of the rough, primitive energy and strength of the "savage" or the "blond beast" as valuable traits *and* the simultaneous recognition of the explosive and dangerous nature of such characteristics. As Walter Kaufmann correctly pointed out, the barbarians or "blond beasts," which Nietzsche refers to in *The Twilight of the Idols, The Genealogy of Morals* and elsewhere, are "ideograms for the conception of unsublimated animal passion."[50] This is, of course, precisely the role that the Emersonian image of the "savage" plays in his thought. Nietzsche does *not* hold up the "blond beast" as a model for present-day men or as a model for men of the future any more than Emerson elevates the "savage" as the cultural ideal for his day or for the culture of the future that he envisioned.

Although we have inadvertently backed into the direct *nexus* between Emerson's awareness of the need to control and master, but *not* extirpate, primitive strength, energy, and power and Nietzsche's explicit conception of the "sublimation" of primitive drives, instincts, and passions in his *Emersonian* ideal or "myth" of the *Übermensch,* the point that is being made is that the "aboriginal" power of precivilized man is prized and is considered as analogous to the subjective "power" or potency that modern man expresses in his diverse means of striving for power. Both Emerson and Nietzsche put considerable emphasis upon the natural potency that seeks its realization in an externalized "search for power" or "striving for power."

One of Emerson's central ideas is that organic life invariably entails an expenditure of energy for the sake of power. What Nietzsche says about this in *Beyond Good and Evil* is, in fact, a theoretical extension of Emerson's understanding of organic existence: "The physiologists should take heed before they assume self-preservation as the cardinal drive of an organic being. A living being, above all, wants to *discharge* its energy—life itself is will to power."[51]

We've already seen that Emerson, before Nietzsche, interpreted the common craving for wealth in modern times as but one form which the striving for power assumes. He, too, views this as the most typical means of seeking power in modern, commercial societies.[52] Nietzsche builds upon and improves upon Emerson's passing remarks on this phenomenon under the influence of F. A. Lange's almost Marxian attack on the egoistic pursuit of wealth through the "accumulation of capital" and his allusions to the "lust of power," in the context of a critique of the *ethos* of capitalism, in his major work, *The History of Materialism.* In addition, Nietzsche was also educated in "political economy" by Eugen Dühring, a very early critic of Marx and a defender of a "national socialism."[53] Lange's linking of the "capitalistic" drive to accumulate wealth with the desire for power only served to reinforce, in Nietzsche's mind, a way of thinking of such matters that Emerson had already impressed upon him. For he, too, had attributed to people in general a fundamental "love of power" that often expressed itself in the pursuit of material or economic gain.[54] Asking himself what men who esteem wealth are seeking, Emerson replies that "power is what they want, not candy;—power to execute their design, power to give . . . form and actuality to their thought."[55]

As an afterthought Emerson comments that men of clear vision see that this tendency to seek power in order to realize one's design and actualize one's thought "appears the end for which the universe exists." Once again, we see that he (and Nietzsche, too) often argues from what he believes is the essence of nature to the psychic or "spiritual" tendencies of man *and* also argues from the posited psychospiritual essence of man to the fundamental characteristic of nature. Both thinkers engage in an anthropomorphic interpretation of the essence of the natural world and then proceed to interpret human nature on the basis of such a conception. Between the two, however, Nietzsche, being a more sophisticated and self-conscious thinker, fully realizes that the human characteristics he transfers to the "essence" of the natural world are expressed in the form of an "hypothesis," a "reduced formula," a metaphorical symbol. In addition, he tries to provide empirical evidence (carefully selected and selectively interpreted) which he thinks will buttress his elaborately constructed myth of the will to power in nature.[56] Even in this regard he follows Emerson's mode of analogical thinking. For he, too, sought to bolster his theories concerning the essential character of nature with poetically interpreted scientific facts and theories. Although neither Emerson nor Nietzsche were serious students of science, they had an intuitive grasp of scientific conceptions and theories of their day and were surprisingly knowledgeable in the sciences.

In his *Nachlass* from 1882, Nietzsche writes: "Will to life? I find in its place always only will to power."[57] So, in effect, did Emerson. If we synthesize his scattered observations, we would see that he argues for the presence of "will" in nature, for the action of a divine power in the natural world, and often points to the analogy between human and natural power. Focusing on the conception of life as a search after power, on the Protean manifestations of power in nature that he refers to, we could construct a notion of reality that is tantamount to Nietzsche's imaginative "ontology" of power. Virtually every aspect of power, every use of the term "power", which Nietzsche refers to or employs, was anticipated in Emerson's writings. In one place or another, he refers to power as psychological potency *(dynamis);* as wealth; as the goal of many religious leaders; as a primary motivational drive in life. Emerson examines the way of life of the "powerful class" and calls attention to the social pursuit of power, and of wealth "as a means to power."[58]

The theme of power, its nature, form and expression, is a dominant one in Emerson's essays and in some of his poems. He refers, in various places, to the increasing power over nature through advances in scientific knowledge; to the magnetism of "personal power"; to the metaphysical "power which . . . makes the whole and the particle its equal channel" in the processes of nature;[59] to the power of a subjective teleology, the power that "resides in the moment of transition from a past to a new state, in the shooting of the gulf, in the darting to an aim";[60] to the power of "illusions" that sustain life and hope; to the rising, negative power of "the masses"; to the "manly" and "noble" power acquired by facing the unpleasant realities of existence and "affronting the horrors of depravity";[61] to an inward experience of inner strength and power (or what Nietzsche calls the "feeling of power"); to the "affirmative power" of faith and ascending life; to the creative/destructive power of nature; to the "scale of powers" (that Nietzsche calls the "order of rank") which runs through the natural world and society; to the power of "beautiful necessity" and fate; to the power of thinkers to imprint their own will upon people, upon entire civilizations;[62] to the energetic creative power of the artist, the power of "the masculine [Michael] Angelo or Celini"[63] (two of Nietzsche's favorite examples of supreme individuals); to the power of the poet to enhance life, to liberate mankind, to inspire and edify with his "*dream*-power";[64] and, finally, to the power of society or "association" to level man, to command "conformity," to punish the "nonconformist," to undermine "individuality," to conspire "against the manhood of every one of its members."[65]

In regard to the social coercion that acts against individuality, it is clear that Emerson's perception of the negative effects of society, combined later with Kierkegaard's criticism of "the crowd" and amplified by Nietzsche's echo of an Emersonian antagonism to the social majority and "public opinion," became one of the central themes of virtually every philosophical tendency associated with existentialism.

Emerson's observations on the "love of power" in man are, generally speaking, not especially critical. Nietzsche, on the other hand, is often critical of the phenomenon in his earliest references to it. The former accepts this primordial desire in man because he believes that it is intrinsic to living beings and is natural in origin. Emerson sometimes does deplore the *means* men use to gain power, but he does not condemn what he construes as a natural drive. He also realizes that "brute force" is not a good in itself any more than the use of immoral means to the end of power is good. Unmitigated "egotism" is not considered morally valuable even though it is rooted in the "life-pulse" of nature.

Emerson shifts his perspective on power and its pursuit quite often and never seems to arrive at an unambiguous, settled opinion on this question. What is interesting in this regard is that we find reflected in Nietzsche's voluminous writings on power precisely this same shifting of perspective. It is when Nietzsche reveals opposing tendencies of thought in his philosophy—specifically in reference to problems raised and discussed by Emerson—that parallel those of Emerson that we see how ensnarled in his modes of thought he was.

Will to Power

Although there is controversy enough concerning the proper interpretation of the meaning of Nietzsche's "theory" of the will to power and about the meaning of his diverse judgments about the role of power in human existence, it is possible to identify a number of key, relatively clear, assertions about power and the will to power in Nietzsche's writings. A fairly straightforward account of his views on this crucial topic may help us to see how closely he followed Emerson's evocative claims about power in nature and in man.

In some of his first observations about power, he conceived of the power-drive as possibly associated with ascetic practices, especially sexual abstinence. He speculates that the Brahmins in the Hindu tradition may have cultivated the experience of a "feeling of power" by virtue of sexual asceticism.[66] In *Daybreak* he once again refers to the Brahmin priests, claiming that they developed "recipes for the feeling of power" by means of heroic self-control.[67] In the same aphorism he goes out of his way to say that Christianity is a religion for those who lack self-control and are unaccustomed to feelings of power. In these references Nietzsche is obviously concerned with a subjective, internalized feeling of power rather than with a public drive for power in the sociohistorical world. Although Emerson sometimes alludes to the "egotism" of religious leaders and to their subjective feelings of power,[68] he focuses mainly on independent, self-reliant persons as paradigmatically possessing a subjective feeling of power.

In a journal entry from 1842, he refers to the richness of the "self-reliant" individual who is the genuine "royalty," who "asks no leave of others' eyes" and who converts lanes into palatial alleys presumably by means of his inner, confident feeling of independent "power."[69] This feeling of mastery and independence is clearly considered a matter of a cultivated, profound "inner" life insofar as it is held that "in the scale of powers it is not talent but sensibility which is best."[70] The point, then, is that Emerson had sketched an image of the independent and self-reliant individual in terms of his subjective feeling of power and had, thereby, anticipated Nietzsche's emphasis upon the enhancement of the subjective sense of power.

Emerson, like Kierkegaard, and almost in his terms, expressed a concern with the "how" of life, with the creation of a "center" for personal, inward existence. At one point, he specifically proclaims that life expresses "not *what*, but how."[71] The feeling of "potency," it is said, enlarges the sphere of our actions.[72] And when we open ourselves to the "fathomless powers" of nature, cultivate our sensibilities, and develop an "inner life," we make our experience of the present "great."[73] Moreover, if we could capture a positive and affirmative principle of life, this principle would express "vast and sudden enlargements of power."[74]

It is clear that Emerson sought to describe, from many different perspectives, the subjective feeling of power that can be attained in an intensified state of spiritual "self-existence." Just as Nietzsche later does, he maintains that the expression of "vigor" is contagious, and whatever makes us either think or feel strongly, adds to our power. Before Nietzsche, Emerson stressed the importance of an inward feeling of power as a goal of existence. Nietzsche seems to complete Emerson's thought by asserting that "the criterion of truth"—a subjective, lived-truth—"is the enhancement of the feeling of power."[75]

In solitude, when a person has only himself as his friend, there is present an indwelling, nameless "Power" that is "superpersonal."[76] This is mysticism, of course, but it is a mode of "mysticism" that is not at all far removed from Nietzsche's concern with a subjective "feeling of power" *(Gefühl des Macht)* that enhances the meaning of our existence. As we shall see, Nietzsche seems to have understood quite well what Emerson was driving at in his poetic-mystical assertions. And he seems to have presented his own version of a peak spiritual experience in what may be called existential mysticism. It was Emerson's combination of calls to self-trust, self-reliance, independence, and "self-existence" with a mystical belief in an immanent "power" that acts through nature and man which provided one of the models for the ideal of a subjective intensification of the *pathos* of existence.

Force/Energy

The metaphysical belief that the complex dynamism of the natural world cannot be explained in terms of mechanistic materialism is shared by Emerson and Nietzsche. In particular, Emerson refers to the power or "spirit" that is within the atom. Nietzsche, too, traces the most primitive expression of the spiritual will to power to atoms and even, in accordance with the eighteenth-century physical theory of Roger Boscovich, to subatomic "centers of force." In his *Nachlass* he designates these hypothetical centers of force "power-units" or "will-points" and conceives of the ultimate constituents of the natural world, as Emerson did, in terms of "human analogy."

The analogies between Nietzsche's thought-experiments concerning the internal dynamics of all phenomena and recent theoretical physics are not coincidental. For Boscovich anticipated, in the late eighteenth century, *some* of the central conceptions of relativity dynamics and subatomic physics. In this regard, Nietzsche goes far beyond Emerson's casual references to microcosmic "atoms." However, it is also the case that Emerson's thinking, starting from the premises of an idealistic metaphysics, provided hints concerning the underlying spiritual nature of reality expressed in material forms that Nietzsche responded to and worked into his general conception of the nature of reality "seen from within."

At the heart of nature, Emerson says again and again, is a "spiritual" process that expresses itself in physical form. When describing this unperceived, though *experienced,* "force" acting through all things, he typically characterizes it as "vital force," "power," or *energy.* In fact, on rare occasions, he even mentions Boscovich,[77] even though what he says about his sophisticated physical theory is insubstantial. The point is that he is the first of a series of thinkers who suggested to Nietzsche that at least *some* physical theories of the structure of the world do not clash with a spiritual voluntaristic conception of reality. In fact, they open the door to precisely such an interpretation. What has been characterized as the "dematerialization" of matter in contemporary physical theory, the reduction of the ultimate constituents of the world to infinitesimal particles of energy, to what amount to dynamic energy-points, was foreshadowed by Nietzsche's philosophical adaptation of Boscovich's startlingly advanced theory of nature.[78]

At the center of all reality, for both Emerson and Nietzsche, is dynamic energy or, to employ the word they ordinarily use, *power.*

Life is a "special case," for both, of this universal force or energy. Now, as previously mentioned, if we grant that power, acting through the organic life of man, comes to self-consciousness (as far as we know) only in man, and if, furthermore, we assume that man is a microcosm, then we can understand why Emerson and then Nietzsche, largely under his influence, interprets the internal dynamics of the natural world in terms of an anthropomorphically construed voluntarism, a metaphorical transference of what is true of man to the natural world.

Power and Growth

In a passage that Nietzsche heavily underlined in his copy of Emerson's *Versuche,* it is said that we admire all "accumulations of power." Elsewhere Emerson applies this notion specifically to the growth of the organism and the consequent storage of "organic power." Such rather vague and general views seem to be carried further in Nietzsche's conception of the nature of organic entities. The distinctive feature of a living being, he contends, is that it "accumulates experiences" and surpasses its previous states.[79] In regard to this specific issue, Emerson quite often hints that there is not only a genetic transmission of traits from generation to generation, but that habits, behaviors, ways of life of our ancestors are transmitted to future generations. Nietzsche, too, believed that acquired traits of character, even feelings, experiences, and valuations, are perpetuated from one generation to the next, that present generations pay a price for the degeneracy of their ancestors. This kind of view is often presented as Nietzsche's "Lamarckian" idea of evolutionary transformation. However, there are only three references to Jean-Baptiste Lamarck in all of Nietzsche's writings and none of them is substantial or marked by enthusiasm for his theory of transformism. Perhaps, as has been plausibly suggested, Nietzsche's understanding of the transmission of acquired characteristics was originally derived from *Emerson,*[80] not Lamarck.

Growth, development, assimilation, the accumulation of memories, experiences, and "valuations" all lie at the basis of organic expressions of the hypothetical will to power. This orientation towards life bears a resemblance to Emerson's iterations concerning "degrees of power" in living beings, the waxing and waning of power in the life-history of organic entities, the tendency in life towards growth and expansion, the increase or decrease of "spirit," "energy," or "power" in the life of the individual, a social class, an entire culture. Emerson posited a tendency in nature towards the creation of new forms of life, as well as the retention, in higher forms of life, of remmants of earlier, more primitive, forms of life. The idea that a primitive "animality" is present in even the most civilized individual, present even in the physical structure of man, was not suggested to Nietzsche by Charles Darwin's theory of evolution by means of natural selection. He had first encountered such views in Emerson's rudimentary sketch of a conception of evolution.

What has been called Nietzsche's "biologism" could easily be seen as a more sophisticated, empirically buttressed, and carefully developed version of Emerson's forays into a bio-spiritual interpretation of actuality. Nature is not, for Emerson, dead, silent, colorless, scentless, soundless; rather, it is dynamic and vital. As Nietzsche later does, he related ascending periods in history to peoples who were energetic. Thereby, he expressed a very general biological conception of cultural development that is quite similar to that of his German admirer. Indeed, Emerson, as Nietzsche after him, strongly suggested the idea, which has long since become a *cliché,* that physiology determines culture. Moreover, he specifically refers to the importance of the effort to overcome "resistances," to the values of difficult circumstances and conditions of existence for an increase in organic strength.[81] This notion that harsh environments or obstacles are contributory to growth and augment power is one that is frequently repeated by Nietzsche. Persistent development and ascending life require a great deal of instinctive drive. Nietzsche practically paraphrases Emerson when he insists that life is imbued with a fundamental "instinct of growth."[82]

Where will to power is lacking, Nietzsche maintains, there is a descending quality of life, even, as he sometimes says, a "will to nothingness." Here this conception pertains to a natural tendency towards growth or development in living beings that is characteristic of the healthy organism. Essentially, the phrase "will to power" (in this context) is a *formula* for the life-process or for a postulated immanent tendency towards increase, expansion, assimilation, or accumulation of power. This notion involves, as it does, in a more subdued way, for Emerson, a transference to nature *in toto* of an anthropomorphic-psychistic propensity: a striving for *more.*

In his protopsychoanalytic psychology, in his various critical analyzes of the concept of "the will," in his biologism, in his ingenious assimilation of Boscovich's dynamic theory of nature, as well as in his tireless explorations of the meanings of, and modalities of, the will to power, Nietzsche transcends Emerson's fertile, experimental reflections. But it is clear that Nietzsche learned as much as he could from Emerson and responded to the stimuli of his rich, original insights.

Among the many treasures that Nietzsche inherited from Emerson there was one conceptual gem that has the power both to fascinate and to petrify: the idea of fate. Thanks to Emerson, Nietzsche struggled throughout his various stages of philosophical development with the riddle of fate or *das Schicksal* that he first encountered in the *Essays*. What is the meaning of fate? And what is the relation between fate and existence, between fate and *my* existence?

Chapter 4 Notes

1. Walter Kaufmann, *Nietzsche: Philosopher, Psychologist, Antichrist*, p. viii.

2. Ibid., p. 179.

3. *Werke* (GOA), IX, p. 297.

4. Kaufmann, *Nietzsche*, p. 180.

5. *SW*, 1, *UB* IV, §8, p. 478.

6. *SW*, 2, *MAM* I, §446, pp. 289–90.

7. "Notes," *COL*, p. 353.

8. *SW* 2, *MAM* II, §226, p. 656.

9. *SW* 3, *M* §23, pp. 24–35.

10. "Notes," *COL*, p. 351, Cp. Nietzsche's claim that "the only power that exists is that of the will" (*Werke* [GOA], XVI, p. 17). Cp. also: "My theory maintains that all productive energy is will to power and that there is no physical, dynamic, or psychological force behind it" (*Werke* [GOA], XVI, p. 152).

11. "Nature," *PE*, p. 31. In his unpublished essay, "On Truth and Lies in a Non-moral Sense" (1873), Nietzsche insisted upon the metaphorical nature of words and the arbitrary designations they express. Language, he claims, simplifies the original experiences it is said to describe. Cf. *SW* 1, pp. 878–79. In later notes Nietzsche asserts that "linguistic means of expression are useless for expressing 'becoming' " (*SW* 13:36).

12. Cf. Lewis Mumford, "The Morning Star," in *The Recognition of Ralph Waldo Emerson*, ed., M. R. Konvitz.

13. *Werke* (GOA), XV, p. 238.

14. Cf. *SW* 3, *FW*. Throughout *The Gay Science* Nietzsche seeks to expose the aesthetic, anthropomorphic and metaphysical basis of man's

scientific interpretations of the natural world. At one point, he asserts that "science is the most exact humanization of things possible" (*SW* 3, *FW* III, §112, p. 473). This jibe at scientific realists may echo Emerson's remark in "Uses of Great Men": "Something is wanting in science until it has been humanized."

15. *SW* 1:875–90. Emerson emphasized the metamorphosis of nature by virtue of the constructive "spiritual" interpretation of natural phenomena. In his *Journals* [VII: 117] he says that "Metamorphosis is the law of the Universe."

16. Sarah Kofman, *Nietzsche et la métaphore*, p. 33.

17. *Werke* (GOA), XIII, 58f. Nietzsche, like Emerson, was a inveterate analogist whose favorite literary device was transference. Sherman Paul correctly links the method of analogy with Emerson's idea of correspondence. Cf. *Emerson's Angle of Vision*, pp. 50, 111, 213–15. Sarah Kofman, under the influence of Derrida, points to Nietzsche's preference for metaphoric language in terms of its uncommonness, its more "noble" nature, etc. However, this is an exaggeration since Nietzsche regards all language as pervaded by metaphors and relies on them himself because he is an analogical thinker and because he holds that there is no "pure" truth, only anthropomorphically colored "truths." In his *Nachlass* he often refers to our categories of thought and our phenomenal knowledge as "true *for us*." Since we cannot see "around the corner" of our evolved way of perceiving and thinking, our "psychology," or our interested perspectives, we cannot attain an impersonal, depersonalized, deindividualized, perfectly objective knowledge.

18. *Werke* (GOA), XIII, 164f.

19. "The American Scholar," *PE*, p. 54.

20. "Nature," *PE*, p. 25. In a journal notation from June 14–15, 1836, Emerson writes that "power is one great lesson which Nature teaches man" (*Emerson in His Journals*, ed. Joel Porte, p. 148).

21. Ibid., p. 50.

22. *Werke* (GOA), XV, 434.

23. "Nature," *PE*, p. 50.

24. "Experience," *PE*, pp. 274–79. Whicher observes that in his middle period Emerson began to conceive of power as a gift of nature, as a product of animal spirits. Human power is derived from natural power. And power in nature is seen as an "aboriginal force." Power is manifested in life, and its ramifications are modalities of "divine energy" (Whicher, *Fate and Freedom*, p. 149). Whicher claims that nature came to lose its "spiritual" associations for Emerson. But it is not so much this as that Emerson has reinterpreted the meaning and expression of the spiritual basis of reality, with an emphasis upon the Protean manifestations of immanent power.

25. "Napoleon; or, the Man of the World," *PE*, pp. 325–45.

26. "Fate," *PE*, p. 361.

27. Ibid., p. 362.

28. Ibid. Cp. Zarathustra's assertion that he has endured the wounds of life by virtue of "something invulnerable, unburiable in him, something rock-splitting: it is called *my will*" (*SW* 4:145).

29. Stanley Hubbard, *Nietzsche und Emerson*, p. 53. Hubbard seems to be reading Nietzsche into Emerson here. For Emerson, unlike Nietzsche, does not explicitly transfer man's interpretive power to all entities. In his "hypothesis" of the will to power Nietzsche attributes interpretation to all actualities, even the nonextended "centers of force" that are posited as the essential processes underlying all dynamic beings.

30. "Notes," *COL*, p. 352.

31. "Experience," *PE*, p. 279. In "The Method of Nature" Emerson virtually epitomizes Nietzsche's picture of nature. "There is something . . . intrusive in the nature of all things; they seek to penetrate and overpower each [other] . . . to prevail and possess" (*RMNAL*, p. 202). Emerson is more explicit in "Uses of Great Men": ". . . every individual strives to grow and exclude and to exclude to grow, to the extremities of the universe, and to impose the law of its being on every other creature." (Ibid, p. 32).

32. "Plato; or, the Philosopher," *PE*, p. 299.

33. *SW* 3, M §204, p. 180.

34. "The American Scholar," *PE*, p. 66.

35. "Plato; or, the Philosopher," *PE*, p. 317.

36. Ibid.

37. *SW* 5, *JGB* §9, p. 22. In *Thus Spoke Zarathustra* Nietzsche attributes the creation of tables of value, the principle of good and evil, as well as the creation of new values, to a spiritual expression of the will to power. Cf. Laurence Lampert, *Nietzsche's Teaching*, pp. 60–61.

38. "Notes," *COL*, pp. 350–51.

39. "Fate," *PE*, pp. 347–48.

40. *SW* 2, *MAM* §61, p. 580. Nietzsche denies he is adopting a "*Türkenfatalismus.*"

41. *SW* 6, G, pp. vi, 8, 96.

42. *The Will to Power*, trans. Walter Kaufmann and R. J. Hollingdale, §712, p. 379.

43. *SW* 12, pp. 507–8.

44. Salter, *Nietzsche the Thinker* pp. 268–69.

45. *SW* 6, ix 48, p. 150.

46. "Power," *COL*, pp. 70–71.

47. Ibid., p. 66.

48. Ibid., p. 71.

49. Ibid. This point is missed in the late A. Bartlett Giamatti's astonishing attack on Emerson's concept of power. He believed that Emerson's secular religion celebrated "political bruisers" and their "unthinking vigor"! The attack on Emerson in "Power, Politics and a Sense of History," in *The University and the Public*, displayed a serious misunderstanding of Emerson's conception of power.

50. Kaufmann, *Nietzsche*, p. 225.

51. *SW* 5, *JGB* §13, p. 27.

52. "Wealth," *COL*, p. 126. The "capitalist" is said not to spend carelessly, but to "hoard for power." Just as Nietzsche worried over the rising "gold aristocracy" or plutocracy of his times, so, too, had Emerson brooded over the effects of the emerging materialism earlier in the nineteenth century: "A question which well deserves examination now is the Dangers of Commerce. This invasion of Nature by Trade with its Money, its Credit . . . threatens to upset the balance of man, and establish a new, universal Monarchy more tyrannical than Babylon or Rome" (*The Journals of Ralph Waldo Emerson*, V:285–86).

53. Cf. George J. Stack, "Marx and Nietzsche: A Point of Affinity," *The Modern Schoolman*.

54. "Wealth," *COL*, pp. 95–96.

55. Ibid., p. 93. Cp. Emerson's early lecture, "Boston." "Wealth is always interesting, since from wealth power cannot be divorced" ("Notes," *COL*, p. 360).

56. George J. Stack, "Nietzsche's Myth of the Will to Power," *Dialogos*.

57. *SW* 10, p. 147.

58. "Culture," *COL*, p. 131.

59. "Nature" (Second Series), *EE*, p. 310.

60. "Self-Reliance," *PE*, p. 152.

61. "Considerations By the Way," *COL*, p. 255.

62. In "Nominalist and Realist," Emerson observes that "each man, too, is a tyrant in tendency, because he would impose his idea on others" (*EE*, p. 332).

63. "Power," *COL*, p. 74.

64. "The Poet," *PE*, pp. 241–65.

65. "Self-Reliance," *PE*, pp. 138–64.

66. *Werke* (GOA), X, 414f.

67. *SW* 3, *M* §62, pp. 62–63.

68. "Nature," (Second Series), *EE*, p. 305.

69. "Notes," *COL*, p. 362. Man's latent power or potentiality enabled favored individuals "to cut loose from nature's determinations and become self-directing agents." Most individuals "belong to the world of fate" (Whicher, *Fate and Freedom*, p. 155). There is a continuity, mitigated by Whicher, between the power of the self-reliant exception described in 1842 and the later increase in Emerson's criticisms of "the many-too-many." Spiritually strong individuals with resoluteness and determination are required to resist or seek to overcome the limitations of fate. The shift from self-reliant individuals to natural aristocrats is not an abrupt one for Emerson.

70. "Success," *Society and Solitude*, p. 278.

71. "Behavior," *COL*, p. 169.

72. Ibid., p. 282.

73. Ibid., pp. 292–93.

74. "Worship," *COL*, p. 213.

75. *"Das Kriterium der Wahrheit liegt in der Steigerung des Machtgefühls"* (*Werke* [GOA], XVI, 45).

76. Ibid., p. 241.

77. "Experience," *PE*, p. 268.

78. Cf. George J. Stack, "Nietzsche and Boscovich's Theory of Nature," *Pacific Philosophical Quarterly.*

79. *Werke* (GOA), XIII, p. 231.

80. Hubbard, *Nietzsche und Emerson*, pp. 32, 80.

81. "Considerations By the Way," *COL*, pp. 254–55.

82. *Werke* (GOA), XI, p. 253.

Chapter 5

Fate and Existence

Nature's dice are always loaded.
[Ralph Waldo Emerson, Nature]

In a preface to *Human, All-too-Human*, written in 1886, Nietzsche refers to Arthur Schopenhauer as his "first and only teacher." His recollection was incorrect on both counts. He had many teachers besides Schopenhauer and he was *not* his first teacher. His first teachers were the ancient Greeks whose language and culture he assiduously studied from an early age. However, aside from the impact of ancient Greek literature and philosophy on his thought, the one thinker who initially seems to have led him to philosophical vistas that attracted him (and helped turn his interest away from philological studies that were beginning to bore him) was Emerson.

Unlike Plato, Kant, Hegel, Leibniz, and the host of technically brilliant thinkers in the Western tradition, Emerson was a literary philosopher, a polished stylist who handled big questions with panache and a deft light touch. Even though Nietzsche had a critical, analytical mind that could chop theories, conceptions, and beliefs to pieces with the best of them, he preferred to present his published thoughts in a nontechnical form and to philosophize in a grand style. Like Emerson, he had a decided preference for the rhetorical argument. His critical thinking usually went on behind the scenes, preserved in journals that rival in length the ten volumes of Emerson's *Journals,* but exceed them in philosophical subtlety and analytical power.

It has been said of Emerson that his *forte* was the vivid and striking sentence. Malcolm Crowley remarks that, at his best, he created genuine sentences in the Latin sense of the word: "ideas briefly and pungently expressed as axioms."[1] This tendency to compress general observations or theoretical points into pithy sentences or compact paragraphs may have contributed to Nietzsche's preference for an aphoristic style. And this feature of his writing obviously affects the way he presents his thought and the way it is received. He doesn't wrestle with a problem or philosophical theme; he duels with it: thrust, parry, riposte.

Before one can duel with a philosophical problem, one must first recognize it, inherit it, have it impressed upon one, as a problem. Given Nietzsche's almost reverential attitude towards Emerson's *Essays* when he was young and his rereading of them over a twenty-six year period, and given his respect for the man and his thought, it would be natural if some of the primary issues in his philosophy centered around themes that were first posed by Emerson. As we've seen, and as we shall continue to see, there are very strong, clearly identifiable, conceptual-imaginative connections between Emerson and Nietzsche in regard to a number of philosophical ideas. The agreement between the two on the question of the meaning of, and role of, fate in existence is one of the strongest of these connections.

The Problem of Fate

With rare exceptions,[2] there is a general tendency to circumvent Nietzsche's conception of fate in many interpretations of his philosophy. To be sure, appropriate passages are usually cited, and there is the obligatory quotation of the phrase *amor fati* ("love of fate"). But there is a conspicuous absence of any extended commentary on this idea and few questions are raised about how Nietzsche's acceptance of fate coheres with his army of exhortations to become ourselves, to "create beyond ourselves," to strive for "self-overcoming," to "remain faithful to the earth," to live in such a way that we would want to have our life eternally repeated. The fact that Nietzsche freely accepts a fatalism governing human life does not stop him from proposing his "morality of strenuousness." Nor does it stop him from barraging individuals with categorical "existential" imperatives. All of Nietzsche's exhortations

imply that we *can* change our lives, that we can change our nature
(or *physis*), that we possess some freedom.

What exactly does Nietzsche mean by "fate"? How does he rec-
oncile, if he does, its overriding power with constant appeals to effort, to striving, creating, willing, acting? If we were nothing but
sophisticated organic computers programmed to feel as we do, to
think as we do, to act as we do, to choose as we do, to be as we
must be, what would be the point of urging us to become other
than we are? Is it not clear that if fatalism, in any strict sense, dom-
inates our existence from birth (and, in fact, in terms of genetic determinism, *before* birth) to death, then freedom is an illusion or a
pathetic delusion?

In his comparative study, *The Image of Emerson in Nietzsche's
Work and Life,*[3] Eduard Baumgarten cites analogical conceptions
and themes and similarities of language that he discovered in the
works of Emerson and the writings of Nietzsche. He hunts down
passages in the body of Nietzsche's works (most of which have already been cited) that he believed, quite rightly, to have been derived from Emerson's essays. What he did not do, and what has
not been done by anyone previously, was to trace substantial and
detailed similarities of thought in the works of the American essayist and the writings of the German philosopher. Baumgarten
does not go much beyond indicating family resemblances between
the language of the two thinkers. The resemblances between key
doctrines, theories, and conceptions in the philosophy of Nietzsche and the impressionistic theories and conceptions of Emerson
are not carefully examined. What is at issue in the relation between
Emerson and Nietzsche is not only a matter of shared turns of
phrase, words, or tropes. Rather, it is a question of a deep, highly
specific transmission of ideas from one to the other, ideas that lie at
the center of Nietzsche's constructive thought and are considered
his original creations.[4] Ironically, perhaps by looking backward to
the original American template of these patterns of thought we
may gain a better understanding of what Nietzsche meant.

We already know that by the summer of 1862 Nietzsche had
read two of Emerson's essays, "Fate" (*Fatum*) and "History" (*Geschichte*). He was still immersed in his classical studies at the Pforta
school and outwardly appeared to accept Christianity. However,
his notes and writings in his youth already showed that he looked
upon the Christian religion as a reflection of the childhood of the
people and viewed a veneration of the "other world," "the beyond," as a theft of the "divinity" of this world. In his earliest es-

say, *"Fatum und Geschichte,"* written in 1862, he criticizes the Christian religion as a belief based upon *"Gewohnheit und Vorurteil"* ("custom and prejudice"), a belief pressed upon individuals in their earliest, formative years. As he will later say, in dramatic voice, the journey into a "sea of doubt" (as a consequence of the rejection of religious faith) could be perilous for man. Surrounded by an "ocean of ideas" that are strange and new, many would long to be on the *terra firma* of faith once again. The title of this essay, as well as its central themes, is derived from Emerson. Its central thrust pertains to the problem of the meaning and implications of fatalism and the relation between fate and history, fate and freedom of the will. In this terse essay there is a reference to the role of temperament in relation to personality and behavior that specifically refers to Emerson's thoughts on this question in "Fate." Nietzsche paraphrases Emerson in the following way: *"Frage geistreiche Mediziner, sagt Emerson, wie viel Temperament nicht entscheidet und was es überhaupt nicht entscheidet."*[5] This somewhat awkward paraphrase is more clearly stated in Emerson's original remark: ". . . ask the doctors . . . if temperaments decide nothing?—or if there is anything they do not decide?"

In his copy of Emerson's *Versuche* Nietzsche underlined the following passage: *"Freiheit ist nothwendig . . . die menschliche Freiheit ein Theil des Fatums . . . so wie der Mensch denkt, ist er frei"* ("Freedom is necessary . . . the freedom of man is part of fate. . . . So far as man thinks, he is free"). What he writes in "Fate and History" is not quite the same as this even though Emerson's meaning is, more or less, captured. He states that ". . . *der freie Wille nichts als die höchste Potenz des Fatums . . . Freiheit des Willens, in sich nichts anders als Freiheit des Gedankens"* (". . . Free will is nothing but the highest potency of fate. . . . Freedom of the will in itself [is] nothing other than freedom of thought").

Fate and Freedom

Having argued that the conditions of human life impose "fatal" limitations on man, that man's temperament determines a great deal of his behavior and values, Emerson seems to locate freedom in man's intentional consciousness. Although his language is simpler and more direct than the language Jean-Paul Sartre uses in *Being and Nothingness,* what Emerson says about freedom in thought is not far removed from Sartre's basic posit: man is free essentially *as* consciousness.

It should be noted that Nietzsche translates Emerson's statement that we are free when we think into the view that "freedom of will" is "freedom of thought." By doing so, he apparently missed a point (which he later picks up) that Emerson makes in "Experience." For there it is said that "I would gladly . . . allow the most to the will of man, but I have set my heart on honesty in this chapter."[6] Thus, Emerson *denies* freedom of the will, but affirms freedom of thought, even in relation to fate. Therefore, in his first response to Emerson's thought Nietzsche mistakenly believes that he intended to equate freedom of will and freedom of thought.

The problem of fate and freedom will haunt Nietzsche's philosophical reflections insofar as he engages in a sustained polemic against the assumption of freedom of the *will,* but, at the same time, he continues to search for some acceptable modality of freedom, a real, if limited, power of freedom. Of all the paradoxes in the philosophy of Nietzsche, the most paradoxical notion pertains to the insistence upon a universal fatalism and the simultaneous assumption of subjective 'power' or a capacity to change one's life, to respond to imperatives, to exercise a presumably negated freedom.

The challenge of "the ought" in Nietzsche's thought would be completely nullified if we understood his commitment to fatalism to mean the obliteration of the possibility of freedom in any form. He asserts that a profound "fatality" pervades our being. In the next breath, however, he implies freedom and responsibility for the kind of life we lead, for the kind of person we are. Nietzsche intensifies the paradox of fate and freedom, which he inherited from Emerson, to a greater degree. The paradoxical acceptance of fate and freedom that Emerson embraced is carried over into Nietzsche's thought and is spread on a larger canvas, exposed to a more intense, dramatic, philosophical illumination.

Nietzsche, relatively early in his development, denied that he defended a "Turkish fatalism." That is, he denies that fate and man are two separate things in diametrical opposition to one another. Fate is not, like the Greek *Moira,* a transcendental power that manipulates men as if they were puppets and determines their destiny. Nor is fate the ineluctable working out of a cosmic destiny as in the Turkish concept of kismet (*qismah*). The characterization of this mode of fatalism was derived from Emerson's depiction of the "Turk" who accepted his foreordained destiny in "Fate." Although he does not adopt this idea of fate, Emerson expresses a distant respect for this mentality: "The Turk, who believes his doom is written on the iron leaf in the moment when he entered the world, rushes on the enemy's sabre with undivided will."

Emerson's interpretation of man as subject to powerful fatalities cast a long shadow on Nietzsche's thought. It is present in the piece of juvenilia he wrote in 1862, "Fate and History," and it reappears in a passionate passage in *Twilight of the Idols* ("The Four Great Errors," §8). Although the language of this passage is far more intense and dramatic than that of Emerson, the ideas expressed in this work of 1888, as well as some of the words and phrases, are Emerson's. *"No one,"* Nietzsche writes,

> is accountable for existing at all, or for being constituted as he is, or for living in the circumstances and surroundings in which he lives. The fatality [*Fatalität*] of his nature cannot be disentangled from the fatality of all that has been and will be. . . . One is necessary, one is a piece of fate [*ein Stück Verhängniss*], one belongs to the whole, one *is* in the whole.

In "The Method of Nature" and especially in "Fate," Emerson characterized the individual as a "necessary" piece of a dynamic cosmic process, as subject to "circumstances" that are out of his or her control, as conditioned by a host of natural "fatalities." And the pithy phrase that is so closely identified with Nietzsche—"a piece of fate"—was derived from Emerson's essay, "Nominalist and Realist." Describing there how he reads authors for stimulation of his imagination, he remarks that he doesn't simply read a particular author (a Plato, say, or a Proclus). Rather, it is "but a piece of nature and fate that I explore."[7] In another place, he characterizes man as a "piece of causation."

Nietzsche accurately expresses Emerson's understanding of the power of psychic, temperamental factors that affect our being, our feelings, and our behavior when, in *Beyond Good and Evil* (§23), he insists that "at our core, intact "deep down," there is . . . something unteachable, some granite of spiritual fate." There are also, as Nietzsche believed (following Emerson's observations), the genetic inheritances that our parents and their ancestors have transmitted to us. And there is the fundamental physiological determination of our nature that is epitomized, in "Fate and History," virtually in the language of Emerson's "Fate": "A fatalistic structure of skull and backbone."[8] The roots of our being run back through the history of nature. And we have inherited, as Emerson puts it, the fate of the "natural history" of our species. If we would

look, with unsentimental eyes, on the condition of all livings beings, we would see that "The book of Nature is the book of Fate."

Even though Emerson emphasized, with a sense of realism that
belies the usual portrayals of him as a glassy-eyed optimist, the
"negative power" of circumstances, the limitations of fate that circumscribe our existence, he insists on preserving the paradox of
necessity and freedom. Although there are, indeed, "immovable
limitations" to which we are subject, we can also "affirm liberty,
the significance of the individual, the grandeur of duty, the power
of character." The individual is and 'becomes' in the world. Nature
or fate places genuine limits on our possibilities. At this point, we
could remind Emerson that he once told us, in *Nature,* that the
world exists *for us*. But if we did so, he might reply that this is the
case from the perspective of subjective consciousness and experience, even though, from the perspective of man's being-in-nature,
it is obscured. In fact, in a rudimentary way, Emerson seems to be
expressing a central point in Heidegger's *Being and Time*. That is,
there is *Dasein* [human being] insofar as there is a world, and there
is a world insofar as there is *Dasein*. The natural world acts upon
us and through us and shapes much of our being. However, for
Emerson, we inevitably interpret the world in anthropomorphic
terms, see it as existing for us as field for our actions, as a Protean
realm of forms we may contemplate, as a source of power, as a
symbolic realm of material poetry. Even though we may not
know *how,* Emerson suggests, we are convinced that "freedom is
necessary," that "a part of Fate is the freedom of man."

The early nineteenth-century preoccupation with the "Spirit of
the Times" (The Hegelian *Zeitgeist?*) detracts us, Emerson believes
(as his Danish contemporary, Kierkegaard, also believes), from the
far more important question of how one ought to live, "the conduct of life." The central question of human life, even in relation to
an acceptance of the fatalism of nature and a recognition of the
spirit of the historical age, is, "How shall I live?" In an assertion
that is reminiscent of Kierkegaard and of Nietzsche's strand of *Existenz* philosophy, Emerson proclaims that "the riddle of the age
has for each a private solution."

"Sacred Courage"

Aware that in his earlier essays he had put the accent heavily on
individuality, self-reliance, independence, and affirmative "self-

existence," Emerson wants to redress the ontological balance in "Fate." Noting that America has a bad name for "superficialness," a reputation that has been exacerbated by time, he wants some honesty about the human condition. Honesty was as much an important existential category and virtue for Emerson as it later became, as *Redlichkeit,* for Nietzsche. His way of preparing us for this honest perception of the condition of man needs no commentary in regard to its affinity with Nietzschean thought and language: "Great men, great nations, have not been boasters and buffoons, but perceivers of the terror of life, and have manned themselves to face it."[9] Emerson, the sensitive idealist, forces himself to face and to think about the terrible realities of life even though this goes against the grain just as Nietzsche, the sensitive, poetic thinker, later forces himself, by an act of "self-overcoming," to face the realities of existence. What is distinctive about the general philosophical orientation of Emerson and Nietzsche is a fundamental idealistic-realism or realistic-idealism. Given the strong influence of the former on the latter, there is little doubt that Nietzsche received his first initiation into the fraternity of philosophical realism from Emerson. Both emphasize the "manly" attitude towards life that a realistic sense of the negativities of existence signifies. When Nietzsche later discovered Schopenhauer, he encountered a veritable *Walpurgisnacht* of realism.

Nietzsche's repeated expression of the need to face "ugly truths," to see reality "as it is," to look into the heart of darkness of existence is, despite the genuine passion behind such admonitions, foreshadowed by Emerson's similar exhortation. Here we find a coincidence not only of thought, but of sincere feeling and rhetorical means of expression.

Emerson and Nietzsche made great efforts to overcome their natural gentleness and sensitivity. They were, on this score, definitely soul-brothers. When he read Emerson, as he admits, Nietzsche felt a surge of recognition, a sense of kinship with the American he would never know. When someone else expresses in writing clearly and effectively what we ourselves feel, believe, or think, it is natural for us to admire these expressions of thought, to quote them, paraphrase them, and, thereafter, unconsciously express them in our own language. Nietzsche's agreement with Emerson on certain important points was so intimate that he quite often underwent an unconscious process of cognitive-linguistic assimilation.

The beauty, spectacle, order and creative tendencies of the natural world are only one side of a larger canvas that has a very dark side indeed. Nature is beautiful and cruel; awesome and chilling; creative and destructive. If we would deepen ourselves and develop our character, Emerson advises, then we must face "the horrors of depravity" in order to gain "nobilities of power." The order of nature certainly reveals a balance, but it is a "balance of beauty and disgust, magnificence and rats."[10] If we would overcome excessive sensitivity and dreamy romantic fantasy, we must "replace sentimentalism by realism, and dare to uncover those simple and terrible laws which . . . pervade and govern."[11] In a decidedly proto-Nietzschean mood, Emerson laments the proneness to hypersensitivity of scholars, thinkers, and theologians who are shocked by the actions of people in "the street," who are horrified by a publicized "brutal act." We should learn to look the brutality in nature and in man in the eye. We should not be cowed by the moral monsters of history or by their horrible deeds. Rather, we should be able to accept, in a natural way, the reality of "beast-like men" and hope that these remnants of nature's brutal past shall one day pass away. If we insist on being thinkers, Emerson writes, "we must think with courage."[12] And if we aspire to emulate the "courage of genius," we must recognize that this requires a certain "quantity of power."[13]

In dozens of places, Emerson urges his readers to cultivate a "manly courage," to have the intellectual courage to face the truly terrible and ugly realities of existence. He typically speaks in martial language to the scholar, the thinker, the person of faith, encouraging tough-mindedness and a disciplining of the mind and heart. As if overcompensating for his own sensitivity (as Nietzsche does *con brio*), Emerson advises the thinker to study the "dangers which . . . invade men," "to familiarize himself with disgusting forms of disease, with sounds of execration, and the vision of violent death."[14] Given the psychological kinship that he felt with him, there is little doubt that Nietzsche adopted the attitudes that Emerson prescribed for existence and thought, that, in point of fact, he continued to convey them to others, intensifying Emerson's message. Doesn't he claim often enough to practice what is clearly recognizable as what Emerson preached? In *Ecce Homo,* for example, he announces that "my truth is terrible." He claims to have uncovered "ugly truths" and to have torn the veils of illusion from actuality. He has seen, he tells us, into the primordial and terrible reality that lies beneath the veneer of civilized existence. Observing that there is a great deal that man does not know about himself, that man's body conceals from him the subtle organic processes that maintain his vital physiological functions (a distinctively Emersonian observation), Nietzsche bemoans "that fatal curiosity that might one day have the power to look out and down through a crack in the chamber of consciousness and then suspect that man is sustained in the indifference of his ignorance by what is pitiless, greedy, insatiable, and murderous—as if hanging in dreams on the back of a tiger."[15]

Following Emerson's advice, Nietzsche takes every opportunity to dig beneath the surface of life, to peek behind the coulisses and expose realities that are typically unpleasant. We contain within ourselves, Emerson once said, a natural history that recapitulates the forms of life that have appeared on earth. This natural history links us to the "ferocity" of nature itself. Nature conceals from us, by means of deceptive appearances and "illusions," the coarse details of our primitive being. This general approach to *homo natura,* including the proto-psychoanalytical suggestions of what Freud later calls the *Id,* the primordial unconscious source of aggressive and sexual instinctive drives, was originally suggested to Nietzsche by Emerson.

Not only in nature, but in society as well, Emerson finds deception and illusions galore. Normally, he says, we live amidst "surfaces." However, the elemental springs of our life are "related to all nature" and especially to the natural history of man. The powers of man are comprised of his multiplicity of affinities. An individual's life "is intertwined with the whole chain of organic and inorganic being."[16] In fact, the individual may be construed as a "bundle of relations" that is bound to the highest powers of nature and to other, more sinister, forms of life. "The habit of snake and spider, the snap of the tiger and other leapers and bloody jumpers, the crackle of the bones of his prey in the coil of the anaconda,—these are in the system, and our habits are like theirs."[17]

We should remind ourselves that Emerson is not suggesting a Darwinian theory of evolution by means of natural selection insofar as he expressed his own conception of the evolutionary continuity of nature many years before the appearance, in 1859, of Darwin's *The Origin of Species.* The point about Emerson's ideas concerning man's place in nature is that man is related to the natural history of life and is inextricably a part of the web of associations of the natural world. Man partakes, as Nietzsche will later say, of the uncanny duality of nature and has, therefore, an antagonistic character. Whether we look out to external nature or into ourselves (ourselves as microcosms reflecting the whole of actuality), we find this struggle of, or antagonism of, forces. Later, when Nietzsche identifies as a chief characteristic of reality the "antithesis character of existence,"[18] he is espousing an Emersonian conception of nature and of man-in-nature.

Fate and Freedom

In his interpretation of Nietzsche, Karl Jaspers refers to the essay written by a young Nietzsche (i.e., "Fate and History") and points out that he then held that fate places man in organic relation to the total development of nature. And he cites a variation on this theme that he did not recognize as Emerson's: "Absolute freedom of the will without fate would make man into God." While, on the other hand, a complete acceptance of a "fatalistic principle" would make of man an "automaton."[19] In his early philosophical foray, it would seem that Nietzsche had simply drawn out the consequences of what Emerson had said about fatalism. He did not, however, present a view that was inconsistent with Emerson's paradoxical assertion that "freedom is necessary," that man is conditioned by "fatalities" that shape his being *and* that he possesses freedom, albeit a limited, finite freedom.

In regard to the necessitations of life, Emerson maintained that as soon as the individual is born "the gate of gifts closes behind him." Some people are, by temperament, prone to concentrate their energy in sexuality and "digestion." If such people give birth to a "superior individual," they and their ancestors are soon forgotten. In the context of this discussion, he expresses a harsh judgment that is by no means uncommon in his writings and one which, like other similar remarks, will infiltrate Nietzsche's thought and seep into his language. Commenting on the demise of certain types of individuals, he says: "The more of these drones perish, the better for the hive." For a man who writes glowingly about love and who sometimes proclaims his loving concern for all humanity, Emerson is quite capable of stern judgments about those he considers lesser mortals, judgments that will be echoed in the sound-chamber of Nietzsche's thoughts about *homo sapiens*. Despite his philosophical idealism and "transcendentalism," or because of it, Emerson is definitely not a sentimentalist about men. This aloof, disdainful, aristocratic attitude of mind plays an important role in his blueprint for exceptional types of human being, a blueprint that Nietzsche saw clearly and understood so well that he co-opted it in *his* design for "supreme men."

Returning to the question of the relation between fate and freedom, it is probable that by the time he wrote *Daybreak,* Nietzsche had adapted Emerson's notion that freedom is part of fate to his own reflections and, in the following passage, he adds the Emersonian idea that we all live, for the most part, on the surface of things. He observes that "our thinking is superficial and content with the surface. . . . the realm of thought appears to be, in comparison with the realm of action, willing and experience, a *realm of freedom:* while in reality it is . . . only a realm of surfaces and self-satisfaction."[20]

As the above illustrates, Nietzsche rarely simply appropriates an idea from another thinker. Rather, he works it over in his mind; examines it from many angles, pares it, reshapes it so that a new perspective is revealed. Thus, he criticizes the notion of *absolute* freedom of consciousness. He agrees with Emerson in holding that we live, for the most part, at a surface level of consciousness. He also agrees that our freedom, as limited as it may be, is relatively greater in thought than it is in action, willing, and experience. As he shows in his later writings, Nietzsche believes that our conscious thinking is often influenced by socially adaptive, typical, ordinary ways of thought that reflect inherited linguistic habits and the "genius of the species" or the patterns of thought that have proven useful to the survival of the species. More than that, he contends that *unconscious* thought-processes take place and unintended thoughts come as, and when, they will. To this extent, there is a certain unfreedom in human consciousness.

What Nietzsche is concerned with, in part, is to deny that our ordinary consciousness is free. He wanted to avoid the cognitive pathway that later led from Kant to Sartre. If he had agreed with Kant that freedom is rooted in "consciousness-in-general," then it would be but a step to the position that Sartre later adopted: that is, that consciousness is the basis of our (presumed) "absolute" freedom. In point of fact, Nietzsche viewed the world of conscious thought as "a second degree of the phenomenal world."[21] He argued that cognitive content that becomes overt in our field of awareness is a *terminal* process that results in an organized, schematized, simplified notion that is an 'inner' phenomenon. Although it would be out of place here to track the various aspects of Nietzsche's complicated account of the cognitive process, there is an obvious connection between him and Emerson even in regard to this particular aspect of his reflections. In addition, what he had repeatedly implied is made explicit by Nietzsche: ideally, thought and knowledge ought to become *instinctive*.

Instinct versus Intellect

In his essay, "Intellect," Emerson refers to the growth of the intellect as "spontaneous" and relegates much of our thinking to the "web of unconsciousness." Thinking that has not yet become congealed in an impersonal object is a receptive process. "We do not determine what we will think." Indeed, despite common beliefs on the subject, we actually "have little control over our thoughts." Prior to the emergence of logical or scientific thinking, he claims, there is a spontaneous, instinctive, unconscious cognitive process that is dominant.

The process of abstract thought takes us beyond "the circumstance of daily life" in which we are "open to the mercy of coming events." Emerson construes ideas separated by the intellect from a living context, as converted into something "impersonal and immortal." And the image he uses to describe this process of elevating and preserving abstract concepts obviously caught Nietzsche's eye. When concepts are separated by the intellect from the actual circumstance of life, Emerson writes, they are "embalmed. A better art than that of Egypt has taken fear and corruption out of [them]. . . . [They are] envicerated of care . . . offered for science."[22]

What was for Emerson a rather mild ironic comment on the eternalizing of concepts is, in Nietzsche's critical remarks on reason in philosophy, converted into a polemical barrage. However, the metaphorical image of this habit of intellection is the same as that of Emerson. Nietzsche lambastes philosophers for their "Egyptianism" because they make a "mummy" of the process of "becoming" and produce "conceptual mummies."[23] Although we've strayed a bit from our main concern here, we can see, in this instance, as in many others, how closely Nietzsche follows Emerson's most casual suggestions and how receptive he is to his language and images. This same process of assimilation is found in his way of dealing with the paradox of fate and freedom.

What has been shown thus far is that Nietzsche more or less agrees with Emerson about the *relative* freedom of consciousness and the superficial nature of ordinary patterns of thought. However, he wants to undermine the conception of man as an intentional thinking agent capable of creating or discovering truth by means of pure reason. Nietzsche, like Emerson, but with considerably greater philosophical finesse, wants to deny the absolute value of pure reason in order to preserve the value of instinctive thinking, spontaneous thought, or the contributions of the unconscious to our understanding.

Our cognitive roots run back into the natural, prelogical world, into the primitivity of "instinct." Committed to such a view, Nietzsche characterizes pure reason as a pure fiction. This is precisely the point that Emerson made in his discussion of intellection. For he gives priority to spontaneous intuition over "the arithmetical or logical." Logic is the terminus of a procession that follows from the unfolding of intuition and spontaneous, instinctive cognition. The proper order of the development of human understanding is: instinct, opinion, knowledge. And, as we might expect, we are urged to trust our "instinct." Emerson insists that the cognition of the "genius" is neither discursive nor follows in accordance with the pattern of deductive inference. Rather, it is essentially "spontaneous." The repeated emphasis on spontaneity or "naturalness" (*die Ungezwungenheit Natürlichkeit, Spontaneität*) in Nietzsche's positive philosophy is indebted to vintage Emersonian attitudes and values.

Even though Emerson praises the creations of the intellect and admires the class of conceptual geniuses ("these great spiritual lords"), it is quite clear that he was fascinated by the presence of the nonrational in life and human nature. As Nietzsche later did, he attempted to defend the paradoxical view that reason and logic emerged out of the primordial, nonrational dimensions of the self. Intense life, deep feeling, spontaneity, intuition, instinct, and the subjective enhancement of existence have as much priority over rationality for him as they later have for Nietzsche. No doubt Nietzsche was temperamentally attracted to this message of Emerson's, and he characteristically exaggerated it.

A great deal that is condemned by some in Nietzsche's philosophy—in this instance, the preference for life over reason, for spontaneity over cool reflection, instinctive thought over logical inference—is actually found, in embryo, in Emerson's calmly stated, but then philosophically radical, insights. The petard of a philosophy of spontaneous life was first employed by Emerson before it was used by Nietzsche in a later philosophical combat.

Pieces of Fate

Returning again to the question of the relation of fate to existence, it can be seen that Emerson laid the groundwork for Nietzsche's theme of the place of man in the total system of relations comprising nature and for his understanding of both the positive and negative meaning of fate. Man in nature, for both, exists in a series of temporal relations and is a part of the web of relations that runs through the cosmos. The individual, at every moment of his or her existence, is intricately involved in a serial and momentary system of relations. Nietzsche brings these notions together in his most exotic philosophical conception: the idea of the eternal recurrence of the same.

The suggestion put forward by Emerson that each individual is linked to nature, history, and society in a complex web of relations is later reinforced in Nietzsche's mind, from a scientific point of view, by F. A. Lange. For Lange had argued that nothing exists in isolation; that all beings are interconnected in a "relations-world."[24] If it were possible to remove an entity from all relations to other beings, it would no longer exist. There is no "subject-in-itself."

Following Emerson and Lange, Nietzsche conceived of existence as relational. The individual conceived of (as in Max Stirner's philosophy of radical individuality) as the "single one" is, strictly speaking, an exaggeration, an "error." What we call "the individual" is, Nietzsche asserts, "the whole *single* line of man up to himself."[25] Although this is sometimes taken to be a *denial* of the reality of the individual, it is actually an attempt to place the individual in the contexts of nature, history, and society. It is a denial of the atomistic, isolated, anarchic 'individual' portrayed, for example, in Max Stirner's *The Ego and His Own*.

Emerson and Nietzsche, despite their respect for, and promotion of, individuality, were primarily concerned with superior types of human beings who would rejuvenate culture, who would provide a center about which a higher, ennobling, life-enhancing culture could be spun. The streak of existential individualism that runs through the writings of Emerson and Nietzsche is real enough and sincere enough, but atomistic individualism was not the goal of their philosophical aspirations. They both wanted to project a philosophy of culture or a stimulating, rejuvenating, disciplinary cultural ideal.

The assimilation of Emerson's emphasis on fatality in existence in Nietzsche's conception of an eternally recurring sequence of "the same" events and lives does present him with problems in regard to his defense of genuine, innovative individuality and a presumed potentiality for becoming oneself, for change, for "self-overcoming." These problems are foreshadowed in Emerson's dual defense of individuality and fatalism. Nietzsche inherited from him (and exacerbated) this tension between an emphasis upon affirmative, independent *Existenz* and both the concept of the dominance of fate and the "hypothesis" of a will to power *acting through* man. For both thinkers, the individual is circumscribed by, and limited by, "circumstances" or "conditions of existence." Man is acted upon by the physical, historical, social, and cultural factors without and by the physiological and psychological factors within the self. Neither hold that man is absolutely free or absolutely unfree. They stress the paradoxical tension between spontaneous, creative freedom and the "tyranny of circumstances." They wanted to admit the determinations of nature that act upon us and to preserve the springs of creative, innovative individuality.

An amateur geneticist, Emerson ponders the question concerning the procreation of the "superior individual" and sketches the decline of generations by virtue of a draining of "vital force" into specialized development to a point at which a potentially talented person finally appears, only to turn out to be unhealthy and unable to reproduce. This reflection leads Emerson to admit the deep influence of fate on human destiny and to worry about the "despotism of race," the despotism of genetically transmitted defects that lead to decline and eventual dissolution. Although he often applauds the advances of transformational development, he also saw that the genetic changes in the human population from generation to generation sometimes engender devolution.

The accumulation of past traits and propensities and their effects upon a person's abilities or limitations gives credence, Emerson believes, to Schelling's judgment that "there is in every man a certain feeling that he has been what he is from all eternity, and by no means became such in time." Although he does not accept such an ultrafatalistic notion, he broods over the determining factors that shape human nature. As if anticipating sociobiological thought, Emerson grants the importance of physiological determinants of behavior, even to the point of admitting their influence on social and political values. We feel free and we believe in our "positive power," but we tend to forget the limitations on our freedom and power imposed on us by the "negative power" of circumstances. In an image that Nietzsche will remember, Emerson points to the "thick skull," the "ponderous, rock-like jaw" that virtually "necessitated action" and inclines an individual in a "violent direction."

Generalizing from reflections on genetic and physiological determinism, Emerson sees the same conditioning process at work in entire nations and peoples. Many groups of people are doomed to hard work, drudgery, and premature death. And the behaviors of large numbers of individuals seem to obey impersonal statistical laws. A predictable fatality seems to haunt human existence. Large populations tend to produce, over a period of time, out of millions, a genius here and there. Events that appear on the surface to be fortuitous actually occur with a kind of "mechanical exactness" or statistical regularity. Our life is not what it seems to be from our subjective, psychological perspective. We *experience* chance, openness, contingency, and freedom, but "our life is walled up." The force of circumstances, the mass of contingent factors that act upon us, make our feeble protests ridiculous. We are like a "minority of one, under compulsion of millions." This awesome reality of circumstances can neither be denied nor surpassed. "No picture of life can have any veracity that does not admit the odious facts. A man's power is hooped in by a necessity which, by many experiments, he touches on every side until he learns its arc."[26]

A "ring of necessity" surrounds our life, and limitations run through our entire existence, through all of nature. There appears to be a "rank in the scale of nature" that is difficult, if not impossible, to alter. This reference to a natural order of rank was no doubt the earliest imprint that Nietzsche received of a conception he later introduces into his constructive philosophy: he wants to institute an "order of rank" (*Rangordnung*) that will be "natural" and which will recognize gradations of value in the world, will negate "sameness" or the valuational equality of all things and of all persons. This is a theme we will return to later when we look at the influence of Emerson's thoughts on a scale of rank in nature and society on Nietzsche's "aristocratic radicalism."

Physical traits, psychic dispositions, morality, and character are all conditioned by factors outside the individual's control. If Emerson stopped at this point, he would have had to abandon all of his exhortations to self-development, to becoming a genuine person, to courage, to self-reliance. He would presumably have to resign himself to the dispensations of fate no matter what they might be. But he contends that fate is matched by power. Although the fatalities of nature certainly limit power, power is antagonistic to fatalism. In his *Journal* of 1852, Emerson reflects on this paradox.

On the one hand, there is the force of natural laws that crush human wishes, the gross and insidious factors that impose limits on our nature and action. But what, he asks himself, is limited? Power. The exertion of power.

Despite the limitations circumscribing our existence, we have thought and insight and the capacity to exercise our will. Our subjective sense of choice and our feelings of "sovereignty" in a restricted domain develops a "strong will."[27] The duality in nature between fate and power is recapitulated in the antagonistic nature of man. Nietzsche seems to have such an idea in mind when he refers to the antithetical nature of all existence.[28] As in the case of Emerson, this understanding of nature and reality is anthropomorphically conditioned insofar as we are told that "Nature must be represented by analogy to man, as erring, experimenting, good and evil, as struggling and overcoming itself."[29] This is a fundamentally Emersonian-Nietzschean propensity: to move freely from natural analogy to man and from human analogy to nature. Nature is construed as an antagonism of forces because man (the microcosm) is understood in that way. And man is construed as an antithetical confluence of forces because nature (the macrocosm) is conceived of in this way. Emerson poetically expresses this intimate relation between man and nature proclaiming that

> the lightning which explodes and fashions planets, maker of planets and suns, is in him. On one side elemental order . . . and on the other part thought, the spirit which composes and decomposes nature,— here they are . . . god and devil, mind and matter, king and conspirator . . . riding . . . together in the eye and brain of . . . man.[30]

Many of Nietzsche's equally poetic descriptions of man, especially "superior" types of men, will embody and express variations on this recurring theme. The conflicting urges that often produce divided, alienated, unhealthy individuals are, if they are mastered, if they are kept in a tension that intensifies life, the *means* to the cultivation of a higher type of individual. Such a person would represent in his or her existence the *"antithetical character of existence."*[31] Antagonistic tension is necessary for development, growth, and an increase of strength. Creativity, too, requires this mastery of antithetical drives, passions, or urges.

Man, according to Emerson's considered view, has within him the energies of nature. And he also inherits the numerous, specific limitations of the species, of *homo natura*. But these inherited aspects of the self can be shaped, formed, controlled, and mastered by an individual of "strong will," by someone who has the "living instinct," the "insight," the power to make efforts to shape his destiny. Life is "prospective" despite the inherited limitations of man's natural history and despite the limiting actual circumstances of the present. At this point, Emerson embraces a "contradiction": "freedom is necessary . . . a part of fate is the freedom of man." By virtue of his or her positive powers, a person can "use and command" the unchangeable facts of his or her life. A strong individual can *use* fate and emulate the powerful "elements" of nature and thereby "show his lordship by manners and deeds on the scale of nature."[32]

Emerson uses every trick in his rhetorical book to extricate his thought from the very fatalism that he so strongly affirmed. The central paradox of his essay, "Fate," can be succinctly expressed: "The material of freedom consists of necessities."[33] Although some philosophers are fairly comfortable with such paradoxes, we must ask ourselves, what exactly does this mean? To my mind, neither Emerson nor Nietzsche ever satisfactorily resolves the antagonistic conflict between the complete acceptance of fatalism and the persistent presupposition of freedom, as finite as it may be, in their conceptions of the condition of man. Both continually try to retreat from the stronghold of a fatalism they affirm in the most forceful terms.

Emerson believed that we all have a sense of the powerful reality of circumstances, conditions, natural forces, and the force of destiny. He tells an amusing story in order to illustrate that even men of faith, in crisis situations, bow to the reality of "circumstances." Two bishops, on board a ship during a terrible hurricane, ask the ship's captain if there is any hope. When he replied, "None but in God," they turned pale, and one says to the other, "And has it come to *that!*"[34]

As much as we hope, wish, and believe that constricting or threatening circumstances can be overcome, we are also painfully aware that this is, in certain dire circumstances, simply impossible. We recognize the power of fate when we are in a situation in which we are impotent to prevent an undesirable, unfortunate outcome.

Emerson urges us to cultivate a "fatal courage," to face whatever dangers we encounter. He interprets fate in a negative and a positive way, sees its harm, as well as its good. Although it is a limited capacity, we do have the power to resist the "savage accidents" of the universe.[35] Even though we are often victims of circumstances, we are also, at times, creators of circumstances. We are constituted and restricted by countless factors beyond our control, but we are constituting agents as well. We have the power of resistance against some of the multiple forces that would act upon us, shape us. And we can engage in "the rugged battle of fate, where strength is born."[36] Our resistances, our actions, our efforts, and our power of will are not for naught. Although we are, as Emerson puts it, a "piece of causation," we are also determining actors who act upon the world, upon our environment, and on ourselves, as well as others.

Even though Emerson insists that the dice of the god nature are loaded, he means by this that we are subject to the dispensations of fate *a tergo,* and at present we are capable of changing circumstances, of resistance, and of producing effects in the social and natural world. Everything has "two sides," even fate. Thus, "if Fate is so prevailing, man also is part of it, and can confront fate with fate."[37] With characteristic hyperbole, Nietzsche exaggerates, but accurately expresses, Emerson's point when he asserts that "I myself am fate and *condition existence for all eternity.*"[38]

Man, for Emerson, as well as for Nietzsche, is a "piece of fate." As such, he is able, to some extent, to influence the course of events. More importantly, he is able to resist external influences and to control his attitude towards events, towards fate itself. The complete acceptance of fate is given an almost mystical significance by Emerson. By virtue of this his reflections on fate are related to some of Nietzsche's later dithyrambic affirmations. He exalts the "beatitude" of the order and succession of nature and life. And he says that we could participate fully in it if we opened ourselves to the revelation of thought. If we could celebrate "the great day of the feast of life," we would see with the "inward eye" the clarity of "the Unity of things." We would see "that what is must be and ought to be, or is the best." Not forgetting the negative facts of nature, the "hints of ferocity in the interiors of nature,"[39] he affirms fate, nature, life and existence nonetheless. He thereby transcends the destructive and creative rhythms of existence and dares to "speak for nature" and immerse himself in its beatitude. Here Emerson is obviously expressing an experiential sense of the reconciliations of dualities, antagonisms, the positive and negative powers of fate, in order to forge in his consciousness "The silver seat of Innocence."[40]

Existential Mysticism

What Emerson attains within the span of a single essay, it will take many years for Nietzsche to develop and express. Emerson's sparks of insight are fanned into the flame of theory. Nietzsche was, from the beginning, sensitive to the destructive powers of nature and man. A study of Schopenhauer, combined with his own observations, made him keenly aware of the horrors of existence. These were to be overcome, as he says in *The Birth of Tragedy,* by the illusions of art and the ideal of the artistic thinker and creator who would redeem existence by means of aesthetic transformation. But even this aesthetic justification of the world is later called a product of his "first period," one in which he practiced a "Jesuitism." That is, "the conscious adherence to illusion and compulsorily incorporating it as the *basis of culture*."[41] After this period began the destructive phase of Nietzsche's development: the critique of traditional morality, the critique of modern man and society, the critique of modern values. In the wake of this assault, there was a new realism that tried to strip away the cultural veils that hide the tragic aspects of life. Put in place of the philosopher during this period was "the free spirit . . . who plumbs the irrational nature of existence, without becoming Jesuitical."[42] From this time forward, he asserts, the necessity in events will be seen as beautiful (compare Emerson's "beautiful necessity") and nothing will be accused.

The Gay Science and *Thus Spoke Zarathustra* marked the beginning of the creation of a new table of values. "Dionysian pessimism" was turned against "Romantic pessimism," and became the watchword of a Dionysian faith that embraced even "the ugly" that cannot be deleted.[43] This was to be a faith that no longer says "no" to actuality or to the past. The fatality in existence is to be squarely faced and affirmed as an inescapable reality. The genuinely strong person accepts his life as affected by "the fatality of all that has been and will be."[44]

It is in his last period of philosophical lucidity that Nietzsche emphasized more and more intensely a Dionysian affirmation of existence. By accepting the dreadful consequences of an objective nihilism, the loss of meaning and value, the sense that nothing has worth or value, and by pushing it to its ultimate limit, Nietzsche sought to annihilate the negating power of nihilism and to attain an overcoming of nihilism in existence, in *pathos.* Here his thinking begins to resemble—admittedly in a more vibrant, intense, and urgent form—the earlier insights of Emerson in regard to a similar reversal of attitude towards the "negative power" of fate, towards the ugly realities of life. Even though Emerson obscures or deflects the personal meaning of life-affirmation in face of his own profound personal losses (while Nietzsche stresses the tragic *pathos* of this attitude towards life), one can imagine how much self-overcoming and courage were needed in order to accept as fatalities his own bouts with illness, his failing eyesight, and, most of all, the cluster deaths of those he loved. No doubt he had to fight off the demon of self-pity as much as Nietzsche later did in his own case. Emerson had already lived through and thought through what Nietzsche later christened "Dionysian pessimism."

In a note from the late 1880s, Nietzsche proclaimed that "this very *pessimism of strength* ends with a *theodicy*...with an absolute yea-saying to the world . . . to the conception of this world as the actually *attained highest possible ideal*."[45] This 'theodicy' is not a justification of the ways of God to man. Rather, it is a justification of life, a recognition of the sacredness of life and existence. It is an affirmation of the value, beauty, and goodness of life despite its transitory nature, despite its painful contradictions and sufferings. Redemption is attained by the total affirmation of actuality *as it is*. It is attained by embracing, rather than rejecting, everything in human history and in one's own life-history, the wonderful and the terrible of what has been. In *Thus Spoke Zarathustra* ("Of Old and New Tables-of-Law") what is required is succinctly stated: "To redeem man's past and to transform every "it was," until the will says: "But thus I willed it! Thus shall I will it: This did I call redemption; this alone did I teach them to call redemption." Nietzsche lucidly articulated what was implicit in Emerson's essays in a more dramatic and detailed way. When Nietzsche links his Dionysian stance with *amor fati* and pantheism, he economically expresses what Emerson meant: "The word *"Dionysian"* means: an urge to unity . . . the great pantheistic sharing of joy and sorrow that sanctifies and calls good even the most terrible and questionable qualities of life."[46]

In Emerson's writings there is a prolepsis of virtually every element that is found in Nietzsche's Dionysian religion of life. He, too, celebrates life with a "sacred affirmation," a pantheistic philosophy of immanent power the source of which "is hidden." And the "negative facts," all that is odious, are encompassed in this affirmation. Man is a microcosm of nature and is the repository of "all spiritual being."[47] How vague and amorphous are Emerson's musings about the "Over-soul" compared to his crisp delineations of man, fate, vital energy, and the paradoxes and opposing aspects of existence! Although there are those who are quick to remind us that, for Emerson, self-reliance is balanced by reliance on the

divine other, the predominance of the theme of an immanent primordial "Power" acting through nature and man, as well as that of
man's "search after power," overshadows the echo of Christian
dependency.

In nature, Emerson believes, is found a "sanctity which shames
our religions."[48] Creating nature (*natura naturans*) expresses itself in
Protean forms and appears "through transformation on transformation, to the highest symmetries."[49] If we could perceive the forces
of nature striving through us, we would experience the "fathomless
powers" of life "pre-existing within us in their highest form"[50] In
tracing Emerson's images of divinity, it becomes increasingly evident that the God of Emerson does not live in splendid isolation,
separated from nature and man, viewing the cosmos from a transcendental palace. His 'theology' is one of life-affirmation, a religion of nature and life. One which envisions currents of power
running through the natural world and microcosmic man and
judges the whole dynamic, polarized process "holy."

Ultimately, Emerson's poetic image of man as letting the
energy-imbued river of becoming flow through him and as yielding to the unitary power immanent in actuality involves the self-
suppression of assertive individuality as an end in itself. It is, in
effect, a foreshadowing of precisely the same transformational
movement of thought that is found in the convoluted development
of the philosophy of Nietzsche.

In the progression of their thought both Emerson and Nietzsche
follow a path of nature-mysticism that leads far beyond the human, all-too-human world, that leads to a Promethean emulation
of a divine vision of a creative and destructive cosmos. Both have
their feet firmly planted on the ground of nature and both propound a deliberately paradoxical *existential mysticism*.

For both Emerson and Nietzsche, the "circle" is the ideal representation of reality. The individual's encounter with nature, society, history, and fate ought to lead from the inner subjectivity of
the genuine person to a vision of the dynamic, energetic cosmic
spectacle and back again to a transformed individual whose existence has been intensified, enhanced, and vivified by the "affirmative principle" of nature and of life. For Nietzsche, this movement
of thought involved a long, painful journey from the perspective
of natural egotism to the self-suppression of *this* modality of individualism by virtue of a process of creative "sublimation." The
circle is completed when the individual lets go of egotism and
fully affirms the dynamic natural process and participates in the

meditative, momentary transcendence of the subjective, human standpoint and of the endless flow of "becoming."

In both Emerson and Nietzsche, radical individualism is affirmed, negated, and reaffirmed in a transfigured guise. Both espouse a paradoxical conception of the condition of man: men are *unique* individuals (or ought to be) *and* they are conduits of the spirit, power, and creative energy of a divine force (Emerson); men are *unique* individuals (or can become such), who are capable of peak experiences of *Existenz, and* they are an expression of a universal, impersonal "will to power," are themselves "will to power—and nothing besides" (Nietzsche). This notion of "will to power" is not only a "metaphor," but a mystical image that pertains to the presumed underlying *nisus* in the cosmos, the *pathos* that strives for form, being, life, knowledge, value, and, ultimately, for the apogee of divinity itself.

In his youth, Nietzsche had denied God as creator of the cosmos and as all-seeing moral judge. But his deeply rooted religious impulse, as he himself admits, had a way of appearing suddenly, without warning. The will to power, his "interpretation" of reality as if seen "from within," is his answer to Leibniz's and Schopenhauer's question: "why is there being rather than nothing?"—on condition that we read *becoming* for "being."

The *spiritual* energy of a willing-to-power is the fundamental, underlying *nisus* in actuality that acts through the universe just as Emerson's "supreme Power" inevitably seeks expression, manifestation, and embodiment in a variety of natural forms. For Nietzsche, as well as for Emerson, the essential reality of all things, despite their appearances in material forms, is *spiritual.* Nietzsche asserts that "spirit is life."[51] And life is one expression of the "will to power."

In regard to the "fatalities" of existence, Emerson held that if we look upon ourselves as conditioned links in an enormous chain of mutable beings, and if we measure our puny forces against those of nature, we would easily see ourselves as "the sport of an insuperable destiny."[52] And, to a large extent, Emerson does believe that we are subject to numerous deterministic factors. But even though we are a "piece of nature," we also have our share of energy and power. We are able to strengthen our will, expend effective effort, control and channel the "primordial impulses" of nature in order to shape, within limits, our character. And character itself is a "natural power," the measure of which is "the resistance of circumstances."[53] Resistance to "forces" that would inhibit our personal growth more than it already is by circumstances and by the negative inheritances of the past, the inheritance of temperament, requires a strenuous disciplining of the self.

Nonconformity, self-trust, self-sufficiency, autonomy, indifference to "public opinion," striving for genuine "self-existence," courage in face of the dreadful realities of existence, accepting the fatalities of our life, all of these enable us to resist extinction or suffocation as a "genuine" self. The powers of the self are as real as the power of fate. They are the means by which we express a finite freedom to constitute ourselves, to strive for an ideal self. When Nietzsche later says, "Be yourself" or "Become who you are," he is not only echoing Pindar, but he is also expressing the sentiments of Emerson.

Fate, then, comprises the restraints and constraints that nature and circumstances impose upon us. And our power is our capacity, our potentialities. It is our possibility (*posse*) or *po-esse*, our "power to be." Considering the essential features of Emerson's portrait of the conditions of man, it is startling to realize that the projection of the ideal of authentic existence that is articulated in Heidegger's *Being and Time* was influenced not only by Kierkegaard's existential ethics, modeled on the Socratic "hero" and his stress on the "potentiality-for" (*kunnen*) in man, but is connected by the thread of continuity that leads from Emerson through Nietzsche to Heidegger. At least some of the central themes of the fermentation of existential philosophy that were imported in America from Europe were originally of domestic vintage!

Despite all that he grants to the "coils of necessity" that surround human life, Emerson still sees the importance of the "how" of existence, the power of resistance, the "creative impulse" in man that enables him to abridge and select what he will out of the panorama of experience.[54] The fate of nature comes to self-consciousness in man and a "plastic," spontaneous element evolves out of the sphere of natural necessity. If an individual develops a "strong will," if he achieves a unity of the entire "energy of body and mind," then there would emerge "power." Insight and feeling ("affection"), if synthesized, generate a strong "energy of will." If there is "jet of chaos" in the individual, it may be converted into a positive "force."[55] Or, as Nietzsche poetically expresses the same notion in *Zarathustra*, "one must have chaos in one, to give birth to a dancing star."

It is not only the individual who has this plasticity that can be shaped and directed towards novel ends. For man collectively has already displayed his power to transform nature, to adapt to changing circumstances, to master the forces and powers of nature, to augment his power by means of creative and innovative knowledge.[56]

On the one hand, the dispensations of fatality—the transmission of detrimental genetic traits, the inheritance of proclivities towards "vice"—are very "odious" indeed. On the other hand, the prospective openness of the future suggests the possibility of liberty. Man has the ability to accumulate experience, feeling, insight, and knowledge. He lives prospectively. Paradoxically, then, human freedom seems to emerge out of fate. Imperceptively, "fate slides into freedom and freedom into fate."

The spiritual "impulse" presumed to be acting through nature and through man assumes millions upon millions of forms of life. And life essentially entails the absorption of materials and "self-direction." "Life," Emerson declares, "is freedom."[57] The "ascending effort" of the organic being in which life achieves self-consciousness is not without effect. It achieves its aims by means of the "ore and quarry" of fate. Freedom and fate are intertwined and man's "double consciousness" enables him to recognize fatality in himself, as well as to discover power and freedom in his being. Although the individual obviously does not have the power to rearrange the enormous order of nature, he does have the power to respond creatively to fate, to resist external and internal forces, to think the possible, the "better, the best," to learn how to use the "beautiful necessity" in nature for his own ends.[58]

Even though man's power is infinitesimal in the hierarchy of nature, it is sufficient enough to provide finite freedom, a freedom that is itself part of the system of reality. Emerson never quite resolves the paradox of fate and freedom any more than anyone else does. But he suggests that "insight" into our condition and nature, in coordination with a full acceptance of fatality, raises us above fate in thought. We have the ability to transcend, by virtue of insight into the operations of fate, the stultifying limitations of our being. We are each a piece in the cosmic puzzle of fate. But we are a living, self-directed, self-conscious piece of fate. Our thoughts, our insights, our feelings, our efforts, our capacity to affirm "beautiful necessity," carry us, at least at peak moments, beyond the bounds of the tyranny of fate. Even though Emerson never explicitly refers to a "love of fate," he says everything that would be included in that conception.

Amor Fati

In his notes and in his published works, Nietzsche struggles with the meaning of, and implications of, the notion of a cosmic fatality even as he presupposes man's freedom to change his thought, his values, his feelings, his attitudes, his entire existence. He exacerbates the significance of fate and man's relation to it in his conception of the eternal recurrence of the same, his ultrafatalistic myth. But before we examine this hyperbolic affirmation of fatalism, we must have some sense of Nietzsche's way of understanding what limiting circumstances mean.

In the *Nachlass* of the mid-1880s, he asks how he can decide his own actions if everything is "necessary." He answers that even though many "forces" press upon us, "thoughts and beliefs" are also determining influences on us that, in fact, may be more powerful than other influences. While it is true that our environment changes and determines our behavior, our opinions also change and determine our actions. Therefore, the *thought* of the fatality of even an eternal recurrence, if it is fully appropriated, will "transform" us.[59] This is, with the notable exception of the specific conception of an eternal recurrence of "the same," a variation on a suggestion implanted in Nietzsche's mind by Emerson. For he held that *how* one relates oneself to fate matters, that our thought *about* fate obviates the fate-idea of "the Turk." More than that, the affirmative celebration of a universal fatalism may generate a beatific attitude toward our condition in existence.

Nietzsche applies to the *thought* of eternal return what Emerson says about the power of thought to take "man out of servitude into freedom" and place him in a state of "beatitude" in which he affirms "that what is must be and ought to be."[60] What Emerson struggles to say about this paradoxical insight is later articulated lucidly by Nietzsche: "My formula for greatness in a human being is *amor fati:* that one wants nothing to be other than it is, not in the future, not in the past, not in all eternity. Not merely to endure what happens of necessity, still less to dissemble it . . . but to *love it.*"[61]

This ecstatic affirmation of fate is an exaggerated expression of what Emerson had called for: "fatal courage" or the courage to accept and beatify the harsh and wonderful dispensations of a cosmic fate. Invariably, Emerson relates the wholesale acceptance of the fatalities of nature to courage. And, in a journal entry, he practically anticipates the frequently cited Nietzschean "formula for greatness" (*amor fati*): "The great . . . in . . . man is . . . [when] he sees what must be, and that it is not more that which must be, than it is that which should be. . . . To be, then becomes the infinite good."[62]

Even the specific philosophical connection between the appropriation of the thoughts of fate and "eternity" (or what Emerson refers to, in one place, as "the Eternal Necessity") is already implied by Emerson despite the fact that it is not articulated as a "theory" of the eternal necessity of the return of "the same." However, it should be noted that at least in *one* interpretation of Nietzsche's most exotic conception, there is a discernible similarity between some of Emerson's descriptions of what may be called peak experiences and an existential interpretation of the meaning of the "thought" of the eternal recurrence of the same.

Emerson's encouragement of "the rugged battle of fate" and his claim that this is "where strength is born" already have about them the tone and attitude that Nietzsche will later express. That we shall come to "love what is dictated by . . . [our] nature" may also be taken as a foreshadowing, in miniature, of the idea of *amor fati*.

An early notice of analogies between many of Nietzsche's philosophical themes and those of Emerson can be found in Salter's *Nietzsche the Thinker*. However, he typically treats these analogical relations of thought or language as *coincidental* and never refers to derivations from one to the other. In a dozen or so instances, he calls attention to similarities of thought or rhetorical expression between Nietzsche and Emerson. But he never suspects that what he has seen is the result of direct influence. Thus, in one of a number of instances, Salter claims that the conception of a *Rangordnung* or "order of rank" in nature and society is such that Nietzsche would agree with Emerson's beliefs about the persistence of a genuine aristocracy.[63] Would agree—he not only agreed with Emerson on this point, but appropriated and elaborated on Emerson's valuation of a natural "scale of rank."

In the case of the conception of *amor fati*, a typical process of appropriation and elaboration seems to guide Nietzsche's thinking. He combines, in a provocative way, the disjointed, fragmentary insights scattered in Emerson's writings and forges them into philosophical themes, doctrines, or countermyths. If we focus on the influence of Emerson's reflections on fate and his affirmation of life as sacred, it would not be surprising that there are foreshadowings of the notion of love of fate in Nietzsche's notes from the early 1860s. When in notes from 1888 he calls *amor fati* his formula for an affirmative, Dionysian attitude towards existence, Nietzsche joins together two themes in Emerson's essays which are presented separately.

In an ingenious way, Nietzsche synthesizes and enriches ideas that Emerson tosses aside as casual observations or remarks in passing. Nowhere is this more evident than in his elaboration upon Emerson's comments *en passant* concerning the experience of "the eternal" in time or the experience of "immortality."

In *The Gay Science,* Nietzsche adopts an affirmative attitude towards existence by negating the negations of romantic pessimism and by accepting what has been and is, by passionately embracing a love of fate. In the same work he offers the existential test of the thought of the eternal return of every detail of one's life. How would we react, he asks, if a demon whispered in our ear and told us that every event in our lives would be repeated in precise detail forever? Would we throw ourselves to the ground and gnash our teeth? Would we, on the other hand, accept such a thought and bless the "demon" as a god because we once experienced a "tremendous moment"? Eternal recurrence is a "weighty" thought that is designed to give depth, profundity, and significance to human life.[64] The appropriation of the *thought* of the eternal recurrence of the same may either crush us or "transform" us.

What underlies this exotic philosophical myth is the repeated experience of a "tremendous moment" in our lives, a peak experience. Like Emerson, he maintains that everything is entangled in a "web of relations." A single event in history or in the life-history of an individual required the entire process of cosmic development up to that moment. Thus, Nietzsche contends that "all eternity was needed to produce this one [momentous] event"—and in this single moment of affirmation all eternity was called good, redeemed, justified, and accepted.[65] If, as is said in *Thus Spoke Zarathustra,* we say yes to a single moment of joy, then we say yes to all the experiences that led up to it because all events are "entangled, snared," linked in a complex network of relations.

Although Nietzsche tried to work out "scientific" arguments for eternal recurrence in his notes, he was never satisfied with these attempts to show that his visionary conception was compatible with scientific theories or empirical possibilities. Without getting into the twists and turns that his defenses of his central conception take, there is *some* evidence that he began to think of eternal return primarily in terms of its existential meaning.

Bernd Magnus has argued[66] that the appropriation of *the thought* of the eternal recurrence of the same was intended as a test for the "overman," a test of courage and strength. The acceptance of the eternal return of the same served to intensify existence, to abolish the last shred of negativism towards the world and life. Whoever could appropriate the dreadful thought of the recurrence of *all* events in one's own life, and in the world, would have faced fatalism in its most awesome, its most terrible, form. The affirmation of life and existence in relation to such a colossal fatalism would require a maximum degree of courage and a defiance of fate itself. The "thought" of eternal return and the total affirmation of existence would "deify" life and existence and radically transform the individual who could endure such a horrendous thought. In *Ecce Homo,* this thought is said to be one that expresses "the highest formula for a Yea-saying to life that can ever be attained." Paradoxically, then, the negative power of fate would be thoroughly negated in existence by virtue of its complete appropriation and affirmation. The negativities of existence are negated by means of the affirmation of life as it is, has been, and will be in face of the appropriation of the thought of the most extreme modality of fatalism.

The Thought of Eternal Return

Focusing on this approach to the existential meaning of the idea of eternal recurrence, let us look at some of Nietzsche's statements about the nature of this "abysmal thought." In an Emersonian spirit, he declares that "Fate is an uplifting thought for he who comprehends that he belongs *to it*."[67] If we ourselves are fate, then we are part of the processes of fate, and, in a sense, we "condition it for all eternity." This rather strange notion may not be as odd as it seems. As a "piece of fate," each of us is part of the total series of occurrences comprising what is called "fate." In this sense, we are *necessary* to the continuity of fate. Whether we have a maximum effect on the world or whether we have minimal effects on it, neither we nor our actions and effects can be subtracted from the process without totally changing it. In this sense, it is plausible to say that each of us has, to some extent, "conditioned existence for all eternity." It is not that we have conditioned the total cosmic process *ab extra,* but that our being has been central to the entire process as it actually occurs. We are, of course, conditioned by a multiplicity of events that have contributed to our nature and being. But, at the same time, we condition the world by means of our existence, our presence, our actions, reactions, or inactions in the relational system of actuality.

In the same terse notation there is an allusion to what may be called an esoteric conception of the meaning of the idea of eternal recurrence. In the full acceptance of the "thought" of the eternal return of all events we may be said to constitute "existence for all eternity" in the sense that we constitute anything that is an object of thought. This would be the freedom of thought that Emerson referred to when he claimed that through insight into the workings of fate, into the laws of nature, we rise above the process we are a part of by means of thought. In Emerson's account, this intensification of insight into the "necessity" in existence augments our "organic power." For whoever "sees through the design, presides over it, and must will that which must be."[68] Our understanding of the power of fate strengthens us and leads us to proclaim, "I am immortal." In notes from 1881 Nietzsche replicates Emerson's exclamation without explanation: *"This life—your eternal life!"*

Cementing the connection between Emerson's mystical notion of the power of the insight into the eternal necessity in becoming and Nietzsche's reflections on this idea is a passing, but revealing, remark in "Fate." The insight into the immanence of fatalism separates those who can endure it from those who cannot. Those who are strong enough to think through such a conception are not members of "flocks and herds."[69] This remark finds its way into Nietzsche's reflections on the eternal recurrence of the same when he claims that it is a "selective principle" that separates those who have the strength and courage to affirm and appropriate the thought of eternal return from the majority who, presumably, would be crushed by the thought of an eternal, circular process of recurrence.

The appropriation of the thought of eternal return is treated by Nietzsche, in some of his formulations of its meaning, as the *experience* of eternity in time. He refers, for example, to the attainment of a feeling of immortality in an *"infinitely small moment"* in which an intensified state of being is experienced as a "lightning flash out of the eternal flux."[70] Elsewhere, he stresses the creation of an "eternalized moment" in which there is a peak experience of "peace" and "light."[71] It is said that a passionate affirmation of life, a deep love of life, does not necessarily demand a *long* life. Rather, the feeling of "love thinks of the moment and eternity—but *never* of length."[72] These sentiments and judgments clearly indicate that attention has been shifted from the idea of an objective, circular, eternal process of which one's life is a part to the notion that eternity can be experienced here and now.

If we concentrate our attention on the experiential attainment of "immortality" in a supreme "moment," we realize that Nietzsche is proposing a state of being in which an individual feels liberated from the circle of time and becoming. This subjective sense of freedom from the flux of actuality is attained, paradoxically, by the complete appropriation of the *thought* of an endless repetition of a fatalistic process. This is clearly mysticism; but it is a kind of existential mysticism that is not at all foreign to the reflections of Emerson on the experience of a transcendence of time in temporality.

In his earliest ruminations, Emerson was very much concerned with searching for what John Milton, in *Comus,* described as

The golden key
Which opes the palace of eternity.

He accepted as a fundamental law of reality "alternation forevermore"[73] and believed that the "circle" is the most appropriate symbol for the entire cosmic process. In the natural world, there is no terminus: "every end is a beginning . . . there is always another dawn risen on mid-noon."[74] Although there is relative permanence, impermanence is the essence of reality. The "circular philosopher" sees that all things "renew, germinate and spring." But nonetheless he lives towards the uncertainty of the future. If we quickly join together the sentiments expressed in "Circles" with the conception of a pervasive fatality, we have the suggestion of an eternal, necessary process that is circular. The necessities woven through the natural world teach us to see that, in actuality, "there are no contingencies."[75]

These conceptions appear to lock Emerson into a theoretical standpoint that excludes freedom. His way out of his self-created dilemma is to affirm the significance of the "how" of existence, the powerful values of thought, attitude, resistance, and insight. Man escapes fatalism by seeing clearly its positive and negative powers, by accepting its dispensations, by embracing it. The free thought of a pervasive necessity combined with an "affirmative principle" and a love of life enables man to transcend fatalism.

At times, Emerson appears to come close to Spinoza's judgment that "freedom is the recognition of necessity" even though he does not specifically argue for such a view. Man's central power is not found in his physical strength (though this is a positive value for Emerson and Nietzsche), but in his thought. "Thought," Emerson tells us, "dissolves the material universe by carrying the mind up into a sphere where all is plastic."[76] When willing and effort are joined with reflective thought, then power emerges. This inner spiritual power is the basis for whatever liberation we are able to attain in life. Such a belief is part of Emerson's demand for a new religion, a religion which, "whatever else it be, must be intellectual." He had long since abandoned religious belief in the form of blind, impassioned faith. The mind of modern man requires a faith that is construed as "science" in the sense of that term in Emerson's day—that is, knowledge. It is probably, for this reason, that he, like Nietzsche after him, encourages a form of religious Prometheanism. He believes that when a powerful intellect awakens in an individual, that individual shares in "eternity."[77]

If the negativity of fatalism is to be transcended, this can be done only by means of thought, knowledge, and insight. Given Emerson's clearly post-Christian conception of religion, this means that the overcoming of the "negative power" of fatalism is essentially attained in a peak religious experience involving feeling, insight, and thought. It is tantamount to what Nietzsche describes, in the context of accepting the thought of eternal recurrence, as a "peak of meditation."

In *Beyond Good and Evil,* Nietzsche engages in an experimental thought about the "play and spectacle" of the eternal return of all things and remarks that this could be construed as "God as a vicious circle."[78] Even though there seems to be a certain toying with this image on Nietzsche's part, it is a notion that appears to have been derived from Emerson's thoughts on nature in one of his early orations. In nature, he observed, "there is never a beginning, there is never an end, to the inexplicable continuity of this web of God, but always circular power returning into itself."[79]

Emerson himself, it would seem, was the "circular philosopher" who associated the endless process of becoming with the limitations and restraints of determinism. All "circular movement," he wrote, is beautiful and the circular process, "the action and reaction of nature," the dynamics of actuality, is connected with our thought of an "ever onward action." It suggests an argument from life for "immortality."[80]

Nietzsche would have had to have read Emerson with meticulous care and sympathetic understanding to have joined together four separately discussed conceptions in one general theory. That is, the idea of a circular eternal process of becoming; the fatalism of nature; the affirmation of life, of the entire circular process; and the notion of a lived experience of immortality. Given the symmetry between Nietzsche's idea of eternal recurrence and his emphasis upon the experience of eternity and Emerson's disjointed remarks on these topics, there is no doubt that he had assimilated and, consciously or unconsciously, synthesized these theoretical conjectures.

This brings us back to the issue of the possibility of experiencing a liberation from the circular cosmic process and the experience, in *pathos,* of immortality. Nietzsche emphasized that redemption could be attained here and now and, in the context of discussing eternal recurrence, he exclaimed that *this* is our "immortal life." There is no doubt that there is an obscurity in such exclamatory remarks. But this obscurity is not at all alien to some of Emerson's very similar assertions. In the course of lamenting that many people who are 'religious' would gladly hear that they will be dismissed through death from the duties and demands of life, he proposes a curious idea of immortality.

Emerson is not at all sanguine about a passive attitude towards a received, a freely bestowed, immortality. "Higher than the question of our duration," he writes, "is the question of our deserving. Immortality will come to such as are fit for it. . . . It is a doctrine too great to rest on any . . . man's experience but our own. It must be proved, if at all, from our own activity and designs."[81]

This is not the only instance in which Emerson suggests the possibility of an immortality attained through effort, insights, and experience. He was preoccupied with the experience of a sense of eternality in the temporal world. Thus, he conceives of the official religious doctrine of the immortality of the soul as too literal and externalized. He seems not at all interested in what he calls "the popular doctrine of the immortality of the soul."[82]

What illuminates Emerson's somewhat vague and obscure allusions to the peak experience of eternity in the temporal world is his repeated emphasis on the full appropriation of the living present. If we could cultivate our sensibilities to the extent of living in the "sufficing present," he assures us, we would achieve a liberating feeling of serenity. If we could affirm the present, live fully in it, we could make this "present great"[83] and experience its sacred nature. We would experience a peace and height that would take us, momentarily, out of the stream of becoming. Above all, we ought to accent the "present tense." "It is," Emerson insists, "the quality of the moment, not the number of days, of events or of actors, that imports."[84] Moreover, strength and happiness come only to the individual who can live "with nature in the present, above time."[85] Later, when Nietzsche claims that the present is not to be justified in terms of the past or in terms of the future, but for the sake of the present itself, he is merely paraphrasing Emerson.

Bearing in mind that living in the present also entails the acceptance of the fatalism of nature that places us in the concrete limitation of the here and now, there is a lived experience of immortality in this unique moment. This state of being, Emerson suggests, must be won by a "sacred courage" to put in action "the invisible thought." The force of a truly transfiguring "thought" is such that it can lift the "mountain of necessity" and be a means to "liberty and power."[86]

The courage that is needed in order to overcome the tyranny of circumstances and the "negative power" of fate is not acquired in a facile way. It requires that we accept reality as it is and face the consequences of the "beautiful necessity" of the natural world. At the same time, we are urged to adopt an "affirmative principle" and to transcend the repetitious surface commonplaces and alluring illusions of everyday life. What is needed, above all, is a "disciplining of the will."[87] By means of this disciplining of the will and of the intellect, by virtue of the acceptance of the power of nature, as well as through the appropriation of the idea of the circular, divine and sacred nature of the cosmos, an individual can attain a synthesis of insight, feeling, and power in the self that is, in effect, the experience of "immortality."

What Emerson proposed was a sea-change in our attitude towards the "how" of our existence. "I wish," he wrote, "that life should not be cheap, but sacred."[88] He sought a way of being in which days would be as "centuries," in which the affirmative feeling of life would be intensified. As is the case for Nietzsche, the eternal is construed as immanent in the intensified present, in "the moment." The individual attains a perspective from which the last vestiges of negativity have been removed from actuality and life and the present is pregnant with value and meaning. The negative facts of fate have been negated by the complete affirmation of the sacredness of the present.

Without getting into the debate concerning the imposition of Being on becoming in Nietzsche's conception of the idea of eternal recurrence, it may be noted that Emerson had earlier suggested a restricted use of the notion of Being in order to refer to the total circular process of reality. In "Compensation," he held that the unity of the recurring cosmic process could be symbolized by "Being" or what he characterized as "the vast affirmative, excluding negation . . . and swallowing up all relations, parts and times within itself."[89] Just as in the case of Nietzsche's thought, the symbol of Being is used to refer not to an absolute, metaphysical reality, but to a thought or experience of unity. Time, becoming, and the limitations of individual existence are transcended in time, in "the moment," by means of the affirmation of the circular process. What is emphasized by both Emerson and Nietzsche is not the objective reality of Being, but the profound experience of the eternal "is." Neither want to surrender the "Protean" diversity in the process of becoming. And Nietzsche is appropriately cautious when he says that the idea of the eternal recurrence of the same would be the closest "approximation" of a "world of becoming" to a "world of Being."[90]

Since virtually every comment and insight that Emerson offers concerning fatalism, the circular nature of reality, the sacredness of the present, the peak experience of "the moment" of liberation from time and becoming, the experience of "immortality," and other related notions find their way into Nietzsche's philosophical experimentation, there is little doubt that the random asides and assertions of the paradigmatic American thinker are incorporated into his "doctrines."

Nietzsche, of course, was more of a philosopher than Emerson, and his thinking is sharper, deeper, more subtle, and more far-ranging than his. But it cannot be denied, in light of the many analogies and parallels of thought and language in the writings of the two, especially in regard to those pertaining to the relation between fate and existence, that Nietzsche could not have constructed this part of his philosophical edifice without Emersonian foundations. In the motto to "Illusions," Emerson's poetic imagination seems to express, in a symbolic vision, "intimations of immortality" or what may be seen as an embryonic version of the myth of the eternal recurrence of the same.

> Flow, flow the waves hated,
> Acursed, adored,
> The waves of mutation;
> No anchorage is.
>
> . . . .
>
> When thou dost return
> On the wave's circulation,

Beholding the shimmer,
The wild dissipation,
And, out of endeavor
To change and to flow,
The gas becomes solid,
And phantoms and nothings
Return to be things,
And endless imbroglio
Is law and the world,—
Then first shalt thou know,
That in the wild turmoil,
Horsed on the Proteus,
Thou ridest to power,
And to endurance.[91]

Chapter 5 Notes

1. *PE*, p. xxxv.

2. One study of Nietzsche's philosophy that takes the question of the meaning of fatalism quite seriously is Joan Stambaugh's *Nietzsche's Thought of Eternal Return*.

3. Eduard Baumgarten, *Das Vorbild Emersons im Werke und Leben Nietzsches*.

4. In a previous work I said more or less the same thing about the extensive influence that Frederick Albert Lange had on Nietzsche's philosophical development. Even at that time I was aware of *some* relationships of similarity between themes in the writings of Emerson and *some* of Nietzsche's basic ideas. In passing, reference was made to the similarity between Emerson's portrait of the independent, self-reliant, nonconformist individual and the Nietzschean idea of the man-beyond-man, the *Übermensch*. However, at the time, I did not realize how profound and pervasive the intellectual and (indirectly) personal influence of Ralph Waldo Emerson on Nietzsche was. Cf. George J. Stack, *Lange and Nietzsche*, p. 153n. What Lange conveyed to Nietzsche was a general phenomenalistic conception of the natural world, a conventionalistic theory of science, a critical and skeptical theory of knowledge, and the idea of the importance of the projection of cultural ideals in order to compensate for the "cold," fragmentary, and nonhumanistic scientific interpretation of reality. Emerson served as Nietzsche's "teacher of the ideal" and provided the content for many of the ideas that Nietzsche put forward from what Lange called "the standpoint of the ideal."

5. *Werke. Historische-Kritische Gesamtausgabe*, II, 58. Five years after this entry was made in his notes Nietzsche writes to his friend von Gersdorff explaining his newly acquired concept of fate as if it were his own. "Indeed it remains within our power to use each event, great and small ac-

cidents, for our improvement and fitness and, as it were, to exhaust it. . . . Thoughtless and immoral men do not know such an intentionality of fate" (*SB* 2:201).

6. "Experience," *PE*, p. 280.

7. "Nominalist and Realist," *PE*, p. 329.

8. Cited in Karl Jaspers, *Nietzsche*, p. 56. Cf. *Werke. Historische-Kritische Gesamtausgabe*, II:58. The possible *locus* of this specific reference might be a citation by Emerson's son, Edward, of an entry from his father's *Journal* from 1851. "There is a thick skull; that is fate" ("Notes," *COL*, p. 339).

9. "Fate," *COL*, p. 5.

10. "Considerations By the Way," *COL*, p. 255. Given all of Emerson's comments about the negative aspects of existence, the American philosopher George Santayana was quite mistaken when he wrote that Emerson "was a cheery, child-like soul, impervious to the evidence of evil" ("The Genteel Tradition in American Philosophy," in *Winds of Doctrine*, p. 197).

11. "Worship," *COL*, p. 215. Vernon Parrington was more insightful in his judgment about Emerson's way of thought than others who only saw the affirmative and optimistic aspect of his reflections. "Despite the jaunty optimism of which he was often accused, [Emerson's] . . . eyes were never blind to reality. . . . He did not shrink from the ugliest fact, and the unhappy condition he discovered men to be in would have discouraged a less robust faith" (Vernon Parrington, *Main Currents In American Thought*, 2:383).

12. "Courage," *Society and Solitude*, pp. 259–60.

13. *Ibid.*, p. 253. Cp. Nietzsche's apparent fusion of two of Emerson's notions—the "scale of rank" and "quantity of power"—in separate journal entries. "What sets off and determines rank is only quanta of power, nothing more" (*The Will to Power*, §855). "The quantum of power that you are decides rank" (*SW* 13:20).

14. "Heroism," *EE*, p. 147.

15. *SW* 1:877. Cf. "On Truth and Lies in a Nonmoral Sense," in *Philosophy and Truth*, trans. and ed., Daniel Breazeale, pp. 79–91. In his deconstruction of this unpublished text, J. Hillis Miller avers that in the passage cited Nietzsche is "describing the human condition as like that of a man hanging in dreams on the back of a tiger." But this is not the normal human condition at all—which is one of dissimulation, self-deception, and skimming the surface of life. Rather, Nietzsche is referring to someone who dares to look beneath the surface appearance of a person and uncover the irrationality within *homo natura*. Cf. "Dismembering and Disremembering in Nietzsche's 'On Truth and Lies in a Nonmoral Sense,' " in *Why Nietzsche Now?* ed. Daniel O'Hara, p. 46.

16. "History," *PE*, p. 124. This statement is incorporated into *"Fatum und Geschichte"* without attribution and without reference to Emerson (*HKG* 2:62).

17. "Fate," *PE*, p. 349. George Santayana noted the curious blend of transcendentalism (idealism) and a "respect for Nature" in Emerson's thought. But he seems not to have looked beyond the poetic depiction of the world in *Nature* insofar as he claims that Emerson saw nature only as "sympathetic" ("The Genteel Tradition in American Philosophy," in *Winds of Doctrine*, p. 200). Stanley Cavell has criticized Santayana's misunderstanding of Emerson, especially in light of "Fate." But he then explicates the meaning of Emerson's "maturity" (or realism) in "Fate" in terms of Wittgenstein, Kant, and Hegel. Naturally, I believe that this is mistaken, particularly because of the obvious affiliation with Nietzsche's reflections on fate (Stanley Cavell, "Emerson, Coleridge, Kant," in *Post-Analytic Philosophy*, pp. 91–98).

18. *Werke* (GOA), XVI, 81.

19. Jaspers, *Nietzsche*, p. 367. Cp. *HKG* II, 62.

20. *SW* 3, *M* §125, pp. 16–17.

21. *Werke* (GOA), XIV, 52.

22. "Intellect,' *EE*, p. 181.

23. *SW* 6, *G* pp. 74–75.

24. Stack, *Lange and Nietzsche*, pp. 103, 131, 135. In "Swedenborg; or, the Mystic," Emerson says that "all things in nature" are "linked and related" (*Representative Men, Nature, Addresses and Lectures*, p. 94). In "The Method of Nature," he claims that each natural effect strengthens every other. "There is no revolt in all the kingdoms from the commonweal: no detachment of an individual" (*RMNAL*, p. 192).

25. *SW*, 6, *G* §33, p. 132.

26. "Fate," *COL*, pp. 19–20. Whicher sees the "fact of necessity" counterbalanced in Emerson by "moral freedom." This is plausible, but it obscures Emerson's stress on the accumulation of power and the antagonism between man's derived power and fate (Stephen Whicher, *Fate and Freedom: An Inner Life of Ralph Waldo Emerson*, p. 167). Although Whicher refers to Emerson's idea of freedom in thought as a source of strength derived from the same nature that dispenses fate, he minimizes this inner power (Ibid., p. 157).

27. "Notes," *COL*, pp. 350–51.

28. *Werke* (GOA), XVI, 81.

29. Ibid., XII, 240.

30. "Fate," *COL*, pp. 22–23.

31. *Werke* (GOA), XVI, 344–46.

32. "Fate,"*COL*, pp. 23–24.

33. "Notes," *COL*, p. 345. Presumably "necessities" refer to what we have inherited from nature or to the causal factors that have conditioned our being. Freedom, then, is the use we make of these determinations of the self. Emerson seems to say that we are retrospectively determined, but prospectively free, in a limited or finite sense. Although this is close to Kierkegaard's view that we have necessity and possibility (potentiality) in our being, Emerson accents fatalism and thereby adopts a position that re-

quires a circuitous defense of freedom. Since both he and Nietzsche prescind "Turkish fatalism," they are actually talking about strict determinism. Emerson, at least, understood this insofar as he refers to fate in terms of "unpenetrated causes." Nonetheless, Whicher is right when he says of Emerson that fate and freedom are "unreconciled in his thought" (Whicher, *Fate and Freedom*, p. 162.

34. Ibid.

35. "The Transcendentalist," *PE*, p. 95.

36. "Self-Reliance," *PE*, p. 156. The Emersonian theme of the power of resistance is a pervasive one in Nietzsche's conceptions of self-assertion and endurance. Thus, in his notes he claims that man needs displeasure in the sense that "every victory, every feeling of pleasure, every event, presupposes a resistance overcome" or a resistance to something (*The Will to Power*, §702. Cp. sections 47, 185, 382, 533, 551, 567, et al.).

37. "Fate," *COL*, p. 24. Here Emerson emphasizes our natural power to resist the power of fate, to expend effort, to strive against the dispensations of fate. Elsewhere, he stresses the freedom of intellect that Nietzsche took note of in his journals. In May, 1859, Emerson wrote that "Fate is the name we give to the action of that one eternal, all-various necessity on the brute myriads . . . in things, animals, or in men in whom the intellect pore is not yet opened." The emergence of thought in man lifts him above the rank of brute necessity. Man then becomes "the maker, not . . . the made" (*Journals*, IX 216–18).

38. *Werke* (GOA), XII, p. 399.

39. "Fate," *COL*, p. 25.

40. "Spiritual Laws," *Poems*. Cited in "Notes," *COL*, p. 349.

41. *SW* 10:507.

42. *Werke* (GOA), XII, p. 215.

43. *SW* 3, *FW* §276, p. 521.

44. *SW* 6, *G* vi, 8, p. 96.

45. *Werke* (GOA), XVI, p. 372.

46. *The Will to Power*, §1050.

47. "The Over-Soul," *PE*, pp. 210, 212. Frothingham discerned in Emerson's essays and poetry a strong streak of pantheism that he neither denied nor defended (Octavius B. Frothingham, *Transcendentalism in New England*, p. 231).

48. "Nature" (Second Series), *EE*, p. 294.

49. Ibid., p. 300.

50. Ibid., pp. 308–9.

51. *SW* 4, *AsZ*, p. 134.

52. "Nature" (Second Series), *EE*, p. 308.

53. "Character," *EE*, p. 256. In "Fate" it is said that freedom is a fact of our experience, but it is limited and partial. Though our lives have been and continue to be acted upon by "hidden causes," we have a limited (or finite) freedom. Cf. Whicher, *Fate and Freedom*, p. 139. Despite the title of his work, Whicher does not delve too deeply into the opposition of fate

and freedom. Rather, he continually contrasts Emerson's various perspectives on life, the self, etc., in order to illustrate his inconsistencies. Whicher does not view Emerson as an experimental thinker who presents a diversity of perspectives on various phenomena. Emerson is a dialectical thinker who always discerns what opposes his own cherished ideas. In "Experience" he argues that different moods, different stages of life and thought, different conditions of life, disclose different and relevant insights, worlds, and realities. Emerson appears to be inconsistent, but only because he is intellectually honest, questioning, restless. Nietzsche understood his intellectual self-overcoming and adopted Emerson's perspectivalism. Before Nietzsche called attention to "the perspectival optics of life," Emerson said that we see nothing and no one directly, that we are 'colored and distorting lenses." Our "subject-lenses" condition all that we experience and we cannot entirely overcome our subjective perspective. Our perception of others is a kind of "optical illusion."

54. "Art," *EE*, p. 193.

55. "Fate," *COL*, pp. 26–32.

56. Ibid., pp. 32–33.

57. Ibid., pp. 36–38.

58. Ibid., pp. 43–48. Nietzsche virtually paraphrases Emerson in *The Gay Science* when he asserts that "I want more and more to learn to see the necessity in things as beautiful" (*SW* 3, *FW* §276, p. 521).

59. *Werke* (GOA), XII, 64.

60. "Fate," *COL*, p. 25. In the course of describing our necessary place in the cosmic process, Emerson touches on the question of eternal return. "I cannot tell if these wonderful qualities [of the spirit] which house today in this mortal frame shall ever re-assemble in equal activity in a similar frame, or whether they have before had a natural history like that of this body you see before you . . ." ("The Method of Nature," *RMNAL*, p. 212).

61. *SW* 6, *EH*, p. 297.

62. *Journal* (1859). Cited in "Notes," *COL*, p. 351.

63. Salter, *Nietzsche the Thinker*, p. 427.

64. *Werke* (GOA), XII, p. 64.

65. *The Will to Power*, §1032, pp. 532–33.

66. Cf. Bernd Magnus, *Nietzsche's Existential Imperative*. In a recent essay Magnus argues that *"The commonplace is deified in the alembic of eternal recurrence."* This precisely captures Emerson's original idea of the experience of the eternal in "the moment" (Bernd Magnus, "The Deification of the Commonplace," in *Reading Nietzsche*, pp. 152–81).

67. *Werke* (GOA), XIV, p. 99.

68. "Fate," *COL*, p. 27.

69. Ibid., p. 26. The selective function of the affirmation of the circular process of becoming is strongly stated in Deleuze's study of Nietzsche. He claims that the negative and "reactive" person "will not return" and that eternal return is an ontologically selective idea (Gilles Deleuze, *Nietz-*

sche and Philosophy, trans. H. Tomlinson, New York: Columbia University Press, 1983, pp. 68–72). In another of his earliest essays Nietzsche had already paraphrased Emerson on this point. "We find that people believing in fate are distinguished by force and strength of will" *HKG* II, p. 60.

70. *Werke* (GOA), XII, p. 45. Whicher claims that Emerson sought the experience of the "Eternal Now" in a precious moment, but from the 1840s on he developed a keen time-consciousness that undermined his desire to live above time in the present (Stephen Whicher, *Fate and Freedom*, p. 98). But the acceptance of transitoriness and the experience of eternity in time is reconciled in what I've called Emerson's (and Nietzsche's) existential mysticism. Both affirm the sacredness of becoming and assert the transcendence of temporality in the intensified value of, and experience of, "the Moment." Nietzsche completes Emerson's reflections in a radical way by presenting the myth of an eternal circular process in which *each* moment is deified and eternalized.

71. *Werke* (GOA), XIV, p. 286. Cp. Emerson's remark in his *Journals:* "A moment is a concentrated eternity" (*Journals*, IV 117).

72. *Werke* (GOA), XII, p. 308. Cp. Emerson's observation that "Every thing admonishes us how needlessly long life is. Every moment [if it has quality] . . . raises us and cheers us [and] . . . a twelve-month is an age" ("The Transcendentalist," *PE*, p. 104).

73. "Friendship," *EE*, p. 114.

74. "Circles," *PE*, p. 328.

75. "Fate," *COL*, p. 49.

76. "Worship," *COL*, p. 240. Harold Bloom's emphasis upon *gnosis* as "poetic knowledge" and the equation of it with Emerson's idea of "Power," as well as his stress on Emerson's assertion that the "great man escapes out of the kingdom of time," reflects Emerson's concern with a religion based upon "science" or *gnosis*. Much of what Bloom says about Emerson's secular religion is compatible with an existential interpretation of his conception of human existence even though he associates the religion of Emerson with America and a literary religion that cuts away from the past and celebrates "discontinuity" (Harold Bloom, *Agon*, pp. 3–15, 145–59).

77. "Notes," *COL*, p. 351.

78. *SW* 5, *JGB* §56, pp. 74–75.

79. "The American Scholar," *PE*, p. 53.

80. "Beauty," *COL*, pp. 293–94.

81. "Worship," *COL*, p. 239. It has been said that although Emerson recognizes a desire for the perpetuation of life enhanced by more knowledge and power, he stresses the attainment, in time, of absolute existence. Depth of life, not length of life, is the goal; and immortality is attained in a way of being (O. B. Frothingham, *Transcendentalism in New England*, pp. 228–31). The relation between Emerson's emphasis on the experience of "immortality" and Nietzsche's proclamation that *this* is his immortal life tends to undercut Nehamas's claim that Nietzsche was concerned with

the representation of a "literary character" (Alexander Nehamas, *Nietzsche: Life as Literature*, Chapter 5).

82. "Nature" (Second Series), *EE*, p. 309.

83. "Success," *Society and Solitude*, pp. 284–93.

84. "The Transcendentalist," *PE*, p. 104.

85. "Self-Reliance," *PE*, p. 151.

86. "Beauty," *COL*, p. 288. The experience of power in a peak "affirmative experience" is described as a liberation from necessity (*Journals*, IX, 221). Elsewhere, the precious moment of hope and joy is characterized as "the secret pass that leads from Fate to Freedom" (*Journals*, VIII, 529). This emphasis upon the experience of freedom in *pathos*, in coordination with some of Nietzsche's quite similar remarks, tends to support the interpretation of the self-suppression of fate in Emerson and Nietzsche as an existential mysticism. Magnus had argued for the existential meaning of the affirmation of eternal recurrence in *Nietzsche's Existential Imperative*, but has since abandoned this view. Earlier, I had argued, in a somewhat different way, for this interpretation in *Lange and Nietzsche*. Given the association between Emerson and Nietzsche on this point, I'm more convinced than ever that the existential interpretation of the meaning of the appropriation and affirmation of eternal recurrence is the most plausible one. Alan White has recently articulated this interpretation in a persuasive way: "This life, with its single and determinate past and its . . . not yet determined future, is my eternal life, the only life I can ever have. . . . To will the eternal return is to will this life, with its ineluctable temporality, both formal and contentual" (*Within Nietzsche's Labyrinth*, p. 101).

87. "Courage," *Society and Solitude*, p. 259.

88. "Considerations By the Way," *COL*, p. 247.

89. "Compensation," *PE*, p. 182.

90. *The Will to Power*, §617. *SW* 12:312. Nietzsche claims that the thought that imprints the character of Being on becoming would be the highest expression of a spiritual will to power. The thought of the eternal return of all things is the closest *approximation* of a world of becoming to a world of Being. The existential significance of this thought is made clear insofar as Nietzsche calls the experience of the thought of eternal recurrence a "peak of meditation" (*"Gipfel der Betrachtung"*).

91. "Illusions," *PE*, pp. 375–76.

Chapter 6

The Paradox of Good and Evil

Nature knows how to convert evil to good.
[Ralph Waldo Emerson, "Success"]

There is probably no other conception in Nietzsche's philosophy that has aroused so much suspicion, ire, and condemnation than his attempt to demolish the dualism of good and evil, to urge, seemingly, the reversal of these ethical categories. His critical approach to the absolute separation of good and evil is expressed in language that was clearly intended not only *épater les bourgeois,* but to amaze and shock everyone else as well. When he defiantly says, "evil be thou my good," he appears to propound a Mephistophelian philosophy of evil.

Nietzsche is notorious for his critique of Christian and traditional morality and for his espousal of what is sometimes called "immoralism." A lackadaisical reader, impatient with serious thought, impatient with the subtle convolutions of his writings on the question of good and evil could misconstrue his thought as a defense of positive immorality. Writing for a select minority, for an "ideal reader," Nietzsche rarely considers the negative effects his radical ideas could have on psychopathic personalities or political thugs. At times, however, he realizes the inflammatory nature of his thought and, as in *Thus Spoke Zarathustra,* he reminds the reader that "this is not said for long ears. . . . These are delicate distant matters." In a preface to a work he never wrote (*The Will to Power*) he is more insistent: "A book for *thinking,* nothing else; it belongs to those for whom thinking is a *delight,* nothing else. . . ."

And, occasionally, in his letters he worries about being misunderstood and suspects that some of his 'followers' will be the kind of fanatics he despised. Unfortunately, his protestations and warnings were muffled by the stentorian nature of his rhetoric.

Of all the combustible material in his writings, Nietzsche's attack on "previous morality" and his prescription of a state "beyond good and evil" are clearly the most inflammable.

The question of the distinction between good and evil preoccupied Nietzsche from his earliest questioning of the values promoted by the Christian *ethos* (and the utilitarian ethics that he treats as a secular consequence of it) to his phenomenology of "master morality" and "slave morality" in *On the Genealogy of Morals*. Although the speculations in the *Genealogy* concerning the origins of the concepts of good and evil, good and bad, as well as the descriptions of the central characteristics of a "slave" and a "master" morality, will be touched upon here, my main focus of concern will be on the relationship between Emerson's idea of "the good of evil" and Nietzsche's more radically expressed, but similar, principle. Nonetheless, it may be said that the notion of a "master morality" that supports an aristocratic ethical orientation is not alien to Emerson's projections concerning a "new morality." For this is central to his projection of a new cultural ideal that, despite the preservation of some Christian virtues, is clearly a post-Christian depiction of what man may yet become, of man perfected. Nietzsche's conception of a positive, affirmative, but strenuous, morality for the few was foreshadowed by Emerson's admiration for, and description of, those he called "exceptions" and "sovereign individuals." Both Emerson and Nietzsche believed that a new, natural morality was a necessary foundation for the creation of a new culture and system of values.

Restoring Dionysus

In *The Birth of Tragedy* (1872), Nietzsche touched upon the cultural phenomenon of the origin of evil in the course of analyzing the meaning and nature of the Dionysian aspect of ancient Greek art and culture. He uncovered a profound strain of irrationalism in this culture that had previously been unnoticed or ignored. Tragedy emerged out of Dionysian festivals in which unleashed primitive energies were centered on "extravagant sexual licentiousness." In these excesses of abandonment, "the most savage natural instincts were unleashed, including even that horrible mixture of sensuality and cruelty which has always seemed to me to be the genuine 'witches' brew.' "[1]

The image of Apollo protected the ancient Greeks from these dangerous outbreaks of Dionysian passion. Nietzsche fully recognizes the evil consequences of uncontrolled Dionysian drives and impulses and, therefore, he values the restraining power of the order, reason, and beauty of the Apollonian cultural and psychic tendency in ancient Greek culture. More than that, he also recognizes, though he deplores its excesses, that the "Alexandrian culture" of rationality, critical thinking, and the accumulation of knowledge (which he claims was inaugurated by Socrates) was *necessary* for the emergence and development of civilization. The anti-Dionysian character of the Socratic valuation of reason and knowledge became excessive when a "culture of knowledge" built upon it replaced genuine, spontaneous, instinctive, mythically imbued culture. The "pyramid of knowledge" raised on the base of the ideal Socratic rationality transferred human energies into "the service of knowledge." If this had not happened, the "instinctive love of life" would have been dissipated in "wars of destruction" and a terrible "ethics of slaughter out of pity" would have arisen. Since Nietzsche held that the unfettered perpetuation of Dionysian impulses would have made civilization impossible, it is an error to believe that the "Dionysian" affirmation of life that Nietzsche later proposes as a new religion (with obvious ethical implications) is tantamount to the original, primitive form of Dionysianism he described in *The Birth of Tragedy*.[2]

The view that Nietzsche proposes in his "Dionysian pessimism" or his "pessimism of strength" a literal return to the form of Dionysian wild abandon that he uncovered in ancient Greek culture is false for a simple reason: it would involve the complete destruction of civilization, a violent, orgiastic nihilism in *praxis*. Nietzsche's later Dionysianism does not encourage social and moral chaos. He acted as a corrective, a champion of a "counter-movement" that undermined the excessive veneration of rationality, assailed the accurately predicted dangers of an unholy marriage of scientific knowledge and practical politics, and criticized all of the leveling and negative cultural and ideational tendencies of modern times. Basically, he sought to find a way of "overcoming nihilism" by means of a positive, naturalistic "morality of growth" and strength that would preserve and conserve a sublimated Dionysian passion.

Before Nietzsche sought to overcome negative moralities or moralities of weakness by recapturing and restoring the Dionysian spirit of life-affirmation, Emerson had celebrated creative intoxication, unrestrained energy, and wild freedom in his poetry ("Bacchus") and had criticized cramped moralities of restriction and prohibition in his prose. In "Bacchus," it has been said, Emerson hails "the reborn Dionysus-Phanes, symbolizing the participation of all things in the whole."[3] In his essays Emerson sporadically returns to the theme of the unconditioned celebration of life, a theme that has obvious affiliations with his Dionysian affirmations. The ideal poet described in "The Poet" not only celebrates the constant fact of life, but is intoxicated with the "nectar" of unrestrained imagination. The poet emancipates and liberates, ravishes the intellect, casts off the shackles of commonsense and the restraints of the understanding. The creative passion that Emerson describes is but a thinly veiled portrait of the Dionysian creative impulse. And the characteristic that Nietzsche attributes to Apollonian art in *The Birth of Tragedy* is said by Emerson (in "The Poet") to be the unique talent of the ideal poet who is not yet: a "*dream*-power" that transcends "all limit and privacy, and by virtue of which a man is the conductor of the whole river of electricity."

In notes from 1887 Nietzsche recalls that around 1876 he "grasped that my instinct went in the opposite direction of that of Schopenhauer: towards a justification of life . . . for this I had the formula *"Dionysian"* at hand."[4] He was right about this, because his absorption of Emerson's thought, his ability to weave together into a unity the threads of ideas that run through his essays, had provided him with the template for the conception of a Dionysian affirmation of life. For Emerson—at least until the writing of "Fate"—invariably sought to accent the affirmative and minimize the negative in life and existence. There is a strong neopagan strain in his writings. It is so strong, in some instances, that it crashes against the reef of his moral sentiments. Emerson's Orphic poet in the section on "Prospects" in *Nature* seems to move towards the ambience of Lucifer, Prometheus, or that of the Roman god of the underworld, Orcus.[5] The spikes of defiance that appear here and there in Emerson's essays often seem to occur in a context in which he is affirming a higher value, an aesthetically imbued value. His aestheticism often leads him beyond the boundaries of conventional morality. Even his affirmation of subjectivity, of the value of the integrity of the inward self, has about it a poetic, Byronic, Promethean tone. There are passages in his essays in which we discover that it was not only the Nietzsche of *The Birth of Tragedy* who believed that "only as an aesthetic phenomenon is life and existence justified eternally." And Nietzsche's subordination of the domain of morality or the moral point of view to an aesthetic perspective is by no means alien to Emerson. It is a propensity shared by these two Dionysians.[6]

Negative Morality

Throughout Nietzsche's writings there runs the recurring dichotomy between moralities of weakness and moralities of strength, negative and positive moralities. The most common form that morality takes is something that Nietzsche treats as if it were barely entitled to the name 'morality': the conformist, herdlike, morality of custom. This is a weak morality in more ways than one. It is basically adaptation to the customary ways of acting in one's immediate social group. Its aim is to encourage us to be like others, to conform to ordinary, typical ways of acting and thinking. Being familiar with Paul Rée's *Der Ursprung der moralischen Empfindungen* (1877), Nietzsche follows him in discerning the origins of a "morality of custom" in animal societies, hence his classification of all such moralities as forms of a "herd morality." What is interesting is that Nietzsche criticizes group "moralities' not only in light of Rée's theory of the analogy between animal group behavior and customary human codes of conduct, but in language reminiscent of Emerson's frequent criticisms of the conformity demanded by society. Emerson often represents group social relations and values as repressive and coercive, as a threat to selfhood. In fact, one can find him anticipating, in a less formal way, the thesis of Rée's that attracted Nietzsche's attention. In "The American Scholar" he laments that modern men have become "the herd" and "the mass." In his "Divinity School Address" he states that the praise of society is "cheaply secured," that the typical "standard of goodness in society" is easily attained. Emerson's opinion of what Nietzsche calls a "morality of custom" is even made plainer in "Self-Reliance." His vituperations against "the crowd" and its "public opinion" anticipate those of Nietzsche and seem to echo those of Kierkegaard. He lashes out against the coercive, anti-individualistic conformity in society which seems to be "in conspiracy" against the manhood and integrity of each person. The central "virtue" in the group morality of society is "conformity." Independence is society's primary aversion, but it values and loves "names and customs." By the time he writes *The Conduct of Life* Emerson's criticism of collective values, attitudes, and behaviors has turned into contempt.

Given his assimilation of Emerson's thought, there is little doubt that Nietzsche's consistent polemics against the "morality of custom" or the belief that *die Sitte* ("custom") is the only "*eigentliche 'Sittlichkeit'*" ("authentic 'morality'") owes something to Emerson's frequent attacks on a conformist group morality. Both criticize this mode of morality not only because it denigrates individuals and individual differences, but because it demands too little. It is primarily a passive morality, a negative morality that plays upon the all-too-human fear of being different, of standing out from the crowd, of genuine independence, of risking the wrath of group disapproval. The bursts of antinomianism in Emerson's works, as well as the explosions of Nietzsche's antinomianism, are primarily directed against what both consider the weakest and most paltry form of 'morality': *die Sittlichkeit der Sitte,* "the morality of custom."

In a subdued, but insistent, way Emerson engages in sniper attacks on the negative features of what is generally accepted as conventional morality. Thus, in "Goethe; or, the Writer," he notes with approval that Goethe and Napoleon are "representations of the impatience and reaction of nature against the *morgue* of conventions."[7] And in his portrait of Swedenborg he suggests the overcoming of the duality of good and evil with reference to Indian thought: "The less we have to do with our sins the better. No man can afford to waste his moments in compunctions. 'This is active duty,' say the Hindoos, 'which is not for our bondage; that is knowledge, which is for our liberation: all other duty is good only unto weariness'."[8]

This passage includes themes that recur in Emerson's writings and are significantly amplified in the philosophy of Nietzsche. That is, the counsel not to wallow in a consciousness of sin, which coincides with Emerson's desire to emphasize the "affirmative principle" rather than dwell upon the negative aspects of moralities of prohibition. What is to be noticed is that this attitude of mind goes against the grain of the traditional Christian stress upon remembrance of sins and the acceptance of our sinful nature. The quotation—presumably from Hindu scriptures or a commentary on them—calls attention to Emerson's valuation of "knowledge" or *gnosis*. Naturally, the idea of liberation from a preoccupation with the opposition of good and evil, which is a common theme in Hinduism in conjunction with the attainment of insight or knowledge, is one that will reappear in Nietzsche's gnosticism, specifically in what he called his "dangerous slogan": "beyond good and evil."

Rather early on Emerson worries over the absolute distinction between good and evil. In "Self-Reliance" he worries whether these are not merely "names very readily transferable to that or this." At times, he hesitates to grant ontological reality to evil, considering it, after St. Thomas Aquinas and others, as a privation of good. Under the inspiration of his "Orphic poet" in *Nature* Emerson foresees a time when the "sordor and filths of nature" will desiccate with "the influx of spirit," when evil will be obliterated. The problem of defect, deficiency, suffering, and evil is a haunting presence in the thought of Emerson, as it is in the philosophy of Nietzsche, as it is in the minds of many. Despite his buoyant tone, Emerson, as much as Nietzsche, was very much aware of the tragic sense of life or what he calls the "old tragic Necessity."[9] His pained acceptance of fate is, as in the case of Nietzsche, closely linked with the tragic aspect of existence. For in an early lecture, "The Tragic," he tells us that "the first and highest conceivable element of tragedy in life is the belief in Fate or Destiny; that the Order of nature and events is constrained by a law not adapted to man . . . careless whether it cheers or crushes him."[10]

Both Emerson and Nietzsche contend with the power of the negative in existence. At first, Emerson seeks to efface its reality in nature and man. Later, as in "Fate," he admits the millionfold negative facts, accepts them as part of the necessity in actuality, and then affirms the value of life and existence in face of them. The painful acceptance of the tragic elements in existence, the stoical embrace of all that is terrible in life and the enthusiastic affirmation of life and world nonetheless is an Emersonian stance before it is christened "Dionysian pessimism" by Nietzsche.

But the problem of moral evil, of immorality, lingers. Emerson, the former Unitarian minister, knows the Christian answers to this question very well. But he has come to question the negative accent of the Christian prohibition. He has come to see that there is no conviction that may not, at some time, have to be renounced, that each person's "christianity, his world, may at any time be superseded and decrease." Perhaps, he suggests in "Circles," the "virtues" prized by society may, like vices, also have to be cast away. After all, many of "the virtues of society are the vices of the saint." The problem is that much that is called "good" in the modern world is not; and much that is called "bad" is good. In fact, as he says in "Self-Reliance," "goodness must have some edge to it" or else it is not genuine goodness. What he does not say directly, but continually implies, is that the negative prohibitions of Christian ethics have been infused, in modern times, into a restrictive, negative morality of conformity. The powerful force of public opinion now dictates how we ought to think, to speak, to act. The "good" man in the modern world has become unattractive, has lost the edge of honesty, is no longer a "true man," a "genuine man." What conventional morality deems good seems to have lost its association with nature, with "the natural." It is a question, Emerson tells us, "whether we have not lost by refinement some energy, by a Christianity, entrenched in establishments and forms, some vigor of wild virtue."[11] The habits of mind cultivated by Christian ethics have not produced strength, beauty, and confidence. Rather, they have encouraged negative judgments of ourselves. Emerson laments the prevalence of "Self-accusation, remorse, and the didactic morals of self-denial and strife with sin."[12] One senses in Emerson a growing weariness with the "shalt nots" of Judeo-Christian morality and a hunger for the positive, edifying, and stimulating "shalt." He decries the fact that "our Religion assumes the negative form of rejection"[13] and observes that virtue can become so narrow, so blind, that it is "vice-like."[14] Emerson is locked in on the target that Nietzsche later expends so much energy firing at: a traditional morality that is negative in form, psychologically debilitating, and, in essence, a "morality of weakness." Although Nietzsche's attack on such a morality is more vituperative, more persistent, and more intense than that of the American thinker, it is entirely consistent with it.

Virtually every criticism that Emerson levels against the ethics of Christianity is repeated by Nietzsche—in a stentorian voice. If Nietzsche had had access to Emerson's journals, he would have discovered that his quarrels with the *ethos* of Christianity were not only occasional red threads woven through the fabric of his essays. As early as 1832 he is recording that "in an altered age, we worship in the dead forms of our forefathers. Were not a Socratic paganism better than an effete superannuated Christianity?"[15] Though wary of Socrates, Nietzsche chooses to return to the atmosphere of the pagan world, not to live there, but to recapture its highest, strongest, most noble virtues. In *The Birth of Tragedy* he interprets the myth of Prometheus as a depiction of a titanic, impulsive action that symbolizes creativity through 'impiety'. In Aeschylus' *Prometheus* especially, Nietzsche sees a defiance, in Prometheus' theft of fire, that represents the artist's defiant creativity as a willful seizure of the divine "fire" of creative power. Even though he suffers for it, man does his best, then, through transgression. This creative good emerging from transgression is contrasted to the Biblical myth of the fall in which curiosity, deception, weakness in face of temptation, and wantonness—all unheroic passions—are considered as the origin of evil. Paradoxically, it is through "active sin" that Prometheus affirms a "virtue." What is expressed in the myth of Prometheus is an antagonism between the aspirations of man and the will of the gods. Prometheus represents the titanic striving of the individual that causes him or her to violate the plan of the gods. This curious double personality of the individual, the fusion of disobedient passion and creative aspiration, conjoins Dionysian and Apollonian tendencies.[16]

Promethean defiance could serve as the motto of Nietzsche's philosophy. However, he is not the only admirer of the Promethean spirit of man. For Emerson has sympathy for this "friend of man" who "stands between the unjust 'justice' of the Eternal Father and the race of mortals, and readily suffers all things on their account" The myth is unlike Christian allegories in that it represents a defiance of god, a resentment of reverence, a willingness to live apart from the god and independent of him. The myth of "Prometheus Vinctus is the romance of skepticism."[17] The image of a victorious friend of man defying the gods seems to be retained by Emerson, in a disguised form, in his praise of daring, energy, and the "search after power." Certainly, Emerson often enough expresses a religious Prometheanism that storms the heavens and seeks to pull the fire of divinity down to earth and implant it in the heart of his "Divine persons [who] are character born . . . victory organized."[18]

Amplifying Emerson's insights considerably, Nietzsche exclaims that Christianity and its *ethos* must be combated because of its power "to break . . . the strongest and noblest souls." Its ideal is designed for "the virtuous average-and-herd man," and its "seductiveness" undermines "the most strongly constituted exceptions," exploits "their bad hours and their occasional weariness," and twists their strength back against themselves.[19] Nietzsche tirelessly attacks the putative "good men" that the moral values of

Christianity promote. In Christian morality "man made harmless to himself and others, weak, prostrated in humility and modesty, conscious of his weakness, the 'sinner' . . . is the most desirable type."[20] In hundreds of ways Nietzsche hammers home the same point: the consequence of the Judeo-Christian morality is a morality of weakness that is poison to the confident, the assured, the noble, and the "healthy" individual. What this successful and enormously influential ethics lacks, among other things, is a healthy respect for the wicked or "evil" passions in man, passions that can be the fuel for great achievement, creative effort, "greatness."

'Evil' into Good

Emerson had said that nature knows the means by which to transform evil into good. And Nietzsche believed him. In an unpublished essay, "Homer's Struggle," he maintained that man is inseparable from nature and partakes of its dual characteristics. It is precisely those of man's "abilities that are terrifying and considered inhuman" that are probably "the fertile soil out of which alone all humanity can grow in impulse, deed and work."[21] This same basic view is defended more forcefully in *Human, All-Too-Human.* What is generally believed to have happened during the geological transformation of the surface of the earth over long periods of time also occurs in the natural history of man. That is, "the wildest forces break the way, destructively at first, but their activity was nevertheless necessary in order that later on a milder civilization might construct its house. These terrible energies— what one called evil—are the . . . architects and road-makers of humanity."[22]

Although Emerson is quite aware that nature "is no saint," he finds in it a long, gradual transformation that is, despite vast imperfections, ameliorating. Culture is the flower of this transformational process. But a harsh and often terrible natural history precedes the emergence of the human cultural world. The process of natural metamorphosis is a long, slow one. The formation of the diamond over extensive periods of time teaches us the *"Natur-langsamkeit,"* the "slowness of nature." Man's natural history emerges out of a more encompassing natural history, and its earlier stages were crude, harsh, and brutal. Emerson accepted and applied a general theory of evolutionary transformation to the development of *homo natura*. What is interesting, especially in regard to his relationship to Nietzsche, is that his conception of evolution places emphasis upon the importance of "effort" and "will" in human development and implies the idea of the transmission of acquired traits and characteristics.

Just as the natural history of the earth has been tumultuous, so, too, has man's natural history. There are many hints in the animal kingdom of the "ferocity" in the natural world. Though he does not say too much about it, Emerson suggests that our ancestors were ferocious too since man is part of the system of nature. Man is like a plant and is nourished by some rather crude fertilizers. What has been true of the human species is true of the individual. "As plants convert the minerals into food for animals, so each man converts some raw material in nature to human use."[23] During the natural history of the species the *nisus* towards civilized modes of existence has been cultivated by crude 'fertilizers' analogous to natural chemicals: raw passions, primitive drives, powerful impulses. From the perspective of traditional moral points of view, these are "wicked" or "evil." And both Emerson and Nietzsche consider them so. However, both reinterpret these primordial traits in man and call attention to their value not only for the survival of our ancestors, but for the cultivation of civilized life and for a naturalistic morality of strength. Thinking of all of the immoralities, all of the cruelty and injustice, that have been part of mankind's development, Nietzsche epitomizes many of Emerson's scattered remarks on this issue when he says that "Culture rests upon a terrible foundation."

Emerson understands the individual and sociocultural processes by which evil is converted to good as comparable to natural processes that accomplish the same thing. By implication he assumes that culture is the outcome of the evolutionary transformation of nature, that it was fecundated by the "evils" that emerged in nature. Although he does not qualify the generalization, this process is what he seems to have in mind when he tells us that "evil is good in the making."[24] The crude raw materials in *homo natura* are essential for the creation of the man of culture. And the wicked impulses of individuals often provide the energy, the passion, necessary for daring actions, creativity, and the sophisticated achievements of civilized man.

Great historical events, Emerson insists, have often been instigated by blunt selfishness, by vanity, by egotism, passion, and greed. Look, he asks us, at what has been accomplished in history by "selfish capitalists." Discreditable means have not infrequently produced valuable ends. Without passion, without a fierce ambition, without a bias in a certain direction, a great deal of art, certainly a great deal of intellectual labor, would not have been produced.

Good and evil are intertwined in nature as well as in history and society. In "Considerations By the Way" Emerson sees through the simplistic dichotomy of good and evil embodied in traditional moral interpretations of actuality. He argues that we must admit that great historical events are quite often effected by paltriness, "coarse selfishness, fraud, and conspiracy." In fact, "most of the great results of history are brought about by discreditable means."[25] He agrees with Mirabeau[26] (and, by implication, Mme. de Staël and Hegel) that nothing great in history has been achieved without passion: "There are none but men of strong passions capable of going to greatness." Even though it is a poor regulator, passion is a "powerful spring" of human action.[27] The theme of malfeasance turned to good is a strong one in the essays comprising *The Conduct of Life*. Thus, for example, the California "gold rush" is offered as an illustration of the way in which crass, immoral motives actually generate prosperity and advance civilization. One could say that, on this question, Emerson not only replicates Adam Smith's conception of the beneficial effects of the behavior of acquisitive, economically self-interested individuals in *The Wealth of Nations,* but that he seems not too far removed from de Mandeville's cynical notion in *The Fable of the Bees* that private vices (e.g., avarice) promote public benefits. Emerson invites this comparison when he remarks that if the criticism of "the thirst for wealth" that issues forth from the pulpit and the press were taken to heart by everyone, then these "moralists would rush to rekindle at all hazards this love of power in the people, lest civilization should be undone."[28]

In *The Gay Science* this particular theme of Emerson's is clearly appropriated. Under the rubric "That Which Preserves the Species," Nietzsche proclaims that the "strongest and most evil spirits have hitherto advanced mankind the most." They "rekindled the sleeping passions" and stimulated the prospect of "the new," "the untried." Using an Emersonian agrarian metaphor, he says that when the "soil becomes finally exhausted . . . the ploughshare of evil must always come once more." Taking a swipe at English utilitarianism, he states that this ethics holds that the good is conservative of the species and evil is detrimental to this end: "But in actuality the evil impulses are just in as high a degree expedient, indispensable, and conservative of the species as the good—only their function is different."[29]

Nietzsche often repeats the Emersonian principle of "the good of evil" in ways that highlight the influence of the American poet and essayist on his thought. Thus, in *Beyond Good and Evil* he maintains that "the plant 'man' has so far grown most vigorously to a height . . . under prolonged pressure and restraint." All that is "evil, terrible, tyrannical" in man's being "serves the enhancement of the species 'man' as much as its opposite."[30] As we've seen earlier, Emerson is the source of this way of construing the passionate, irrational, potentially dangerous, inherited primordial drives of human beings. Individually and collectively human beings are often indebted to their "vices," Emerson tells us, just as a "plant" is fertilized with "manures."[31] The first lesson of life and history, Emerson insists, "is the good of evil."[32] But this "good" is primarily attained in individuals by means of conversion and transformation, by the means used to express "wicked" impulses and drives. Aside from references to the value of man's baser impulses to historical development, this interpretation of Emerson's and Nietzsche's is a psychological theory of the nature of man that traces his energies to their roots in the natural history of man. Neither Emerson nor Nietzsche value the "wicked" in man *per se* or intrinsically. Rather, they are engaged in an unsentimental psychological analysis of the natural instinctive drives of man. It is an error, in my view, to join this analysis to a doctrine of "immoralism."[33] Without fanfare Emerson inaugurated and Nietzsche continued a depth psychology of *homo natura* in order to correct what Nietzsche calls the "forgery" of previously regnant moral psychologies of man.[34] Emerson's stance in this regard is aptly expressed by Nietzsche in *On the Genealogy of Morals:* "Man has regarded his natural propensities with an 'evil eye' all too long."[35]

Emerson and Nietzsche are concerned with correcting the tendency in traditional moralities to value a "goodness" that is tame, mediocre, and conformist. In neither case is the unleashing of passions, drives, or impulses in an unchecked way advocated. The aim is to replace what is considered a negative morality of weakness with an aesthetically conceived ideal of a synthesis of goodness, beauty, and strength. The object of this attack on the *ethos* of Judeo-Christian morality is its antinaturalism, its attempt to extirpate the naturalistic basis of human nature, to make of man a tormented creature at war with what is essential for his preservation, his persistence, his energy, his highest aspirations. St. Augustine's attitude towards the 'virtues' of Greco-Roman culture, seen from a Christian perspective, inadvertently confirms some of Nietzsche's insights. For St. Augustine called the virtues of the pagans nothing but "splendid vices," thereby announcing the Christian "transvaluation of values." In a similar vein, Nietzsche said that Christian morality converted the figures of Eros and Aphrodite (which were, for the pagans, capable of being idealized) into diabolical sexual tormentors.[36] Rather than extinguishing sexual drives, previous morality forced them inward, twisted and perverted them. Before Nietzsche declared that sexuality pervades the entire being of man, Emerson had said that "sex is universal, and not local; virility in the male qualifying every organ, act, and thought."[37] Thus, the attempt to label human sexuality as 'evil' is a libel against natural instinct. In this instance, as in others, the zeal of the moral reformer of man's nature "reacts suicidally on the actor" who seeks to act against his nature. This is the penalty, Emerson tells us, of trying to transcend nature.[38]

Both Emerson and Nietzsche create problems of interpretation by using the term 'evil' in a freewheeling and cavalier way, by not always making clear what they mean by it in specific contexts. What complicates matters more is that Nietzsche invariably seeks to sew together ideas that Emerson does not interrelate. Thus, for example, the *"plus"* factor of vitality and energy he finds in creative individuals such as Cellini and Michaelangelo in "Power" is not related directly to "the good of evil." However, Nietzsche does make this connection, one that is entirely consistent with the direction of Emerson's thought. He affirms what he calls "the evil of power" in association with innovators and creative people who are daring and go beyond the values of the crowd.[39] This coincides with Emerson's enthusiasm for the creative individuals who have superabundant energy, a "surcharge of arterial blood," "positive power," and "coarse energy." Such individuals often have vices enough, but they also "have the good nature of strength and courage."[40] These human types are not 'good' in terms of a strict Christian morality. In fact, Emerson implies, they are prone to what would be designated as "wickedness" by conventional moral standards. Thus, even though Emerson does not explicitly link the good of evil to the human types he admires, he clearly insinuates this in a way that Nietzsche discerned.

Innovators of all kinds, Nietzsche insists, have often been called "evil" or have been looked upon as sinister until their innovations are perceived as beneficial to society or culture. This sense of *böse*

("evil," "wicked," "displeased," "ill-tempered," "angry") is sometimes made plain. "The most powerful man, the creator, would
have to be the most wicked, inasmuch as he carries his ideal
against the ideals of other people and remakes them in his own image. Wicked here means: hard, painful, enforced."[41] Elsewhere, he
uses *böse* to refer to strength or a core of toughness. Socrates, for
example, is said to be harsh towards those who pretend to possess
knowledge.[42] Relying on Emerson's organic metaphor once again,
he tells us that the "plant" man needs to be tested by dangers,
needs heartiness or a wicked tenacity in order to evolve into subtlety and daring.[43] The "will to knowledge" requires "good and
evil" impulses, a harshness towards things or prejudgments.[44]
Sometimes, in an Emersonian voice, Nietzsche simply relates *böse*
to being opposed to custom. "To be evil is to be 'not customary,'
to resist tradition."[45] Virtually all of these senses of 'evil' are derived, by implication, from the essays of Emerson with one proviso: that we see, as apparently Nietzsche did, the ideas, themes,
and images in them superimposed upon one another.

Before turning to a consideration of Emerson's recommenda-
tions concerning the means by which man's natural passions,
wicked impulses, and primitive drives ought to be managed, a
point should be made in regard to Nietzsche's prescription of
wickedness. He is not concerned with defending, in any strict
sense, gross immorality. In his preface to *Daybreak* (1886), he states
that he has attacked traditional morality "out of morality." He is
concerned with the "self-suppression of morality" (*"die Selbstauf-
hebung der Moral"*).[46] The deliberate use of one of Hegel's central
concepts should not be overlooked. For self-suppression implies
cancellation *and* preservation. So what is suggested is the negation
of previous morality in its original form and its preservation and
conservation in another form.[47] In the text of *Daybreak* Nietzsche
says that he does not deny that "many actions called immoral
ought to be avoided and resisted, or that many called moral ought
to be done and encouraged." His main concern is that we learn to
think differently and take morality out of the morass of superstition, custom, and tribal consciousness in order *"to feel
differently."*[48] Like his American inspiration, Nietzsche wants to escape from the labyrinth of a narrow, cramped, restrictive, negative
morality into the openness of a 'morality' of life, health, affirmation, beauty, and "cheerful wisdom."

Before Nietzsche did so, Emerson had already railed against
what the former calls "absolute morality," as well as against the
radical duality of good and evil. In life the two are intertwined.

And it is often the case that what is deemed good by society, what is bolstered by public opinion, is bad for the individual; that a "good man" (*qua* conformist, submissive, dependent, weak) is, in fact, bad. What is wanted is a morality that enhances life, that is positive, that is active rather than "reactive," that is infused with, but not ruled by, Dionysian passion. The healthy individual, Emerson once said, "chooses what is positive, what is advancing . . . embraces the affirmative."[49] But, of course, this affirmative attitude towards existence does not erase or deny the sufferings and pains of life or the tragic dimension of human experience. Nor, as we've seen, does it efface the grounding of our being in nature, the natural history of our species, which must be the foundation for a "new morality."

Emerson's disillusionment with Christendom and customary public morality led him to seek a morality of affirmation and strength, a vitalistic, naturalistic morality. The endeavor to discern the good of 'evil' was central to this quest since it involved a restoration of nature, a recovery of an energy or "vital spirits" that seem to have been lost or subdued by "the smooth mediocrity and squalid contentment of the times."[50] The recovery of the value of what is natural in man entails the denial of the absolute opposition of good and evil in traditional morality. As if retroactively defending Emerson's position, Nietzsche maintains that whoever believes in good and evil as absolute opposites "can never treat evil as a means to good." Then he proposes a conundrum for those who refuse to break with a morality based upon the absolute opposition of good and evil: it makes every teleological worldview impossible.[51] That is, as long as good and evil are radically opposed, any defense of an objective teleology becomes an apology for evil and human suffering. Thus, the traditional ethical conception of the absolute difference between good and evil undermines the justice of a metaphysics of objective teleology because it glorifies historical success at the expense of the misery of the victims of history. The notion that there is an objective teleology operative in the world rationalizes evil for the sake of a supposed purposeful good. This seems removed from Emerson's angle of vision, but it isn't. For in "Fate" and elsewhere he criticizes a "pistareen Providence" and ironically recounts the suffering and genuine evils that a religious teleology too easily embraces. And we may recall that, for him, "the tragic" is an ineludible feature of existence.

Granting to Emerson and Nietzsche the value of, the good of, mankind's 'evil' or wicked traits and propensities, how are these converted or transfigured into constructive, positive use or expression? Surprisingly, it is the American poet and essayist who provided Nietzsche with the rudiments of a theory that is a response to such a question.

Sublimation

The process of guiding, refining, and transforming "evil" drives and passions into good is expressed by Nietzsche on a number of levels. He puts forward a general cultural-history theory (foreshadowed, to some extent, in *The Birth of Tragedy*) that advances the idea that "everything good is the evil of former days made serviceable."[52] This notion is particularly prevalent in his account of the history of punishment in *On the Genealogy of Morals*. For in this he traces the gradual transformation of punishment and its meaning over long periods of time in such a way as to show how entire cultures undergo processes by which brutal means of punishment are symbolically transfigured. Such an interpretation seems to be related to a "thesis" he records in his notes. That is, that "all good is a simulated serviceable wickedness of former times."[53] Since Nietzsche does not assume that there is any overt intentionality in the gradual refinements of customs or procedures in regard to punishment, we may assume that this historical process is unconscious. In another context, he suggests that the bloody physical struggles of the cruel ancient Greeks were, over time, transformed into a form of artistic *agon* in the competitions amongst the tragic dramatists. In *The Birth of Tragedy* he had, of course, traced the same cultural-historical evolution of Greek tragedy (*tragoidia* or "goat-song") out of the earlier orgiastic Dionysian celebrations. These interpretations are usually included in his theory of the "sublimation" of the instincts even though they are sometimes more closely related to Freud's theory of reaction-formation.

Nietzsche invariably looks beneath the civilized behavior or practice in order to infer an earlier mode of behavior or practice that was brutal and cruel. From what he knew and we know about human history, this was not an improbable speculation. However, some of his accounts of how primordial instincts are transformed in a culture over time seem to fit the Freudian model of reaction-formation. For this defense mechanism is a response to drives and impulses experienced as threatening or dangerous. Independent of whether these drives were acted upon or not, reaction-formation involves a repression of such drives and impulses by means of an almost obsessive-compulsive adherence to a socially approved way of acting that is typically the opposite of the original behavioral tendency (or actual behavior) to which one is drawn. Even though the effects of reaction-formation and sublimation are similar, the former relies more upon rigid repression and mechanical rule-following. In his psychohistorical treatment of the cultural evolutionary transformation of punishment in the *Genealogy* Nietzsche seems to be offering a theory analogous to Freud's theory of reaction-formation even though the sublimation of instinctive drives is interwoven into his analysis.

This digression serves to segregate Nietzsche's original anticipation of Freud's theory of reaction-formation (which has no analogue in Emerson's thought) from his theory of sublimation, which is an enhanced elaboration on insights he found in the essays of Emerson.

Although he has no theory of the sublimation of passions, instincts or 'evil' impulses, Emerson provides insights that point to such a theory. What are counted as faults or "vices" are often, paradoxically, the raw materials out of which moral goodness and character are formed. Egotism, infatuation, and strong passion not uncommonly enable individuals to surmount obstacles and overcome resistances that stop prudent individuals in their tracks. In this regard, Emerson quotes with approval an observation of Voltaire's (which Nietzsche later applies to the value of error in the interpretation of actuality): *"Croyez moi, l'erreur aussi a son mérite."* Error, in the sense of moral flaw, has its value. And Emerson proceeds to show us how this is so. It is not necessary to extinguish passion or error (or, as Nietzsche later says, it is not desirable, as some would have it, "to kill the passions"). It would be better, he continues,

> if we could secure the strength and fire which rude passionate men bring into society, quite clear of their vices . . . there is no moral deformity but is a good passion out of place . . . there is no man who is not indebted to his foibles . . . the poisons are our principal medicines, which kill the disease and save the life.[54]

Contrary to popular moral opinions about a good person, each individual is, at some time or another, "indebted to his vices." What is essential is that growth take place. The amelioration of individuals is possible if they can "convert the base into the better nature."[55] The idea of the transformation of evil into good by means of "spiritualization" or "sublimation" that lies at the heart of Nietzsche's naturalistic morality of growth is derived from Emerson's abbreviated sketch of precisely the same conception.

Commenting on the moral climate of his time, Emerson laments that there is a general lowering of the natural "scale of rank," a tendency to put the best on the level of the least. Man, he says, as Nietzsche later does in *On the Genealogy of Morals,* is no longer "in awe of man." And the rank of a person in nobility, integrity, and character counts for little or nothing. What is needed is a moral sense that discriminates rank in terms of genuine qualities of character and preserves a "convenient distance" between independent individuals and the crowd.[56] Just as there are "gradations" in nature, so, too, should there be gradations in the social world, gradations that provide a balanced "distance" between individuals.[57]

These themes—a respect for gradations of rank among people and the need to recognize the "distance" between different types of people—are tantamount to Nietzsche's insistence upon a moral orientation that recognizes an "order of rank" (*Rangordnung*) and his claim that those who seek to accomplish much and demand a great deal of themselves have a *Pathos der Distanz.* A "feeling of distance" separates such individuals from those who seek a comfortable adaptation to the social and moral status quo of their time and place.[58] Nietzsche combines these separated and passing remarks of Emerson's into an *ethos* when he contends that the elevation of man has been the work of an aristocracy of talent which upholds a ladder of gradations and cultivates a "passion for distance" that emerges out of genuine, perceived differences between creative and innovative individuals and those who are not similarly endowed.[59]

In his poem "Uriel" Emerson pictures the circular pattern of the universe in which "all rays return" and, in the spirit of William Blake, proclaims that "evil will bless" as "ice will burn." The 'evil' in those with "coarse energy" and gross impulses can be put to good use, for such individuals possess the constitutional strength to accomplish great things or to serve as benefactors of mankind. To be sure, an excess of grossly immoral propensities is "dangerous and destructive." What are needed, Emerson tells us, are "absorbents" to take the edge off these excesses.[60]

The "pursuit of power" frequently assumes immoral forms. However, culture acts as a restraining corrective of the raw hunger for power in man. What Emerson is suggesting is paralleled in Nietzsche's thought: nature is the primordial source of the drive for power, and it is the origin of "coarse energy" in individuals. Ideally, culture should refine, subdue, and "spiritualize" these strong natural energies, but not destroy them. Both Emerson and Nietzsche conceive of culture, in its best expression, as the sublimated transformation of a morally indeterminate natural energy. However, since culture, for Emerson and Nietzsche, evolves out of nature, it is, in effect, the self-suppression of nature itself insofar as the energy and power of nature are, in a Hegelian manner, negated and preserved in culture.

Nietzsche has often been criticized for calling attention to the natural egoism of each organic entity, especially that of the most self-conscious organic entity, man. He has been attacked for claiming that man's primitive striving for power is an egoistic process. Here, as in other instances, a frank interpretation of the motives, drives, and actions of individuals that is, alas, based upon a substantial amount of factual evidence is mistakenly taken to be a celebration of selfishness or naked egotism. This is not Nietzsche's position. He neither defends nor promotes a morality of selfishness. In his analysis of human motivations and in his denial that *soi-disant* altruistic actions are unegoistic he has affiliations with psychological egoism. But he does not rest there because he admits, in *Beyond Good and Evil,* that every morality entails " a bit of tyranny against nature." The "egoism" that enters into all of our actions is, for him, derived from the organic evolution of the species and is attributed metaphorically to the most minute organisms. In one place, with obvious irony, he notes that "we may consider all that has to be done to preserve the organism as a 'moral' demand."[61] The 'egotism' that Nietzsche uncovers with such relish is not, strictly speaking, a "psychological" egotism; rather, it is a natural, organic egoism. It is this which provides the raw material for an affirmative morality of strength which is a morality of strenuousness. All positive, life-affirming moralities have their ground in nature, in what is natural. Hence, Nietzsche suggests, morality has its origin in what in nonmoral: the energy and power of the natural world. It is for this reason that he condemns antinatural moralities as antilife, as the suicidal turning of life against itself. The natural egoism in man is rooted in the perspectival optics of life itself, in the core of the organic dimension of the self.[62] Although there is more to Nietzsche's analyses of egoism, an examination of them would carry me too far afield of my concern here.

Nietzsche agreed with Emerson that there is a ferocity at the heart of nature, that many of the dreadful traits found in 'inferior' animal species are found in *homo natura,* in his natural history. The evolutionary road to civilization has been a long and painful one in which the primitive drives of natural man had to be, as far as possible, suppressed or controlled. The drives, passions, and impulses inherited by man are powerful and potentially dangerous. In *Daybreak* Nietzsche appeals to the conception of atavism in this regard. The strong, reckless, energetic, violent criminal that frightens the citizenry shows us what we once were, what our ancestors were like. If this naturally inherited energy, minus the violent acting-out behavior, could be harnessed, it could provide the fuel for a morality of strength. If a person is to be mentally and physically healthy, Nietzsche thought, the "wicked" impulses, passions, and drives must not be extirpated. They should be forged, but not melted away.

Given the conventional portrait of Emerson as a naive idealist, it may come as a surprise to some that he had emphasized the importance of "natural egotism" (despite its dangers) in the development of individualism and strong individuals. Even though he deplores selfishness (as Nietzsche in *Thus Spoke Zarathustra* attacked "sick selfishness"), he recognized the value of a natural egotism. And he offers a pre-Darwinian evolutionary explanation of the phenomenon:

> This goiter of egotism is so frequent among notable persons that we must infer some strong necessity in nature which it subserves; such as we see in the sexual attraction. The preservation of the species was a point of such necessity that nature has secured it at all hazards by immensely overloading the passion, at the risk of perpetual crime and disorder. So egotism has its roots in the cardinal necessity by which each individual persists to be what he is.[63]

The individuality that has its origin in man's natural egotism is valuable insofar as it is the basis of culture. Despite the hazards of this egoistic individual determination, the aim of culture "is not to destroy this . . . but to train away all impediment and mixture and leave nothing but pure power."[64] If man's "organic egotism" is disciplined and "meliorated," it can serve as the basis for ambition, social effort, creative action. Education and cultivation are essential to this disciplinary process; but so, too, is physical activity. Physical activities and competitive sports are especially important for the development of young men and women. They offer "lessons in the art of power."[65] What is a *cliché* now was not so in a period in which the physical dimension of human development was neglected. Nietzsche was quick to adopt Emerson's attitude towards the physical development of youths. He incorporated this theme into his criticism of a cultural education based on "words, words, words" and his advocacy of a culture based upon life and vitality in "On the Uses and Disadvantages of History for Life."

Wickedness, in the form of man's "organic egotism," often generates good. Referring to the "Americans" (whom Emerson chastises and criticizes with a severity that Nietzsche later turns on "the Germans"), he remarks that "we are great by exclusion, grasping, and egotism." The Americans have, he continues with dry irony, illustrated the French saying, *Rien ne réussit mieux que la succes.*

Contrary to moral prejudices, egotism grants a momentary strength, a concentration of energy, a directionality that can produce effective or beneficial action. Nature turns this 'evil' into good, "utilizes misers, fanatics, show-men, egotists, to accomplish her ends."[66] What is true of nature is within the power of the individual of "strong will." A "systematic discipline" is needed to transform crude passions into an ascending creative impulse. The problem is to harness and guide primitive drives, to restore natural instincts without releasing them pell-mell. Emerson says it better: "Better, certainly, if we could secure the strength and fire which rude, passionate men bring into society, quite clear of their vices. But who dares draw out the linchpin from the wagonwheel?"[67]

Nietzsche is accused, in another sense, of pulling out "the linchpin from the wagonwheel," even though he doesn't. Rather, he accurately expresses and builds upon the various suggestions in Emerson's essays of a conception of sublimation. His theory of the sublimation or spiritualization of instincts, drives, and passions clearly anticipates (and, despite Freud's denials, influences) the Freudian theory of sublimation. As Freud later does, Nietzsche particularly refers to the "sublimation" (*Sublimierung*) of sexual and aggressive drives, to their expression in a multiplicity of forms. He refers to the transfer of love from other persons to religious objects of veneration as a form of "sublimated sexuality."[68] The impulse to cruelty has not died out in civilized man. Much in higher culture results from a sublimation of "cruelty." The "wild animal" in man has not been eliminated despite millions of years of evolution. It has been transformed, "deified." The enjoyment of tragedy involves a refinement of cruelty. We vicariously enjoy, by way of identification, the spectacle of the suffering hero or heroine. Even the impersonal scientist experiences a refined feeling of cruelty as he discloses, beneath surface appearances, hurtful truths.[69] It is odd that he does not mention, in this context, the cruelty that pervades so much humor and satire, the devastating joking that is appropriately called "nihilistic" comedy. And, given his protopsychoanalytic insights, it is ironic that he did not discern the refined cruelty of his own thought in its nihilistic phases.

Nietzsche laments that virtue (in its modern expression) is losing its attraction. In fact, it has become what it was not before: "vice."[70] A "restoration of nature" is needed in order to generate virtues of strength, virtues of power. What he calls "the wickedness of power" can be a source of positive affects and creative actions. The "moralist's madness" was to demand the destruction of the passions in lieu of restraining, subduing them.[71] These great sources of energy and strength, these "impetuous torrents of the soul that are so often dangerous and overwhelming," ought to be pressed into service.[72] What is needed, he says elsewhere, is "to press the mightiest natural powers—the affects—into service."[73] This notion of the "spiritualization" (*Vergeistigung*) of our drives, passions, and impulses is clearly the completion of Emerson's suggestions concerning the same process. And it differs from Plato's conception of the rational guidance and control of the appetitive and spirited aspects of the self in such a way as to cement the Emersonian connection. For Emerson, like Nietzsche, questions the priority of reason in man and emphasizes that the shaping of the "crescive" or creative self requires a "strong will," a persistent effort of willing towards an affirmative end. In man, as in life itself, there is a willing-towards-an-end, a "search after power" that is virtually Nietzsche's psychological theory of *der Wille zur Macht*. At times, Emerson's expression of this is distinctly Nietzschean: "We only value a stroke of will; he alone is happy who has a will; the rest are herds."[74]

As late as 1887, Nietzsche continues to reexpress Emerson's rudimentary suggestions concerning sublimation. He advises that we ought "To press everything terrible into *service,* one by one, step by step, experimentally: this is what the task of culture demands."[75] Where Emerson speaks of the "economy of nature" that requires expression of the passions in positive, creative ways, Nietzsche appeals to the "economy of life" as demanding the same. Rather than "pressing their power into service," the moralists seek the obliteration of strong desires and passions; they do not see the importance of *"economizing"* them.[76]

It has been said that Nietzsche developed his theory of sublimation through his study of the Hellenes. That is, he held that the sublime and noble culture of ancient Greeks was possible because the Greeks had been "cruel and bloodthirsty." Where there appears the *sublime,* there must have existed previously much that was not sublime. This observation of R. J. Hollingdale's has the appearance of plausibility because of the etymological association between sublime (*erhaben*) and a figurative word for sublimate (*erheben*), which literally means to raise up, to elevate.[77] However, as we have seen, a simpler explanation of the origin of the theory of sublimation is Nietzsche's absorption of Emerson's incisive observations on this process.

The dynamic interpretation of the self that Nietzsche repeatedly expresses is related to his belief that if the basic passions and drives were silenced, this would desiccate the wellspring of constructive, creative actions. Man is conceived of not as a smoothly functioning clockwork of traits, propensities, or dispositions. Rather, he is an "antagonism" of impulses, drives, passions, desires, "forces," reason and willing: "In man, *creature* and *creator* are united: there is in man, matter, fragment, excess, clay, mud, madness, chaos; but there is also in man creator, sculptor, the hardness of the hammer, the divine spectator and the seventh day."[78]

Out of this antagonism of "forces" grows aspiration, creative drive, the striving for more that moves the world. If the "creature" could be deleted from the being of man, the "creator" would also be destroyed. What are called the "immoral" propensities of man—his "striving for the forbidden," his "adventurous courage," his subtle "spiritual will to power"—are all necessary spurs to creative effort, achievement, and the rare attainment of "greatness."[79]

This conception of man is but a slight variation on that of Emerson. He, too, conceives of man as "a stupendous antagonism." He is an ill-disguised quadruped, "hardly escaped into biped," but in him, too, is the "maker of planets and suns," "the lightning which explodes and fashions planets." Side by side in the human being one finds "god and devil, mind and matter, king and conspirator, belt and spasm."[80] Given this conception of man, the moral goal of extracting passion, drives, and raw energy from him is, as Nietzsche puts it, an antinatural goal, a desire for the emasculation of the individual.[81] Both Emerson and Nietzsche sought to create a new morality of strength based upon the dynamic energy in the antagonistic being of man, one that required the willed sublimation of potentially dangerous passions and instincts. It was not Nietzsche alone who had renounced the Christian *desideratum,* the desire for "peace of soul," and projected a natural, strenuous, energetic ethics of health.[82]

If, as I believe, Freud borrowed or simply absorbed Nietzsche's emphasis on the power of the instincts, the expression of the unconscious in life and dreams, the idea of the sublimation of the instincts, as well as the suggestion of the theory of reaction-formation, and if, as has been shown, Nietzsche derived most of these conceptions from Emerson's insights, then Emerson is a hidden presence in Freudian psychoanalytic theory.

Master/Slave Morality

In tracing the genealogy of morals in his impressionistic phenomenology of two dominant forms of morality, Nietzsche argues that a group-morality or a "slave" morality reversed the values of a "master" morality. Even though he admits (in *Beyond Good and Evil*) that in all higher civilizations there are attempts to synthesize these two moralities and that both often reside in the same person, Nietzsche's bias towards the aristocratic, elitist "master morality" is obvious. The "rulers" who exude pride of self, confidence, nobility, and a sense of personal power have a positive, affirmative conception of goodness. They are law-givers and creators of values. It is they who originally define good and bad. The ethics of the majority is "reactive" rather than "active" and encourages mutual aid, group sentiments, sympathy, patience, and humility. Taking the opportunity to implicate J. S. Mill's ethics in this description, Nietzsche claims that a slave morality is fundamentally a "morality of utility." By doing so, he links slave morality to a morality of custom and/or "herd morality."

The ruling class describe themselves as honest, as good, and characterize those lower in "the order of rank" as ignoble, self-abasing, "bad." The categories of good and evil, on the other hand, emerge out of the value-reversals of slave morality. Thus, those who resent the pride, assurance, confidence, and self-respect of the "masters" come to characterize their "good" as "evil." The ascending aristocratic morality is attacked by a slave morality that is negative, reactive, restrictive, resentful, fretful, and suspicious. The "good" person is then redefined by a negative morality of resentment as harmless, safe, good-natured, naive or, in sum, *"un bonhomme."* In the language or the 'logic' of a slave morality, a good person is now one who is undangerous, somewhat simple, overly compliant, nonthreatening. Those who were considered by the ruling caste as of "base character" are, as a result of a "transvaluation of values," now esteemed as "the good." Though the language of morality (good/bad) was created by innovative members of the ruling caste to refer to their own ideal-typical representatives, the new language of "good" and "wicked" displaces the previous moral language. Good and bad, then, were the basic class-determined dualities that, Nietzsche believes, dominated the moral valuations of the Greco-Roman world.

By the time of the early Christians, Nietzsche claims, the resentment towards the Greco-Roman *ethos* emerged. Here he seems to follow the historians William Lecky and Edward Gibbon and pictures early Christian morality as vengeful and negative. Lecky, in his *History of European Morals,* links the rise of Christianity to the rise of the "slave class," to the effect on Roman social and political ideals of the importation of "foreign cults." And Gibbon, of course, blamed the fall of the Roman empire (as Nietzsche does in *The Antichristian*) on the vampiric effects of the *ethos* of Christianity. In his notes Nietzsche accepts the judgment of the Roman historian Tacitus that Christianity is a "most mischievous superstition" whose followers were convicted not so much of the charge of burning the city of Rome, but of a "hatred of mankind."[83] Nietzsche looks upon the Judeo-Christian morality from the standpoint of an ideal-theoretical Greco-Roman noble class and, therefore, views it as the expression of the values of an underclass. In *The Antichristian* he goes further and attributes it to the values of the *Chandala* or the "out-castes" of the Hindu social structure described in *The Laws of Manu.*[84]

Although Nietzsche admires the aristocratic morality of the true or "authentic" exemplars of a "master" morality, this is not, in my view, his considered version of a naturalistically grounded morality of strength that he seeks to shape and reshape in his writings. For his positive morality is not a straightforward neopaganism, particularly because it presupposes a retrieval of what is natural in a post-Christian, postnihilistic atmosphere. Moreover, in his depiction of "supreme" types of human beings he is no longer considering a social aristocracy. The strenuous morality he projects for those who are possible, but not yet, requires the acceptance of a reality and way of existing that would be alien to the "masters" he depicts in his phenomenology of master morality. Without going into too much detail, the new 'morality' he opposes to what he calls "the anemic Christian ideal" is a *"more robust"* ideal[85] that demands a sea change in one's way of interpreting existence and actuality. Among other things, it presupposes that one has lived through a nihilistic stage of feeling and thought, that one has renounced objective teleology and embraced the destructive and creative chaos of the cosmos, that one has been able to will the eternal return of one's existence and all existence, that one has embraced a Dionysian religion of life in face of the genuinely terrible aspects of life, the painful, ineluctable sufferings of existence.

Against this daunting background of requirements, Nietzsche's projected ideal (which is "beyond good and evil," but *not* "beyond good and bad") includes the Emersonian ideals of seeing the necessary as beautiful and, most painful of all, choosing to love one's fate (*amor fati*). Moreover, this ideal requires great self-discipline and a "bit of tyranny against nature," as well as against one's "first nature." It requires giving style to one's life, living in the present, being open to the "innocence of experience," being able to endure solitude, being able to withstand the isolation of standing alone, the neglect or criticism of others, embracing fully the tragic sense of life without despairing. What is needed to endure the demanding requirements of this ideal is what Emerson called "sacred courage." He understood that whoever aims high must renounce ease and popular support, perhaps applying to the effort required for this the saying of Porphyry: "Steep and craggy is the path of the gods."[86]

As we shall see in another context, the intellectual movement from an admiration for the moral values of the aristocrat, the patrician, to the creation of a demanding aristocracy of spirit is already apparent in the reflections of Emerson. He admired the assured "master" who radiates confidence, strength, and good manners. In fact, he was more an admirer of the actual social aristocracy, the social hierarchy of rank, than Nietzsche ever was. He cannot say enough about the heroes of history, "the great," the "transcendent men" whose actions have a magnetic appeal. But he is aware of the flattering light in which heroes are shown, is aware of the value of the commonplace, the need to protect ourselves from the worship of idols. There are stern demands in the effort to be "genuine," to be independent, self-reliant, to develop self-trust. In fact, "it demands something godlike in him who has cast off the common motives of humanity and has ventured to trust himself for a taskmaster."[87]

As in the case of his disciple in this respect, Emerson's ethical ideal is born of antagonism. It is the torpidity, the mediocrity, timorousness, conformity, and untruth of the conventional social morality he sees around him that sends Emerson back to retrieve something of the vitality, strength, and nobility of the Greco-Roman culture. Most men, he says with alarming simplicity, are "slaves." And most of us have inherited "badges of servitude." Given what he believes has happened to historical Christianity, he would rather be "a pagan, suckled in a creed outworn." The Greek and Roman ideal has been "domesticated" in a secular group morality which, Emerson implies, is no longer genuinely Christian. Virtually in Kierkegaard's language he asks: "in Christendom where is the Christian?"[88] On a smaller screen Emerson sketches the trajectory of Nietzsche's movement away from the Judeo-Christian ethics, away from the conformist group morality of the modern age, back towards the Greco-Roman world to recapture virtues of strength, restore pride and self-respect, and then forwards to a new challenging morality that is liberating and demanding, joyful and painful, affirmative and austere.

Before Nietzsche endeavors to adopt it as a central principle, Emerson prescribes a form of "self-overcoming," a difficult process that is generated by the virtue both cherished: truthfulness. In "Experience" it is said that "the life of truth is cold, and so far mournful; but it is not the slave of tears, contritions, and perturbations."[89] Once we firmly grasp the scapel of truth we have to turn it on everything; on our cherished ideals, on others and on ourselves; even on truth itself. What Emerson expressed as an insight years before, Nietzsche presents as if it were a sudden discovery:

> One must fight for truth every step of the way, virtually everything dear to our heart, on which our love and trust in life depend, must be sacrificed to it. It requires greatness of soul: the service of truth is the hardest service—What does it mean to be *honest* in spiritual things? That one is stern towards one's heart, that one despises "beautiful sentiments," that one makes each Yes and No a matter of conscience![90]

This valuation of honesty and of self-overcoming goes a long way towards explaining why both Emerson and Nietzsche seem to be always shedding their skin, engaging in arguments with themselves, invariably seeing two or more sides to everything, hesitating to seek a mediation for fear of resolving antitheses, postponing settled conclusions in order to avoid the security of dogmatism.

It is this practice of self-overcoming, it would seem, that drives Emerson to continually raise the requirements for his ideal of the "central man," the "synthetic" individual in whom antagonistic traits contend under the control of a strong will. If one looks for the foreshadowing of a master morality in Emerson's writings, one can definitely find it. He upholds those "who are intrinsically rich and powerful"[91] as examples of what man can become. Invariably, the "superior" types of people are described as grounded in nature, possessed of natural power and energy, in tune with the natural world. In "Manners" and "Character" in particular, the theme of "a self-constituted aristocracy, or fraternity of the best" is intensified. The master morality that Nietzsche projects into the past is discerned by Emerson in superlative individuals who appear in history sporadically. However, even as he cites El Cid, Julius Caesar, Alexander, Pericles, Cellini, Michelangelo, and others as paradigms of the "energetic class" of men, Emerson also prescribes what those of "heroic character" ought to be. Moreover, though he does not directly say, as Nietzsche does, that there is a distinctive morality associated with the "class of power," he continually insinuates such a morality, especially in contrast to what he almost calls "herd morality" and the morality associated with a religion that utters a "thousand negatives" and "negative propositions" that cause its followers and preachers to "bewail and moan."[92] Emerson and Nietzsche pass through a stage of hero worship, but neither remains there. It is ironic that Nietzsche is so hostile to Carlyle insofar as, up to a point, he has so much in common with him. This is particularly the case if he looked at Emerson's encomium to the English historian. Of Carlyle he says, "this man is a hammer that crushes mediocrity and pretension. He detects weakness on the instant, and touches it. He has a vivacious, aggressive temperament, and unimpressionable."[93]

Carlyle is said to have great "reverence for realities" and to admire "a strong nature . . . previous, it would seem, to all inquiry whether the force be divine or diabolic." Just as Emerson holds that "the great," the noble individuals, will not deign to take things too seriously, so, he tells us, does Carlyle prize humor. "He feels that the perfection of health is sportiveness, and will not look grave even at dullness or tragedy."[94] Naturally enough, Nietzsche counsels, in *Zarathustra* and elsewhere, that the wise and the "supreme men" must learn to laugh. What is positively strange is that Nietzsche recapitulates Emerson's various attempts to sculpt man perfected and, like Emerson, continually raises the standards for such perfection, projecting his ideal into the future. What may be called Emerson's implied master morality is obviously a counterideal to the modern moralities he sees around him, a morality that is incorporated in what will subsequently be shown to be his aristocratic radicalism and his image of a man "beyond-man."

Antinomianism

In the spirit of Emerson, Nietzsche sought to redefine the meaning of 'good,' as well as to transcend the radical dualism of good and wicked or 'evil.' Goodness must be allied with a toughness of spirit, and our virtues, as Emerson said, ought to have a cutting edge to them. In his defense of a rejuvenated idea of goodness Emerson quite often crosses the perimeter of conventional morality. He was quite aware that he tended to play the role of "devil's attorney." If he does so, it is to combat the negative, descending trends in American culture. Struggling to free himself from a morality of prohibition, from a morality of timidity which submits to the power of "public opinion," Emerson sometimes embraces an antinomianism that disturbed his contemporaries. When he does so, it is invariably in order to preserve a place in the world for the "exceptions" who are needed when people grow too much alike. His relaxation of the braces of restrictive moralities for the sake of the beauty, power, and liberating effects of the thought and actions of exceptions is tied to Emerson's desire to escape from the stultifying nets of a morbidly introspective, guilt-ridden, depressive morality. If he is a critic of conventional morality, "this technique of hyperbolic nay-saying is designed to confirm what must be the final . . . yea-saying."[95] It is curious how often American literary critics have appealed to Nietzsche in order to illuminate aspects of Emerson's thought. For, in many instances, as we've seen and shall see, it is Emersonian insights and conceptions that are accentuated and intensified in the philosophy of Nietzsche.

Nietzsche contended that the culture and *ethos* generated by the success of the Judeo-Christian religious worldview and ethics has been, *via* secularization, absorbed into a "herd-morality" that negates individuality and will eventually eliminate exceptions through the force of its leveling tendencies. Modern values are designed for the average type of human being and positively promote mediocrity. They have produced emasculated 'good' people who are more and more intolerant of those who are different. The Christian *ethos,* he claimed, encouraged "faith" dissociated from effort and energy and encouraged the growth of a "herd" consciousness, a uniformity of beliefs, values, and feelings. Though the Judeo-Christian ethics was once needed to tame the wild beasts who were our ancestors, it is now repressive and debilitating. It promotes a negative attitude towards life, instinct, spontaneity. All of the tendencies and valuations of this morality have led to a flatlands in which everything and everyone is "the same." In effect, it has led to the devaluation of life and man, to the emergence of a nihilism that he predicted the people of the twentieth century would inherit to their detriment, if not their total demise.

The "last man" who, in *Thus Spoke Zarathustra,* proclaims that all human beings are "the same," is the spokesman for the devaluation of man, for the triumph of "herd morality." He is the rasping voice of nihilism. In *On the Genealogy of Morals* Nietzsche spells out lucidly what he believes has been the ultimate consequence of the devolution of traditional morality:

> The levelling and diminution of European man is our greatest danger because the sight of him makes us despair. . . . We no longer see anything . . . that aspires to grow greater; instead, we have a suspicion that things will continue to go downhill, becoming . . . more placid . . . cosier, more ordinary, more indifferent. . . . Together with the fear of man, we have also lost the love of man . . . indeed . . . the will to man. Now the sight of man makes us despair. What is nihilism today if not that?[96]

Nietzsche sees what may be called a psychosocial cultural devolution at work in the modern world, one that, if it continues, will demoralize, depress, debilitate, and "destroy" exceptional individuals who think, feel, and value differently than a powerful majority. This injustice to such exceptions strikes at the heart of culture and the possibility of a higher culture. For he agrees with Emerson that we owe an enormous debt to the innovative, creative minority who have elevated the level of civilization, that it is a cultivated minority that sustains and perpetuates the greatest achievements of the human spirit.[97] Since he sees the cultural illness of his times as serious, Nietzsche reaches for strong medications. But one of them—antinomianism—is often misunderstood.

Relative to previous moralities, Nietzsche defiantly calls his own standpoint "immoralism." It is typically associated with what he calls his "dangerous slogan," "beyond good and evil." We've seen that he has already settled the question about those actions deemed morally wrong in traditional morality: he agrees that they ought not to be done. And his writings are dotted with what can only be construed as moral imperatives. "Become thyself!" (an echo of Pindar and of Emerson's admonition "to exist," to become "genuine," to strive to realize the potential self),[98] "remain faithful to the earth," esteem life as "sacred," "live dangerously," affirm *amor fati*, etc. Among these is the imperative to adopt an attitude towards life and existence that is "beyond good and evil." An antinomian slogan that has attracted a great deal of heated criticism.

Emerson's repulsion against social conformity, against the coercive effects of public opinion, against what de Tocqueville and J. S. Mill called "the tyranny of the majority," as well as against the intrusiveness of temporary group passions, is what often leads him to antinomian stances. His defiant defense of the intrinsic value of the subjective person leads him to attack the conventional manners and mores that demand submission to social and ideational norms. In "Self-Reliance" these attitudes are graphically asserted. He tells us that he has his "own stern claims and perfect circle. It denies the name of duty to many offices that are called duties." He repudiates (again, practically in Kierkegaard's language) "our slavish respect for numbers." The "sacredness of traditions" has nothing to do with him. When asked by a friend whether these defiant impulses might come from the devil, he replies that he thinks not—"but if I am the Devil's child, I will live then from the Devil." Emerson was quite aware of the dangers with which his new doctrine flirted. In a journal entry written before his Divinity School Address he reminds himself to "beware of Antinomianism."[99] But he doesn't heed his advice.

Emerson's Carlyle-like admiration for "great men" and "superior chronometers" is a factor contributing to his positive image of rule-breakers who have achieved much, contributed to the advance of civilization, and ennobled man. Under the sway of Carlyle, he asserts that "a strong person makes the law and custom null before his own will."[100] Moreover, he accurately reports that "to the right aristocracy, to Hercules, Theseus, Odin, the Cid . . . Napoleon . . . Walpole, to Fox, Chatham, Webster . . . every thing [except "incest & beastliness"] will be permitted."[101] But he does not settle in this opinion because he continually tries to reform and reshape his notion of antinomianism. Despite his admiration for exemplary individuals and his willingness to overlook their faults, he fights against his own tendencies towards hero-worship. Defeats are also great teachers that strengthen and, in the final analysis, as he says in "Heroism," "Self-trust is the essence of Heroism." As is the case in Nietzsche's existential hero, endurance of "the slings and arrows of outrageous fortune" is also heroic.

It is the aesthetic aura that surrounds heroic figures, as in the case of Nietzsche, that attracts Emerson to them and permits him to overlook their moral flaws. In "Power" he applauds the "affirmative force" in the *plus* man" (or, as Nietzsche would have read this, *die bejahend Kraft* in the *Überschussmensch*) for its "positive power," its energy, its overflowing vitality. Despite our moral qualms, we cannot ignore the value of "a *plus* condition of mind and body" even though we realize that it often appears in an "excess which makes it dangerous and destructive."[102] Although Emerson admires some of the tough virtues in military and political figures (what Nietzsche later called Renaissance-style *virtù*), he reserves his highest praise for creative, artistic innovators such as Cellini and Michelangelo. These members of the "affirmative class," despite their flaws, deserve "the homage of mankind." Even those who are committed to the scientific conquest of nature are obliquely praised in a visionary passage: "[Man] . . . is tempted out by his appetites and fancies to the conquest of this and that piece of nature, until he finds his well-being in the use of his planet, and of more planets than his own."[103]

In the context of "Power," as Nietzsche understood so well, what Emerson is saying is that "all *plus* is good" if and only if it is put in "the right place," guided in the right direction, if its "astringency or acidity is got out by ethics and humanity." The "search after power" or, as Nietzsche puts it, the "will to power," is inherited by man from nature and is his most potentially lethal trait. But it is also a tremendous source of positive energy and the will to excellence.

The admiration of exemplary individuals who achieved much on the stage of history is not the only source of Emerson's antinomian proclivities. His flight from a rigid morality of prohibition and introspective self-laceration, his desire to shake off the "Iceland of negations" of traditional morality, lead him into a spiritual and intellectual antinomianism that serves a higher good. In "The Transcendentalist" he declares that spiritually motivated exceptions "may with safety not only neglect, but even contravene every written commandment." A transcendence of the letter of the law is defended, somewhat vaguely, because it issues from "the determination of the private spirit." In this regard, the German

philosopher Jacobi is cited with approval. Emerson quotes a passage from his *Letter to Fichte,* one that had been noticed by others,
in which Jacobi states that the moral law exists for man and man
does not exist for the sake of the moral law. A defender, before
Kierkegaard, of subjective religious faith, Jacobi expresses a spiritually justified antinomianism:

> I am that atheist, that godless person who, in opposition to an imagi-
> nary doctrine of calculation, would lie as the dying Desdemona lied;
> would lie and deceive, as Pylades when he personated Orestes; would
> assassinate like Timoleon; would perjure myself like Epaminondas and
> John de Witt; I would resolve on suicide like Cato; I would commit
> sacrilege with David; yea, and pluck ears of corn on the Sabbath, for
> no other reason than that I was fainting for lack of food. For I have as-
> surance in myself that in pardoning these faults according to the letter,
> man exerts the sovereign right which the majesty of his being confers
> on him; he sets the seal of his divine nature to the grace he accords.

Emerson often appeals to this positive antinomianism. In one
place he mentions, *en passant,* a friend's comment in regard to public opinions about his views: that he is beyond the praise or blame
of the public. In "Character" he says that some individuals are
above praise and that a self-trusting person "can neither be praised
nor insulted." The depth of Emerson's influence on Nietzsche—if
it is, at this point, even in question—is measured by the fact that
years later he proudly declares that he is beyond "the praise or
blame" of others.

There is little doubt that it was Emerson who first implanted in
Nietzsche's mind the seeds of antinomianism. Certainly, the
former Unitarian minister was familiar with the recurring tendency towards antinomianism in the Christian tradition and the
hostility of the orthodox to it. But what is interesting in regard to
his affiliation with Nietzsche is that Emerson, by implication,
joins antinomianism with gnosticism. That is, the valuation of
knowledge (*gnosis*) over faith (*pistis*). Moreover, Emerson discerns
the same linkage in Hindu thought. And he incorporates this into
the way of being he prescribes. Thus, Harold Bloom's emphasis
on Emerson's valuation of *gnosis* is on target except that, in my
view, it is not, for Emerson, only a "literary gnosticism,"[104] but
an existential gnosticism as well. The new "religion of character"
that Emerson proposes in "Worship," "whatever else it be, must
be intellectual. The scientific mind must have a faith which is science." Here science refers to knowledge in general, scientific
knowledge of the natural world, and knowledge as insight or *gno-*

sis. Nietzsche's "Dionysian religion" will promote and encourage the same modalities of knowledge.

In a notebook entitled "Orientalist" Emerson expresses a view that runs through his writings. "In the history of the intellect," he writes, "no more important fact than the Hindoo theology, teaching that the beatitudes or Supreme Good is to be obtained through science [=knowledge, *gnosis*]."[105] No doubt he saw the similarity between the stress on knowledge (*vidya*), as spiritual insight, in Hinduism and the centrality of *gnosis* in the Gnostic sects. In the same passage he goes on to say that spiritual knowledge is attained by seeing through "the magical illusions" of the phenomenal world, the "*Maias* or illusions" that cloud and obscure our understanding. This espousal of gnosticism interlocks with antinomianism. That is, that redemption is attained through insights that lift us out of the circle of becoming at peak moments of liberation in which, as Hindu scriptures say, "good and evil" are left behind.

Emerson expresses very little interest in "the beyond" or "the other world" and, in fact, shows virtually no interest in the traditional doctrine of immortality. Insofar as redemption is possible, he suggests in a number of places, it is attained, as Nietzsche says in *Thus Spoke Zarathustra,* in the here and now, in "time and becoming." This coincides with my previous reference to Emerson's emphasis upon Heraclitean flux, on the value of life despite its transitory nature, on the experience of an *ekstasis* in immanence.

Nietzsche was quite familiar with Emerson's sympathy with oriental thought. Later, of course, Schopenhauer reinforced his interest in Buddhism and Hinduism. And, finally, he had the advantage of a friendship with the then-leading European expert on Hinduism, Paul Deussen. He expressed his admiration for his *Das System des Vedanta* (1883) in a series of letters to Deussen. Moreover, Nietzsche was far more knowledgeable concerning Eastern philosophy than many have suspected. As early as 1875, in a letter to his friend Carl von Gersdorff (December 13, 1875), he praised the Buddhist scripture *Sutta Nipata* and went on to say that "the rendering of the unworthiness of life and of the deception of all goals often impresses itself upon me so strongly, particularly when I'm lying in bed ill, that I long to hear something more of it, but not amalgamated with Jewish-Christian idioms."[106]

Since he had been reading Emerson assiduously since 1862, it is clear that Nietzsche had already been exposed to oriental concepts. This had a powerful impact on his thought. As we've seen, Emerson had already instilled in his mind the idea that we ought to put

our sins and moral errors beneath and behind us. Emerson's quotation to this effect from "Hindoo" scriptures was reinforced in
Nietzsche's mind by his reading of a far more detailed account of
this point in Deussen's *The System of Vedanta*. He found there a
central doctrine of esoteric Hinduism: that whoever has disciplined
the self, renounced all attachments, and attained *vidya* (or *gnosis*)
enters a spiritual state "beyond good and evil." It is this phrase
from Hindu scripture that is used as the tital of one of his books
and is adopted as his "dangerous slogan."

Although both Emerson and Nietzsche were aware of the dangers implicit in this esoteric Hindu doctrine for adepts, this "overcoming," as Hindu scriptures express it, of "good and evil works"
and past deeds, this antinomianism of the spirit based on "knowledge," neither was probably aware that the history of Hinduism
had already spawned perversions of this volatile doctrine. India
had already experienced the emergence of religious cults that encouraged active immorality in order to demonstrate a total freedom from moral conventions or because of belief that salvation
was indifferent to morality. The orthodox, quite naturally, were
horrified by these aberrations and put them down.[107] Any historian of East Indian civilization could have told Nietzsche, in depressing detail, how "dangerous" his slogan really was.

Nietzsche was more familiar with the dangers of antinomianism
than Emerson by virtue of his acquaintance with Joseph von Hammer's *History of the Assassins Out of Middle Eastern Sources* (1818).
For this study showed the religiously motivated terrorism of the
Ismailis sect, the *hashshāshin,* whose ostensible motto was "Everything is permitted."[108] This was a nihilism in *praxis,* an extreme
form of religiously inspired antinomianism from which Nietzsche
had to dissociate himself. Nowhere does he, his character Zarathustra, or his imagined "beyond-men" support or promote this
kind of active nihilism. Unfortunately, because he refers to the Assassins and their nefarious slogan in his writings he invites an association that theologians, philosophers, and contributors to
popular culture have exploited and used against him.

Nietzsche uses the principle "beyond good and evil" sparingly.
The antinomic stance he defends is but a more intense, dramatic,
and volatile version of what he originally found in the writings of
the "genteel" Emerson. The principle is invoked in a context in
which "free spirits" are distinguished from those who desire a
"green-pasture happiness of the herd." It is associated with the
Emersonian notion of the good of wickedness for the enhancement

of the strength of the "plant" man. After virtually paraphrasing Emerson's assertions about the value of "everything wicked, terrible, tyrannical in man" for the growth of the species and the individual, Nietzsche cements his relation to Emerson in his description of his intellectually courageous "free spirits." He asserts that "we are born, sworn, jealous friends of *solitude,* of our own most profound, most midnightly, most middaily solitude: that is the type of man we are, we free spirits!"[109] This is the turn that Emerson takes after announcing his antinomic principle in "The Transcendentalist." For his transcendentalists "repel influences . . . shun general society . . . find their tasks and amusements in solitude." Being beyond good and evil pertains to a way of being, an attitude towards life, existence, and actuality. One of its ingredients is accepting the value of our "wicked" traits that link us to the natural world. Speaking for his free spirits, Nietzsche asserts that we should be "grateful to god, devil, sheep, and worm in us" because our highest spiritual aspirations are dependent on the intermixture of these antagonistic traits, of what is usually considered as "good and evil." The dialectical interaction of polarities in nature and that "piece of nature" that is man, absent any facile Hegelian mediation, that is so much a part of Emerson's thought is wholeheartedly embraced by Nietzsche. In the *Nachlass* from the late 1880s he writes that "love and hate, gratitude and revenge, good nature and anger, affirmative acts and negative acts, belong together. One is good on condition that one knows how to be wicked; one is wicked because otherwise one would not understand how to be good."[110]

One sense of beyond good and evil is being beyond the radical bifurcation of good and evil in traditional morality. In nature, as in the individual, good and evil are intertwined. The goal, as we've seen, is to refine, cultivate, creatively channel passions, drives, and desires that are volatile by a self-conscious process of sublimation. This is a persistent, dynamic process that requires discipline, effort, and struggle.

It is not the case that "to be beyond good and evil is to combine all of one's features and qualities, whatever their traditional moral value, into a controlled and coherent whole."[111] Nehamas models an interpretation of Nietzsche's thought on his ostensible conception of literature and the arts. Thus, he not only pulls the teeth of Nietzsche's emphasis on the "how" of *Existenz,* but converts the prescription to live and be "beyond good and evil" into a tropic filigree.

The Dionysian religion that Nietzsche proclaims is character-ized by the affirmation of life and existence as it is, "without sub-straction, exception or selection." This is the negation of a nihilistic Romantic pessimism insofar as the contradictions, antith-eses, the "detested and notorious side of existence" are accepted not because they are acceptable, but because the valuation of life and existence requires the affirmation of everything. Being beyond good and evil is a "divine" way of viewing actuality, an aesthetic interpretation of the world, that is included in the tragic optimism of the "Dionysian faith." It would take what Emerson calls "sov-ereign individuals" (Nietzsche's *souveränen Individuen*) to take the long step to this liberation from a (traditional) moral interpretation of actuality. Such individuals, who have "sacred courage," must have submitted to a "voluntary discipline . . . an art of under-standing *beyond* the affects" and must, at times, be able "to think in a 'supra-European' way."[112]

Nietzsche illustrates this Emerson-inspired, *gnostic,* supra-Euro-pean way of thinking in a context in which his conception of thinking and living "beyond good and evil" is made clear. In *On the Genealogy of Morals* he remarks that the insight into the illu-sions of desire and overattachments to the things of the world is a "state beyond good and evil." Under the influence of Deussen, he quotes from the Vedantists: "Neither what is done nor undone gives him (the sage) pain; his dominion is no longer marred by any action; he has left both good and evil behind."[113] Although Nietz-sche is critical of aspects of Hindu thought, specifically attacking the idea that in profound sleep (*sushupta*) there is a union of the soul with Brahman, he is *not* critical of the belief that redemption is achieved not merely through faith or good works, but chiefly by means of knowledge (*vidya*). Since he has become quite familiar with the esoteric doctrines of Hinduism both from his study of Deussen's works and his acquaintance with the Hindu code of laws, *The Laws of Manu,* he knows that "emancipation" and "lib-eration" (*moksha*) entails attaining a psychic and intellectual state "beyond good and evil." And this is precisely what his demanding and "dangerous" principle means. Like that of Emerson, Nietz-sche's antinomianism is a way of thinking, a form of spiritual knowledge, that is *not* activistic. Nor is it related to the licentious-ness and active immorality that has been justified by impassioned antinomians in the Western, Eastern, and Near Eastern religious traditions.[114] In a strict sense, what Emerson suggested and Nietz-sche emphasized (without sufficient qualification) was actually more a form of hypernomianism than, say, the antinomianism of St. Paul, which held that, after the revelation of Christ, the Mosaic law was given secondary significance in relation to the higher spirituality of the total love of God.[115] The Gnostics also viewed the Mosaic law as too formal and as lacking in spirituality and criticized it in the name of "knowledge" (*gnosis*) and a more strenuous asceticism.

In one place Nietzsche offers a description of the ideal teacher that suggests the orientation of an East Indian guru. The ideal teacher "never says what he himself thinks, but only what he thinks about something in connection with the benefit he brings to the student. . . . Such a teacher is beyond good and evil, but no one dare know that."[116] Being "beyond good and evil" is first projected as an ideal for the "new philosopher" in *Beyond Good and Evil*. Later it is a trait of spiritual aristocrats, a characteristic of "good Europeans." And, finally, it is the attitude of the "beyond-men" of the future or those who are able "to think in a 'supra-European' way." In *The Antichristian* Nietzsche makes his valuations plain and seems to be thinking of his American "soul-brother" once again:

> The most spiritual men, as the *strongest,* find their happiness where others would find their destruction: in the labyrinth, in severity towards themselves and others, in experiment; their joy lies in self-constraint: with them, asceticism becomes nature and instinct. They consider the difficult task a privilege, to play with vices which overwhelm others a *recreation.* . . . Knowledge—a form of asceticism. They are the most venerable kind of human being: this does not exclude their being the most cheerful, the most amiable.[117]

This image of spiritually strong individuals occurs in a passage that refers to Brahmin priests, but seems to allude to Emerson as well. For Nietzsche says that for "the most spiritual, the affirmative instinct," "*The world is perfect.*" Every "imperfection" is beneath them and they feel a *pathos* of distance between man and man. The reference to the world become perfect is reminiscent of a comment Nietzsche made twenty-two years earlier about a passage in Emerson's *Nature*. The ego-less experience of the beauty of nature described there is paraphrased by Nietzsche, and he says that "then Nature became perfect."[118]

While Nietzsche rejects a morality that insists upon the absolute opposition of good and evil, he does not, in spite of the presentation of the highest spiritual state as being "beyond good and evil," abandon a 'morality' (if such it may be called) of "good and bad."

All morality, even his own ethic of affirmation and endurance, is a "bit of tyranny against nature." In a letter to Paul Rée he seems to belie his own slogan of "immoralism" by expressing surprise that others say he has no morality. He exclaims that "I believe that I have a *stricter* morality than anybody!"[119] From his new perspective "bad" is substituted for what was previously called *böse:* it is whatever is antinatural, antilife, whatever proceeds from weakness, from envy, from resentment, from vengefulness, a nihilistic "will to nothingness," the inability "to resist a stimulus," a debilitating sympathy, hiding within the crowd, conformity, a lack of "self-reliance," lacking an "instinct for growth," meanspiritedness, rigid dogmatism, and much more. If a morality is a "table of values," then there is no doubt that Nietzsche has a morality despite his self-described "immoralism."

Although Nietzsche extends Emerson's search for a new morality of beauty, strength, and discipline beyond the boundary of his discourse, he is clearly infused with the spirit of the American thinker. Surprisingly, some of the most volatile aspects of Nietzsche's thought have, as we've seen, their roots in the fertile soil of Emerson's imagination and thought. Insights he spins out from that "zero of indifferency"[120] from which he thought harsh truths should be spoken are worked up, enhanced, intensified, and, at times, overheated in Nietzsche's texts. It is astonishing to see how much of the philosophy of Nietzsche has been written on a palimpsest on which one can detect traces of the essays of Emerson.

Chapter 6 Notes

1. *SW* 1, *GT* §2, p. 32.

2. The most recent fusion of these two modalities of Dionysianism can be found in Ofelia Schutte's *Beyond Nihilism: Nietzsche Without Masks,* Chapter 1, "Truth and the Dionysian." Erik Thurin claims that a difference between Emerson and Nietzsche lies in the fact that Nietzsche criticized Socrates (or Socratism) because he laid the groundwork for the decline of Greek civilization in that he "deemphasized 'Dionysian' unity and wholeness in favor of an 'Apollonian' sharpness of vision." In contrast, Thurin holds, Emerson looks favorably upon the Socratic-Platonic turn in ancient Greek culture (Erik I. Thurin, *Emerson as Priest of Pan,* p. 245). This is contestable given Emerson's inclination towards Dionysian affirmation and his sense of "the tragic" in existence. In "Intellect" in particular he criticizes abstraction and the elevation of ideas or thought

into "impersonal and immortal" objects. Thought that is "disentangled from the web of unconsciousness" is "embalmed." "A better art than that of Egypt has taken fear and corruption out of it" (Intellect," *EE*, p. 181). This observation is incorporated in Nietzsche's attack on " 'Reason' in Philosophy" in *Twilight of the Idols*. Thus, he criticizes the "Egyptianism" of philosophers, their sanctification of "conceptual mummies." What they have bracketed, as Emerson already suggested, is "Death, change, age . . . procreation and growth." Moreover, Emerson's frequent positive references to the importance of "spontaneity and instinct," his emphases on willing, his valuation of "the superiority of the spontaneous or intuitive principle over the arithmetical or logical" ("Intellect," *EE*, p. 182), to say nothing of his Dionysian celebration of the ecstasy of life, entail strong anti-Socratic and anti-Platonic valuations. Hence, despite his respect for reason, its value and its use, his considered position on this score is obviously very closely related to that of Nietzsche.

3. R. A. Yoder, *Emerson and the Orphic Poet in America*, p. 100.

4. *SW* 12:354–55.

5. Yoder, *Emerson and the Orphic Poet in America*, p. 36. The pronouncements of the "Orphic poet" are located by Yoder in the section on "Spirit," but they are actually found in "Prospects."

6. Cf. Rudolf Schottlaender, "Two Dionysians: Emerson and Nietzsche," *South Atlantic Quarterly*. In his notes Nietzsche avers that aesthetic judgments, especially those of "taste," are the "ground of *moral* judgments." In the same place he states what was clearly his aim: *"Reduction of morality to aesthetics!!" ["Reduktion der Moral auf Aesthetik!!"]* (*SW* 9:471). In regard to Emerson's Dionysianism, it has been said that "Emerson . . . conceives of Nature as a Dionysian force, with overflow and intoxication in it, and his imaginative symbols for it are all of this order" (George E. Woodberry, in *The Recognition of Ralph Waldo Emerson*, ed. Milton Konvitz, p. 130). Cf. "The Poem" (Ibid., p. 132).

7. "Goethe; or, the Writer," in *RMNAL*, p. 275.

8. *RMNAL*, p. 132. The connection between Emerson's antinomianism and Hinduism is not dealt with in studies of Emerson.

9. "Art," *EE*, p. 201.

10. *The Early Lectures of Ralph Waldo Emerson*, III:105.

11. "Self-Reliance," *PE*, p. 162.

12. "The Method of Nature," *RMNAL*, p. 195.

13. "Lecture on the Times," *RMNAL*, p. 268.

14. Ibid., p. 266.

15. *Emerson in His Journals*, ed. Joel Porte, p. 83.

16. *SW* 1, *GT* §9, pp. 64–71.

17. "History," *PE*, p. 131.

18. "Character," *EE*, p. 263.

19. *The Will to Power*, §252. Ironically, Kierkegaard, who strongly defends New Testament Christianity, admitted that the very Christian faith he championed was "poison" for many types of human beings. He

contends that when it is "preached in truth to the happy, those who enjoy life, then Christianity becomes a kind of cruelty" (*Søren Kierkegaard's Journals and Papers*, ed. and trans., H. V. Hong and E. H. Hong [Bloomington and London, 1978] 6:189).

20. Ibid., §248.

21. *SW* 1:783. Insofar as Christian morality insists upon the absolute disrelationship between good and evil, this means, from Nietzsche's standpoint, that it denies the value of man's natural drives and, therefore, expresses an "antinatural" attitude. It has accurately been pointed out that Nietzsche "thinks that the traditional assumptions incorporated into Christianity are that the good is purely good and the evil purely evil. His analysis . . . has shown that these assumptions are false: the good and evil are intertwined with one another . . . they are not thoroughgoing opposites" (John Wilcox, *Truth and Value in Nietzsche*, p. 96).

22. *SW* 3, *MAM* §246, p. 205.

23. "Uses of Great Men," *RMNAL*, p. 14.

24. "Fate," *PE*, p. 365.

25. "Considerations By the Way," *COL*, p. 256.

26. Honoré Mirabeau (1749–1791) was a French politician and writer who served in the National Assembly during the early phases of the French revolution. He wrote a book of "recollections" and eight volumes of "biographical memoirs."

27. "Considerations By the Way," *COL*, p. 259.

28. "Wealth," *COL*, pp. 95–96.

29. *SW* 3, *FW* §4, pp. 376–77.

30. *SW* 5, *JGB* §44, pp. 61–62.

31. "Considerations By the Way," *COL*, p. 254.

32. Ibid., p. 253.

33. This is a feature of Philippa Foot's essay: "Nietzsche's Immoralism" (*New York Review of Books*, pp. 18–22). She mentions Emerson's *Essays* as an influence on Nietzsche and says that this work sheds interesting light on Nietzsche's thought. However, she doesn't state any relation between the latter and Emerson's idea of "the good of evil." At one point she attributes the idea of "the image of a tree which to flourish had to have its roots in the mud" to Nietzsche, mistakenly locating this reference in section 171 in *The Gay Science*. No doubt she was thinking of the metaphorical description of man as a plant. As far as I know, there is no statement such as she cites in Nietzsche's writings, even though he does refer to man as a "tree," but in a quite different sense. That is, "we are . . . always growing, changing, shedding our bark each spring, becoming younger, higher, stronger. We grow like trees—that is hard to understand, like all life!—not in one place, but all over, not in one direction, but equally upwards and outwards as inwards and downwards" (*SW* 3, *FW* §371, p. 623).

34. *The Will to Power*, §786.

35. *SW* 5, *GM* 2, §24, p. 335.

36. *SW* 3, M §76, p. 73.

37. "Swedenborg; or, the Mystic," *RMNAL*, p. 122.

38. "The Conservative," *RMNAL*, p. 286.

39. *Werke* (GOA), XII:92.

40. "Power," *COL*, pp. 56–65.

41. *The Will to Power*, §1026.

42. *SW* 5, *JGB* §212, p. 146.

43. *The Will to Power*, §44.

44. *Werke* (GOA), XII:86–87.

45. *SW* 2, *MAM* §96, p. 93. The invitation to "evil" in *Thus Spoke Zarathustra* is correctly said to refer to this opposition of 'evil' to 'good' construed as "customary" (Laurence Lampert, *Nietzsche's Teaching*, 318n). The problem is that throughout *Zarathustra* Nietzsche uses the same term to refer to evil in its traditional sense and in his revised sense of *böse*. What makes matters worse, he speaks of the transformation of man's drives into something good without using the concept of "spiritualization" or "sublimation" that he employs elsewhere. Without any signal, the sense of "evil" shifts back and forth virtually throughout *Zarathustra* as Nietzsche uses it now in a traditional sense, then in his special sense, even sometimes in the same paragraph. Here polysemy is the reverse of harmless.

46. *SW* 3, M, "Vorrede," p. *16*.

47. Stack, *Lange and Nietzsche*, pp. 75n, 310. Recently, Nietzsche's endeavor to adopt a stance beyond morality has again been interpreted in terms of what Hegel called "sublation" or negation and preservation in an appropriate way. "The distinctions between weak and strong, active and reactive, displace good and evil . . . [and] are formulated in terms of quantities and relations of power." Hence, they seem to be nonmoral distinctions. But they clearly have a "moral charge" in Nietzsche's writings. That is, "Nietzsche approves strength and condemns weakness in a way that is structurally identical to moral approval and condemnation, so that the 'transvaluation' of the old categories [of good and evil] starts to look like their *Aufhebung*" (Henry Staten, *Nietzsche's Voice*. p. 21).

48. *SW* 3, M §103, pp. 91–92.

49. "Success," in *Society and Solitude*, p. 289.

50. "Self-Reliance," *PE*, p. *147*.

51. *Werke* (GOA), XIII:126.

52. *The Will to Power*, §1025.

53. *SW* 12:413.

54. "Considerations By the Way," *COL*, p. 258.

55. Ibid., p. 259.

56. "Behavior," *COL*, p. 175.

57. "Notes," *COL*, p. 409.

58. *Werke* (GOA), XIV:101.

59. *SW* 5, *JGB* §257, p. 205.

60. "Power," *COL*, p. 71.

61. *Werke* (GOA), XIII:170.

62. Ibid., XVI:114.

63. "Culture," *COL*, p. 134.

64. Ibid.

65. Ibid., p. 143.

66. "Success," *Society and Solitude*, p. 273.

67. "Considerations By the Way," *COL*, p. 257.

68. *SW* 2, *MAM* II §95, pp. 414–15.

69. *SW* 5, *JGB* §229, pp. 165–67.

70. *The Will to Power*, §324.

71. Ibid., §383.

72. Ibid.

73. Ibid., §386.

74. "Notes," *COL*, p. 352.

75. *The Will to Power*, §1025.

76. Ibid., §383.

77. *Twilight of the Idols* and *The Anti-Christ*, Appendix F, p. 193.

78. *SW* 5, *JGB* §225, pp. 160–61.

79. Ibid., §227, 162–63.

80. "Fate," *PE*, p. 358.

81. *SW* 5, *JGB* §200, pp. 120–21.

82. *SW* 6, *G* v, §3, p. 84. That *Twilight of the Idols* (1889) includes a number of Emersonian themes—the "Egyptianism" of abstract rationalism, the idea of each of us being "a piece of fate," the reprise of the theme of "fatality" in man's being that reverts back to his early essay, "Fate and History," the idea that the genius *"expends himself,"* the tragic optimism of "Dionysian affirmation," as well as minor notes of the American writer—belies the occasionally expressed view that Nietzsche was impressed by Emerson "in his youth."

83. *SW* 9, p. 274. Cf. Stack, *Lange and Nietzsche*, pp. 80–82.

84. The reversal of values that Nietzsche attributes solely to the importation of Judeo-Christian religious and moral values into Roman civilization had already appeared in the teachings of Stoicism, which emerged in Greece with the teachings of Zeno in the third century B.C. The incipient reversal of pagan moral values is shown by the Stoics' humane attitude towards slaves, their emphasis upon the "brotherhood of man" (a theme sounded earlier by Alexander the Great, who advocated universal brotherhood and equal rights for all rational human beings, who encouraged the intermarriage of Greek soldiers and Persian women), nonresistance to unjust treatment, benevolence towards all people, and the endurance of suffering. It was they who averred that "true nobility of virtue is within reach of the slave." The synonymy between the ethical values of the Stoic emperor Marcus Aurelius and those of the Stoic slave, Epictetus, indicates that, *before* Christian morality was recognized in the Roman world, an internal transformation of moral values was taking place at all levels of Roman society. Given that the original *stoa poikile* was established by Zeno in Athens in 294 B.C., it could be said that Stoicism emerged out

of the educated, ruling class in ancient Greece. This tends to undermine Nietzsche's account of the evolution of what he calls "slave morality." Cf. R. D. Hicks, *Stoics and Epicureans*, (New York: Charles Scribner's Sons, 1910), pp. 3–152. In *A Study of History* Arnold Toynbee calls attention to Alexander's ideal of a universal harmony (*harmonia*) or concord among all men (Arnold Toynbee, *A Study of History*, one volume abridged edition, [New York: Oxford University Press, 1946], p. 495).

85. *The Will to Power*, §361.

86. "Culture," *COL*, pp. 162–63.

87. "Self-Reliance," *PE*, p. 156.

88. Ibid., p. 162.

89. "Experience," *PE*, p. 287.

90. *SW* 6, *A* §50, p. 230.

91. "Uses of Great Men," *RMNAL*, p. 10.

92. "Notes," *COL*, pp. 389–90. Cf. "Success," in *Society and Solitude*, p. 291.

93. "Carlyle," *PE*, p. 623. The image Emerson uses to describe Carlyle's traits immediately suggests the subtitle of *Twilight of the Idols*, "*How to Philosophize with a Hammer.*"

94. Ibid., p. 625.

95. Gertrude R. Hughes, *Emerson's Demanding Optimism*, p. 113. Hughes's study corrects the belief of Stephen Whicher that Emerson denied in his thought "the tragic sense of life" (Whicher, *Freedom and Fate* p. 46). She clearly sees the "strenuous strain in Emersonian optimism" (Ibid., p. 55).

96. *SW* 5, *GM* I, §12, pp. 277–78.

97. "Considerations By the Way," *COL*, pp. 246, 248. Philippa Foot criticizes Nietzsche for encouraging a "*pathos* of distance" from the majority and argues that a sense of equality, which Nietzsche lacks, is probably necessary for justice ("Nietzsche's Immoralism," *New York Review of Books*, June 13, 1991, p. 20). Emerson would be subject to the same kind of criticism. However, it is difficult to know why advising a feeling of distance as a way of being, an attitude, a "how" of existing, would imply 'injustice' towards others, as Ms. Foot suggests. Unfortunately, there is a value-orientation here that cannot be resolved insofar as Nietzsche insists that a belief in the equality of all persons, in all respects, is not only "unjust," but a *pia fraus*. Has any significant social system, even the most democratic, ever actually operated in accordance with a literal, undifferentiating principle of equality? Here a healthy dose of Nietzsche's most prized virtue—*Redlichkeit* or "honesty"—is in order.

98. Whicher, *Fate and Freedom*, p. 58. These imperatives, as well as some of the other traits of Emerson's "genuine man," as is mentioned in the text of this study, find their way, *via* Nietzsche, into Heidegger's conception of *Dasein* (human being) as a "potentiality-for-being-a-Self" in *Being and Time*. Kierkegaard, too, had held that no "authentic existence" was possible without living through "the ethical." Genuine existence is,

for him, the *telos* of man, the endeavor to realize one's "potentiality-for."
In the case of Heidegger's conception of the *eigentlich Existenz* or "authentic existence" of *Dasein*, elements of Emerson's and Kierkegaard's thought coalesce. Stanley Cavell has said that Emerson was an epistemologist of moods and links him to Heidegger's analysis of moods in relation to the "how" of man's being-in-the-world. But here, too, there is an overlap of ideas. For both Kierkegaard and Emerson emphasize the importance of moods, apparently independently, in man's experience of the world and himself. Cf. Stanley Cavell, "Thinking of Emerson," *New Literary History*, p. 168.

99. B. L. Packer, *Emerson's Fall*, p. 13.

100. "The Conservative," *RMNAL*, p. 296.

101. *Emerson in His Journals*, p. 371.

102. "Power," *COL*, p. 71.

103. Ibid., pp. 88–89.

104. Cf. Harold Bloom, *Agon*.

105. "Notes," *COL*, p. 426. This coincides with Emerson's insistence that the new religion he proposes will be "intellectual" and will have "science for symbol and illustration." Again, 'science' is used in the sense of 'knowledge' ("Worship," *COL*, pp. 240–41).

106. *Sämtliche Briefe*, 5:128.

107. *The Hindu World* (New York: Praeger, 1968), 1:51–54.

108. Nietzsche found a summary of the essential contents of Hammer's study in F. A. Lange's *History of Materialism*, a work he called a "treasure-house." What is curious is that this study, which is far more than a history of materialism, which he read some four years after discovering Emerson, includes many themes in Emerson's essays: the need for a "new religion" and a new ethics that would find a place for man's natural egoism (though not for selfishness); the recognition of a "lust for power" in man; the need (often expressed by Emerson) to effect a *"Selbstüberwindung"* ("self-overcoming") of a debilitating sympathy; theories concerning a cosmic circular process of becoming; a critique of a negative, repressive, and depressing Christian ethics; the interrelationship of all beings and events; speculation about monadic "spiritual atoms"; references to Boscovich's theory of unextended centers of force as the ultimate constituents of the natural world; the "social question" concerning the rise of the masses; political economy; the need for a stirring, new cultural ideal in face of the decline of traditional religion and the rise of science; the personification and humanization of nature in science; and other incidental points of reference. One observation of Lange's bears a relationship to an insight of Emerson's that finds its way into Nietzsche's *On the Genealogy of Morals*. That is, that the religious valuation of nature, as the creation of God, in Christianity was secularized into the valuation of the conscientious study of nature in the emerging scientific world-interpretation. Emerson's insight is related to this general view, but is more specific. "Exactly parallel," he writes, "is the whole rule of intellectual duty to the

rule of moral duty. A self-denial no less austere than the saint's is demanded of the scholar. He must worship truth, and forego all things for that, and choose defeat and pain, so that his treasure in thought is thereby augmented" ("Intellect," *EE*, p. 189). Superimposing Lange's generalization about science growing out of religion on Emerson's comment about the religious discipline of the "scholar" seems to yield the following notion of Nietzsche's: that scholarly work is the "noblest and latest form" of the "ascetic ideal" and that "science is closely allied with the ascetic ideal" both psychologically and "physiologically" (*SW* 5, *GM* 3 §23, §25).

109. *SW* 5, *JGB* §44, p. 62.

110. *The Will to Power*, §351.

111. Alexander Nehamas, *Nietzsche: Life as Literature*, p. 227. Elsewhere Nehamas offers a circuitous understatement of Nietzsche's reclamation of the *böse* impulses of man and skirts around his spiritual-intellectual antinomianism or "hypernomian" (as Emerson calls it in "Experience") principle. "To be beyond good and evil is not simply to discard these terms of valuation and the system to which they belong. Since it is not even necessary to abandon all the qualities that this system commands, to be beyond good and evil is to see how good and evil qualities have been thought to be related in fact, and to reconsider that relationship and all that it implies" (Ibid., pp. 206–7).

112. *The Will to Power*, §132.

113. *The Genealogy of Morals*, p. 269.

114. Cf. "Antinomianism," *The New Schaff-Herzog Religious Encyclopaedia*, vol. I. Cp. *Hastings Encyclopaedia of Religion and Ethics*, 1:581–82.

115. Despite his strong criticism of the (ostensible) ethics of Nietzsche, John Bernstein insightfully sees that Nietzsche and a religious figure he never fails to attack, St. Paul, are in agreement in their criticism of the letter of the law. This aspect of Nietzsche's thought, he believes, is "the most legitimate aspect of his own 'immoralism' " (John A. Bernstein, *Nietzsche's Moral Philosophy*, p. 171). Bernstein seems not to have noticed that Nietzsche *was* familiar with the relation between St. Paul's antinomianism and that of Hindu thought. Relying on Paul Deussen's works on Hindu religious thought, he notes that "neither in the Indian nor the Christian way of thinking is it held that . . . redemption can be *attained* through virtue, through moral improvement, no matter how highly both regard the . . . value of virtue" (*SW* 5, *GM* 3:17).

116. *SW* 11, p. 580.

117. *SW* 6, *A* §57, p. 243. Despite some passages in his notes that suggest otherwise, Nietzsche's considered notion is one of inner strength, a "feeling of power" he attributed to Brahmin priests in *Daybreak*. He states that "we do not find the task of the higher beings to consist in the guidance of the lower," as, for example, in Comte's utopia (*The Will to Power*, p. 901). Elsewhere he explicitly states that "it is absolutely not the idea to consider the latter [exceptions, "beyond-men"] as lords of the former [the majority]; the two types are to exist alongside one another—as far as

possible separated" (*Werke* (GOA), 14:262). In the same context he says that exceptional individuals may, at times, serve as "shepherds" whose function is to preserve the majority and provide models of what man can be. This suggests Emerson's "bellwethers," not dominating individuals. As if answering his critics in advance, Nietzsche insists that the "higher natures" he values are characterized as "being different," as "incommunicable," as feeling a "distance of rank." Moreover, what distinguishes such types—their value—lies *nich in irgend welchen Wirkungen"*—"not in an effect of any kind." And, specifically, contrary to the views of the English historian Henry Buckle, their value does not lie "in the ability to set masses in motion" (*SW* 13:498).

118. *SB* 2:120. (Letter to Carl von Gersdorff, 7 April 1866). The same image of the experience of the world as perfect recurs in *Thus Spoke Zarathustra* and is associated with "noontide."

119. *SB* 6:309 (letter to Paul Rée, December, 1882).

120. "Considerations By the Way," *COL*, p. 270.

Chapter 7

Aristocratic Radicalism

It is natural to believe in great men.

[*Ralph Waldo Emerson, "Introduction" to*
Representative Men]

In *A Century of Hero-Worship* Eric Bentley had a great deal to say about the idea of heroism in the writings of Carlyle, Nietzsche, Wagner, Spengler, and D. H. Lawrence. But, even though he mentions his name, he did not notice how prominent the ideal of the hero was in the essays and poems of Ralph Waldo Emerson. To some extent, the apotheosis of the hero in Emerson's works reflected the influence that Thomas Carlyle exerted on him. However, his reading of Carlyle, as well as his personal acquaintance with him and his correspondence with him, did not implant the admiration of heroes in Emerson's mind. For as early as 1837 one can detect a burgeoning hero-worship that presaged his later increasing concern with the future emergence of "well-turned-out" individuals who would exemplify the best qualities of humanity.

In his earliest book, *Nature,* Emerson not only praised the power, glory, and beauty of the natural world, but he also insisted upon its human characteristics. Frankly anthropomorphic in his thinking, he construed nature as pervaded by human qualities. At the same time, he celebrated consonance with the natural world, claiming that communion with nature would make us vibrant and youthful. When he counsels man to build his own world, with roots shooting down into the restorative power of nature, he is speaking to all men. He has not yet drawn that thick line between mankind *en masse* and strong, highly cultivated individuals who are distinguished from the vast majority of human beings by their manner, their style, their power, their creative energy. The "convenient distance" that he believed should be established between each and every independent human being eventually becomes a considerable distance between the "mediocre" and the rare "great man." A psychological sense of distance between man and man became an ontological distinction between different types of human beings.

The Authentic Scholar

In his oration, "The American Scholar," we hear the first sound of Emerson's battle for preservation of, and adulation of, a spiritual aristocracy. Calling the "scholar" to his or her tasks, he laments the "sluggish and perverted mind of the multitude" and he deplores its slow response to rationality. By way of contrast, he points to the forward-looking genius, the creative person who is able to translate experience and thought into action.[1] Scholarly work is a test of various powers. It requires "total strength" and is an activity that is rooted in life. The ideal scholar should think and live deeply and should remember that character is higher in value than intellect.[2] This sturdy scholar must never sacrifice his good opinions to "popular judgments."[3] Warming to his subject, Emerson begins to up the ante for qualification as an authentic scholar. The requirements are: self-reliance, self- direction, self-confidence, an avoidance of popular appeal, steadiness, patient observation, self-trust, freedom, and bravery.

A genuine student will be able to see through the pretentions of the world and unmask its lies, will hold greatness before him or her as an edifying ideal and will project great aims for himself or herself. As Nietzsche later does, Emerson projects for the ideal "scholar" higher and higher goals. He attributes to this ideal-type heroic characteristics. This depiction of the authentic scholar is clearly the model for the ideal of "the warrior of knowledge" in *Thus Spoke Zarathustra*.

Culture versus Politics

A perceptive individual, Emerson believes, can clearly see that man's value is declining in history. People who are "well-turned-out" are becoming exceedingly rare. Instead of wholeness, we find in people a partial, one-sided development. A "great person" is sorely needed for the inspiration of the young and for the presumed need on the part of people in general to admire exceptional individuals. The ordinary man, in his own way, either aspires to achieve something in life or admires those who do. Cultural heroes are needed for their edifying effect on whole societies. Mankind has to be awakened to the meaning and value of a higher culture and learn to "leave government to clerks and desks."[4]

What is the aim of a genuine culture? It is "the upliftng of a man." This simply stated theme is restated often by Emerson and is reiterated by Nietzsche. Governments or the State must serve culture, not vice versa. In his early lecture, "The Future of Our Educational Institutions" and in "Schopenhauer as Educator," he strongly argues for this Emersonian priority. As we know too well, this message was ignored in history, and national governments have grown more and more powerful. Nation-states have influenced, controlled, coerced, and manipulated various cultures for their political, military, and economic aims. The results of elevating governments above culture have been devastating.

Today, in an anti-Emersonian America, a dominant belief is that education (a significant aspect of culture) must first and foremost serve the practical, material needs of the State, local governments, and their prosperous supporters and beneficiaries. And the situation is far worse in communist/socialist countries where "ministers of culture" shape artistic and educational values. The political domination of culture and utilitarian control of resources invariably produces far-reaching negative effects. Instead of a free building of a higher culture, which ought to be the aim of advanced civilizations, we have a mind-numbing stress on practical skills, practical and commercial arts, and the endless development of military technology. As a consequence, we have a social atmosphere of practical materialism in which, as Emerson once said, "Public and private avarice make the air we breath thick and fat."[5] Or we have an environment in which, as Nietzsche said in *The Gay Science,* the contemplative-intellectual, nonutilitarian life is devalued and in which those who seek to live it are made to feel ashamed or are ridiculed by the "practical" majority.

Preoccupied with a rejuvenation of culture, Emerson's energies are more and more focused on the unique, single person. He proposed what could readily be called a humanistic, existential ethics. The world exists for man, not man for the world. Not only the "scholar," but every reflective individual should create a center of reality in himself and have cultural avatars for consolation and company. Such individuals must walk alone, stand apart from the crowd, and speak his or her mind without fear.[6] These admonitions to seek independent self-existence are later amplified in Emerson's hortatory essay, "Self-Reliance," and are prescriptions which are retained in his various attempts to depict those he described in "Uses of Great Men" as "the exceptions which we want, where all grows like."

Christianity

In his address presented at the Harvard Divinity College in 1838, Emerson continues to advocate self-trust, independence of mind, a "solidity of merit," an avoidance of imitation, and "endurance." However, there is an additional theme sounded that shocked the assembled theologians who came to applaud politely, but gasped instead. What they could not help but notice was also noticed by Emerson's avid German reader. It is a theme that is closely related to Emerson's repeated attempts to forge a novel, affirmative ethico-religious ideal that would emphasize the centrality of character, autonomy, and strength. Against the background of the then-startling discussion of Christianity in the past tense, Emerson was beginning to promote an aristocratic ideal that Nietzsche appropriated as his own, as much out of predisposition as out of admiration.

The need for veneration and faith is, Emerson insists, a profound need of humanity. It has, obviously, taken many forms and, in Western civilization, it has centered on the Judeo-Christian tradition of faith and morality. The sublime teachings of Jesus Christ, however, have been gradually converted into a "mythus." Christ was a "true man" who, alone in history, "appreciated the worth of man." But his exemplary existence became part of a dogma and Christianity became historical. This fact has undermined the essence of the teachings of Christ. "Historical Christianity has fallen into the error. that corrupts all attempts to communicate religion."[7] Official rituals and doctrines have replaced the message of the living Christ. The believer is required to accept the official interpretation of Christianity and to submit to a monarchial God. Against this attitude, what fortifies *him* is whatever shows the divine in man and elevates the value of the spiritual inwardness of the self. Official religion blights the beauties of *this* world and Christ's "glad tidings" are presented as sad tidings.

Institutional religion, Emerson continues, has become so deeply entrenched that men refer to the revelation as something long since past and as no longer relevant to the living present. It is "as if God were dead."[8] Reflecting on the sharpness of this remark, we may wonder if this was not, given Nietzsche's meticulous reading of Emerson, the *locus classicus* of the announcement of the madman, in Nietzsche's *The Gay Science,* that "God is dead."

Emerson questions the validity of the teachers of the ancient religion and avers that not just anyone can show the way to God. It is only a person who has, who can give: only he or she "who is" or is genuine can create. The truth and the value of faith must be made fresh and vital once again. He reluctantly reports his sad conviction that there is a decay of religious faith, almost a death of faith, in modern society. The life of religion and faith seems in jeopardy. People go through the motions of religious practice, but their hearts are no longer in it. Preachers have succumbed to a "hollow, dry, creaking formality." The spark of genuine faith is no longer present. In short, "historical Christianity destroys the power of preaching, by withdrawing it from the exploration of the moral nature of man, where the sublime is, where are the resources of astonishment and power."[9]

On the basis of evidence of the decline of religious faith, Emerson declares, practically in the words of Kierkegaard, that "the true Christianity . . . is lost."[10] And, in the wake of this, the morality that was central to it has yielded to the paltry, "common degrees of merit" dictated by society; the easy merit acquired by meeting the facile "standard of goodness in society." In lieu of a conformist public morality that encourages mediocrity, there is a need for an ethical reformation that will draw on resources of man as yet untapped. Closing his address, Emerson calls for the "new teacher" who will announce an ideal in which duty, knowledge, beauty, and joy are combined.

A fresh ethico-religious ideal is needed, Emerson fervently believes, in order to rejuvenate aspiration and spiritual effort. Even though he retains the conception of God in the ethereal form of the "Oversoul," he is very much concerned with introducing an ethico-religious ideal of immanence in the form of an appreciation of, an admiration for, great men. This is an aristocratic morality that, at times, eulogizes strength, energy, and power in ways that cut against traditional moral notions in general, and against Christian morality in particular.

The transcendental idealism that refers faith to an eternal spiritual being, an "Oversoul," and supports "other-reliance" is actually tepid, vague, and amorphous, especially when it is compared to Emerson's rhetorical apotheosis of the sculpturesque ideal man. More than that, his idealism is frequently undercut by a realism that puts sentimental idealism on ice. To this must be added a quick current of skepticism that runs through his writings and is often justified in the name of honesty. At times, he expresses his valuation of honesty with surprising bluntness. In a journal entry from 1842, for example, he writes: "I will speak the truth also in my secret heart, or think *the truth* against what is called God."[11] Elsewhere, he acknowledges that, through an "excess of candor," he sometimes makes the argument for atheism too strong. And, finally, he maintains that "a just thinker will allow full swing to his skepticism."[12]

To see how Emerson was led to project a cultural ideal into the future in order to rejuvenate man's faith in life and what he saw as the highest forms of human life, we should complete the mental picture he had of the state of traditional religious belief in his time.

From a realistic perspective, he sees a divine providence that does not spare man disease, deformity, accident, misfortune, or corrupt societies. If we flatly assume a direct relation between the providential nature of God and events, we would have to admit this divine presence in "passions, in war, in trade, in the love of power and pleasure, in hunger and need, in tyrannies." Faith can do many things, but it cannot erase the tragic dimension of existence. An overly optimistic appeal to divine providence could easily backfire on religious faith. Later, when Nietzsche refers to God as "the greatest immoralist in deeds that has ever existed," he only dramatically expresses what Emerson had said in his usual understated way.

Emerson describes his age as a "transition period," a time during which the "old faiths" that comforted millions "seem to have spent their force."[13] There is much that is childish and insignificant in religions and much that is "unmanly." This is a constant theme of Nietzsche's—that the morality and culture of traditional religion are emasculating, debilitating, and cultivate timidity.

Reporting on the godlessness of large populations, the materialism rampant in modern society, the general lack of enthusiasm and belief, Emerson wonders how so many people can continue to live such aimless lives. All in all, he laments, "there is a feeling that religion is gone."[14]

The "universal decay of religion" seems to have given rise to a skepticism about the value of man, a distrust of human nature, a callous cynicism, and a wholesale pursuit of comfort and pleasure as the primary goals of life. Such a description of the condition of modern man is recapitulated by Nietzsche in his portrait of a crepuscular world in "Schopenhauer as Educator." Although he never uses the word, Emerson describes a period of spiritual dissolution and indifference that is clearly one in which *nihilism*—a loss of a sense of meaning, purpose, and direction in life—is emerging.

In spite of, or because of, this deplorable state of affairs in modern society, Emerson believes that a resuscitation of the ethico-religious spirit, in conjunction with an affirmative cultural ideal, is possible and necessary. The rising *culture* of natural science produces marvels, but it gives no direction, no sense of meaning, to human life. There are, nonetheless, some good signs. The energetic activity of the modern world seems to spin out and promote individualism. Perhaps out of this tendency a "religion of character" might be developed.

Although there is a decline of traditional religion, and the morality of Christianity has become a watered-down, secularized 'morality' of conformity, a "dawn of faith" may be on the horizon. What should be avoided, at all costs, Emerson insists, is a religion that enfeebles, enervates, and "demoralizes." If a new religion is to guide men of the future, it will have to be intellectual in nature and include elements that would satisfy the "scientific mind."[15] This religion will use "science for symbol and illustration" and will entail a "stern and exigent" morality. It will have at its center the spiritually strong, independent persons who will bypass the supplicating manners of society. Such individuals shall expect no cooperation and "walk with no companion." They will rely on the "nameless . . . Power," the "superpersonal" source of energy and "vital force."[16] This religion will require a morality of "great duty" and will establish itself in "the neighborhood of the great."

Emerson passes on quickly from a description of the decline of religious belief and of the aimlessness and demoralization of modern life to a commentary on the factors that he believes contributed to the dissolution of previous values. Unlike Kierkegaard, he does not seek to restore "primitive Christianity" or revitalize its moral principles. He seeks a new direction for man in a 'religion' of nobility, character, integrity, affirmation, and "joyful wisdom." As in the case of Nietzsche's constructive philosophy, he recommends a faith based on knowledge and compatible with science, especially with the sense of realism found in the "exact sciences." Thus, Nietzsche follows him by basing his religion of life, his affirmation of existence, on general scientific ideas. Science reveals the dynamism of nature and transforms the face of the earth, but it does not give us a goal for our lives. However, science "gives the *presuppositions* with which the new goal must agree."[17]

Exceptions

In Stanley Hubbard's study of the influence of Emerson on Nietzsche, he goes out of his way to say that the latter was not an "Emersonian." But given the parallels between the thought of these similar radical thinkers, we may wonder if Hubbard fully understood what an Emersonian was. There is no doubt that both intellectually and in a curiously personal way, Nietzsche *was* a kind of ultraradical Emersonian who transcended this standpoint in scope and depth and by dint of his philosophical acuity. Nietzsche adopted Emerson as one of his chief, though certainly not exclusive, mentors. This is especially the case in regard to his reverence for great men and his profound valuation of an aristocratic morality.

When, in "On the Uses and Disadvantages of History for Life," Nietzsche proclaims that "the *goal of humanity* cannot lie in the end, but only *in its highest specimens*," he is paraphrasing Emerson. The significance of this is made apparent if we accept Walter Kaufmann's considered judgment that this single assertion is the most "basic statement of Nietzsche's philosophy." Moreover, Kaufmann finds in this proposition "the most crucial point of his philosophy of history and theory of value—no less than the clue to his 'aristocratic' ethics and his opposition to socialism and democracy."[18]

Granting that this is a valid judgment, we then have a basis for arguing that, particularly in regard to an aristocratic scale of values, Nietzsche *was* replicating and enhancing one of Emerson's basic themes. Thus, it is no exaggeration to say that, in certain crucial respects, Nietzsche *was* something of an Emersonian. "Exceptions" and "great men" were a lifetime preoccupation of a thinker who is said to have represented "the golden mean of New England transcendentalism" and to have been a "genial critic" and a "constructive idealist."[19] In fact, Emerson was more a proponent of a golden extreme than of a golden mean; more a philosophical immanentalist than a transcendentalist; as much a hard-headed realist as a constructive idealist; and more a radical than a genial critic. Ironically, given the way in which he cultivated and brought to fruition his insights and his sketches for a philosophy, it could be said that Nietzsche had a more profound understanding of Emerson than did many of his American admirers and interpreters.

Emerson firmly believed that genius had not yet been "incarnated in any powerful individual," in individuals with a passion for what is extraordinary. He wanted to see goodness and virtue committed to action; to see beauty in action. His conception of exemplary human beings was imbued with an "aesthetic spirit." What is wanted in the world are magnetic persons who follow their own genius; who are not afraid to enter "uninhabited deserts of thought and life"; who travel heroic pathways alone on "the highway of health." Society needs rare and gifted individuals who serve as "superior chronometers" by which we may measure the spiritual quality of life. The authentic great man is possessed of the "heroism and grandeur" that accompany self-reliance. The ideal person, as Nietzsche will later remember, must be open to the reality of experience and have a positive attitude towards the world. He slightly modified Emerson's formula for such an orientation towards existence and used it as a motto for *The Gay Science*.[20]

The genius, Emerson tells us, observes the "monad" as it assumes different masks and participates in the "metempsychosis of nature." This stylish *aperçu* will be elaborated on by Nietzsche and, with the aid of Roger Boscovich's sophisticated physical theory of point-centers, will eventually become the "hypothesis" that reality is comprised of "monads" or "will-points" from which emanate a pervasive "will to power," expressed in Protean forms.[21] In this interpretation of the internal reality of the cosmos he, like Emerson before him, looks for an analogical relation between the macrocosm and the microcosm in accordance with a consciously adopted anthropomorphic model.

As Emerson polishes his images of the genius in particular and greatness in general, his reflections are guided not only by a profusion of analogies and tropes, but by a fundamentally *aesthetic* model of embodied perfection. For, he contends that "a profound nature awakens in us by its actions and words, by its very looks and manners, the same power and beauty that a gallery of sculptures or of pictures addresses."[22]

This aesthetic aspect of excellence appears again and again in his writings, and it has its origin in romanticism. In some random notes on "beauty," Emerson quotes with approval from Keats' *Hyperion*:

> For 'tis the eternal law
> That first in beauty should be first in might.[23]

He continually states or insinuates the association among beauty, will, nature and power. And this romantic fusion plays an important role in his attempts to describe the paradigm of "the great man" who is said to be the goal of culture. The cultural ideal would be the apogee of valued human traits embodied in a living aesthetic synthesis, a "central man."

Outstanding individuals exude robust or "extraordinary health." Such human types are frequently harshly compared to the average types of human beings who, *en masse,* manifest "imbecility." Even heroic individuals are not immune to such inbecility except at peak moments of their lives. They, too, are "victims of gravity, custom, and fear."[24] Once more, we see that Nietzsche must have read Emerson with microscopic care. A passing remark, an image thrown away, is plucked out of this passage from "Power" and is later christened "the spirit of gravity" by Nietzsche. That is, the attitude of dull seriousness that pulls even the best down with its dead weight; the spirit characterized in *Thus Spoke Zarathustra* as one that "draws downward toward the abyss . . . dripping lead into my ears, leaden thoughts into my brain."

In his sweeping account of the ancient Greeks, Emerson is obviously sympathetic to the naturalness, the spontaneity, the buoyant health, the grace, energy, and childlike genius of these idealized historical characters. He is especially impressed by the reverence they show for personal qualities: self-command, courage, demeanor, sense of justice, strength, swiftness, a loud voice, a broad chest. Such human types are extravagant human beings who only appear in history at long intervals. What their behavior discloses are "new facts in nature" that show what human beings *can* be.[25] In the same context in which he extols the virtues of the ancient Greeks, Emerson expresses admiration for Prometheus (who is characterized by him as "the Jesus of the old mythology") and views him as a benefactor of man who defies the gods and represents an attitude that recurs when objective theism is dominant in a culture. Nietzsche agrees with him when he praises Prometheus' compassion for mankind and the sacrifice he made for men.[26]

Emerson argues that history offers actual and symbolic images of man as heroic, defiant, daring, as superior to the typical modern man. Nietzsche, too, goes through this same stage of idealizing selected ancient Greeks and admiring heroes in history.

However, this orientation does not entail setting up shrines to great personages of the past. He shares Emerson's belief, expressed in "The Uses of Great Men," that "Great men exist that there may be greater men." This is precisely the attitude that Nietzsche adopts to the recorded instances of greatness in history. These are signs that man is the, as yet, not fixed species.

The characteristics of the exceptional individual found in Emerson's writings are, over a period of time, linked together in a chain that entwines his earlier sketch of the genuine person. Emerson repeatedly insists on the rarity of such authentic individuals. Like Nietzsche after him, he escalates the requirements for entrance into the circle of the elite. His radical aristocratic valuations lead him, as they lead Nietzsche, to place his faith in a future in which there may emerge men who, relatively speaking, will be beyond man.

Solitude

When the wandering hermit, Zarathustra, praises solitude and urges that we live far from the marketplace and avoid the congregating crowds, he is speaking directly in the voice of Emerson. In fact, Zarathustra is largely modeled on Emerson. Like Zarathustra, Emerson extolled the virtues of solitude and affirmed that the "great man is he who in the midst of the crowd keeps with perfect sweetness the independence of solitude."[27] This valuation of solitude, combined with a critical attitude towards society is a point of direct consonance between Emerson and Nietzsche. It has been said that both had a "temperamental dislike of association in any form."[28] There is no doubt that this is true. But it is also the case that Nietzsche felt a deep affinity with Emerson and his personal values. In this particular case there are two factors at work: intellectual influence and temperamental affinity. The sentiments pertaining to solitary existence and the counsel to avoid the crowd that are found in *Thus Spoke Zarathustra* incorporate virtually every judgment Emerson ever made on this score. Solitude and a practiced aloofness towards the everyday world of social existence are mutually shared aspects of Emerson's and Nietzsche's aristocratic radicalism.

The select person, Emerson believes, is one in whom there is an accumulation of power and force of character. Such an individual is unique and has his or her center in himself or herself. Because of a disdain for, or indifference to, public opinion, the genuine individual is often misunderstood. In fact, one who is great is invariably "misunderstood." It may be remembered that in the margins of Emerson's essays Nietzsche had written *"Ecce Homo."* This is not intended to refer to Emerson or to what he has written. Rather, it is meant to refer to an idea, an insight, a saying of Emerson's that Nietzsche wanted to include in his autobiographical work, *Ecce Homo.* He is very close to Emerson's spirit and thought, in more ways than one, in his unusual autobiography. For it is there that he refers to his antipathy towards social existence and characterizes *Thus Spoke Zarathustra* as "a Dithyramb of solitude."[29]

Greatness, Spontaneity, and Instinct

In his autobiography, *Ecce Homo,* Nietzsche expresses what we've seen to be a distinctively Emersonian formula for "greatness": "love of fate." In this unusual autobiography there are also found echoes of one of Emerson's central imperatives: to look always into the heart of reality and behold its terrible facts without blinking, without despair. This courageous sense of reality is immediately related by Nietzsche to greatness. For what is needed is "the kind of man [who] . . . conceives reality *as it is;* he is strong enough for this—he is not estranged or removed from it, he is himself the reality; in him can be found all the doubt and terror of reality; *only in this way can man have greatness."*[30]

Before writing *Thus Spoke Zarathustra* and before composing *Ecce Homo,* Nietzsche immersed himself once again in the writings of Emerson, in his psychic and literary ambience. He treats his scattered insights and pithy asides as points of inspiration for his own thought, as dynamic, imagistic centers from which his own reflections radiate.

The essence of genius, Emerson tells us, is that of life and virtue: "Spontaneity or Instinct."[31] These two attributes are directly appropriated by Nietzsche in his depiction of the traits of outstanding individuals. Instinct, Nietzsche believes, is something that accumulates over generations of *praxis* and has become, for some, a spontaneous intelligence. It is an "assimilated virtue" that is the basis for "every kind of mastery, of every kind of perfection, in the art of life."[32] Instinct has been assimilated by fortunate individuals over a long period of time and is attained by the "accumulated forces" that are under the control of a firm will. Such conceptions of the accumulation of force or energy find their way into Nietzsche's attempts to formulate the nature of growth. And a person with natural *virtù* is said to possess instinctive knowledge and becomes a "prodigy of force."[33] Like Emerson, Nietzsche moves easily from theories of organic growth to conceptions of the development of a positive morality of strength. Spontaneity, too, is a highly desirable human trait for Nietzsche. And, as is the case for Emerson, it is usually associated with the types of creative artists who are typical models of paradigmatic men.

Nietzsche reverses common opinion by claiming that creative or accomplished individuals are actually *more irrational* than others insofar as they follow their "impulses" and intuitions and, in their best moments, reason "*lapses* altogether."[34] In this regard, once again, he assimilates Emerson's praise of the "plastic power" of spontaneity and creative unreason.[35]

The "genuine man," Emerson insists, is not afraid to say "I am," to assert a strong sense of his prerogatives. Such a person respects and reveres the present, derives strength from living, with nature, "in the present, above time."[36] We've already seen how Nietzsche makes the act of living in the present an esoteric doctrine of experiencing "eternity" in time and becoming. Although he carries this idea beyond Emerson, he does not deviate from his emphasis upon the importance of living in and focusing on the "sacred present." Once again, a passing insight of Emerson's is converted into a doctrine, one which is linked to the exceptional individual's power of affirmation. Thus, thinking of a person having a moving inward experience, he says that "if the individual experienced it as *his* fundamental characteristic, [this] would drive the individual to affirm triumphantly each moment in general. The crucial point would be that one experienced this basic characteristic in oneself as good, valuable."[37]

This orientation towards experience seems similar to Emerson's stress upon the affirmation of the present, to the deification of the moment. Moreover, it is he who first joins this ability to hold fast to the present to a "sacred courage," to the insight into the necessities of existence. The concentration of thought, feeling, and energy in the still point of "the moment" raises the individual out of the stream of ordinary existence and generates a feeling of liberation and power. Nietzsche was perceptive enough to discern in this experience of the "inward eye" (as Emerson called it) the seeds from which he could cultivate his conception of the self-suppression of fate by means of its complete affirmation. He reproduces Emerson's transition from the recognition of a "tragic necessity" in life to the transformation of it into an affirmation of "beautiful" necessity. And, in turn, Nietzsche links this positive attitude towards the necessities in existence to "courage."

The ethics of self-reliance demands "godlike" capacities because it requires a stern independence of the conventional beliefs, values, and motives of others, a deep sense of "self-trust." Whoever exercises self-trust thereby acquires "new powers." "In self-trust," we are told, "all the virtues are comprehended." From the moment at which a person spontaneously acts from a center in himself or herself and throws the laws, books, idolatries, and customs of the world out the window, we know that this person is a teacher who "shall restore the life of man to splendor."[38] Emerson and Nietzsche share a benign attitude towards a liberating iconoclasm. Neither seems to entertain the possibility that smashing the venerable tables of value of the past could be a prelude not to splendor, insight, and glory, but, rather, a propaedeutic to something sinister, to the nightmares of social and political nihilism that have plagued this destructive century.

Overcoming Sympathy

One of the recurring themes in Emerson's writings that is associated with his aristocratic morality is one that reappears in the philosophy of Nietzsche. That is, his strong hostility towards sympathy. He sometimes characterizes what many would normally consider a virtue as "base." Self-help is emphasized so much that Emerson is led to say that instead of crying with others and hence becoming additional objects of sympathy, we should impart to those who are suffering "truth and health in rough electric shocks."[39] He often laments the numerous causes that elicit our time, energy, and money. Health and psychic strength require a careful husbanding of our resources. If, through an excessive sympathy, we try to aid all those who need help, we ourselves will soon be depleted. We have to overcome our sympathetic inclinations in self-defense because, as he says in his journals, "Our sympathy is too strong for us."

Although Emerson may seem to be cold and aloof in regard to the suppression of sympathy, his point is well taken. Inspired as it may be by humane and charitable motives, sympathy can subvert and debilitate whoever is too generous in its dispensation. Excessive sympathy is an expensive virtue. And a fundamental principle of life (for Emerson, as well as Nietzsche) is economy: psychophysical health is maintained through an economic use of one's energies.[40] Emerson sometimes wonders, as many others probably have, how much of our sympathy is, in fact, wasted. Again, it is not so much that he is indifferent to the sufferings of others as that he realizes the value of strong, healthy, productive individuals who, he believes, ought not to be sacrificed at the altar of sympathy.

Nietzsche seems to have Emerson's views in mind when he urges that we ought "to create circumstances in which every one can help himself, and he himself decide whether he shall be helped."[41] He also seems to have shared or absorbed Emerson's contempt for self-pity. Despite his awful string of physical and psychological sufferings, Nietzsche checks every temptation to self-pity in himself. Emerson was quite intolerant of self-pity and is critical of individuals who are, as he puts it in "Considerations By the Way," "insatiable cravers of sympathy." Nietzsche responded so positively to his opinions and judgments that he seems to have completely assimilated his belief that in order to retain spiritual or psychological strength it is important to overcome the weakening feeling of pity or sympathy.

Self-reliance is "the basis of behavior." It guarantees that our "powers are not squandered" by expending our energies in a persistent sympathy for others.[42] If we are to assist others, we may best do so by imparting comfort by our "security and good nature to all."[43] Nietzsche expresses more or less this same sentiment when he has Zarathustra say: "Not your pity, but your bravery has hitherto saved the unhappy."[44] Although there is a kind of psychological optimism in such views, they are not implausible. Does misery truly love company? Perhaps "misery" needs cheerfulness, healthy attitudes, affirmative sentiments, needs to see the edifications of life in others rather than a sad, morbid reflection of itself.

Another related point can be found in Emerson's unorthodox reflections on the feeling of sympathy. Bearing in mind the fragility of genius, he may have been thinking that such a type might lose his or her core of strength if he or she became too involved in a draining sympathy for those who are prone to suffering. Artistic and intellectual work, especially, requires great concentrations of attention and energy. Such work could easily be spoiled by too many demands made on a creative person's energy and emotional resources.[45] Although Emerson sometimes seems to be covertly referring to himself, especially since here and there in his journals he complains about his limited resources and his need to concentrate all of his energies on his work, he is also thinking of creative and productive people of all kinds. Curiously enough, he may have discovered an affinity between the German poet and novelist, Goethe, and himself on this score, particularly since his admiration of Goethe is rivaled only by that of Nietzsche. Rittelmeyer, in his work, *Friedrich Nietzsche und die Religion,* mentions that Goethe knew that he risked being branded an egoist because he refused the importunities of strangers. He remarks that Goethe would have committed a crime against humanity if he had sacrificed himself to such importunate people and, as a consequence, failed to have produced his immortal works.[46] This notion seems to lie behind Emerson's attitude towards those who would consume his energy, time, and creative powers by an insatiable demand on his sympathy. And this is generalized to pertain to all who are committed to a life of creativity.

In sum, given a choice between a sympathetic altruism that required that we "live for others" and a creative, demanding, independent existence, Emerson invariably chooses the latter. Both he and Nietzsche seriously question the value of, the validity of, and the rationale for, the popular ethics of altruism.

Having at one time embraced Schopenhauer's ethics of compassion and sympathy, Nietzsche was better trained than Emerson in the personal and cultural dangers of the expansion of a "morality of pity." If this type of morality spread throughout a culture, it might end in a "will to nothingness" insofar as life is construed as so filled with suffering, both physical and mental, that the extinction of the self may be seen as a *good.* Of course he knew that, in this regard, Schopenhauer's morality of pity and sympathy was a variation on the perceptions and values of Buddhism. The cultivation of a morality of pity was seen as the reverse of harmless.

Emerson's influence on Nietzsche in regard to the negative effects of excessive sympathy was significant. In *Thus Spoke Zarathustra* the temptation to pity is considered as the most difficult aspect of affirming the thought of the eternal recurrence of the same. The self-overcoming of sympathy or pity is presented as an ultimate test of courage. Self-pity is condemned and pity for others is criticized because they debilitate the individual who strives for an affirmation of life and a strengthening of will. Nietzsche had seen in the *pathos* of the moral sentiments presented in the music-dramas of Wagner and in the morality of pity of Schopenhauer, both of which he had been attracted to in his early thought, the danger of becoming so oppressed and preoccupied with human suffering and the pain of existence that one would turn against life and embrace a nihilistic "will to nothingness."

Emerson's mild comments on the need to defend oneself against excessive sympathy are superficial compared to Nietzsche's analyses and criticisms of a morality of pity. However, the suggestion of the need of a self-overcoming of a human propensity to sympathy for others was originally conveyed to Nietzsche by Emerson. It was later reinforced by F. A. Lange's surprisingly similar views in *The History of Materialism*. Briefly, Lange's view is that the effort to avoid a tendency to become overly involved in the life and interests of others requires a great deal of *"Selbstüberwindung"* or "self-overcoming." He pointed out that, in a paradoxical way, an over-extension of sympathy to others has harmed civilizations. Specifically, Lange advises that the suppression of a "self-denying altruism" may be necessary for the "moral and intellectual progress" of mankind.[47]

Nietzsche insisted upon the overcoming of excessive sympathy because he understood very well its psychological power to undermine faith in life, affirmative attitudes, courage, inner strength, and cheerfulness. It is a mistake to see him as an advocate of harshness towards the real or imagined sufferings of others any more than to believe that Emerson encourages hardness of heart. The self-overcoming of his own inclination to be overwhelmed by pity or sympathy is one of his central concerns. The same was no doubt true of Emerson as well.

Nietzsche's attitudes toward sympathy can be found in his works of the 1870s and elsewhere. He was surprisingly understanding of Richard Wagner's early radical, socialistic activities and he believed that Wagner became politically active "out of pity for the people." More than that, he maintained that "one cannot be happy, as long as everything suffers and creates suffering about us; one cannot be moral, as long as the course of human events is determined by violence, deceit, and injustice; one cannot even be wise, as long as mankind . . . does not lead the individual in the wisest way to life and knowledge."[48]

In his early writings, Nietzsche often expresses concern for, and sympathy for, the well-being and just treatment of the very people he later typically refers to as "the masses." Such sentiments are usually presented in the context of ideals of social justice, and they are rarely seen for what they obviously are: humanistic, sometimes quasi-socialistic, sentiments.

Nietzsche denounces the bourgeoisie who seek profit at the expense of the underprivileged; attacks the wealthy class for their ostentatious and provocative extravagance; predicts that Europe will have to pay for the "exploitation" of workers; criticizes the egoistic, anarchic pursuit of self-interest at the expense of culture; laments the "superfluous" members of the wealthy class for using money as a means to power and influence; and attacks the social atomism that is produced by the pursuit of naked self-interest and purely egoistic ends. In *Human, All-Too-Human,* Nietzsche sarcastically refers to the then-emerging "merchant's morality," characterizing it as a "refinement on piratical morality." In *Daybreak* he lashes out at the "legalized fraud" that is practiced by the upper classes. One of the objects of his wrath in "Schopenhauer as Educator" is what may be called the industrial-military complex of Germany in the 1870s. He hurls invectives at the "greed," the "egotism," and the "selfishness" that he believes runs through the German society of his day. Some of these attitudes and value-judgments were picked up from Emerson, but they were also strongly expressed by the philosopher and political economist, Eugen Dühring, and through him, as well as through F. A. Lange, Nietzsche absorbed some of the critical ideas of a then-obscure political economist, Karl Marx.[49]

By the time he wrote *Thus Spoke Zarathustra,* in part under the sway of Emerson, Nietzsche came to see the necessity to overcome the temptation to a weakening sympathy if a life-enhancing way of existence was to be possible for "exceptional" individuals. The overcoming of a tempermental tendency towards pity in his youth, which is particularly evident in his caring for and self-sacrificing feelings for seriously ill, wounded, and dying soldiers during his military service as a medical aide, was, despite outward appearances in his bravado prose, a very painful process of self-overcoming. In a letter to Malwida von Meysenbug (March 24, 1875), he expresses a personal sentiment, which there is no reason to assume is not sincere. "I have wished," he writes, "that I could daily do some good things for others. This autumn I proposed to myself to begin each morning by asking, Is there no one to whom you could do some good today? . . . I vex too many men by my writings not to feel obliged to attempt to make it up to them somehow." Given other random bits and pieces from his personal life and private feelings, there is no doubt that his own prescription of a "self-overcoming" of sympathy or pity required heroic efforts.

Growth

In nature, as in life, especially in the life of an integrated healthy person, the underlying tendency is towards growth. This requires that one deal with one's faults and come to understand how they can contribute to personal growth. We really don't understand an existential truth until we have contended against it. It is self-knowledge that enables us to discover these lived-truths of defect or talent. Paradoxically, the strength of superior individuals owes a great deal to their prior weaknesses. A great individual is even willing, at times, "to be little." Such a person can learn from defeat, failure, shipwreck, and misfortunes. Emerson insists that if we would grow as individuals, then we should not flee the dangers, without and within, of life. Adversity educates and strengthens. He does not literally say what Nietzsche later asserts, but he means it. "Whatever does not kill me makes me stronger." This motto of Nietzsche's epitomizes Emerson's reflections on the value for personal growth of danger, misfortunes, and adversity. He and Nietzsche are convinced that the effort to overcome misfortune and "resistance" leads to the enhancement of psychospiritual strength. Here is yet another form of "the good of evil."

The somewhat vague, but challenging, goals that Nietzsche projects for "higher men" are an echo of Emerson's portraits of his "exempts." Such individuals should be impulsive, spontaneous, open to new perspectives, experimental in life and thought, should regard as good what follows from their nature and grows out of the self. Whoever would surpass common social sentiments must learn to select out of the panorama of experience what is appropriate for himself or herself and to reject what is unfit. Such a person must learn, as Nietzsche later expresses this Emersonian advice, to say Yes and No, in regard to people or circumstances, and proceed in a straight line. Nietzsche repeats the counsel of Emerson in regard to the "conduct of life" in a slight variation on his theme: we must learn what, in life, enhances our sense of existence and what is detrimental, negative, or poisonous *for us*. This is deceptively simple in statement and very difficult to execute in practice.

Many of the values that Nietzsche attributes to himself in *Ecce Homo* and elsewhere are, in point of fact, stated fulfillments of Emerson's practical wisdom. He seemed to have adopted Emerson as his teacher of the "how" of existence, and it is not surprising that, in his personal life, he tried to emulate the Emersonian ideal.

The idealized "genius," "hero," or "great man" is described as one who adopts an affirmative philosophy of life in face of "the testimony of negative facts." This is a terse summary of Emerson's thoughts on this question, and it is also a reduced version of the essence of Nietzsche's Dionysian pessimism; the passionate affirmation of life in light of a full realization of its terrible negativities and antitheses.

It is in the interior drama of existence that the Emersonian "hero" chooses *to be* rather than to seem. This is the "real action" that takes place in silent moments. For, as Emerson puts it, the significant epochs in our lives often occur in thought, especially in "thought which revises our entire manner of life." The ancestor of external action is always a thought; thought *is* action.[50] Contrary to popular opinion, Emerson asserts that it is a rich mind, an active mind, that can be contented, be natural, lie in the sun, and, if so inclined, sleep. In one form or another, Nietzsche incorporates these and other *obiter dicta* of Emerson into the fibers and the fabric of his *Zarathustra* tapestry. The sayings of the "sage of Concord," paraphrased or slightly modified, appear often in this work. If one went from a careful reading of Emerson's essays (let's say a Nietzschean reading!) to *Thus Spoke Zarathustra,* one would repeatedly have the experience of *déjà-vu.*

"Aristocratic radicalism." This was the summary phrase that Georg Brandes, the Danish literary critic, applied to the philosophy of Nietzsche in a letter to him. In response, Nietzsche approved of the designation and praised Brandes's insight into his central idea.[51] Brandes himself, in an essay on this subject that appeared two years later, said that what Nietzsche emphasized was that humanity should work for the production of solitary great men. He quotes Ernest Renan and Gustave Flaubert to the same effect and claims that others as well have seen the need for preparing the groundwork for the cultivation of great men.[52] He does not mention Ralph Waldo Emerson in this context even though it was he who presented the original outline for the "aristocratic radicalism" that Nietzsche adopted as his own.

Although, at first, Emerson speaks of man-in-general as capable of becoming more than he is, as able to strive for a "great possibility," in almost the same breath he elevates the superior person and admires his "grandeur" and lack of ordinary prudence. This same move from encouraging all men to strive to realize their higher self, to the praise of the superlative, but imprudent, great man who expends himself in creative expression can be traced in

Nietzsche's writings. Both thinkers begin as teachers who seek to lead all human beings out of the herd and end as elitists who separate the common man from the insurpassable paragons of their philosophic and aesthetic imagination.

Emerson praises, in "Circles," the strong individual who is able to shrug off catastrophe, to *forget* calamity, who always moves "onward." This passing remark of his becomes the theme, in Nietzsche's writings, of knowing how and when to forget in order to be free for the openness of the future. To experience "happiness" man needs "the ability to forget." A healthy individual, he tells us, in the manner of Emerson, is one who is able to forget at the right time, to let go of the past.

The Poet

Literary critics have said that the essay, "The Poet," served as an inspiration to Walt Whitman and his conception of the role of the poet in the modern world. There is no doubt that this is correct. But it was not only the American poet of the "open road" who found inspiration in this essay. For Nietzsche, too, was affected by its programmatic ideals for the new poet.

Presenting a portrait of the poet as cultural hero, Emerson contends that he represents the complete person amongst a host of partial individuals. The ideal poet expresses in language natural powers and is a representative person who "traverses the whole scale of experience." A poetic mind is sensitive to the use of symbols and is aware of the symbolic form of nature. In tune with the living powers of nature, the true poet translates the emblems in nature into the symbolism of the world.

New facts are conveyed through poetic power, facts that enhance the pervasive fact of life itself. Turning the world to "glass," the poet discerns within the forms of life the "force" that ineluctably seeks expression in higher form. Words and language, the expression of life, were once wholly poetic; they symbolized the world. The images and tropes in language pass into common use, and their creative, dreamlike poetic power is gradually lost. Here Emerson seems to be restating his conception of the metaphorical character of language in "Nature." And this understanding of the original quality of words is quite similar to Nietzsche's treatment of language in "On Truth and Lies in a Non-Moral Sense." Thus, for example, he avers that the creators of language designate "the relation of things to men" and express this relation in bold metaphors. Our concepts, too, are metaphors that we use to represent things. What later comes to be called 'truth' is a "mobile army of metaphors, metonymies, and anthropomorphisms." When these truths become established, they become metaphors drained of their original poetic force. They are, he says, like "coins that have lost their embossing and are now considered as metal and no longer as coins."[53]

The language of the poet and the melodies of this language have an ascending motion and seem to pierce the depths of "infinite time." Despite this power of poetry, nature has an ever-higher goal: to generate ever-new individuals, to create higher forms through *"ascension."*[54] Poetic language attempts to duplicate, as far as it can, the organic forms of the natural world, the "text in nature."

In *Beyond Good and Evil,* Nietzsche presents his counterinterpretation of the "text" of nature, one that is made competitive with the physicists' interpretation of the natural world. He alludes to his training as a philologist as equipping him for his interpretation of "the text in nature."[55] In a similar vein, Emerson says that the paradigmatic poet should seek, by transference, to express in language the silent poetics of nature, to tap the energy in the nature of things, to supplement his private power with the "great public power" immanent in nature.[56]

Emerson's ideal poet should express cheerfulness and sunlight, employ symbols that exhilarate and emancipate men. Through the imaginative use of tropes and poetic forms, the poet creates worlds, spins a subtle metamorphosis, and serves man as a liberating god. Poetry carries us out of the ordinary into the extraordinary, unlocks the chains of thoughts that keep us prisoners. Although Nietzsche, in his aphorism "In Prison," emphasizes the way in which our senses enclose us in a "prison" from which we have no access to the actual world, the image he uses was probably borrowed from Emerson.[57]

In typical fashion, Emerson announces that he looks in vain for the ideal poet he describes, the artist in language who celebrates the ecstasy of life. The inspired reconciler, the new man, and the "new religion" are not yet given by time or nature. He calls out to the poet of the future and asks that he draw out of himself the *"dream*-power" that transcends all private power and become "the conductor of the whole river of electricity" that runs through nature.[58]

If Walt Whitman responded to Emerson's call and challenge, so, too, did Nietzsche. This is especially the case in his most poetic philosophical work, *Thus Spoke Zarathustra*. But more than that, he seems to have translated many of Emerson's evocative images into his vision of the great man who will be instinctive, spontaneous, courageous, self-trusting, and . . . poetic. The celebration of life is certainly carried forward by Nietzsche and considerably amplified. And the image of a power emerging from nature, a pervasive power that surges through all things, is incorporated in the idea of the will to power.

By synthesizing Emerson's assertions about this energetic power and joining them to the idea of the presence in man of a "search after power," Nietzsche fashioned the conception of a universal "will to power" acting through actuality without at all distorting what Emerson had said, in a disjointed and truncated way, about this conative cosmic energy. Passing from Emerson's mystical idea of an immanent power in nature to Richard Wagner's music-dramas (in which the quest for power is a central *Leitmotiv*), and then to F. A. Lange's description of the various physical theories of force in the nineteenth century, as well as *his* identification of a "lust for power" in man, Nietzsche received strong reinforcement, and powerful imprints, of virtually the same general conception.

Nobility

What is required, especially in times of spiritual need and danger, is "intrinsic nobleness," a belief, if only in imagination, in a "circle of godlike men and women . . . between whom subsists a lofty intelligence." Our disappointments with actual society, with the quality of human behavior, with even the "virtuous and the gifted," should not extinguish our hope that great and noble individuals are still possible. Patience is needed for this hope. We must, Emerson counsels us, respect the "slowness of nature" (*Naturlangsamkeit*) that "hardens the ruby in a million years."[59]

To the end of creating the conditions for the development of superior persons, the "natural aristocracy" amongst men must be acknowledged and preserved. Emerson would agree with Jefferson that this natural aristocracy is "the most precious gift of nature, for the instruction, the trusts, and governments of society."[60] Nature,

Emerson insisted, is *not* democratic. The scale of rank in nature ought to be preserved in the social world. And a "convenient distance" should prevail between man and man, particularly between "exceptions" and the majority.

Emerson insists, again and again, that the aim of culture is the "perfection of man." He deplores the decline in the spiritual quality of human lives, the excessive concern with "numbers," the abandonment of the pursuit of excellence, and the general lowering of standards in modern society. As Nietzsche did later, he saw signs of decadence in modern men.[61]

The cultural hero proffers an antipodal model for mankind in a time in which man appears to have lost natural spontaneity, "animal spirits," "undaunted boldness," fortitude, and endurance. The genuine hero, however, is no saint. Even though there is something unphilosophical in such a personality, we revere such individuals nonetheless. The hero is typically proud and self-confident, "not holy." Such a human type represents "the extreme of individual nature." The acts of the hero are not subject "to the censure of philosophers or divines." There is an admirable rashness in the hero that is negligent of comfort, safety, health, security, and of life itself. Such a person has a strong and forceful will and persists in face of obstacles, resistances, and adversity.[62]

There is, Emerson contends, a nobility and greatness in the authentic hero that raises him above the crowd and elevates the standard of virtue. Such an individual is natural, poetic, cheerful, healthy, and lacking in ponderous seriousness. These human types combine "Greek energy" and "Roman pride." Or, as he suggests in the motto for "History," they are an expression "Of Caesar's hand, and Plato's brain, / Of Lord Christ's heart, and Shakespeare's strain." Modern society has obscured and overdominated such strong and valuable traits. No matter how democratic our sentiments, we must admit that the "heroic cannot be the common, nor the common the heroic."[63]

At the center of the envisioned perfected man is the hard core of character. Such an individual is one who does not accept conventional beliefs, who is independent of social opinion and "accidental distinction." A person of character knows that existence entails "incessant growth" and is, as Emerson says in "Uses of Great Men," a "noble endogenous plant which grows, like the palm, from within outward." Capable of enduring misfortune, and having cultivated a sense of self-respect, such people feel, as Nietzsche says of himself in *Ecce Homo,* beyond praise and blame.[64]

The exemplary person combines insight with "tart virtue" and steady accumulations of power. Construing idealized sculpture as disguised history, Emerson avers that the strong and beautiful forms of Greek sculpture suggest what man could be in flesh and blood. The ideal traits that the ancient sculptors combine embodied in a work of art are traits originally taken from life. And the artistic representations of ideal human types testifies that "we are born believers in great men."[65]

Virtually everything that Emerson says about ideal types of human beings is, more or less, repeated by Nietzsche. That there is a family resemblance between the Nietzschean apotheosis of "supreme men" and Emerson's earlier poetic, aesthetically formed, portraits of such paradigmatic human beings is patently obvious.

Not only did Nietzsche model his exceptional individuals on Emerson's image of man perfected, but he adopted Zarathustra as his prophetic cultural hero on the basis of Emerson's description of this Persian "sage." In his worn copy of Emerson's *Versuche* he wrote *"Das ist es!"* ("That is it!") in the margin next to the following passage in "Character"[66] which creates a charismatic picture of "Zertusht."

> We require that a man should be so large and columnar in the landscape, that it should deserve to be recorded, that he arose and girded up his loins, and departed to such a place. The pictures most credible to us are those of majestic men who prevailed at their entrance, and convinced the senses; as happened to the eastern magian who was sent to test the merits of Zertusht or Zoroaster [Zarathustra]. When the Yuani sage arrived at Balkh, the Persians tell us, Gushtasp appointed a day on which the Mobeds of every country should assemble, and a golden chair was placed for the Yuani sage. Then the beloved Yezdam, the prophet of Zertusht, advanced into the midst of the assembly. The Yuani sage, on seeing the chief, said, "This form and this gait cannot lie, and nothing but truth can proceed from them."[67]

Emerson constantly refers, with poetic passion, to the magnetic power of greatness, to the daring and boldness of superlative individuals. Always he seems to be contrasting, by implication and insinuation, such paragons to the domesticated modern man whose 'morality' is one of custom, timidity, and fear. His counterethics is one of self-discipline, self-trust, and affirmation. It is conjoined with what could be called a religion of life.

This is not a "literary religion" and it is not, as Nietzsche's response to it shows, an exclusively "American religion." It is a secular, aristocratic 'religion' that expresses the hope that at least some men will, *in futuro,* transcend man as he has been and exemplify, in practice, what man ought to be.

The Hoi Polloi

Before turning to a comparison between Nietzsche's lifelong idealization of exemplary human types and Emerson's encomia to greatness, there is a residual issue remaining that pertains to Emerson's assumption of a natural aristocracy and his proposal of a radical aristocracy of spirit which should be considered.

Nietzsche frequently writes with disdain about "the masses," "the herd." This is usually taken to be a reflection of his arrogance, his snobbish elitism, or his "megalomania." In point of fact, it is simply an accurate duplication of the basic attitudes, perceptions, and valuations of Emerson.

As much as he desired to be a philosopher of the common man, Emerson was never quite able to carry it off convincingly. To be sure, he originally said that he called out to the individual to return to his center, and he spoke of lifting individuals out of the herd. Incidentally, as has previously been noted, Nietzsche also, at first, wanted to be a liberator, a "physician of culture" who would heal all men. Even in this respect, in his shift from a compassion for the weaknesses, foibles, and crudeness of the majority to a harsh condemnation of its opinions, values, and its "herd morality," Nietzsche, consciously or not, replicated the same change of attitude toward the majority of people as Emerson had earlier displayed.

In "Considerations By the Way," Emerson's attitude towards the majority is transparent. Although he avers that "nothing is so indicative of deepest culture as a tender consideration of the ignorant,"[68] this apparent charity is quickly scotched. For he proceeds, throughout this same essay, to lambaste, to excoriate, "the ignorant." Nietzsche sometimes showed the same ambivalence. When he was in a considerate mood, he counseled that a hatred of mediocrity is not worthy of a philosopher. It is because the philosopher is an "exception" that "he has to take the rule under his protection; he has to hold all the mediocre in good heart."[69] Needless to say, this does not stop him from engaging in a sustained polemic against "the mediocre." Emerson made inconsistency a virtue. And, at least on some issues, Nietzsche seems to have done the same.

Emerson laments, as we have seen, that men have become a conformist, anonymous "herd" and have long since neglected to think of realizing their higher possibilities. The people, he tells us, are corrupted by the means used to acquire distinction or aspirational possibilities, and they easily desert ideal ends. A higher culture, such as he proposes, which would display "the rank of powers," is but a mere name to the majority.[70]

An ideal form of education is needed to "meliorate" the quality of life of men in society. Such an education is rarely pursued. And many are unable or unwilling to recognize the "transcendent" character of exceptional individuals. The discipline of thought, work, and character needed for a higher culture is scrupulously avoided by the vast majority. If we contemplate the "transcendent power" of a Goethe, a Beethoven, a Wellington, or a Napoleon, we deplore the "glib-tongued tribe, who live for show, servile to public opinion," in our modern cities. Everywhere we look, Emerson sighs, we find "myrmidons" taking control and gaining positions of power, deepening the slough of mediocrity.[71]

The mediocritization of society forces the "genius" into solitude, "the stern friend, the cold, obscure shelter" which is a safeguard, protecting him or her from "the crowd."[72] This theme of solitude and its value is, of course, reiterated with a vengeance in *Thus Spoke Zarathustra*. Zarathustra advises the creators of new values to go "away from the marketplace," to avoid "the multitude." It turns out that Zarathustra is the spokesman for a great many of Emerson's distinctive sentiments and ideas even though he is much more than this.

In Emerson's considered opinion, man *en masse* retains a great deal of an earlier "quadruped organization." Even though we speak casually of a million *men,* "they are not yet men." The light at the end of the tunnel, however, is that there is a natural, compensatory tendency towards a "melioration" of man, towards the realization of "the Better in the human being." Although this is a general evolutionary tendency, is it not inevitable. It cannot occur without effort, without projecting higher personal and cultural goals for mankind.

Emerson is not a naive evolutionary optimist even though he does believe that the general directionality of nature, its "organic effort," is towards the creation of higher forms of life.[73] As his son remarks in notes to "Culture," his father accepted and propounded a general conception of ascending evolution before Darwin presented his biological theory of evolution by means of natural selection. What Emerson insisted upon, in his sketch of a theory, is that *effort* is a significant factor in evolution, and it is that which enables an organism to overcome adverse forces or circumstances. In order for man to survive and advance, voluntaristic "organic action" is necessary.[74]

The benefactors of mankind, Emerson believes, are always a minority. Many of the majority of people are coarse, torpid, spiritual invalids, and malefactors. We judge a country not by its total number of citizens, but by the quality of its minority. The "masses" are "pernicious in their demands and influence." They should not be flattered and cajoled, but "schooled." If he could, he would seek to draw potential genuine individuals out of this amorphous multitude. The world does not need more and more people. It needs better human beings, those who will strive for excellence.

Society is composed of many "drones," of many who, in short, are a "calamity." Emerson refuses to join in the "hurrah of masses." And he would like to see each person that is born be essential. Unfortunately, society continues the careless, excessive methods of nature: for every fifty "melons" that are of poor quality, there is one that is good. "In mankind she is contented if she yields one master in a century." Unfortunately, he sadly observes, the "mass" is largely rooted in primitivity and is too much motivated by "quadruped interest." The pity is that the social majority "have the advantage of number." Therefore, by sheer force of numbers, they are fast becoming "masters" in the modern world. Exceptions, "innovators," "geniuses," the "independent," and the psychospiritually strong are simply outnumbered.[75]

That Emerson encouraged Nietzsche in the proclamation of his aristocratic radicalism and directly influenced his conception of the radical distance between the creative, innovative minority and the majority is indisputable. Moreover, the specific notion that the "sovereign individual" is vulnerable because he or she is massively outnumbered by a recalcitrant majority is directly appropriated by Nietzsche. For he holds, contrary to thinkers like Herbert Spencer, that the evolutionary process, especially in its relatively recent psychosocial form, has *not* been progressive, has not been ameliorative. It has not by any means led to the survival of the "fittest," but has led to the survival and propagation of the average members of the species.

In obvious agreement with Emerson, Nietzsche describes exceptional individuals as complex "mechanisms" that are continually subject to damage from without and within. Persons who are independent, self-motivated, possessed of freedom of intellect and inner direction tend to move away from crowds and one another. While they tend to keep their own counsel, the insecure, the self-doubting, and outer-directed flock together for reassurance and protection. Immersion in the social group is the most primitive self-protective organic response. It is a response that genuinely independent individuals have outgrown or transcended.

The "herd-mentality" is so prevalent, Nietzsche believes, simply because it serves organic, practical, adaptive needs so well. Although, in isolation, a member of the social group may be relatively "weak" (in a psychospiritual sense), when he or she bands together with others of like sentiments or nature, then the individually "strong" are easily overpowered. The power of a social majority is enormous. It thrives on whatever augments its collective uniformity and it avoids, coerces, isolates, attacks, criticizes (via "public opinion"), demoralizes, or destroys, in one way or another, independent, self-existent, exceptional individuals. If a group, any group, has instinctive unity, it easily subdues a minority, especially what Emerson calls "a minority of one." This view of Nietzsche's, [76] though sometimes misconstrued as paradoxical (i.e., that the 'strong' are rendered 'weak' by group cohesion), is a perfectly plausible one, one which is readily confirmed. And it is clearly an annotation on a theme in Emerson's essays.

The exceptional individual who is "strong" is "weak" in relation to a conformist group that shares basic fears, sentiments, and values and flocks together in an anonymous herd. Nietzsche surpassed Emerson by seeing clearly and accurately the social and political implications of this modern shift of valuation from outstanding individuals to masses of human beings who have one essential imperative: be like us. What he opposes to the phenomenon of the rise of mass-man, the growth of group-mentality and group-values, is the cultural ideal of a spiritual, creative aristocracy. This is a theoretically embellished amplification of Emerson's original sketch of an aristocratic radicalism.

It is certainly ironic that what has been criticized by so many American writers and thinkers as an elitist cultural ideal that is presumed to be a Germanic aberration that is alien to the naturally egalitarian American spirit was put forward, in embryonic form, but in terms at least as forceful as those of Nietzsche, by a man regarded as a quintessential American poet and essayist.

Kierkegaard, Emerson, and Nietzsche shared one central belief: the rise of mass-man and mass-society and the consequent elevation of public opinion, coupled with a leveling of values, threatens the continued existence of autonomous individuality. Kierkegaard

offered as countermovements a return to a Socratic ethics of subjectivity or a rejuvenation of the practice of New Testament Christianity. Emerson and Nietzsche responded to the challenge of a
commercialized, value-leveling, mass society by projecting the
cultural ideal of the genius, the "great man," and the cultural
'hero'. Both wanted to undermine, if possible, the rising tide of
collective mediocrity and conformity. Both hoped to reverse this
sociohistorical trend towards the devalution of "the exception "
and the elevation of the average.

Spiritual Aristocracy

Nietzsche followed Emerson's lead very closely by condemning
the emerging "merchant's culture," the rising "gold aristocracy"
(or the kind of plutocracy that still survives and prospers), the
spreading commercialization of human life, the sacrifice of genuine culture for the immediate gains of financial interests, and the
dominance of purely utilitarian criteria of value. This is a prominent theme in *Untimely Meditations* and *Daybreak*. It surfaces, here
and there, in *Thus Spoke Zarathustra* in an obviously Emersonian
form. In the spirit of the American thinker, the wealthy are criticized as "superfluous" and charged with accumulating riches for
the sake of power. "They desire power and first of all the lever of
power, much money—these impotent ones."[77] Emerson attacked
materialism and condemned the economic system that was becoming a "system of selfishness" that corrupts so many institutions,
that encourages "fraud" and promotes legalized theft.

Ironically, about four years after discovering the *Essays,* Nietzsche found in F. A. Lange's *History of Materialism* a reinforcing criticism of the political economy of capitalism and of the 'culture'
based upon the pursuit of wealth, comfort, and pleasure as ends in
themselves.[78] Although this point was touched upon earlier, it is
curious that most critics of Nietzsche seem to be unaware that he
was, especially in his youth, sympathetic, at a distance, with the
workers who, he said, were being "exploited" at the expense of a
stable future. He, like Emerson, severely criticized the selfish and
egoistic interests of "capitalists." It is ironic that the Marxian literary critic and philosophic thinker, Georg Lukács, charged Nietzsche, in *The Destruction of Reason,* with being an apologist for
capitalism, for there is considerable evidence that Nietzsche (under
the influence of Emerson and that of the socialist, historian, and

economist, F. A. Lange) was a serious *critic* of the political economy, the practice, and the culture of nineteenth-century laissez-faire capitalism.[79] However, neither Emerson nor Nietzsche were critics of the excesses of capitalism in the nineteenth century because they harbored socialist values or ideals. They criticized it for its deleterious effects on social behavior, public morality, and cultural values. They propounded something that seems to puzzle past and present defenders of the capitalist social ideal: a nonpolitical, moral, and valuational critique of the system.

Nietzsche argued that capitalism corrupted the politics of the State, led to anarchic social atomism, encouraged selfishness, and promoted an egoistic morality of personal gain. It undermined the creation of a higher culture, generated an educational system devoted solely to practical utilitarian ends, and denigrated nonutilitarian cultural values. Where his criticism of the *ethos* of laissez-faire capitalism differs significantly from that of Marxists is revealing because of its clear relationship to the thought of Emerson.

In *Daybreak,* Nietzsche remarks that the "same volcano" of the "lust of power" still smolders in modern times even though its means have changed. What was once done "for the will of God, is now done for the love of money . . . what today gives man . . . the highest feeling of power."[80] This is practically what Emerson had said, specifically in "Power." For he had maintained that the "love of power" in the modern world takes the form of the wholesale pursuit of practical, utilitarian, and materialistic interests. In his oration of 1837, "The American Scholar," he had already linked the pursuit of wealth with the pursuit of power. In his later essays, he gave priority to man's striving for power in his rudimentary sketch of a theory of human motivation.

In his *Untimely Meditations,* Nietzsche celebrated the genius of Arthur Schopenhauer and insisted that the aim of culture is the production of outstanding examples of the artist, the philosopher, and the saint. Culture should have priority over the State and should serve to promote the cultivation of higher types of individuals. People in general have value insofar as they prepare the way for "the rarest and most valuable specimens" of humanity. Deploring, in the manner of Emerson, the uniformity of the populace, he argues that everyone should further the emergence of exceptional individuals in the world and should emulate them, as far as possible, "within." Like Emerson, he, in some of his earlier works, extended an invitation to his valuational perspective to *all* men, not only, as he later did, to a select few. Nonetheless, he continued to polish the image of the "great man," referring to Goethe and Wagner (whom he later demoted from that status) as paradigms, and persistently added to the list of their virtues.

Exemplary individuals are said to have a strong sense of selfhood, a "rugged masculinity," an independent attitude, a determined will. Like Emerson, Nietzsche attributes military characteristics to the outstanding types he admires: bravery, courage, a willingness to fight for and defend what they value. However, these virtues are not at all meant to be in the service of any State-sponsored military ideal. The "warrior of knowledge" is not modeled on military heroes, but is an augmentation of Emerson's early description of the authentic "scholar."

A distinctive characteristic of those who, because of their unusual insight, or creativity and sensibility, are exceptional is that they typically feel a deep sense of distance from others who live in the utility-driven world of everyday *Gemütlichkeit:* they experience a *Pathos der Distanz.* Or, in other words, precisely the sense of "distance" that Emerson had identified, described, and advocated. While Emerson had, at first, presented a general notion of the psychic distance between man and man, he also insisted upon the sense of distance between the exceptional individual and the typical social group, between the genuine thinker and the proverbial 'man on the street'.[81]

In a note to Nietzsche's remarks on "greatness" in *Beyond Good and Evil,* Walter Kaufmann refers to the similarity between Nietzsche's prescription of "greatness of soul" and Aristotle's image of the great-souled man in his *Nicomachean Ethics.*[82] There are certainly some bases for this comparison. However, his portrait of greatness owes far more to Emerson than to Aristotle, for greatness is specifically described by him as entailing "being noble, wanting to be oneself, being able to be different, standing alone and having to live independently." When the herd-man "receives and dispenses honors," he wages war on "all that is rare, strange, privileged, the higher man . . . the abundance of creative power and masterfulness."[83]

For Nietzsche, a just assessment of persons is said to require making distinctions, discerning an "order of rank" (or, for Emerson, "scale of rank"), and frankly judging inequalities of talent, skill, energy, discipline, nobility, integrity, and independence. If we obliterate such differentiating characteristics and say, with "the last man" in *Zarathustra,* that *everyone is the same,* then we reveal ourselves as the enemies of any genuine higher culture. In effect, we express a loss of faith in any higher values and a contempt for what is best in man: we would be advocates of nihilism.

Nietzsche's countermovement sought to preserve and conserve the values of "supreme men." This is incorporated into his natural morality of growth and is basic to his affirmative religion of life. Aristocratic radicalism is his considered answer to the leveling tendencies of the modern era and to the debasing mentality of mass 'culture'. The English philosopher, John Stuart Mill, defending liberal democracy, spoke of the possible "tyranny of the majority" in regard to politics, public policies, and sovereignty. But Nietzsche probed more deeply into the value-structure of an equalizing cultural system and saw that under a scheme of values created by and sustained by the majority the "exceptions" would suffer and would eventually be "destroyed" by one means or another.

The ideal social order, Nietzsche said in *The Antichristian,* would be a "cultural pyramid" in which there is preserved an "order of rank." It would be a genuine meritocracy not only based on talent or abilities (as in Mill's "aristocracy of talent"), but on natural qualities, on *being,* on psychospiritual strength and character. This is what is truly revolutionary in Emerson's and Nietzsche's visionary cultural ideal: the idea of the creation of a cultural system that is not based on brute force, inherited social status, wealth, stealth, deviousness, cunning, tradition, group sentiments, social contract, class interest, custom, kinship, or economic self-interest, but on the basis of *character.* Power in society ought to be in the hands of "the best" or those who do not crave power. The *aristoi* would not be political rulers or leaders, but bellwethers, shepherds. Although this cultural ideal may seem quixotic in a cynical and skeptical age, an age that wears egalitarian disguises, and deceives with egalitarian shibboleths, it at least has the merit of having never been pursued or adopted.

Nietzsche's rough draft of an aristocratic cultural system is compared by Salter, at one point, to Emerson's view that a superior minority appears and reappears in history despite the efforts of the majority to eliminate it by a "strong hand" or violence.[84] Once again, Salter was right to discern the similarity between Nietzsche and Emerson.[85] And once again he failed to see that there is a *direct* connection between the two thinkers on the value of aristocratic qualities or the promotion of aristocratic elites. Both recognize a natural historical tendency in healthy cultures, at peaks of human development, for a kind of *natural* aristocracy to arise. It is countervailing antiaristocratic social forces that divert this natural course of things or prevent its occurrence.

Between the two, Emerson is far more sanguine than Nietzsche about the natural tendency for the "best" to rise to positions of leadership in society. Nietzsche is much more skeptical about any naturally evolving social aristocracy of creative power, leadership, and strength. He was aware, as the twentieth century has been made painfully aware, that there are times in history when "the lowest one is *worth more* than the one up there."[86] His basic point is that there are many examples of "higher men" in history who have appeared in *diverse* cultures from time to time. But these individuals were "lucky accidents." They were not prepared for, cultivated, or willed. Thus, he follows Emerson's Jeffersonian idea of a natural aristocracy up to a point, but then goes beyond it. His cultural ideal involves the "cultivation" (not the "breeding" in any direct biological sense) of an aristocracy of character that he thought would be "supranational" and would take one thousand years to develop.

As in the case of Emerson, Nietzsche thinks of an ideal aristocracy as comprised of *spiritually strong* individuals who are open to experimental thinking and an experimental attitude towards life. Such individuals would be those who take pleasure in subduing the self; who pursue knowledge as a form of asceticism; who are cheerful, independent thinkers; who "rule" others not in a political sense, but in the sense in which Emerson felt that "magnetic" personalities "rule": by virtue of what they are.[87]

Contrary to the belief of Nietzsche's critics, he is not proposing a despotic, closed social system. He proposes a "cultural pyramid" in which there is social mobility based on knowledge, ability, skill, creativity, and personal qualities. He criticizes a closed caste system such as he found in the Hindu *Laws of Manu*. A genuine aristocracy, he contends, continually takes new and fresh elements into it throughout its evolutionary development.[88]

The cultural ideal proposed by Emerson and disposed by Nietzsche is designed for an imagined spiritual-cultural aristocracy. Even though he, far more than Nietzsche, tends to believe that people attain in society their proper place in the "scale of rank," he is aware that the "persons who constitute the natural aristocracy, are not found in the actual aristocracy."[89] Hence, such select individuals must be encouraged, promoted, valued, challenged, disciplined, and "bred" over long periods of time.

In a strict sense, Emerson says, with subtle irony, "we have never seen a man," a genuine man, a "complete man," but only the "prophesy of such." The historical examples of "greatness" are only "beginnings and encouragements" which point in the direction of even higher human possibilities.[90] As Nietzsche often did after him, he discerned defects in historical heroes (as he shows in his positive and negative portrait of Napoleon) and stressed the vulnerability of exceptional, more complex, individuals. He continually raises the requirements for admission into the category of "the great." Nietzsche later reiterates this pattern of thinking.

Although he refines, polishes, and embellishes his conception of exemplars, there is a sense in which Nietzsche never abandoned the standpoint he adopted as early as 1875: "My religion, insofar as I can still call it so, lies in the work for the production of genius."[91] But he did not have a naive belief in the intrinsic value of those who possess outward, popular social status. He knows well enough that corrupt political systems or corrupt societies have elevated "petty tyrants," incompetents, and madmen to power and have hailed them as "geniuses" and as "great" leaders. This happened, for example, in the case of the Roman emperors, Nero and Caracalla, to say nothing of other unlikely 'rulers' in modern times. He realized that rulers and ruling classes have not infrequently been inadequate, inept, or corrupt.[92]

The "higher men" that Nietzsche repeatedly refers to are *not* measured solely by their effects on the behavior of masses. The "higher nature" he extolled is much closer to Emerson's self-trusting, independent, nonconformist, for the personal traits of such an individual lie in "being different, in incommunicability, in distance of rank, not in an effect of any kind."[93] The fact that actual members of an aristocracy and actual aristocratic classes have, in history, occasionally been deficient, decadent, or corrupt, proves nothing, for Nietzsche, about the cultural necessity of a radical "new aristocracy."

From many different perspectives Nietzsche examines the nature of, the meaning of, the genius, the hero, "the great" who ought to be the central concern of a higher culture. Despite his perceptive insight into the imperfections of such types, he never loses faith in their value. Nor does he lose faith in the possibility of an order of rank based upon spiritual strength, creativity, and achievement. The form and manner in which he expressed his faith in the capacity of some individuals to transcend the human-all-too-human was suggested to him by Emerson's scattered remarks and observations.

Anti-Nomos

Nietzsche follows Emerson's views so closely that he adopts his archly presented suggestions that exemplary "law-giving" individuals need not conform to conventional conceptions of morality. For Emerson, in an antinomian spirit, suggests (as we've seen) that "noble" persons are not always subject to the letter of moral laws. Naturally, Nietzsche tends to exaggerate Emerson's occasional flitations with an "immoralism" of attitude and perspective. As is the case with Emerson, his impatience with a putative morality of conformity and custom, his valuation of a life-affirming, antitraditional morality leads him to extreme expressions of a liberation from the restrictions that are necessary for any genuine morality. As he says in his preface to *Daybreak,* if he attacks traditional conceptions of morality, it is "out of morality." This is but a completion of Emerson's truncated reflections on the problem of morality.

In the unlikely setting of an essay on "The Transcendentalist," Emerson announces that the free-spirited "transcendentalist" may, "in action," open himself to the charge of "anti-nomianism" or an opposition to the letter of moral laws by "his avowal that he . . . may with safety not only neglect, but even contravene every written commandment."[94] But only for a higher, constructive good.

There is a deep irony in the development of a tendency toward a decidedly risky "immoralism" in some of Nietzsche's portrayals of his attitude towards morality insofar as one form of the antinomianism that Emerson occasionally espoused (and conveyed to Nietzsche) emerged out of Christian culture. For it is the belief that a true Christian is freed from the moral law by virtue of grace, the conviction "that the believer in whom God dwells cannot sin and is superior to all law, both civil and moral."[95] Although this late medieval, radical Christian idea never became prevalent in the historical development of Christianity, it is curious that, in the name of the "freedom of the Spirit," this strand of the Christian tradition unwittingly recapitulated an esoteric teaching of Hinduism. That is, that the liberated Brahmin or "liberated man" (*jivanmukta*) is freed from the duality of good and evil. Steeped in the oriental literature available during his lifetime, Emerson was cognizant of this theme in Hinduism. And, of course, he was quite familiar with antinomic tendencies in the Christian tradition, as well as with Jacobi's version of antinomianism.

Antinomianism surfaces, as we've seen, as the idea of, and the valuation of, living "beyond good and evil." As previously noted, the earliest imprint of this notion was received from Emerson. Later, through his study of Hinduism, specifically in the works of his friend, Paul Deussen—*The Sutras of the Vedanta, The System of the Vedanta,* and *The Philosophy of the Upanishads*—he discovered that the esoteric teaching of Hinduism had proclaimed that the adept who attains true "emancipation" is "free from good and evil" or is "beyond good and evil."[96] He presents his "dangerous slogan" in *On the Genealogy of Morals,* alluding to Christian, Hindu, and Buddhist expressions of it and emphasizing that his slogan does not mean "beyond good and bad."[97] It is intended as a way of thinking, feeling, and being that is far removed from activistic, gross immorality.

Chapter 7 Notes

1. "The American Scholar," *PE,* p. 35. From as early as 1824, Emerson believed that "Aristocracy is a good sign." It would be, he claims, "the greatest calamity to have it abolished" (*Emerson in His Journals,* ed. J. Porte, p. 40). In "Uses of Great Men" he had not yet separated his image of an ideal person from actual social aristocrats. "I like a master standing firm on legs of iron, well-born, rich, handsome, eloquent, loaded with advantages, drawing all men by fascination into tributaries and supporters of his power" (Uses of Great Men," *RMNAL,* p. 27).

2. "The American Scholar," *PE,* p. 61.

3. Ibid., p. 62.

4. Ibid., p. 66.

5. Ibid., pp. 70–71.

6. Ibid., p. 71.

7. "Divinity School Address," *PE,* p. 78.

8. Ibid., p. 81.

9. Ibid., p. 85.

10. Ibid., p. 87.

11. "Notes," *COL,* p. 398.

12. "Worship," *COL,* p. 201.

13. Ibid., p. 207.

14. Ibid., p. 209.

15. Ibid., p. 240. Without necessarily accepting Harold Bloom's personal image of Emerson as an "American Orpheus," the emphasis in Emerson on a "scientific" religion or a religion of knowledge dovetails with Bloom's interpretation of Emerson's new religion as based upon "gnosticism." Cf. Harold Bloom, *Agon,* pp. 145–78.

16. Ibid., p. 242.

17. *Werke* (GOA), XII, 357.

18. Kaufmann, *Nietzsche,* p. 149.

19. Herbert W. Schneider, *A History of American Philosophy,* p. 248.

20. "History," *PE,* p. 121.

21. Cf. George J. Stack, "Nietzsche and Boscovich's Theory of Nature," *Pacific Philosophical Quarterly,* pp. 69–87. Although neither Nietzsche nor Emerson have a patent on the picturing of nature as Proteus-like, it is curious that this frequently used Emersonian image for the mutable forms of the natural world should appear in a crucial passage in Nietzsche's *Nachlass.* Saying that he calls reality that system of appearances that resists transformation into a "truth-world," Nietzsche designates this reality "will to power." This is, he explains, a designation of reality "from within" and not in terms of its "inconceivable, fluid Proteus-nature" (*SW* 11:654).

22. "History," *PE,* p. 123.

23. "Notes," *COL,* p. 415.

24. "Power," *COL,* p. 54.

25. "History," *PE,* pp. 127–29.

26. *SW* 3, *FW* §251, pp. 515–16.

27. "Self-Reliance," *PE,* p. 143.

28. Henry N. Smith, "Emerson and the Problem of Vocation," *New England Quarterly,* p. 56.

29. *SW* 6, *EH* §8, p. 276. Nietzsche's valuation of solitude and animosity towards social existence was largely temperamental. However, it is possible that he may have been encouraged in these attitudes by Emerson. In his lecture of 1837, "Human Culture," he described society as "A Routine which no man made and for those whose abuses no man holds himself accountable [and which] tyrannizes over the spontaneous will and character of all the individuals." In the social world, "We are overpowered by this great Actual." Cf. Stephen Whicher, *Fate and Freedom,* p. 61. There is a curious synonymy not only between Emerson's and Nietzsche's attitudes towards social being, but between these attitudes and those of Kierkegaard in regard to "the crowd" and Heidegger's description of the anonymity of the being of man or *Dasein* in the "they-world" of everyday ordinary being in *Being and Time.*

30. Ibid., §5, p. 370.

31. "Self-Reliance," *PE,* p. 149.

32. *Werke* (GOA), XV:193. In notes from 1870–71, Nietzsche refers to unconscious instinct as a "primal intellect"—(*Urintellekt*) (*SW* 7:111).

33. *Werke* (GOA), XVI:358.

34. *SW* 3, *FW* §3, p. 374.

35. Hubbard, *Nietzsche und Emerson,* p. 79.

36. "Self-Reliance," *PE,* p. 151.

37. *SW* 12:214.

38. "Self-Reliance," *PE,* pp. 156–57.

39. Ibid., p. 158.

40. "Considerations By the Way," *COL*, p. 266.

41. *Werke* (GOA), XIV:261.

42. "Behavior," *COL*, p. 190.

43. Ibid., p. 189.

44. *SW* 4, *AsZ* I, "On War and Warriors."

45. "Wealth," *COL*, p. 114.

46. Cited in Salter, *Nietzsche the Thinker*, p. 508n. At one point in his *Journal* Emerson characterizes himself as the Goethe of America (8:62).

47. Cf. George J. Stack, *Lange and Nietzsche*, pp. 278–80.

48. *SW* 1, *UB* 4, §4, p. 252.

49. Cf. George J. Stack, "Marx and Nietzsche: A Point of Affinity," *The Modern Schoolman*, pp. 23–29.

50. "Spiritual Laws," *PE*, pp. 201–3.

51. Letter to Georg Brandes (December 2, 1887), in Georg Brandes, *Friedrich Nietzsche*, p. 64.

52. Ibid., pp. 12–23.

53. *SW* 1:880–81.

54. "The Poet," *PE*, p. 254.

55. *SW* 5, *JGB* §22, p. 37.

56. "The Poet," *PE*, p. 255. Commenting on *Thus Spoke Zarathustra* in *Ecce Homo*, Nietzsche says, in the manner of Emerson, that "it . . . seems . . . as if the things themselves offer themselves as metaphors" *SW* 6, *EH*, p. 340).

57. *SW* 3, *M* 2, §117, p. 110.

58. "The Poet," *PE*, p. 261. This image may have suggested to Nietzsche the idea of the dream-power of Apollonian art he describes in *The Birth of Tragedy*.

59. "Friendship," *EE*, pp. 115–19. Whicher correctly identifies Emerson's "ethics of culture" as "patrician," as "an ethics for the superior man," as "an aristocracy of character" (Whicher, *Freedom and Fate*, p. 163). However, he assumes that these "patricians" are an actual class of aristocrats and that Emerson is concerned with "class feeling." This underestimates Emerson's futurism and his concern with a new scale of rank based on character. And it ignores his aside to the effect that the ideal persons he imagines are *rarely* found in the social class called "aristocrats."

60. Letter to John Adams (October 28, 1813). Cited in *The Annals of America*, Chicago: Encyclopaedia Britannica, Inc. 1976, 4:333. Although Thomas Jefferson believed in the possibility of the *moral* education of "the great mass of the people," he had a definite inclination towards a modified form of elitism. In this regard, it has been said that "for all his faith in the people and their ultimate possibilities and achievements he had no love for what he called 'the rabble'. His early education made him an aristocrat, and an aristocrat of the intellect he remained to the end of his days" (Gilbert Chinard, *The Literary Bible of Thomas Jefferson*, p. 1).

61. "Heroism," *EE*, p. 140.

62. Ibid., pp. 141–42.

63. Ibid., 143–46. Needless to say, this was one of the numerous passages in his copy of the *Essays* that Nietzsche underlined. In his translation it read: "Das Heroische kann nicht gewöhnlich sein, noch das Gewöhnlich heroisch." Cf. Hubbard, *Nietzsche und Emerson*, pp. 85–86.

64. "Character," *EE*, pp. 258–62.

65. Ibid., p. 263.

66. This marginal comment is found in the heavily underlined copy of Emerson's *Essays* found in Nietzsche's library. That is: R. W. Emerson, *Versuche* (Essays), trans. von G. Fabricus, Hanover, 1856, S. 361.

67. "Character," *EE*, pp. 263–64. This passage is heavily underlined in Nietzsche's copy of the *Versuche* (361), and the German reads *Zarathustra* for "Zertusht."

68. "Considerations By the Way," *COL*, p. 260.

69. *SW* 12:559–60.

70. "Wealth," *COL*, p. 111.

71. "Culture," *COL*, pp. 151–53.

72. Ibid., pp. 153–54.

73. Ibid., pp. 165–66.

74. "Notes," *COL*, p. 343. Nietzsche, too, emphasizes effort and striving in organic development and criticizes Darwin for stressing adaptation to an environment. He claims that all organic entities strive for *more*, seek to expend energy. This is the biological dimension of the "hypothesis" of "the will to power" (*SW* 5, *JGB* §13, p. 27). One sense of the will to power is derived from "the strongest of all urges which has directed all organic evolution thus far" (*Werke* [GOA], XVI:101).

75. "Considerations By the Way," *COL*, pp. 248–53. Against Darwin, Nietzsche argued that the individually "weak," because of their number and their tendency to band together, can overpower the happiest and spiritually strongest individuals. Independent individuals can be overpowered "if they have organized herd instincts, if they have the timidity of the weak, the majority, against them" (*Werke* [GOA], XVI:149).

76. *Werke* (GOA), XVI: 149.

77. *SW* 4, *AsZ* I, "Of the New Idols."

78. Stack, *Lange and Nietzsche*, pp. 275–80.

79. Cf. Stack, "Marx and Nietzsche: A Point of Affinity," *The Modern Schoolman*, pp. 23–39.

80. *SW* 3:202.

81. In a journal entry of 1859, Emerson refers to the "perception" (in the sense of sensibility and insight) that "distances" genuine individuals from the "mob" ("Notes," *COL*, p. 352). It has been said that Nietzsche recapitulates this distinction between, and *distance* between, the practical majority in society and "the nation of thinkers." Stanley Hubbard, *Nietzsche und Emerson*, p. 70. Emerson observes that everyone is involved in a "search after friendship," a search that is often stunted by the feeling of "infinite remoteness" between oneself and others ("Friendship," *EE*, pp. 113).

82. Friedrich Nietzsche, *Beyond Good and Evil*, trans. with commentary by Walter Kaufmann, 138n. Robert Solomon restates this comparison in stronger terms. For he claims that the *Übermensch* is none other than "Aristotle's *megalopsychos,* 'the great-souled man' . . . " (Robert Solomon, *From Hegel to Existentialism,* New York: Oxford University Press, 1987. p. 115).

83. *SW* 5, *JGB* §212, pp. 145–47.

84. "Manners," *EE,* p. 274.

85. Salter, *Nietzsche the Thinker,* p. 247.

86. *Werke in drei Bänden,* ed. Karl Schlechta, III:427.

87. *SW* 6, *A* §57, p. 243.

88. *Werke* (GOA), XIV:226.

89. "Manners," *EE,* p. 284.

90. "Character," *EE,* p. 266.

91. *SW* 8:46. Referring to "persons who are intrinsically rich and powerful," Emerson said that "our religion is the love and cherishing of these patrons" ("Uses of Great Men," *EE,* p. 10).

92. *Werke* (GOA), XIV:340. In this regard, Emerson was a more uncritical hero-worshipper than Nietzsche was. In a note from 1847, he includes "Hercules, Theseus, Odin, the Cid, and Napoleon" in the "right aristocracy" and asserts that, because of their incomparable superiority, they are permitted a wide range of immoralities (*Emerson in His Journals,* p. 372). His later double-edged depiction of the positive and negative traits of Napoleon in *Representative Men* indicates that he had modified his veneration of heroes somewhat and no longer spares them from moral criticism.

93. *SW* 13:497–98.

94. "The Transcendentalist," *PE,* p. 96. Cp. "Plato; or, the Philosopher," *PE,* p. 324.

95. A. C. McGiffert, *A History of Christian Thought,* 2:356. Religious antinomianism can be traced back to the gnostic religions of the Greco-Roman world just prior to the fall of the Roman Empire. Various forms of antinomianism are found in the heretical sects of the Bogomils, Cathars, Albigensians, Manicheans, and Waldensians. Hans Jonas has argued that there are parallels between gnosticism and existentialism. He avers that the "gnostic individual" aspired, as the existentialists do, to "exist authentically." Against the background of Nietzsche's extensive uncovering of, and description of, the phenomenon of nihilism, Jonas specifically points to the antinomianism found in gnosticism and nonreligious forms of existentialism (especially that of Martin Heidegger in *Being and Time*). Jonas claims that "antinomian Gnosis appears crude and naive in comparison with the conceptual subtlety and historical reflections of its modern counterpart" (Hans Jonas, "Gnosticism, Existentialism, and Nihilism," in *The Phenomenon of Life,* p. 224). Jonas does not consider the possibility of the transmission of antinomian orientations by way of the Christian tradition. This is certainly more likely the case in regard to Emerson. The

parallels that Jonas discerns between gnosticism and existentialism may be accounted for in terms of the transmission of such a notion from Emerson to Nietzsche and then to Martin Heidegger. Nietzsche certainly seems more self-consciously aware of the parallels between Christian-Gnostic negative attitudes towards the letter of the law (*nomos*) and restrictive norms and the Hindu conception that the truly liberated adept assumes a stance "beyond good and evil." Emerson's radicalism in this regard was recognized by his contemporaries, for they labeled his "latest form of infidelity" as a form of "Antinomianism" (Stephen Whicher, *Freedom and Fate* "Note D." p. 179).

96. In *On the Genealogy of Morals* Nietzsche explicitly refers to the idea of redemption in Hinduism and Buddhism in terms of the attainment of "knowledge," the releasement from desires and acts, arriving at "a state beyond good and evil" (*SW* 5, *GM* III §17, p. 380). This notion of redemption through knowledge coincides with Harold Bloom's accurate identification of Emerson's "gnosticism."

97. *SW* 5, *GM* I, §17, p. 288. Among the many things that Nietzsche thought were "bad" were the following: (1) the idea of a moral world order; (2) the concept of a moral God who judges and punishes his creations; (3) the notion of the moral justification of the sufferings of humanity. He came to think of the entire cosmic "aesthetic spectacle" of the creation and destruction as itself "beyond good and evil." In his notes from the late 1880s, he entertained the possibility of a God "beyond good and evil" (a conception already found in Hinduism and some forms of Christian mysticism). Finally, he refused to deny, explain away, or "justify" the very real injustices, contradictions, and sufferings in existence. Being, thinking, feeling, and living "beyond good and evil" entails, for Nietzsche, a sanctification and deification of life and existence—in effect, the tragic optimism of a Dionysian religion of life. Cf. Stack, "Nietzsche's Antinomianism," *Nietzsche-Studien*, pp. 109–33.

Chapter 8

The Image of the *Übermensch*

Can rules or tutors educate
The semigod whom we await?

[Ralph Waldo Emerson, Motto
to "Culture"]

In a monograph that appeared in 1937 the impact of Emerson on German thought and letters was examined, and it was noticed that there were certain common features in his writings and in the ideas of Nietzsche. Their mutual opposition to historicism and their criticisms of "historical Christianity" were cited. A contrast was made between the optimism of Emerson and the pessimism of Nietzsche; the former's idealism and the latter's paganism; Emerson's "Christian humanism" and Nietzsche's "Dionysian anti-Christianity."[1] Only a surface relationship between the thought of the American and the German radical thinker was touched upon, and some specific points of differentiation are, at best, questionable.

As we have seen, Emerson's optimism was balanced by a strong sense of realism. A principle of affirmation of life was embraced in relation to the "negative facts" that pervade nature and impinge upon human life. When Nietzsche counsels a Dionysian affirmation of life in face of the antitheses and sufferings of existence, he is but heightening and dramatizing Emerson's basic standpoint. And Emerson extols the virtues of "paganism," especially in relation to the culture of Christianity and to the secularized version of Christian morality in the form of a conventional morality of custom.

And the statement about Emerson's Christian humanism reveals a misunderstanding. For he became disillusioned with conventional Christianity and, in his "Divinity School Address," he argued that the teachings of Jesus Christ were victims of "distortion," that "historical Christianity" emphasized the person of Christ in an exaggerated and "noxious" way.[2] He epitomized his unorthodox 'theology' in a notation from 1834: "When we have lost our God of the tradition and ceased from our God of rhetoric then may God fire the heart with his presence."[3]

Emerson, like Nietzsche after him, stressed the value of life and proposed immanent values in a cultural ideal, one that was, in part, modeled on a version of Greco-Roman morality. He was not immune to the appeal of 'pagan' cultural images and values. And he put more faith in the experience of "immortality" in finite existence than in the official Christian doctrine of immortality. Because of his commitment to temporal ethico-religious values, his faith in the perfectibility of man, his lack of concern with "the beyond," and his emphasis upon future cultural ideals, to say nothing of his sympathy with the ideas of Hinduism, Emerson had already assumed a post-Christian orientation towards life and the condition of man.

Although vague and loose associations have been made in previous treatments of the relation between Emerson and Nietzsche concerning the constructive conception of the *Übermensch*,[4] no one has delved into the profound nature of the relationship between Emerson's fragmentary remarks pertaining to transcendent human types and the image of the "beyond-man."

In Hubbard's *Nietzsche und Emerson* it is accurately reported that during the "Zarathustra period after 1880" Nietzsche occupied himself, in an intensive way, with Emerson. It is then held that the precise proofs in *Zarathustra* for this influence are "very sparce."[5] However, as we have seen, the evidence for Emerson's influence on a great many specific conceptions, insights, images, and valuations in Nietzsche's writings—including *Thus Spoke Zarathustra*—is the opposite of slight. And the "proofs" of the presence of Emerson's language and thought in *Zarathustra* permeate this poetic-philosophical *tour de force*.

In Salter's *Nietzsche the Thinker* there is a discussion of Nietzsche's physical and psychological sufferings and the way he overcame them. His affirmations are characterized as "a warrior's joy," not the "unruffled optimism of Emerson."[6] But the affirmation of life despite personal suffering and the sufferings of existence in general, which Nietzsche expresses, is simply an exponential assertion of an idea that he found in Emerson's writings. It need hardly be said, given the attention that has been focused on Emerson's dark side, that his optimism was not "unruffled." Nietzsche understood this and, in his personal life, he tried to practice what Emerson preached. This was especially so in regard to his will to health and his strenuous efforts to overcome his illnesses.

What is even more unusual about Salter's eye for Emerson-Nietzsche connections is that he specifically identifies a strong relationship between Nietzsche's valuation of "great men" and a passage in Emerson's essay, "Character." That he noticed this relationship indicates that he had a lucid understanding of Nietzsche's concept of the *Übermensch* even though he simply concludes that Emerson's portrait of the superlative individual "perfectly illustrates Nietzsche's thought."[7] But, it is Nietzsche's conceptual models of the man "beyond-man" that illustrate, in a more dramatic way, aesthetically conceived images of exceptional individuals which were originally presented in Emerson's impressionistic descriptions of such distinctive human types.

As Emerson looks beyond the "masses" and above the mediocrity he sees everywhere in the world around him, he looks back nostalgically to the great thinkers and men of action, to the geniuses and "masters" of the past who represented the "energetic class." As Nietzsche later does, he extols great artists, poets, spiritual leaders, courageous, activistic individuals and accomplished people of all kinds and views them from many perspectives. He speaks with equal fervor of religious or philosophical heroes, literary heroes, and heroic men of action. His cultural paladins are, like those of Nietzsche, exclusively *masculine* figures. In fact, he refers to "manliness," as Nietzsche does, as a fundamental requirement for "greatness." Apparently neither he nor Nietzsche considered the value of creative women or women of action, even though such have had an impact on history and culture, and despite the fact that they continue to do so. One need only think of Sappho, Cleopatra, Joan of Arc, Queen Elizabeth, Saint Teresa of Avila, Mme. de Staël, Queen Isabella of Spain, and numerous others. And certainly someone like Catherine the Great of Russia possessed the qualities, both good and bad, that Emerson and Nietzsche freely ascribe to their "manly" avatars.

The preoccupation with what can only be called *machismo* and the attempt to discover its essential features is one which Emerson seems to have transmitted to his unknown German champion. The "*plus* man" (which Nietzsche would have read as the *Überschussmensch*) that Emerson evokes in "Power" has vivacity, surplus energy, robust health, and magnetic "personal power." He has that accumulated power that enables him to take the "step from knowing to doing." Such capacities are exemplified in creative artists such as "the masculine [Michael]-Angelo or Celini."[8] These strong, highly talented personalities have a magnetic effect upon those around them and, whenever they appear, "immense instrumentalities organize around them." Compared to such individuals, the majority of men seem caught in the quagmire of "mediocrity." Unlike the "strong" individual, "the multitude have no habit of self-reliance or original action."[9]

Over and over again, in the essays of Emerson and in Nietzsche's mobile army of aphorisms, we come upon the same all-or-nothing contrast between superior, creative, powerful, self-reliant individuals and the "mediocre," the uncreative, unheroic, always anonymous, vast majority. It is an overworked and hyperbolic theme in their otherwise polished and persuasive writings.

It has been said that the conception of the man "beyond-man" may have been suggested to Nietzsche by the German poet Goethe. But he is supposed to have given it a "new meaning."[10] Actually, he first uses the term *Übermensch* (in his published works) in *The Gay Science,* specifically in reference to heroes and gods in contrast to "undermen" such as dwarfs, satyrs, centaurs, demons, etc.[11] This distinction is introduced in the context of an interpretation of the moral meaning of polytheism. The reference to *Übermenschen* of all kinds is similar to a remark Nietzsche probably noticed in his study of F. A. Lange's *History of Materialism* concerning the way primitive people project into the circumambient natural world "superhuman human beings."[12]

The full-blooded version of the idea of a person who has "overcome" man as he has been and is does not appear until *Zarathustra.* However, Nietzsche had early on proclaimed that he imagined "something higher and more human above me." And he had envisioned a new man "who is full and measureless in knowledge and love and vision and power."[13] Such an individual would be faithful to nature and would take his place as the judge and evaluator of things. This apotheosis of such a human type is expressed in the context of a concern with the "circle of culture" and a critique of the quality of modern German culture. An overriding theme of "Schopenhauer as Educator" is that society *ought* to work for the production of great men. This is what Nietzsche refers to in his early notes as his "religion." In the manner of Emerson, he even claims that the personified, intentional "nature" that is eulogized "works" towards the creation of "the individual higher specimen." *Ergo,* culture ought to continue this process by creating the conditions for the possibility of the emergence of "great redeeming men."

What may be called an argument from nature, as well as the correlative assumption that culture ought to be a continuation of a natural process that somehow has been perverted in many instances, is typical of Emerson's reasoning. Nietzsche follows him by first projecting a particular and ameliorative conception of nature and then trying to draw an 'ought' out of the 'is' of this idealized image of nature. In fact, Emerson claimed to find an unspecified morality immanent in the organic unity of nature. Both he and Nietzsche were convinced that culture is a continuous development of nature, but both criticize modern culture because it is defective, inadequate, mediocre, and *not* natural. The presumption, in both cases, is that the essence of nature is clearly known and that many cultures are deviations from a norm that is genuinely *natural*.

An idealized, selectively represented, and often inconsistently interpreted, model of nature is upheld by Emerson and Nietzsche as the criterion of what culture (which has presumably developed *out of nature*) ought to be. But both conceive of an ideal culture as a transformed and aesthetically embellished nature. Therefore, neither wants a literal "return to nature" for the simple reason that, if this *were* possible, culture, in any viable form, would be precluded. Given their developmental conception of nature, one can understand why they were led to proclaim a modality of *futurism,* despite the fact that they are both admitted "circular" philosophers. For Emerson and Nietzsche, the ideal transformation of nature into culture is exceedingly rare and, in fact, has never been perfectly executed in the historical process. Hence, the belief in the promise of the future, a belief which, especially in the case of Nietzsche, seems to crash against the reef of eternal recurrence.

Given Nietzsche's theory of the eternal recurrence of *the same* (if it is taken as an ontological reality), the "great men" and the *Übermenschen* of the future that he sings hymns of praise to are really beings of "the past," even of an infinite number of "pasts." Holding him to his claims about eternal recurrence as an *objective* reality, we could say that he exercises himself too much over the issue of the possibility of the emergence of *Übermenschen* of the future. For, if there *were* such superlative individuals, then, *a forti-ori*, there *will be* such exemplary beings; if there never have been such types, then there never *will be* such men "beyond-man."

If superior individuals are inevitable "in the future" (because they have already recurred innumerable times in "the past"), then all of the elaborate theoretical preparations for their (re-)arrival are superfluous. If, on the other hand, these paradigmatic individuals have never existed in an indefinite "past," then the preparations for their arrival are futile. This entire issue centers on the question of what Nietzsche came to mean by the *thought* of the eternal recurrence of the same and what function it served in his experimental philosophy. A possible resolution of this question was tentatively put forward earlier in the discussion of Emerson's emphasis upon the experiential encounter with "eternity."

There is evidence in Nietzsche's writings that the existential meaning of the appropriation of the thought of eternal recurrence replaces the tentative attempts to argue for the objective reality of eternal recurrence on the basis of scientific hypotheses.[14] Fortunately, the details of this difficult question fall outside the range of my chief concerns here. Suffice it to say that Nietzsche's emphasis upon the *experience* of eternity in "the Moment" is an elaboration on Emerson's *obiter dicta* concerning the experience of rising above the stream of temporality in the "concentrated eternity" of the "moment."

Before examining in detail Emerson's description of his "exceptions," his paragons, it should be mentioned that his theory of "correspondence" plays a role in this regard. For the idea of correspondence is based upon the notion of microcosmic analogies. Each entity in the natural world epitomizes the order and structure of nature *in toto*.[15] The essence of the cosmos is believed to be reflected in the microcosmic atom. Man is, as far as we know, the only self-conscious microcosmic being. And, for Emerson and Nietzsche, the interpretation of nature is ineluctably anthropomorphic. In this regard, Harold Bloom is on target when he says that Emerson's *Nature* could just as well be called "Man."

A difference between Emerson and Nietzsche here is that the former completely embraces and affirms the anthropomorphic understanding of the natural world while Nietzsche exposes it, criticizes it, and then, in the final analysis, accepts the inevitability of interpreting the essential nature of the world according to "human analogy." Between the two, Nietzsche clearly has a deeper and more critical grasp of the anthropomorphic interpretation of nature. Despite his critical awareness of the "anthropocentric idio-syncrasy" of man, he eventually offers a hypothetical interpreta-tion of reality in terms of an underlying "will to power" acting through all things that is put forward on the basis of human anal-ogy. The macrocosm is understood in terms of what we know about the essential nature of microcosmic man. Even the elemen-tary subatomic particles or "force-points" that Nietzsche provi-sionally posits are construed, after man's volitional nature, as "will-points."

Nature/Morality

Emerson extracts from the panorama of the natural world a 'mo-rality' which, in fact, involves a synthesis of nature *and* spirit. In the broadest sense, what both he and Nietzsche do is to propose an ethico-aesthetic ideal: the dynamic synthesis of nature and spirit in an idealized individual in whom there is a dialectical tension of an-tagonistic, but mastered, characteristics. The antithesis-character of nature is modeled upon the antithetical nature of man. When the metaphysical chips are down, Emerson and Nietzsche give prior-ity to a spiritual *nisus* acting through nature and man.

The natural religion of Emerson is basically a pantheism,[16] just as Nietzsche's interpretation of reality "seen from within" is a mo-dality of supramoral pantheism. Emerson's claims about the spiri-tual power pervading nature are based upon a metaphysical intuition whereas Nietzsche is self-consciously aware that his "hy-pothesis" of the will to power is an experimental thought, an "in-terpretation" of the text, a palimpsest, of man-in-nature and nature in man.

The religion that Emerson sought to develop is centered on the belief in the emergence of higher forms of human life. And this notion is connected with his approval of what he considered as a then-recent tendency for morality to be *aesthetically* construed. He often speaks of the fusion of beauty and will, beauty and power, beauty and strength. The extraordinary person is described in ar-tistic, sculpturesque terms, as if he or she were a kind of living sculpture in which nature and art have been dynamically synthe-sized. All of this is intimately associated with his romantic, poetic, and aesthetic understanding of nature. The supreme individual will embody the power of nature in a living aesthetic unity. The separation of morality from nature and its beauty, he suggests, has led to the development of an unattractive, negative morality of weakness.

Emerson balances his romantic conception of nature by vividly depicting the wastefulness, the destructiveness of the natural world. The "fatalities" of nature that reveal ferocity, violence, and destructiveness are not reconciled by Emerson with his typical image of a benevolent, creative, poetic, and ascending unity of nature. Against him, it could be argued that the "moral law" that is ostensibly revealed in natural processes is, unfortunately, either ambiguous or questionable. The Greek Sophists contrasted the conventions of civil society to the grim realities of nature and justified what Plato portrays as a harsh version of 'natural' morality. In Plato's dialogue, *Gorgias,* a tough-minded spokesman for the Sophists' distinction between nature and convention, Callikles, argues that "nature . . . demonstrates that it is right that the better man should prevail over the worse and the stronger over the weaker. The truth of this can be seen in a variety of examples, drawn from the animal world and from the complex communities and races of human beings; right consists in the superior ruling over the inferior and having the upper hand."[17]

Nietzsche appears to follow the Sophists up to a point by espousing a morality modeled on natural growth. But, even in this case, he recapitulates Emerson's paradoxical understanding of nature. For, despite his praise of what is natural, he, too, is quite aware of the negative aspects of the natural world. In *Beyond Good and Evil,* he criticizes the ancient Stoics for imposing their morality "on nature" while pretending to prescribe "living according to nature." He argues that if man literally emulated nature, he would be "wasteful beyond measure, indifferent beyond measure, without purposes and consideration, without mercy and justice, fertile and desolate and uncertain at the same time."[18] This surely indicates that a direct imitation of nature, strictly followed, would be disastrous for life and would lead either to brutality or indifference. By implication, he suggests that his own naturalistic morality does not involve a literal acting in accordance with nature.

In an early essay, *Homer's Contest,* Nietzsche had referred to the "uncanny dual character" of nature. This at least had the merit of a neat consistency. To claim, as Kaufmann did, that the idea of the will to power (as a monistic hypothesis) resolves this dualistic character of nature because it emphasizes "the continuity of nature and culture"[19] actually creates difficulties for his thought that are similar to those encountered in Emerson's praise of natural, energetic, bold, and unrestrained "heroes" and "great men." For the culture (and the 'morality') that ostensibly emerges out of nature can take, and has taken, many diverse forms, most of which would be (and, in fact, were) repugnant to Emerson and Nietzsche. Thus, not *any* culture that is (presumably) derived from nature is considered good, valuable, or consistent with the ostensibly positive characteristics of the natural order of things. Certainly, for Nietzsche, a culture that, in his view, counsels a "will to nothingness" is not construed as "natural." Nature generates many cultures and they are not all viable, creative, affirmative, or "higher" cultures.

The transformation of natural tendencies into cultural values and systems may take highly destructive or highly creative forms. However, Emerson selects out of the panorama of natural phenomena and qualities only those he believes ought to be present in a complete, perfected human being. That is, he wants to preserve the "vital force," the spontaneous, creative, dynamic energy of nature while prescinding the *excesses* that would lead to social, personal, and moral chaos. This is clearly shown in his anticipation of the conception, which later appears in Nietzsche's thought, of the *spiritualization* of natural propensities. Thus, it is said that the "*plus* condition of mind and body" is often found in an "excess that makes it dangerous and destructive"; hence, the need for restraints or "absorbents" that take the edge off it. Even "physical force" has no great value if that is all there is. We want, to use Emerson's image, not a conflagration, but fire enough to warm our hearth.[20]

Nietzsche elaborates on Emerson's suggestion and argues that the (natural) passions, drives, or urges ought to be "sublimated." Retaining its original meaning in chemistry, sublimate means to refine or purify something, with the additional sense of transforming a substance which, in its primary form, would be corrosive, dangerous, or noxious. If Emerson, as far as I know, does not use this particular term, he intends its meaning in his remarks on the need to restrain the primitive natural tendencies in man. It is, in effect, the postulated primordial will to power in man which, like Emerson's "search after power" or "love of power," must be controlled, channeled, and mastered by a "synthetic," "complete," or "central" man. "Your will to power," Zarathustra warns candidates for *Übermenschlichkeit*, "is your greatest danger."

Despite the reiterations of Emerson and Nietzsche that they want to see a fully *natural* human being who embodies the raw energy of nature, they do not idealize the negative, wasteful, blindly destructive aspects of nature. Presumably, then, the evolution of culture out of nature involves *a transformation of nature* that entails some restraint and constraint; requires an inhibition of crude impulses. Nature, then, provides the raw materials (in the form of organic values) for the creative evolution of culture. And culture must be built upon stated or unstated tables of moral values even if these evolved out of premoral organic valuations or even if they are reversals of dangerous instinctive tendencies. The point is that if culture has evolved out of nature, then this involves a transfiguration of nature into culture. What is suggested is an unconscious or unarticulated immanent process of sublimation of purely "natural" energies and tendencies. Expressed in Hegelian terms, culture could be construed as the self-suppression of nature by which it is negated in its original untamed form and preserved in a "spiritualized" expression.

Nietzsche's natural history of morality is a fascinating, imaginative, and speculative experiment in thought. What is especially arresting is the thesis (originally suggested to him by Emerson) that good impulses and virtues are derived from propensities that were originally evil or immoral. The negative affects (hatred, envy, covetousness, and the lust to dominate) are regarded as essential to the "economy of life." They must be "enhanced if life is to be further enhanced."[21] This is central to his psychology of morality. And, of course, it is clear that he does not mean that these lethal "affects" should be "enhanced" in their coarse, natural form. Rather, they must be transfigured into positive feelings and drives. No morality worthy of the name, not even Nietzsche's naturalistic morality of growth, encourages an uninhibited expression of primordial natural drives. For, as he says in *Beyond Good and Evil,* "every morality is . . . a bit of tyranny against 'nature'. "[22]

The "immoralism" that Nietzsche wears as a defiant emblem of rebellion is only a relative designation of his attitude towards morality. It is immoralism in relation to traditional morality, to Judeo-Christian morality, to a "morality of pity," to a "herd morality." If it were an absolute or literal immoralism, he would then be embracing the very "return to nature" that he forcefully repudiates. And he would be negating the very foundation of culture, to say nothing of the aristocratic culture that he projects into an imagined future. In *On the Genealogy of Morals* he says that he wants to go beyond the duality of good and evil, but not abandon the distinction between "good and bad." In his preface to *Daybreak* he tells us that his critique of 'morality' is "out of morality," in the service of a "higher" morality.

Nietzsche prescribes a morality of affirmation that is antiutilitarian and positive, a morality in which nature, art, and culture would be sustained in a dialectical tension in the existence of spiritually strong individuals. He wanted to make room for an aristocratic morality designed for exceptions. And he sought to undermine the idea that there is *one* type of morality for all individuals, one dictatorial morality that prescribes how all human beings ought to live.

"Herd Morality"

Many of the features of the so-called "herd morality" that Nietzsche criticizes with such fervor are practically synonymous with the traits of modern man that Emerson had earlier attacked. Modern European morality of the late nineteenth century is characterized by Nietzsche as a code for temperate people, for the "mediocre," for the domesticated, the timid, the tame. It is a morality of utility designed for the "greatest number," the average members of a community. It disvalues whatever seems threatening or dangerous to group sentiments. Thus, it slanders any high and independent spirituality, the will to stand alone, "self-reliance." Such a group morality is said, in the manner of Emerson, to value conformity, submissiveness, modesty, timidity, and a "mediocrity of desires."[23]

In order to reverse what Nietzsche, following Emerson, sees as a disastrous undermining of an independent moral consciousness, he proposes a "revaluation of values" in the form of a new morality and a cultural idea centered on sovereign individuals. Like Emerson before him, he foresees what can yet be made of man and projects for the few his aesthetically conceived image of the *Übermensch* in direct opposition to what Emerson called the "quadruped" nature of men.

In *Beyond Good and Evil* Nietzsche refers to his harshness in speaking of human beings as animal herds, but, in his own defense, he argues that, for him, the danger of the cultural dissolution entailed by the rising morality of the masses is so great that strong language and powerful criticisms are needed. Emerson also spoke of the majority in equally harsh tones, but he never deigns to notice it. And the metaphors he uses to characterize "the mass" are as cutting as any Nietzsche ever employed.[24]

Emerson's son, Edward, aware that his father's views sound quite harsh, explains that he only wanted to return to man his dignity and self-respect. His father thought that, to this end, the individual must be drawn out of "the herd." Edward claims that his father's harshness "was directed to the man who sacrifices his manhood for the mass."[25] What his son says of Emerson's aim in this regard could be said, with equal justice, of Nietzsche himself, especially in his *Zarathustra* period. At one point in *Thus Spoke Zarathustra* the prophet practically quotes Edward Emerson's comment about his father's attitude towards "the herd" when he says: "To lure many away from the herd—that is why I have come."[26] The proviso would be that those who want to leave the security of the horde must remain faithful to the earth and embrace a religion of life that entails a morality of strenuousness. But even then, Emerson had already foreshadowed this positive, disciplined attitude, this natural morality of life-affirmation, surplus energy, and health. He had seen the need for "universal" men who would seem "superhuman," who would serve as bellwethers of a higher culture.

Emerson's cultural hero, his paradigm of what man ought to be, will be self-legislating, spiritually strong, possessed of a confident self-respect, and "noble" in comportment. A premium is placed on being able to look at the ugly and disturbing realities of life and existence without flinching. The "sovereign individual" must be willing to discover and examine the unpleasant and deplorable characteristics of man, to know the "horrors of depravity," to face the dreadful and heartbreaking necessities of nature, the accidents and catastrophes that destroy human beings as if they were insignificant dolls. Precisely this deliberate and persistent staring into "the heart of darkness" of actuality advocated by Emerson is made one of the chief requirements of Nietzsche's *Übermensch.*[27]

When Nietzsche praises the individual who sees reality as it is and adds that such a person should discover in himself or herself the "dubious and fearful qualities" of this same reality, he combines two of Emerson's prescriptions that were presented separately. That is, the necessity of facing and accepting the disturbing and terrible aspects of reality and the need to discover the same disturbing realities in the antithetical and antagonistic nature of the self. What Emerson called the "fire," coarse energy, and explosive potentialities of "passionate" individuals are construed by him as necessary for "greatness." The long and often painful journey to greatness requires steel-like endurance, intense energy, and strong passions. For Emerson believed that in culture, as well as in personal life, "everything is worked up and comes in use,—passion, war, revolt, bankruptcy . . . folly . . . blunders, insult, ennui."[28]

As we saw in the discussion of Emerson's rudimentary theory of development, sinister and potentially dangerous propensities lurk in the being of each individual because each of us carries within our biological nature remnants of traits found in ferocious, inferior species. Nietzsche paraphrases Emerson quite often on this score, but nowhere so transparently as he does in *Thus Spoke Zarathustra*. After Zarathustra announces that he teaches that man is something to be overcome, he asks: "do you want to be the ebb of this great flood and even go back to the beasts rather than overcome man? . . . You have made your way from worm to man, and much in you is still worm."[29] This passage echoes not only Emerson's concept of evolution, but the concluding lines of his motto to "Nature": "striving to be man, the worm/ Mounts through all the spires of form." And his belief that a reversion to animality is possible is merely a stronger version of Emerson's opinions about the "quadruped nature" of the majority and the declination of man and society. Emerson hinted, from time to time, about the possibility of devolution, but Nietzsche considered it a real possibility. Here, as elsewhere, he is inclined to follow Emerson's beliefs about 'evolution' rather than those of Darwin. Although Darwin considers instances of "retrograde development" in which there is poorer organic organization at later stages of an animal's development than in earlier stages in *The Origin of Species,* he does not consider wholesale retrogression of a species. In *The Descent of Man* Darwin makes two references to "reversion" in the sense of the appearance in members of a species of traits that were previously deleted by means of natural selection. But he says nothing about the possibility of the devolution of an entire species.

Emerson's general notion of natural development is not tantamount to a Darwinian theory of evolution by natural selection. Rather, it is a conception of a spiritual tendency towards gradual perfection immanent in the natural world. A tendency towards the development of higher, more complex, forms of life. A corollary to this general tendency is that retrogression is possible. This is especially possible in the domain of what later comes to be called psychosocial evolution. If the cultural conditions of life discourage self-reliance, autonomy, independence of mind, innovative intelligence, nonconformity, maverick ways of thought or, in effect, exceptional individuals, the remaining social group may regress and the quality of individual lives decline.

A mass-society promotes mass-consciousness, conformity, pseudovalues, corrupted language, and a form of vicarious thought that filters upwards through the entire cultural system. Emerson and Nietzsche were highly sensitive to the coercive power of customary thought and values. They believed, with good reason, that the *ethos* of a mass-society cannot tolerate exceptional individuals or those who "stand alone"; it cannot tolerate genuine individuals.

Despite the improvements of the general welfare in successful mass-societies, or because of them, the welfare of the minority which cannot or will not adapt to common values and interests is undermined or neglected. The overt or covert values of leveling societies tend to act as selective factors that discourage the development of, or weed out, certain types of individuals. A dominant cultural bias functions steadily, as Nietzsche suggested, as a principle of selection until a cultural system declines and is replaced. Although Emerson is never quite as specific as this, he did see, early in the nineteenth century, the rise of mass-man and deplored the consequences of this historical tendency. In addition, he proposed a countermovement that was diametrically opposed to the sociocultural atmosphere he saw around him, one that emphasized, as Nietzsche's later countermovement did, the importance of an edifying image of what man may yet become.

"Plus Men"

Emerson and Nietzsche admire creators, innovators, those who envision new cultural ideals. Even though they both admit the determinations of nature that act upon man, they also presuppose a plasticity and power in culture and in man that permits the transformation of the human world and the forging of cultural values. Nietzsche's project of a "transvaluation of values" (which articulates what Emerson sought in a meandering way) requires and assumes creative freedom. Man is a "piece of fate," but he is not only conditioned by factors outside of his control. For he is a conditioning being that acts on others, on society, culture, history, and the world. Both thinkers adopt the same attitude towards the power of culture as they do towards the "fatalities" of nature. For they emphasize the enormous power that a dominant cultural 'ideal' has over individuals *and* they insist that *some* individuals can see through the illusions and idols of their own cultures, can liberate themselves from their nets, can become value-creators.

As much as Emerson and Nietzsche insist upon the determinisms of human existence, on the power of cultures to demoralize or drive out select individuals, they both affirm the freedom of at least *some* persons to transcend these natural and cultural forces and project an ideal for man that assumes a freedom for possibility. Their frequent exhortations and existential imperatives entail a belief in human freedom, as finite as it may be.

Emerson was very much concerned with promoting the development of "demi-gods" who would be possessed of "transcendent power." He desired the creation of a superior culture in which man's natural striving for perfection could be realized. His models for hints of what is still possible for man to attain were taken from historical examples of superlative individuals. It is the "affirmative class" that has been the spearhead of civilization. History affords us some distinctive examples of members of this 'class'. In a characteristic way, he observes that "aboriginal might gives a surprising pleasure when it appears under conditions of supreme refinement. . . . Michael Angelo . . . surpassed his successors in rough vigor, as much as in purity of intellect and refinement."[30]

All "plus-men" have a "positive power," an overflowing vitality, a robust health, a power of concentration, a capacity to overcome "resistances," a deep sense of purpose, a strength of will, a self-discipline, that separates them from others and persuades them to recognize their "transcendent superiority." In modern society, Emerson laments, we find very few "finished men," not to speak of individuals possessing indisputable excellence. Outstanding accomplishments require the "courage of genius" and this, in turn, arises out of what he calls a 'quantity of power," a phrase that easily suggests Nietzsche's notion of individuals possessing varying "power-quanta" at different times or the idea of directing one's "quantity of force" into constructive channels.

Emerson wavers between emphasizing *what* his ideal individual does or is imagined as doing and stressing the "*how*" of his existence. Manner, comportment and style, as is the case in Nietzsche's picture of the *Übermensch,* count for a great deal. A "complete man" needs no "auxiliaries to his personal presence." He exudes "personal power" and the power of "manners," the good manners that naturally flow from self-reliance.[31] Such an individual will have integrity and character. Through the unique individual's actions there will run a discernible "great style."[32] This highly specific characteristic immediately suggests to mind Nietzsche's remark that the one thing needful is "To 'give style' to one's character."[33] This is described as a rare art, a shaping of one's first and second nature, a self-imposed constraint of strong passions, a disciplining of the crudeness of nature in oneself. Although Nietzsche expresses this idea more fully and more dramatically than Emerson ever did, he combines his images in a dynamic synthesis that captures exactly what he meant.

In his restorative study of Nietzsche, Walter Kaufmann reached back to the Chinese philosopher Lao-tzu in order to find analogies to Nietzsche's linking of character, style, and subjective power.[34] He could have found better ones in the period of the American literary renaissance or, more specifically, in Emerson's essays. And if he had seen these obvious 'analogies', he might have found the original, poetic, American template of the ideal of the *Übermensch*.

Emerson lamented that there has not yet been a man (in a superlative sense) just as Nietzsche lamented, in *Thus Spoke Zarathustra,* that "there has never yet been an overman."[35] This is one of numerous instances in which he consulted the heavily underlined passages in his copy of Emerson's *Versuche.* In "Character," from which this slightly modified line is extracted, Nietzsche also underlined the following: "This great defeat is hitherto our highest fact."[36]

The integrated, affirmative, "noble" individuals that Emerson lauded are especially prevalent in *The Gay Science.* We've already cited the view that "noble" natures expend their energy carelessly and act impulsively as a co-opted theme of Emerson's. Nietzsche also agrees that passionate, 'immoral' individuals have "advanced mankind the most" (their malfeasance, as Emerson put it, producing public good). Despite this acknowledgment, Nietzsche criticizes the bourgeois commercial class in language equal in censure to that of Emerson and contrasts members of this growing class to those with "noble presence." He goes out of his way to identify the "vulgar" commercial type with America. Do we have to wonder, at this point, where he may have gotten *that* impression of *Amerika?*

The theme of a "joyful wisdom" as a central trait of the life-affirming person is, as Allen and Baumgarten have said, directly derived from Emerson's poetic ideal. It is associated with a new "manliness" which will "carry heroism into knowledge," wage a war of ideas, and generate "warriors of knowledge," the same militant scholars Emerson envisioned in 1837.

Even the (ostensibly) distinctive Nietzschean advice that we should "be our own experiments" and adopt an experimental attitude towards life and thought is, as we've seen, specifically mentioned in Emerson's self-description: he is a *Versucher* in the fields of thought and life.[37] Practically in Emerson's language, and certainly in his style, emancipated, liberated individuals are described by Nietzsche as "the new, the unique, the incomparable, making laws for ourselves and creating ourselves! And for this purpose we must become the best students and discoverers of all the laws and necessities in the world."[38]

Against the biological theorists who assume the priority of the drive toward self-preservation, Nietzsche maintains that the fundamental instinct of life is *"the extension of power."*[39] This aim, as Emerson had said, is often reckless of prudential self-preservation. This conception of an underlying striving for more, this conception of a psychological tendency in man to "search after power" is not a fully developed theory in Emerson's presentation of it. But it is certainly an implicit theory about the springs of human conduct. Although Emerson and Nietzsche are quite aware of the dangerous aspects of this primal will to power, both believe that it provides the raw materials for strength and great achievements. In "Power" Emerson tells us that where there is "a great amount of life" it is often "gross and peccant." However, with the application of "checks and purifications" this "force" can be the source of "positive power," creative activity, and morality.

As in the case of Emerson, Nietzsche experiments with images of the "higher" types of human beings he envisions. In *The Gay Science* we are given portrayals of what may be called an 'existential hero'. Every major trait of this human type that Nietzsche cites is analogous to a characteristic of Emerson's self-existent individual. The specific invitation to think and "live dangerously," the apotheosis of "cheerfulness" and a "new Healthiness," the challenge to live with an attitude of openness towards an uncertain future, and other existential imperatives for the would-be liberated person are traceable to Emerson's impressionistic prescriptions for *his* protoexistential individualist.

The depiction of the free-spirited, supremely healthy individual in *The Gay Science* is the clearest expression of Nietzsche's existential stage of thought. And it is a foreshadowing of the as yet undeveloped "image" (*Gleichniss*) of the *Übermensch*. The conception of a being with superabundant health, boldness, strength, and joyful knowledge is juxtaposed, as in Emerson's writings, to the "man of the present day" who no longer inspires anyone, not even himself. Nietzsche looks forward and upward to the "ideal of a humanly superhuman well-being and good-will" that will appear, to the populace, as "inhuman."[40]

Even as he escalates the qualifications for superiority, Nietzsche retains the characteristics of his earlier personal, cultural ideal of man. However, every model of the "higher" individual (the genius, the heroic man of action, the great person, the superlative artist, the liberated existential hero) that was, at one time or another, idolized by him is eventually discarded as unsatisfactory.

Sometimes Nietzsche sculpts his *Übermensch* in such grandiose forms that he does what he accuses theists of having done in relation to the being of God. That is, he attributes to his supreme individuals all of the noble, heroic, creative, poetic, and venerable characteristics that actual human beings have exemplified in hard-won experience, in time and becoming, in difficult circumstances, and in the penumbra of the threat of illness, madness, and death. Then we are asked to venerate and admire this perfect transhuman being as an alien perfection. Thinking of the concept of God, Nietzsche held that

> All the beauty and sublimity with which we have invested . . . imagined things [are] . . . the creation and property of man: as his most beautiful apology. Man as poet, as thinker, as god, as love, as power . . . he has lavished gifts upon things in order to *impoverish* himself and make himself feel wretched . . . he admired and worshipped and knew how to conceal from himself that *he* was the one who created what he admired.[41]

"A Victory to the Senses"

As if aware of the deificatory tendency of his thinking about the man "above-man" of the future, Nietzsche sometimes presents a modified version of this ideal person that at least has the virtue of being attainable by some. However, even this less-exalted version of what a true man should be is indebted to his sympathetic understanding of Emerson.

A guiding valuation in Emerson's delineations of man perfected is that the advanced moral attitudes of his time, as well as "religious and benevolent enterprizes," focus upon an "aesthetic spirit," an ideal of beauty in action. We now look, he says, for "genius . . . united with every trait and talent of beauty and power." Indeed, we hope for the embodiment of moral-aesthetic ideals in a "powerful individual." The ethico-religious "hermits" who projected moral ideals for mankind ought to be manifested in "beauty and strength," ought to be reorganized in the crucible of nature.[42]

Although Emerson's prescriptions are somewhat vague, we know, on the basis of his other valuational formulae, what he was driving at. He was simply saying that morality is related to aesthetic taste; that ethical and aesthetic ideals are intertwined; that reflective and concerned modern men desire to see moral goodness joined with beauty and power in a *living* being; that men are no longer satisfied with paying homage to ethereal moral ideals that are embodied nowhere and in no one. There is the spirit of romanticism here, but it is no longer a dreamy, fantasized elevation of an ideal far beyond the world of actuality, no longer an ideal that only frenzied, intoxicated, and passionate poetic feeling and imagination can envision. It is a *practical romanticism* in which beauty, truth, goodness, and power are construed as able to be present in the being of a living, human, plastic work of art.

Emerson was not being facetious or merely clever when he said that he conceived of sculpture as history and of men as living sculptures. His aesthetically formed ethico-religious ideal demonstrates this clearly. The sense of beauty and the manifestations of beauty meant so much to him that it would seem that Nietzsche was not the only one to suggest that life and existence may be justified eternally as aesthetic phenomena.

A key to understanding Nietzsche's dithyrambic delineation of the *Übermensch* is found in *his* translation of morality into aesthetics or, what amounts to the same thing, his fusion of the two. Disagreements about ultimate values are not primarily rational disagreements; they are, in the final analysis, serious disputes about *taste*. Reversing the old Latin adage, *de gustibus non est disputandum* ("there is no disputing about tastes"), Nietzsche contends that, in regard to tables of values, there are *only* disputes about tastes.

In *Thus Spoke Zarathustra,* life is metaphorically pictured as seeking always to overcome itself, creating temples that represent symbols of ultimate value. What is called a "divine" contest of values is positively encouraged. Life itself requires *a conflict of values* in order to "overcome itself," in order to ascend. Most "tables of value" have been, more or less, tables of moral value. Moral ideals, like artistic creations, can only project ideal images of man;

they cannot, in the last analysis, be demonstrated. In his notes, Nietzsche seems to articulate Emerson's inchoate suggestions about the nature of moral value when he claims that it is fundamentally "aesthetic judgment" or judgments of *taste* that are the foundation of "moral judgments." He specifically insists upon the "reduction of morality to aesthetics."[43] In a far more casual and informal way, this is exactly what Emerson repeatedly implies in his endeavor to project for mankind a transcendent image of man.

In agreement with the ancients, Emerson proclaimed that beauty is something divine; that it is, in fact, "the flowering of virtue."[44] Like all things excellent, beauty has a "rainbow character" that defies any attempt to appropriate it or use it. The magnetic power of sovereign individuals is expressed in a living synthesis of character, style, and beauty. When he describes the moral effect of a "true master," he uses poetic or aesthetic images, images that infiltrate *Thus Spoke Zarathustra.* "A river of command seemed to run down from his eyes into all those who beheld him."[45] Such individuals are said to have a dynamic "presence" or, as we would say today, they exude charisma.

Again and again, Emerson commingles ethical and aesthetic attributes. A person of character is said to express self-sufficiency in his or her face and is "beatified." Strong character engenders natural nonconformists. The wise man is a "fountain"; is self-moved, absorbed, a commanded commander; one who expresses in his existence "the instant presence of supreme power."[46] Emerson seems unable to speak of a moral ideal or an ideal human being without employing a catena of tropes. In his cognitive-affective world nothing is what it is and everything bears an analogical relation to something else.

All of Emerson's habits of thought and language contribute to his efforts to sculpt his image of a "god-like" human being. And, consciously or unconsciously, Nietzsche follows his lead. He strains his poetic abilities to present *his* image of the "synthetic," perfected man. Just as Nietzsche says in *The Antichristian,* Emerson claims that "at long intervals" in history there appear a class of men who are so "eminently endowed with insight and virtue," so possessed of an accumulation of power, that they have been called "divine." Such unique individuals are "character born . . . victory organized."[47] Except for the rare appearance of such individuals, history is, for the most part, a mean affair, and "our nations have been mobs." The "divine form" of a "universal" man we have not yet seen. We have only "the dream and prophesy of such." The "majestic manners" of such a person are as yet unknown even though we have hints of "grandeur of character" in the outstanding historical figures who encourage us to hope for further greatness.[48] Many historical "documents of character" encourage us to look to the future for more complete individuals in whom nature will be exemplified in its highest form. That Emerson is here on the grounds of a faith that is ethical, aesthetic, and religious is unquestionable. It is a faith that is reiterated in Nietzsche's belief in the possibility of the *Übermensch*.

Sometimes Emerson puts in question not only ancient religious myths, but the Christian religion as well. He observes that the religions of mankind have exulted in the manners of youths who owed nothing to fortune, who exemplified pure natures, and who "transfigured every particular into a universal symbol." An epic splendor surrounded the facts of their *death*. The religious documents of character show us the *pathos* of the death of virtuous, pure, inspiring youths. His comment on these religious images is instructive: "This great defeat is hitherto our highest fact." What he seems to be saying is that for too long mankind has been raised in the shadow of religions of death, even religions that are centered on the *pathos* of the death of a virtuous youth. In the next breath, he appears to propose a positive, natural religion of life. For, he says, "the mind requires a victory to the senses, a force of character which will convert judge, jury, soldier, and king; which will rule animal and mineral virtues, and blend with the courses of sap, of rivers, of winds, of stars and of moral agents."[49]

Just as is the case for Nietzsche, Emerson's aristocratic radicalism leads him to seek ever-higher levels of idealization. Neither is completely consistent in his artistic shaping and reshaping of powerful, moral-aesthetic or quasi-religious living works of art. By multiplying the attributes of this imagined superlative being, often without necessity or in a flurry of poetic images, both thinkers try to bring into being, at least in a conceptual-imagistic way, a paradoxical personage that takes on mythological proportions.

There is no doubt, given his familiarity with his works and his personal acquaintance with the man, that Emerson was influenced by Thomas Carlyle's veneration of great men and courageous heroes, as well as his claim that history is the biography of outstanding individuals. *On Heroes, Hero Worship, and the Heroic in History,* with its praise of "greatness" and its theme that the leading figures in history cooperate with the real and "natural" tendency of the world, certainly seems to have left its imprint on Emerson's thought. However, even though Emerson sometimes expressed himself in the manner of Carlyle, he does not simply embrace the cultural ideal of the fearless, reckless, dominating hero in history, for he projects an image of man in which there is passion and self-control, vital energy and relaxed grace, strength and gentleness, a strong sense of reality and an aesthetic sensibility.

Emerson's paragons are not ruthless conquerors who achieve heights of power by trampling others underfoot. Not only that, but he considers poets, philosophers, and artists as "heroes." Carlyle's heroes, for the most part, are "men of action" who directly influence the course of history. Carlyle seemed to have worshipped historical success no matter what questionable form it took. This is a parting of the ways for Emerson and, later, for Nietzsche as well. For their paladins are often described as disdainful of "public opinion," as solitary, reflective (though capable of action), and skeptical of what the world typically venerates as "success." The power of Emerson's independent self-reliant individual is not power "over others," but, rather, a subjective feeling of power, a power over oneself. In a similar spirit, Nietzsche chides the Germans for only being able to recognize power in a military-political sense, for being blind to the "power" of Goethe.

Emerson's supereminent person has *sensibility* as a core character trait, and Nietzsche's *Übermensch* is sometimes depicted as a creative artist endowed with sensibility and intuitive taste. Carlyle admired Napoleon I without reservation, whereas Emerson admired his courage and boldness but criticized his egotism, selfishness, and crudeness. And later Nietzsche summarizes his judgment of Napoleon by calling him a strange combination of an *Übermensch* and an *Untermensch* (an "underman" or animal). This characterization practically epitomizes that of Emerson.

In one of his early lectures, presented under the rubric "Religion," Emerson foreshadowed his later delineations of the confident, self-mastered individual in terms that certainly can be found in Nietzsche's writings. In the notes appended to *The Conduct of Life,* we find the following passage quoted from the sixth of these lectures:

> The man of this age must be matriculated in the university of sciences and tendencies flowing from all past periods. He . . . should be taught all skepticisms and unbeliefs, and made the destroyer of all card houses and paper walls, and the sifter of all opinions, by being put face to face from his infancy with Reality.[50]

Such a tough-minded person will, in addition, become accustomed to viewing the circumstances of his life as "mutable," will carry personal relations, possessions, and his opinions in his hand. Such an individual will pierce through to the core of morality and thereby transcend the skepticisms that have been lived through. This vision of what man should become encompasses what is most "affecting and sublime" in our personal relations, our happiness, our personal losses. Such an edifying image seems, Emerson says, "to uplift us to a life so extraordinary, one might say superhuman."[51]

When Nietzsche first read this passage, he probably had no idea that years later, when he sought a being to replace in man's faith the God who had, in a cultural-historical sense, "died," he would recover this image of a superhuman or *Übermenschlich* (as Nietzsche would have read it) possibility. Emerson elaborated on this early visionary idea by attributing to his "superhuman" being a string of positive, enriching traits of character. To moral character he quickly added might and beauty; insight and will; power and wisdom.

Asking himself, in his journals, why we invariably seek out beauty anywhere we can find it, he answers that we search for and imagine beauty "as an asylum from the terrors of finite nature."[52] Some years later, Nietzsche will explain that the ancient Greeks saw clearly "the terror and horror of existence" and, in order to endure life, to overcome this painful insight into actuality, to avert their eyes from it, they created the illusory dream-world of art.[53]

Zarathustra tells us that man is not the goal of existence; but someone beyond-man, the *Übermensch,* is. As in the case of protagonists in religion and mythology, this idealized figure is somewhat enigmatic. We learn, from what is said in *Thus Spoke Zarathustra,* that such an avatar is courageous, courageous enough to endure the "abysmal thought" of the eternal return of all things. To will not only the return of one's own life, but the return of all the joy, pain, boredom, suffering, and misery of human history and human lives, would require that one have the highest degree of life-affirmation. Whoever could positively will the eternal recurrence of all things with a full understanding of the positive and negative consequences would have passed the entrance requirement for the school of "overmen."

In describing the condition and attitude of "sublime men," Zarathustra chastises them for not having overcome the "beast" in themselves. Although the "heroic will" and riddle-solving knowledge of such types are admirable, Zarathustra says that he sees in them only "the neck of the ox." The "eye of the angel" is missing.

The "sublime" person has not yet learned good cheer, and "his gushing passion has not yet grown tranquil in beauty." A smoldering, violent will *cannot* attain this graceful beauty. Obviously thinking of the *Übermensch*, Zarathustra exclaims:

> To stand with relaxed muscles and unharnessed wills; that is the most difficult thing for you sublime men to do! . . . I desire beauty from no one else as much as I desire it from you, you men of power. May your goodness be your final self-overpowering.
>
> I believe you capable of any evil; hence, I desire of you the good. . . .
>
> You should aspire to the virtue of the column. The higher it rises, the more fair and graceful it grows; but inwardly it is harder and better able to bear more weight.[54]

The images, the tone, and the content of this significant allusion to the qualities of the *Übermensch* are surely derived from Emerson. To the *true* individual, he contended, action and inaction are alike. And the virtues of such an individual should have an "edge" to them. Such virtues are acquired by means of discipline and self-control. It is the assured and powerful person who is natural, who can relax gracefully, whose power is expressed "obliquely and not by the direct stroke."[55] There is an "energy of health," "animal spirits," a synthesis of the natural and the poetic, a "wholeness," a "completeness," a coiled capacity for "spontaneous action," at the heart of the "exempt" whose being is like a living statue that has many aspects.[56] "A great man is a new statue in every attitude and action." The character of this spiritually strong person is "a reserved force" that acts on others simply by its presence. His or her inner strength is only half-used on any given occasion.[57] Emerson consolidates his thoughts on this lifelong preoccupation with greatness embodied in a living synthesis of power and grace and compresses them into a literary image:

> O Iole! how did you know that Hercules was a god? "Because," answered Iole, "I was content the moment my eyes fell on him. When I beheld Theseus, I desired that I might see him offer battle . . . but Hercules did not wait for a contest; he conquered whether he stood, or walked, or sat, or whatever thing he did."[58]

Hercules, like Nietzsche's sculpturesque man of power, conquers with relaxed muscles even though, as Greek legend recounts, he was capable of swift and violent action if the occasion called for it. Such a person has that "plus" factor that Emerson extols and possesses a "coarse energy" that has "the good nature of strength and courage."[59] The emblems of the well-made person are repose and cheerfulness, "repose in energy."[60] In the comportment of such commanding individuals "every gesture and action shall indicate power at rest."[61] Illustrations of the parallels between Nietzsche's depiction of the *Übermensch* and Emerson's scattered descriptions of sovereign individuals could be multiplied beyond necessity.

There is no doubt that Nietzsche remembered, or culled out of Emerson's writings, most of the characteristics of the new being who would appear to the all-too-human man as 'superhuman'. The Emersonian connection is especially apparent in the metaphorical image of the man of power as "columnar." For it is precisely this image that Emerson uses when he introduces the figure of Zoroaster (Zarathustra). After saying that we are all "born believers in great men," he adds that we require "that a man should be . . . columnar in the landscape."[62] This image seems to be associated in Nietzsche's mind with Emerson's view that we should construe virtue as height, should see that a person "plastic and permeable to principles . . . must overpower and ride all cities, nations, kings, rich men, poets, who are not."[63] Elsewhere he thinks of the "height" of man as "the deity of man"—"to be self-sustained, to need no gift, no foreign force."[64]

Bestowing Virtue

Interwoven in the tapestry of *Thus Spoke Zarathustra* is a theme that is closely related to the image of the man "beyond man." It is that of a "bestowing virtue," a notion that is traceable to the thought of Emerson. As we would expect, Nietzsche is only interested in those virtues that are positive and flow from strength. Virtues derived from weakness are really not genuine virtues at all. He identifies four cardinal virtues: honesty, courage (in relation to one's enemies), magnanimity (towards the defeated) and courtesy.[65] Elsewhere, he adds insight, solitude, and sympathy.[66]

The fact that Nietzsche includes sympathy as a chief virtue indicates that it is not the feeling of sympathy, in its proper place, that he is opposed to in his critique of morality, but a morbid morality of pity, a morality that weakens man by its excessive demands on his sympathetic feelings. It should be noted that prominence is given to "insight," a distinctively Emersonian 'virtue'. And what is said about solitude as a virtue strengthens the association with Emerson's scale of virtues.

Solitude is considered a virtue by Emerson because, as Nietzsche expresses his view, all communal association "makes men—somehow, somewhere, sometime 'common'. "[67] He makes a virtue of solitude as something deep and organic. We usually, he believes, descend to meet others in the social world. And if solitude is sometimes proud, society is often "vulgar."[68] What society considers a 'virtue'—conformity—is a vice for the "central man." The tendency of social relations is to level all people; and society conspires against our manhood. If we would become ourselves, we must walk alone, cherish solitude.

In "Self-Reliance" and elsewhere, Emerson opposes his ethic of individuality, self-trust, and nonconformity to the customary, leveling *ethos* of the modern social world. The synonymy between Emerson and Nietzsche on the issue of the value of solitude is practically perfect. And, of course, both are self-consciously aware of the paradox and danger of this opposition between society and solitude. Being independent and solitary, Nietzsche believes, is a "privilege of the strong." But solitude can be dangerous insofar as one can be torn apart by a "minotaur of conscience" and, having cut oneself off from others, find oneself bereft of "fellow feeling" or "human compassion." Emerson puts the dilemma succinctly: "Solitude is impractical, and society fatal."[69]

The most prized virtue, the virtue specifically related to the *Übermensch,* is a free, gift-bestowing virtue. This is exemplified in the difficult task of willing to create beyond oneself. It is manifested in the overcoming of "sick selfishness," the desire to lead upward beyond the ordinary human species to the "superspecies." A bestowing virtue is one in which its possessor is "beyond praise and blame."[70] It is a virtue concentrated in a "single will."

At the center of this bestowing virtue is power, an edifying feeling of power that is "faithful to the earth." A power that sanctifies life. A bestowing virtue centers on life and the body. It lies at the basis of the effort to create a human meaning for the earth. It is the virtue of joyful, experimental knowledge. Nietzsche expresses the sacrificial aspect of this virtue when he celebrates the willing overcoming of the self, the voluntary "going under" for the sake of the *Übermensch.*

Bestowing virtue is a love of life and of this world of becoming; a means to the creation of meaning. Here there is a deep faith in the value and meaning of life, a retrieval of the "innocence of becoming," the self-suppression of the all-too-human *through* man. With a significant difference, Nietzsche incorporates in this virtue the traditional religious conception of sacrifices. He praises those who have faith enough and will enough to hope for a being beyond man as he is and as he has been. The difference, of course, is that this faith is directed toward the anticipation of paragons who will embody the virtues that had previously been transferred to a transcendental divinity. In describing the ramifications of this free, gift-bestowing virtue, Nietzsche is, like Emerson before him, seeking to articulate a chief virtue of an affirmative religion of immanence.

A Religion of Life

Despite the "skepticisms" he prescribes, Emerson acknowledges man's *"universal impulse to believe,"*[71] just as Nietzsche acknowledges the continuation of man's "need for metaphysics" even as he attacks metaphysical claims to truth and states in his notes from the 1880s that truth is a "valuation," that something must be held to be true for the sake of the valuation of a higher human type and a higher culture, even though we do not *know* that what we project from "the standpoint of the ideal" is true. Emerson diverts his impulse to believe away from the "Oversoul" to life, existence, and the promise of man perfected. As is the case for Nietzsche, his earlier existential humanism eventually leads him to a belief in the possibility of a superhumanism. True Christianity, he believed, is declining or is "lost." It has been undone by its conversion into a historical phenomenon, by the moral decline of Christian culture, by the waning of the spirit of Christian societies. A spiritual vacuum has emerged in the modern world in the wake of a desiccation of authentic Christianity. It is still possible, however, that there can be a spiritual renovation, a new religion that will affirm the sacredness of life.[72]

Emerson embraces a religion of life and weaves it around paradigmatic men of character who have their center in themselves. If such a "perfect man" were possible, he would be "the center of the Copernician system."[73] Although he doesn't literally say that man perfected would give a human meaning to the earth, as Nietzsche says of the *Übermensch,* what he does say is compatible with such an idea. As Nietzsche later does, Emerson sought meaning, fullness, and redemption in the ever-changing stream of life-experience and in hope of "He That Shall Come."

The aim of science, even the aim of alchemy, Emerson proclaims, was projected in the right direction: "to prolong life, to arm with power."[74] But the activity of science, like that of politics, must *serve* culture, must function as a means to a higher culture. Fundamentally, man admires "what streams with life, what is in act or endeavor to reach somewhat beyond."[75] The tendency of nature is towards the expression of energy or power in a beautiful form. Such an embodied, energized beauty is a cosmic quality, a new virtue, a power that suggests a relation to the whole that transcends egoistic individuality.[76]

Emerson turned away from the Christian motto, *memento mori*—"remember death"—and chose instead Goethe's motto: "Think on living."[77] And this thinking on living celebrates the ecstasy of life, the possibility of the unexpected, the hope of a "new influx of light and power." Whoever could affirm life and value its sacredness would have inner power and would want to share his or her goodness; would express a "bestowing virtue" for the sake of higher life, greater life. As Emerson wrote in his "Boston Hymn,"

> I cause from every creature
> His proper good to flow;
> As much as he is and doeth,
> So much he shall bestow.[78]

What Emerson himself "bestows" is the future promise of persons in whom power and beauty, energy and grace, and all the positive and best attributes of men will be embodied in nature perfected. In such sovereign individuals nature and art will be joined together. These types will appear, as nature does, at its best, as "art perfected."[79] The general tendency of nature, despite detours, deviations, and distortions, is towards perfectibility. If men were not corrupted by fear and weakness, if they did not erect unconditional group moralities that filter down through cultures for ages, if they could recapture and spiritualize *physis* as natural growth, then this movement towards perfection would work its way upwards.

Creative Nature

Emerson and Nietzsche, as well as Spinoza before them, conceive of nature as creative nature—*natura naturans*—a force that manifests itself in Protean forms of "indescribable variety." The natural process moves, as Emerson puts it, "through transformation on transformation to the highest symmetries, arriving at consumate results without . . . a leap."[80] Reflecting on the creative transformations of nature, Nietzsche later describes the cosmos as a "self-creating work of art." In doing so, he epitomizes an Emersonian idea virtually in his language.

The paradox that jams Emerson's and Nietzsche's thinking on this central issue is that both claim that there is a morality present in nature. This ostensible morality is carried forward in the transformation of nature into culture. This implies that a given morality embodied in a culture, even the kind of morality that is considered as one of timidity, conformity, mediocrity or a morality of custom, must also have emanated from nature. Thus, even what is considered as 'anti-natural' in morality must have its origin, paradoxically, in nature.

When Emerson and Nietzsche try to create a demanding morality that is natural and centered on man as perfected, they propose a singular moral ideal which their conception of a multifarious nature does not justify. One could even argue that what Nietzsche calls a "herd-morality" is compatible with nature and may even be considered as natural, all-too-natural. If a species survives and prospers by means of a "herd-morality," then this morality seems consonant with what is deemed "natural."

At times, Nietzsche seems to be aware of the problem of presenting a single morality as *the* morality given the Protean character of nature and its variety of organic values. In a note that refers to his existential stage of thought, he remarks that "an impulse to live individualistically exists. I think in its service. Others who do not have this impulse cannot be obligated by me."[81] He proceeds to defend his way while denying that he has a monopoly on *the* way. On the other hand, he was quite aware of his tendency to promote a single moral ideal and, given his commitment to a diversity of value-perspectives, he sees this as a difficulty for his thought. "Rule? Force my type on others? Horrible! Is not my happiness just in contemplating a variety of types? Problem."[82] Needless to say, time seems to have eroded his liberal attitude towards a diversity of values, especially moral values. Eventually, he came to believe that some values, certainly some 'moral' values, are detrimental to the highest expression of human life, are subversive in relation to excellence, and are nihilistic in consequence.

The effects of some systems of value are disastrous for the possibility of the emergence of exceptional individuals and are destructive of mavericks who turn their backs upon and criticize the cultural and moral values of their time and place. The tyranny of a majority morality could make exceptions, geniuses, and maverick thinkers endangered species. It could level an entire culture or pull down a complex civilization. The equalization of all values is disastrous for any higher values and, in fact, leads ineluctably to cultural nihilism.

Emerson and Nietzsche argue that a truly *natural* form of morality is one that preserves aristocratic valuations. It is a morality that is centered on an aesthetic ideal fused with an imaginative-conceptual notion of a natural tendency towards completeness, health, growth, energy, and creative expression. The incarnation of these selective features of nature, including aesthetic qualities, would serve as the goal of culture and history and thereby would become the meaning of the earth. For both, a morality entailing a "scale of values" is based upon a highly selective interpretation of nature as a whole and of "the natural."

One of the things that Nietzsche was seriously concerned with was the need for a new ideal to fill the spiritual vacuum in Western culture and to overcome the nihilism manifested in man's loss of love for, reverence for, and hope for, man. In order to go beyond this weariness of man, he believed that we ought to envision "a man who will justify the existence of mankind, for whose sake one may continue to believe in mankind."[83] In stating this rationale for the projection of the image of the *Übermensch,* he was articulating the aim, concern, and hope that suffuse Emerson's reflections on the future of mankind.

Anti-Politics

Emerson and Nietzsche are extremely critical of institutions and the political State. Both project a goal for man that is rooted in culture, a goal centered about supereminent human types. When, in *Zarathustra,* Nietzsche calls the State a lying, cold monster that has become the new idol of superfluous people, he echoes his earlier polemic against the military-commercial State in "Schopenhauer as Educator." There he attacks the selfishness of the State and criticizes its utilitarian attempt to make education and culture subservient to its ends. He cites the corruption of the ideal of Christian culture because it was "used in a hundred ways to drive the mills of the State."[84]Historical Christianity became hypocritical. As nation-states absorbed Christian culture for their own political goals, that culture became morally compromised.

Nietzsche has often been called an apolitical thinker. In point of fact, he is quite often more than this. For, he is an antipolitical thinker. The modern nation-state, he accurately reports, attempts to create for itself an *ersatz* 'culture', a veneer that thinly veils its will to military power and its insatiable economic interests. The nation-state supports either a "merchant-culture" or a military 'culture' and often both at once. He correctly predicted that the growth of a plutocracy that has loyalty only to itself will end by corrupting entire cultures. And, despite his sympathy in youth with the plight of workers and the victims of modern capitalism, he has no faith in the socialists' or communists' drastic solutions to injustice or socioeconomic inequities. These political movements follow the leveling tendencies of the modern age, and their aim is not really social justice, but merely a shift of power in their favor.

All forms of mass movements are disastrous for the development of a genuine culture. Nietzsche was equally critical of bourgeois capitalism as a practice and as an ideology. What the capitalist wants is not wealth *per se*, but power or social dominance. The preoccupation with *national* political economy is seen as narrowminded and shortsighted. Nietzsche is an internationalist who envisions the dissolution of artificial national boundaries. Anarchy is at least as bad as nationalistic self-glorification, if not worse than it. The one thing the *Übermensch* will *not* be is a political ruler.

Nietzsche was hostile to political ideologies, especially those that spouted slogans such as *Deutschland über Alles*. He was antinationalistic and was critical of military cultures (even though he, like Emerson, admired *some* military virtues). He was not enthralled by the industrial-commercial movement in Europe in the late nineteenth-century and claimed that it created an army of industrial "slaves," converted men into "commodities," and undermined cultural, intellectual, and artistic values. The modern world, he thought, would make slaves of us all.

Instead of a politically determined "master-race," Nietzsche envisioned an international class of *Übermenschen* who would not rule over others directly, but who would exist alongside the collectivity.[85]

As in Emerson's view, a "*pathos* of distance" would separate those who have an excess of strength for beauty, for bravery, for culture, for autonomy, for manners, those who are self-assured and affirmative, from the vast majority. For Nietzsche, the superiority of these paragons would *not* be based upon nationality, "pure blood," or ethnicity. He thought in terms of a "European" or international, loosely associated, class of individuals who exemplified an aristocracy of character. He insisted that Germany offered the least promising soil in which such types could be cultivated. He not only opposed German nationalism, but condemned all forms of narrow nationalism, even proposing a "United States of Europe."

There is a terrible irony in the use and abuse of Nietzsche's thought by mass political movements. They confirmed his worst fears about the subterranean working of a lust of power in individuals, groups, and nations, if it is expressed in its crudest form, if it is not channeled into constructive, creative pathways. The "lust of power" is identified as an "evil" in *Thus Spoke Zarathustra* and the drive for power of the "petty tyrant" is characterized, with ironic accuracy, as ending with a desire to destroy everything, even itself. Nietzsche has the sad distinction of having predicted a coming European "nihilism of action" and then being *blamed* for having provided the atmosphere for its emergence.

The aesthetically conceived, self-legislating, sovereign individuals Nietzsche hoped for would require, under ideal cultural conditions, *at least* a thousand years to cultivate. The mass movements of the twentieth century appeared in the time frame of the century of violence, war, and revolution that he predicted: the age of a nihilistic conflict of values. Unlike all the optimistic cheerleaders of progress through science in the nineteenth century, he saw the nightmarish possibilities for the future if scientific knowledge and techniques were combined with a utilitarian ethic and practical political interests *without* the cultural unity and wisdom needed to control these powerful forces.

As early as 1872, he predicted, in his notes, that the marriage of scientific knowledge, utilitarian values, and national politics would have disastrous effects on Western civilization. In spite of the benefits to mankind that have been provided by means of the value of technology, the value of utilitarian ethical aims, and the value of political organization, it must be said that this troika of forces has generated an incredibly destructive and demoralizing period in human history. The synthesis of utilitarian values and the awesome technology of applied science under the control of a variety of political ideologies unleashed enormously powerful forces that have severely damaged the fabric of civilization.

The continuation of this table of values has created a geopolitical situation in which nuclear weapons are proliferated at an insane rate and are freely used as global-political bargaining chips. The very existence of such monstrously destructive weapons overshadows every other significant aspect of human culture, overpowers nations, societies, and individuals, casts a shadow over future generations, and guarantees the perpetuity of politico-military power and influence as long as their production continues. Ironically, the same utilitarian, scientific, and political forces have combined to create, under the influence of humane values, the conditions for the possibility of the technical and material substructure that Nietzsche believed could be the basis for "the enhancement of human life" and the building of a great international civilization. Emerson and Nietzsche's concerns are not irrelevant to the future of Western civilization. If artistic and intellectual cultures are not made to serve political, economic, or military interests (as they all-too-often have been in this century), they are devalued or rendered irrelevant to the main thrust of societies. As Nietzsche to a great extent, and Emerson to a lesser extent, feared, an aesthetic-intellectual culture could be crushed by the rise of what Emerson called a "culture of science" and the growth of mass culture.

There is some evidence that Emerson was one of Nietzsche's models and inspirations for his consistent antagonism towards political and social institutions. In "Politics," Emerson argues that the State is not aboriginal. Its institutions, contrary to popular belief, are *not* superior to the individual citizen. Every institution was once the creation of a single man or of individuals. Every law or common practice was once the expedient of a man to meet a particular case. Institutions are not permanent fixtures; they are malleable to the efforts of people to change them. Responding to the then 'radicalism' of democracy in America, Emerson looks once again to his favorite paradigm: the natural world. "Nature," he explains, "is not democratic."[86] This fundamental belief lies at the basis of his conception of natural aristocracy which, in turn, informs his aristocratic ethical ideals.

The praise of 'Society' at the expense of real individuals is either myth-making or blatant lying. What is hailed as the wisdom of collective society (say, what is shown in the fictional idea of Jean-Jacques Rousseau's "general will") is actually comprised of "an ignorant and deceivable majority." A mass-society, Emerson repeatedly says, is primarily comprised of conformists, opportunists, the fearful, the gullible, the deluded, and the ignorant. Once again, we see that there is hardly a vituperative judgment about the populace in Nietzsche's writings that could not be matched by the acerbic barbs of the "gentle optimist."

The true purpose of government is "the culture of men." Politics itself is the art of "cunning," deception, disguising and obscuring the actual agenda. With his usual candor and directness, Emerson asserts that every "actual State is corrupt." Neither the radical democrats nor the conservatives aspire to any worthy good. Whichever party is in power, the people can expect no benefit to art, humanity, or culture that is commensurate with the vast resources of the nation. Given these perceptions, it is natural for him to hold that "the less government we have, the better." The only antidote to the abuses of government is the positive influence of "private character" or genuineness. The continuing tendency of nature in a social context is towards the development of character. A citizenry of men and women of character would render the State unnecessary. In fact, actual societies are often "barbarous," and the influence of character on society is, unfortunately, minimal. But then character is still in an embryonic form. Governments based on force are only necessary evils that exist primarily because of the selfishness and barbarity of the people. Emerson (and Nietzsche after him) puts no faith in *political* institutions for the desired transformation of individuals and culture.

Only a revolution in thought, sensibility, feeling, attitude, and values, a revolution in culture, a regeneration of individuals, could bring about a natural "scale of rank" in the world. Emerson sees the common attacks on institutions as indicating that "society gains nothing whilst a man, not himself renovated, attempts to renovate things around him."[87] Nietzsche, too, will not propose a political revolution as the means of turning the modern world right side up. Instead, he will insist on the need for a transvaluation of values.

This digression serves to show that many of Nietzsche's critical judgments of the State, politics, and institutions are in the spirit of Emerson. The idea of a *pathos* of distance between exceptional individuals and the majority population that is central to Nietzsche's elitist conception of the best social order is one which was originally expressed by Emerson with virtually the same meaning. The strong antipolitical sentiments of Nietzsche are compatible with those of Emerson and were probably encouraged by them. In "Politics" Emerson resents the fact that we "pay unwilling tributes to governments founded on force." Reversing the dominant state of affairs in the twentieth century, both Emerson and Nietzsche placed politics close to the base of their envisioned cultural pyramid. Both were concerned with the transformation of, and elevation of culture, with what might be called a 'deconstruction' of centralized political power and dominance.

Sovereign Individuals

The converse of the political 'leader' for Emerson and Nietzsche was the self-trusting, independent sovereign individual who would influence others indirectly by his presence, integrity, and character. Emerson's valuation of "*plus*-men" who are self-assured and possess a relaxed sense of inner power was assimilated by Nietzsche. His description of the "sovereign individual" who leaves behind the coercive morality of custom and who is genuinely "autonomous"[88] is a transcription of all that Emerson says about this human type. Although Nietzsche's discourse concerning sovereign individuals (particularly in *On the Genealogy of Morals*) is more reckless and intense than that of Emerson, his thinking is in the spirit of the American writer.

The aesthetic, metaphorical images of the *Übermensch,* who is described as sculpturesque, columnar, a living work of art comprised of the goodness of strength, beauty, and the courage of independence reproduce Emerson's portrayals of his paragons of the future. Although both Emerson and Nietzsche admired some of the traits of historical political figures, neither, in the final analysis, envisioned their "sovereign individuals" as political personalities.[89] What is needed in order to create the cultural conditions for the emergence of autonomous "sovereign individuals" is not a new political system, but what Nietzsche called, after Emerson's intimations of the same idea, "a transvaluation of values."

Whenever Nietzsche reaches for a fresh adjective to apply to his transcendent individual, he often returns to Emerson. The well-turned-out person will have "wholeness"; will be a "complete" individual; will be "symmetrical."[90] The "semigod" that Emerson awaits is akin to Nietzsche's "victoriously completed one" who expresses an "excess of life," who possesses "genuineness" (*Wahrhaftigkeit*), and expresses a self-sufficient "nobility" (*Vornehmheit*). The parallel between the characteristics of Emerson's "sovereign individual" and those of the *Übermensch* is so obvious that any notion of coincidental ideas or separate speculations about paragons of the future is out of the question. That Emerson not only sketched the models for the cultural ideas of the perfected "genius," the reflective "hero," the "noble spirit," and "great man" that Nietzsche tries to flesh out, but directly influenced the conception of, and image of, the *Übermensch,* is an overdetermined thesis.

Gentlemen?

What banishes any hint of skepticism about the link between these radical thinkers, specifically in relation to the countercultural ideal of sovereign individuals that is directed *against* the leveling of cultural values and of the value of man, is a passing remark in *Ecce Homo.* Commenting on the essential content of *Beyond Good and Evil,* Nietzsche avers that it focuses upon a certain type of man,

> an antithetical type who is as little modern as possible, a noble, an affirmative type. In the latter sense the book [*Beyond Good and Evil*] is a *school for gentlemen;* that concept taken more spiritually *and radically* than it has ever been taken. One has to have courage in one even to endure it.[91]

A *"Schule des gentilhomme"*—a "school for gentlemen"? On the face of it, this is an odd designation, especially since it refers to the powerful, strong, "commanding" type of individual, to the *Übermensch.* What is even stranger is that this particular characterization of a fearless, independent countertype to modern man, expressed in the language of *manners,* is one that is obscured in Nietzsche's other writings. Why does he now, in *Ecce Homo,* present his cultural ideal of man in the guise of well-bred "gentlemen"? What does he mean by "gentlemen"?

It is very rare for interpreters of Nietzsche's thought to even wonder why he conceives of his noble, life-affirming, enduring, and inwardly powerful sovereign individuals as . . . gentlemen. Perhaps one of the reasons for this is that they have not taken the evidence for the intimate relation between the thought of Emerson and the philosophy of Nietzsche seriously enough. In his essay, "Manners," Emerson asserts that we ought to preserve "the heroic character" that the true "gentlemen" possesses. He makes his understanding of the term and the type quite clear.

> The gentleman is a man of truth, lord of his own actions . . . expressing that lordship in his behavior, not in any manner dependent and servile, either on persons, or opinions, or possessions. Beyond this fact of

truth and real force, the word denotes good nature or benevolence: manhood first, and then gentleness.[92]

This description of the authentic gentleman is an elaboration of his self-reliant individual of noble character who is independent and skeptical of external authority and public opinion. The true gentleman has a "sense of power" and "original energy," a "great range of affinity," the ability to stand "in his own right." He works by his own "methods," is "bold," and imbued with "animal spirits." The impressive gentlemen of Europe and Asia, Emerson writes, "have been of the strong type: Saladin, Sapor, the Cid, Julius Caesar, Scipio, Alexander, Pericles. . . ." Such individuals were natural aristocrats who were "working heroes." They are examples of the members of that recurring "minority" that perpetuates and sustains civilization. They attain a natural status in the gradations of rank that "depends on some symmetry in . . . structure." Such types exude "good breeding," "personal superiority." They have a "strong will" combined with "good sense and character."

Emerson's masterful gentlemen are "self-content" and have "composure." They project a strong sense of reality; they are courteous, have "noble manners," and possess a rare "graceful self-respect." Such self-assured individuals are aware of the "metaphysical isolation of man" and are taught independence by it. As he says elsewhere, these distinctive persons have a sense of *distance* and respect the separate nature of others. This, of course, is converted by Nietzsche, especially in *Beyond Good and Evil*, into an essential trait of those who would enhance "the type 'man' " and encourage the continual process of the "self-overcoming of man": a *Pathos der Distanz*.

Natural aristocrats are not often found in the actual social class of aristocrats. In fact, in their most complete form, they are yet to come. However, they are promised by the historical examples of the perfectibility of the human character. Emerson seems to have in mind such exemplars when he appeals to the prophecy of the gods in John Keats' "Hyperion":

As Heaven and Earth are fairer far
Than Chaos and blank Darkness. . . .
And as we show beyond that Heaven an Earth,
In form and shape compact and beautiful;

. . . .

So, on our heels a fresh perfection treads;
A power, more strong in beauty, born of us,

And fated to excel us, as we pass
In glory that old Darkness:
—for, 'tis the eternal law
That first in beauty should be first in might.

What is being proposed is a "romance of character" embodied
in those with a love of beauty who have "the power to embellish
the passing day." Emerson envisions men of the future whose
character shows through their every gesture and word; whose
moral quality emanates from their being and presence; whose nature rivals "the majority of the world." These romantically, aesthetically conceived "original and commanding" persons express a
"large, flowing, and magnanimous deportment" and, with a
"holiday spirit," stimulate the imagination by opening up vistas of
"new modes of existence."[93]

As Emerson embellishes his living works of art shaped by a
disciplining of the powers of nature, he fashions the "superhuman"
individuals he imagined earlier in his life. Practically all of the
traits and qualities that he ascribes to what we may rightfully call
his Übermenschen of the future are employed by Nietzsche in his attempt to create an appropriate image of the true "gentlemen."
When, in his notes, he characterizes the "joyful science" of the
conduct of life as the "Unity of minstrel, knight and free-spirit,"[94]
it is clear that he is thinking of the attributes of a truly "symmetrical" individual in a way that is indebted to the inspiration of
Emerson.

In his poetry, Emerson continues the preoccupation, which
runs through his journals and essays, with a burnished image of
man that his German disciple will later appropriate. The motto of
"Power," for example, could be inserted in *Thus Spoke Zarathustra*
without a hint of incongruity.

His tongue was framed to music,
And his hand was armed with skill;
His face was the mould of beauty,
And his heart the throne of will.

"Immoralism"

If Nietzsche's *Übermensch* is sometimes depicted as overly harsh or
as a bold 'immoralist', this is only a slight amplification of Emerson's romantic, metaphorical descriptions of his archetypal man.

In his enthusiasm for his "exempts" and their independent power and strength, he sometimes grants them license to go beyond the bounds of conventional morality.

To the extent that Emerson conveyed to Nietzsche the impressive image of powerful, energetic individuals who create their own laws and who may occasionally break the chains of public morality because of their superior nature, he must, ironically—given his lofty moral consciousness—be given some responsibility for having created the intellectual atmosphere in which a dangerous moral ambiguity could flourish. This is a feature of Emerson's thought that Nietzsche completely accepts and then, characteristically, exaggerates. And, *via* Nietzsche, Martin Heidegger, in *Being and Time,* seems to absorb and reflect this orientation in his delineation of a resolute, independent, forward-moving, authentically existing *Dasein* whose stern self-existence is constrained by no clearly expressed moral restrictions, whose way of being is given a covert sense of 'moral' validity in the absence of any enunciated moral principles.

Authentic existence is a way of being, a "how" of existence, that is *not* given ethical meaning by Heidegger even though this mode of being is described in moral tones. Man or *Dasein* is authentic, in large part, through the activation of a "potentiality-for-beinga-Self." Since Heidegger insists upon a descriptive approach to the being of man, there is no clarified or unambiguous "ought" for man and no moral circumscriptions are offered. Thus, the intensification of self-existence, for Heidegger, entails no moral obligation or constraints.

In an earlier study of an existential ethics,[95] I called attention to the way Heidegger appropriated central conceptions pertaining to authentic human existence from Kierkegaard and suggested that the moral neutrality of Heidegger's concept of authenticity veered away from the Kierkegaardian model. For Kierkegaard, an authentic existence is not possible unless the individual has lived through the mastered irony and discipline of the ethical stage of existence. Thus, the striving for moral excellence and an ironic self-mastery are central to Kierkegaard's version of authenticity, but are absent from Heidegger's ontology of authentic existence, from his "phenomenological description" of the being of *Dasein* or human existence. What was then a suspicion in my treatment of the ideal of authenticity is now a conviction that the moral ambiguity of Heidegger's projected authentic way of being is vulnerable to a morally nihilistic interpretation.

Granting the Kierkegaardian influence in regard to Heidegger's conception of authentic human existence, there are also strong indications that Heidegger's conception of an individuated, self-standing, self-existent *Dasein* includes a subdued, reduced, and compromised version of Nietzsche's image of the *Übermensch* that accentuates the disquieting absence of ethical limits or restraints on Nietsche's paragons. And, if my tracing of this thread of moral ambiguity or the implied transcendence of moral laws (in certain unspecified circumstances) back to Emerson is plausible, then he is also theoretically implicated, despite his deep concern with moral issues and values, in this unfortunate, easily abused, tendency of thought. There is no doubt that Emerson had transferred antinomianism from a religious context in which it was questionable to a secular context in which it is an invitation to immoralism.

Heidegger's description of *eigentlich Existenz* or "authentic existence" is an eclectic one that fuses Kierkegaard's earlier impressionistic phenomenology of a non-Christian ethical existence and some aspects of a tamer, formal, unpoetic version of Nietzsche's *Übermensch*. What Heidegger certainly did not realize was the extent to which Nietzsche had developed his aesthetic construction of the *Übermensch* according to Emerson's original specifications. Given Heidegger's rather disdainful personal attitude towards American thought and thinkers, there is a certain poetic justice in the realization that the centerpiece of his existential phenomenology, the reflective, realistic, and 'heroic' authentically existing *Dasein*, conserves and preserves the images, insights, and thought of an *American* poetic philosopher.

The Future Perfect

Again and again, in his prose and poetry, Emerson returns to the theme of "sacred persons" who are "silver admist the bronze population," who are perhaps only five or six out of a generation, and who are as "conspicuous as fire in the night." He has so much faith in these rare human beings that he believes that they can perform "some deed of the Impossible."[96] What may be taken to be Nietzsche's hyperbolic description of a godlike human being is, in point of fact, only a slight exaggeration of Emerson's visionary faith in the unlimited perfectibility of man.

Before Nietzsche said that life was endurable only because he anticipated the emergence of the *Übermensch*, before he lamented that there has not been a new god for two thousand years, Emerson had already expressed similar hopes and sentiments. In "Song of Nature" he asks:

> But he, the man-child glorious
> Where tarries he the while?
> The rainbow shines his harbinger,
> The sunset gleams his smile.
>
> . . . .
>
> My creatures travail and wait;
> His couriers come by squadrons,
> He comes not to the gate.

Emerson, then Nietzsche after him, awaited a "semigod" who would bring to earth what the former pictures, in his poem, "Spiritual Laws," as "heaven"—

> Forging through swart arms of Offence,
> The silver seat of Innocence.

In all probability, this particular image suggested to Nietzsche the liberating ideal of "the innocence of becoming." Emerson's new religion, like Nietzsche's religion of life, had, as one of its main tenets, the "affirmative principle" of the sacredness of life and the attainment of beatitude and redemption in the world of time and becoming. His personal and cultural ideal is one that is projected into the future, into an actuality deemed sacred. And this same ideal is continued, intensified, and amplified in Nietzsche's affirmative "Dionysian faith." Both Emerson and Nietzsche turned away from the traditional religious culture they had assimilated. They rejected the morality and the culture of Christianity. They decried the emerging practical, commercial, mass-culture that followed in the wake of the sedimentations of Christian values. And they turned away from the figure of Christ, whom they nonetheless respected as a teacher, for reasons that were quite similar.

Emerson does not uphold Christ as a prototype or model for his avatars because he lacked "cheerfulness." In a journal entry he asks himself: "Do you ask me if I would rather resemble Jesus than any other man? If I should say Yes, I should suspect myself of superstition."[97] In *Thus Spoke Zarathustra,* in "Of the Higher Men," Nietzsche, obviously referring to Christ, writes: "He—did not love sufficiently; otherwise, he should also have loved us, the laughers." Often enough, he repeats Emerson's criticism of Christian culture and attacks its morbid death-consciousness and its deadening "spirit of gravity," its lack of healthy cheerfulness. The accent on the negative in Christian culture and morality is deplored by both.

Emerson and Nietzsche set out on a voyage of discovery in uncharted and dangerous seas. They discovered, in a conceptual-imaginative way, exciting, new cultural horizons, unexplored territories of the mind. The ship on which they sailed, at different times and from different ports, might have been called, in Nietzsche's phrase, "The Great Perhaps."

Aside from elaborate depictions of sovereign individuals of the future that Nietzsche presents with increasing fervor, to the point at which his paladins begin to take on mythical proportions, there is another, more modest, version of the *Übermensch* that is often barely noticed. In *The Antichristian,* he had spoken of the "most spiritual men" who have a profound sense of the beautiful, who have an affirmative instinct, who see the world as "perfect," as models of the *Übermensch.* Such individuals are strong insofar as they can survive in the labyrinth of reflection, are severe with themselves, and have a natural asceticism of instinct and needs. They are venerable, amiable, and joyful. They "rule" others only by virtue of their personal power, because of what they are.[98] This vision of a *spiritual* aristocracy that has an attitude towards life and a discipline that are entirely unlike that of the general populace is, in fact, the final state of the formulation of what Nietzsche's paradigmatic persons will be like. It includes, among other things, Emerson's idea of a fundamental attitude of skepticism towards objective, global claims to truth combined with spiritual strength, integrity, and life-affirmation. Those who live such a life of self-discipline conjoined with an experimental attitude towards existence will seek to avoid the prisons of strong convictions and dogmatic claims to absolute truth.[99]

Self-existent independence, flexibility of thought, and a spontaneous openness to the future are the hallmarks of a genuine individual. Emerson's "religion of character" pertains to those who manifest "power and grace," who remain outside and above the mutable stream of public opinion, who are consistently independent of mind. Such persons, he believes, will be judicious thinkers who "allow full swing to . . . skepticism."[100] Nonetheless, they will have positive values and be capable of a "sacred affirmative" attitude towards life and existence.[101] It is obvious that this synthesis of skeptical habits of mind in regard to absolute claims to truth and a valuational affirmation of life—construed as "sacred"—that is central to Nietzsche's constructive philosophy of life is an Emersonian prescription.

The impermanence of ideas and theories is embraced by Emerson and so is the encouragement of new, bold generalizations, of an experimental attitude of mind. When Nietzsche avers that strong convictions are "prisons" and advocates an experimental attitude towards life and thought, he thereby replicates central ideas of Emerson. He certainly appropriated his belief that

> every thought is . . . a prison, every heaven is
> also a prison . . . we love the poet, the inventor,
> who in any form . . . has yielded us a new thought.
> He unlocks our chains and admits us to a new scene.[102]

A Practical Übermensch

There remains a final affinity between the Nietzschean image of a man "beyond-man" as he has been and Emerson the man and "the teacher" of practical wisdom. It is one that is based upon Nietzsche's profound admiration for the man himself and his orientation towards life.

In one of his numerous sketches of exceptional individuals, Nietzsche pays Emerson the highest compliment. He describes a more subdued version of the *Übermensch* in terms that strongly resemble his own image of Emerson's personal existence. Thus, he says that strength is often found in "simple, mild, and pleasant people" who have no desire to rule others overtly. The passion to rule others directly is actually "a sign of inward weakness." Genuinely powerful natures "dominate" others even though "they need not lift one finger," even if, during their lifetimes, "they bury themselves in a garden house."[103]

Even though it cannot be conclusively demonstrated that Nietzsche had Emerson in mind in this notation, he certainly was deeply impressed by the man and had enormous respect for him and his simply way of life. The reference to a solitary person leading a quiet life in a garden house strongly suggests Emerson because Nietzsche was quite familiar with his way of life. He was aware of his habit of remaining at home, when not presenting lectures or writing, working in his garden. In fact, Nietzsche once wrote to one of his friends indicating that, in order to be more self-sufficient, he planned to develop a vegetable garden. Even though he didn't do so, we see, once again, a strong desire to emulate his soul-brother. The allusion to those who rule by virtue of their presence and being is a typical Emersonian observation, one that may have been taken straight out of "The Transcendentalist." For there it is said that "strong spirits overpower those around them without effort."[104]

In a note from 1887, Nietzsche returns to the theme of the demythologized conception of the *Übermensch* and, once again, seems to allude to Emerson. He contends that the coming period of nihilism he predicted, a period during which the previous values that sustained Western man for millenia will no longer be vital, operative, or functional, will put vast numbers of people through an endurance test. Who will be strong enough to endure in a time in which nihilism is pervasive? First of all, such a crisis will promote "an order of rank" in accordance with the degree of spiritual strength individuals have and in accordance with the ability to preserve physical and mental health. Those who will be able to live through such a destabilizing and disturbing period in history must have inner power and strength. They will be the "most moderate" of people. Such individuals are distinguished by their lack of a need for "extreme articles of faith." They are able to face and accept the accidents, misfortunes, and incongruities of existence without psychological disintegration. Such moderate individuals are able, Nietzsche continues, to think of man-in-general as considerably reduced in value *without* becoming petty, small, mean-spirited, and weak because of this.

The survivors in a nihilistic world must be rich in surplus health and have an inner core of strength. In effect, such moderate, but exceptional, persons are "human beings who are *sure of their power* and represent the *attained* strength of humanity with conscious pride."[105] If we add to this, the world-affirming attitude of such a person, conjoined with the ability to look into the heart of darkness of existence, the resemblance of this modified version of the *Übermensch* to Emerson's projected self-image is uncanny.

We must remind ourselves that Emerson's "superhuman" sovereign individuals and Nietzsche's *Übermenschen* are *human* beings who are subject to suffering, subject to the vicissitudes of life and to the antithetical forces of society and nature. They are vulnerable to disease, injury, accident, and death. They are able to endure life in a chaotic universe because they *create* meaning and carry a core of meaning within themselves. Such individuals strive to overcome resistances and prize honesty, integrity, self-trust. These avatars force themselves, against their tender-hearted tendencies, to face the ugly and unpleasant facts of existence. The strength of such exemplars is more a matter of an inner strength of character than it is a public, muscular display of strength. What power they have is an assured sense of themselves, a "feeling of power" that does *not* depend upon dominance over others.[106]

Post Scriptum

The problem of the modern world, as Nietzsche saw it, is not that of the literal creation of an entirely new species that is *über-Mensch,* "beyond-man." The pressing problem is: what *type* of human being is Western culture going to cultivate and will as more valuable, as worthy of life, as the future hope of mankind? There have been historical instantiations of well-turned-out human beings. But these have been "lucky accidents." The aim should be to create the conditions for the possibility of the cultivation of such "higher types."

Whatever one may think of Nietzsche's dramatic and extensive elaboration on Emerson's preliminary sketches of an image of the man who would be beyond man as he has been and is, it is not an impossible cultural goal, especially as it is presented in the more subdued form of the ideal-type. Certainly, the exalted, hyperbolic, aesthetic *imago* of the *Übermensch* is projected as an article of faith in what is a remote, but realizable, possibility. The more realistic version of the type is attainable as a way of being that scrupulously avoids all forms of fanaticism; which fully accepts the antitheses, incongruities, and negativities of life; that values life as sacred despite its transitoriness, and is capable of enduring the absence of objective meaning or absolute truth by virtue of a profound sense of subjective meaning and inward self-assurance.

In his study of Nietzsche, Heidegger says that the thought of the beyond-man does not arise out of Nietzsche's "arrogance." He is certainly right about that. He then avers that this thought has its origin "in the innermost decisiveness by which Nietzsche submits himself to the essential necessity of consummate subjectivity."[107] Although I would agree with the image of the beyond-man as someone who intensifies subjectivity and accepts the intrinsic value of the self, in lieu of Heidegger's elaborate account of its origin we may substitute a simpler explanation: the image of the man beyond-man is an appropriation of Emerson's conception of such a being and the attempt to elaborate on such an image and include it in the multicolored tapestry of a philosophy of culture and life.

For both Emerson and Nietzsche, this complex being would be a self-conscious synthesis of antagonistic tendencies or traits and thereby would reflect the antagonistic characteristics of nature and existence. When Nietzsche suggests that the exceptional person would be a Julius Caesar "with the soul of Christ," he presents an epitome of a "synthetic" man that symbolizes precisely the vision of what man can be that Emerson sought, in many different ways, to portray.

A variation on the theme of the superlative individual is the ideal type of the aristocratic gentleman who would be outside and above all actual social classes. In an early lecture, "Aristocracy," Emerson described such a type in terms that Nietzsche understood very well and appropriated in a modified form. In the true "gentleman," he said, there should be "a secret homage to reality and love." There should reside in such a person "the steel hid under gauze and lace, under flowers and spangles."[108] This image of the civilized and graceful person who retains the "steel" of nature beneath the aesthetics of refinement is precisely the one that Nietzsche projects in his vision of the gentleman who will be a "noble" and "affirmative type" in whom there is a synthesis of gentleness and strength, grace and power.

Neither the American poet and essayist nor the philosopher who felt he was his soul-brother ever formulated a definitive or completely satisfying conception of their man "beyond-man." However, as we've seen, Nietzsche incorporates (and elaborates upon) virtually every characterization of Emerson's "sovereign individuals" into his image of the *Übermensch*.

Spiritual strength, naturalness, civilized gentleness, self-assurance, personal knowledge, courage, autonomy, nonconformity, energy, creative drive, integrity, self-respect, honesty, self-reliance, and self-trust—a scintillating array of positive traits embodied in individuals who unify spirit and nature, art and actuality. Hasn't this been one of the aspirational ideals of Western civilization? In spite of periods of decline, cynicism, decadence, numbing stasis, mediocrity, moral and intellectual regression, and nihilism, there is a recurring concern with the possibility of the perfectibility of man, with the possibility of living embodiments of excellence who would not manifest a distorted one-sidedness. Emerson often lamented the fact that people are, at best, parts of a possible complete or "synthetic man." And, as late as 1887, Nietzsche was still thinking about Emerson's lamentation. In his notes he remarks that "most men represent pieces and fragments of man: one has to add them up for a complete man to appear." Both for Emerson and Nietzsche such a complete person was not presented *only* as a literary, aesthetically embellished work of art.[109] It was the promise of a living, breathing human being, vulnerable to suffering and the hazards of chance, who would embody a wholeness that had not yet been attained.

Emerson and Nietzsche wanted to project a new image of what man may yet become, to project an immanent, realizable *telos* for mankind. Both accepted the polarities and antitheses of existence and wanted them to be manifested in a spiritually strong individual whose effort of willing could control the dialectical tensions in the self. Plato prescribed the control of the appetitive and spirited aspects of the self by reason. But Emerson and Nietzsche saw that man's natural history linked him with the dark, usually unconscious, ferocities of the natural world. They thought that there is health and vitality at the heart of instinctive life and looked upon a hypertrophy of reason as detrimental to growth, as dangerous as an unmitigated release of passions. The cognitive-affective multiplicity in the self must be willed into a dynamic unity.

Both Emerson and Nietzsche saw clearly the danger, for individuals and entire cultures, of the overdevelopment of a "Corinthian" refinement, the danger of the expression of crude, potentially lethal, natural drives, and the danger of a hyperrationality alienated from natural, instinctive energy, from life. And both deplored the emergence of, and the growing tyranny of, mass-consciousness and mass-values, the spread of conformity, the domination of public opinion, and the contagious mediocrity that would soon no longer be able to tolerate genuine independence, exceptions, or individuality.

Although he had no access to Emerson's journals, Nietzsche fully understood and shared his desire for an "exhibition of character" to the senses. Rather than despair of humanity entirely, he embraced Emerson's hope that "he that shall come shall do better" than Christ, than all of the soulful, spiritual figures who are remembered for their sacrifice, whose fate signifies "a great Defeat."[110]

Because Emerson and Nietzsche desired a "victory to the senses," they sought and hoped for a living embodiment of an aesthetico-ethical ideal and turned away impatiently from the ancient promise of a perfection that transcends the world of time and becoming. They hoped for a creative, self-creative, independent person who could escape the powerful nets of the all-too-human

and cultivate an affirmative, distinctively individual style of
thought and existence. They tried to teach mankind a difficult
faith, a faith far more demanding than a belief in a distant, perfect,
omniscient, but hidden and strangely silent, deity: a faith in man
and his capacity for self-overcoming.

Chapter 8 Notes

1. Cf. Julius Simon, *Ralph Waldo Emerson in Deutschland, 1851–1937.* A
"Dionysianism" has been found in Emerson by a number of literary critics, and even though he is not overtly anti-Christian, his post-Christian
sentiments emerge now and then. Thus, he chides the mystic Swedenborg
for clinging too much to the "Christian symbol" and for not seeing that
in a strong morality there are "innumerable christianities, humanities, di-
vinities . . ." ("Swedenborg; or, the Mystic," *Representative Men,* p. 130).
Elsewhere he asserts that "this great, overgrown, dead Christendom of
ours still keeps alive at least the name of a lover of mankind." Perhaps
"one day all men will be lovers, and every calamity will be dissolved in
the universal sunshine" ("Man the Reformer," *Selected Essays,* ed. Larzer
Ziff, p. 146).

2. "Divinity School Address," *PE,* p. 78. Erik Thurin exaggerates when
he states that Emerson's man of the future is "a kind of Antichrist." However, he correctly sees the relationship between the one Emerson called
"He That Shall Come" and Nietzsche's beyond-man. He also sees the
post-Christian nature of Emerson's "new teacher" and accurately points
out one reason why he adopted this stance. He cites Emerson's belief
"that Jesus failed to give us the 'victory to the senses' needed to prove
complete spirituality and godmanhood; he did well, but he that shall come
shall do better" (Erik Ingvar Thurin, *Emerson as Priest of Pan,* p. 216).

3. *Emerson in His Journals,* ed. Joel Porte, p. 129.

4. Cf. Stanley Hubbard, *Nietzsche und Emerson,* p. 73. Cf. also: G. W.
Allen, *Waldo Emerson,* p. 378. Allen suggests that Nietzsche's concept of
the beyond-man was influenced by Emerson's image of the "Over-Soul."
This is somewhat exaggerated. In his notes he refers to *"die Überseele"* as
Emerson's "truly highest cultural result." However, he characterizes it as
"a phantasm in which everything good and great has been worked up"
(*SW* 8:562). The name of Emerson's divinity, *die Überseele,* was given to it
by Nietzsche since the translator, Fabricus, translated it as *"höhere Seele"*
or "higher soul" in the *Versuche.* So it is possible that the *name* of the divinity made an imprint on Nietzsche's mind. One could say that he brings
the image of the Over-Soul down to earth and joins it to Emerson's prescriptions for human greatness. In his study of Emerson, Whicher pointed
out that beneath Emerson's " 'good conduct' theory of heroism . . . we

can see the sayer's envy of the doer's power. The Nietzschean Superman is already half-explicit in Emerson's hero" (Stephen Whicher, *Fate and Freedom* p. 69).

5. Stanley Hubbard, *Nietzsche und Emerson*. Cp. Charles Andler, *Nietzsche, sa vie et sa pensée*, vol. 1.

6. William Salter, *Nietzsche the Thinker*, p. 20.

7. Ibid., pp. 520–21.

8. "Power," *COL*, pp. 74–75. In "Schopenhauer as Educator" Nietzsche praises Cellini as a "man in whom everything, knowledge, desire, love, hate, strives towards a central point" (*SW* 1, *UB* 3:342). In his notes he describes Michel Angelo as an "ideal" that "only a man with the strongest and highest life-intensity" could match (*SW* 11:471).

9. Ibid., p. 54.

10. Walter Kaufmann, *Nietzsche*, p. 308.

11. *SW* 3, *FW* § 143, p. 490.

12. George J. Stack, *Lange and Nietzsche*, p. 153.

13. *SW* 1, *UB* 3, § 6, p. 385.

14. George J. Stack, "Eternal Recurrence, Again," *Philosophy Today*.

15. Richard Tuerk, "Emerson's *Nature*—Miniature Universe," *American Transcendental Quarterly*. Sherman Paul does not emphasize this aspect of Emerson's theory of correspondence, but he does stress the primacy of perception for access to nature, Emerson's organic conception of mind, and the convergence of the "rays of the universe" in the self (Sherman Paul, *Emerson's Angle of Vision*, pp. 220–23).

16. Laurence Buell correctly observed that "natural religion, which Transcendentalism essentially was, has strong pantheistic tendencies . . ." (*Literary Transcendentalism*, pp. 150–51).

17. Plato, *Gorgias*, p. 78.

18. *SW* 5, *JGB* § 9, pp. 21–22.

19. Kaufmann, *Nietzsche*, p. 193.

20. "Power," *COL*, p. 71.

21. *SW* 5, *JGB* § 23, p. 38.

22. Ibid., § 188, p. 108.

23. Ibid., § 201, pp. 121–23.

24. "Considerations By the Way," *COL*, p. 251.

25. "Notes," *COL*, p. 403.

26. *SW* 4, *AsZ* "Prologue" § 9, p. 25.

27. *Werke* (GOA), XV, p. 122.

28. "Considerations By the Way," *COL*, p. 262.

29. *SW* 4, *AsZ* "Prologue" § 3, p. 14.

30. "Power," *COL*, p. 72.

31. "Behavior," *COL*, pp. 181–86.

32. Ibid., p. 188.

33. *SW* 3, *FW* § 290, p. 530.

34. Kaufmann, *Nietzsche*, p. 252.

35. *SW* 4, *AsZ* II, p. 119.

36. Cf. Hubbard, *Nietzsche und Emerson*, p. 72.

37. "Circles," *PE*, p. 238.

38. *SW* 3, *FW* § 335, p. 563.

39. Ibid., § 349, p. 585.

40. Ibid., § 382, p. 637.

41. *SW* 13:41. Emerson expresses this same idea when he remarks that "the great Pan of old, who was clothed in a leopard skin to signify the beautiful variety of things and the firmament, his coat of stars,—was but the representative of thee, O rich and various Man" ("The Method of Nature," *RMNAL*, p. 196).

42. "The Transcendentalist," *PE*, pp. 98–100.

43. *SW* 9:471.

44. "Love," *EE*, p. 104.

45. "Character," *EE*, p. 255. Throughout *Thus Spoke Zarathustra*, a commanding presence is related to natural excellence. There Nietzsche also relies on Emerson's image of the commander commanded. The commanding individual, as in "Character" and "Manners," is described in terms of manner, style, and panache. In a note from 1884 Nietzsche refers to future philosophical legislators of values as "commanders"— *"Gebieteren"* (*The Will to Power*, § 972). In "Of Self-Overcoming," Zarathustra speaks, if in a loud voice, in the tone of Emerson. He exclaims that "he who cannot obey himself will be commanded," that "commanding is more difficult than obeying." He asks, "What persuades the living creature to obey and to command and to practice obedience even in [self-] commanding?" He answers in terms of what Emerson understood as "the search after power": "the will to power" (*Thus Spoke Zarathustra*, trans. R. J. Hollingdale, p. 137).

46. Ibid., pp. 258–59.

47. Ibid., p. 263.

48. Ibid., p. 266.

49. Ibid., pp. 266–67.

50. "Notes," *COL*, p. 399.

51. Ibid., p. 400.

52. Ibid., p. 424. Nonetheless, despite the negativities of finite existence, Emerson elsewhere condemns, in a proto-Nietzschean manner, the denigration of the finite world for the sake of the adulation of the infinite. "Statements of the infinite are . . . unjust to the finite, and blasphemous" ("The Method of Nature," *RMNAL*, p. 190).

53. *SW* 1, *GT* § 3, pp. 35–36.

54. *SW* 4, *AsZ* II, 152.

55. "Experience," *PE*, p. 280.

56. "Art," *EE*, p. 196.

57. Ibid., p. 201.

58. "Character," *EE*, p. 253.

59. "Power," *COL*, pp. 64–65.

60. "Culture," *COL*, p. 159.

61. "Behavior," *COL*, pp. 195–96.

62. "Character," *EE*, p. 263.

63. "Self-Reliance," *PE*, p. 153.

64. "The Transcendentalist," *PE*, p. 95.

65. *SW* 3, *M* § 556, p. 325.

66. *SW* 5, *JGB* § 284, p. 232.

67. Ibid.

68. "Solitude and Society," *PE*, pp. 390–93.

69. Ibid., p. 394.

70. In "Character" Emerson refers, with approval, to a theologian's admonition that a genuine "man can neither be praised nor insulted" (*EE*, p. 262). Nietzsche, considering the physical and mental suffering he endured, also thought of himself as "beyond praise or blame." The relation between solitary independence and gift-giving virtue is stressed in a recent study of *Zarathustra* without any reference to Emerson's similar notion and without reference to his subdued passion for "He that shall come." Cf. Laurence Lampert, *Nietzsche's Teaching*, pp. 74-75. Lampert makes two references to Emerson in this work. He relates the teaching of eternal recurrence to Nietzsche's early quotation of Emerson's vision of "a new center of tremendous forces" which would "revolutionize the entire system of human pursuits" (Ibid., p. 352n). Elsewhere, he cautiously relates Zarathustra's question—"Did not the world become perfect just now?"— to Emerson's reference to nature's perfection (Ibid., p. 355n).

71. "Experience," *PE*, p. 283.

72. "Considerations By the Way," *COL*, p. 247. The affirmation of life and the world, despite the antitheses and negativities of existence, as well as the recognition of the sacredness of *this* world, are central to Nietzsche's Dionysian faith. Cf. *SW* 13:266.

73. Ibid., p. 278.

74. "Beauty," *EE*, p. 282.

75. Ibid., p. 292.

76. Ibid., p. 303.

77. "Notes," *COL*, p. 412.

78. Ibid., p. 409.

79. "Art," *EE*, p. 197.

80. "Nature," (Second Series), *EE*, p. 300.

81. *Werke* (GOA), XI:220–21. Cp. John Wilcox, *Truth and Value in Nietzsche*, p. 27: ". . . there is not just morality, there are moralities, there are a great many types of value systems in the world, past and present. Philosophers, not aware of the extent to which this is true, have failed to understand the difficulty of providing a rational foundation for morality, and have wound up merely giving expression to the morality of their own time and place." Wilcox correctly points out that Nietzsche based morality on an aesthetic foundation—"taste" (Ibid., pp. 28–29).

82. *Werke* (GOA), XII:365.

83. *SW* 5, *GM* I, § xii, pp. 277–78.

84. *SW* 1, *UB* III, § vi, pp. 388–89.

85. *Werke* (GOA), XIV, p. 262.

86. "Politics," *EE*, pp. 310–11. Cp. Nietzsche's remark that it is not Manu (the ancient author of the Hindu lawbook, *The Laws of Manu*) who "separates from one another the predominantly spiritual type, the predominantly muscular and temperamental type, and the third type distinguished neither in the one nor the other, the mediocre type." It is "Nature" that does (*SW* 6, *A* § 57, p. 242).

87. "New England Reformers," *EE*, p. 344.

88. *SW* 4, *AsZ* "Prologue" § 5, p. 19.

89. *SW* 13:498. Cf. "Politics," *EE*, pp. 310–23 and "New England Reformers," *EE* pp. 338–58.

90. "Nominalist and Realist," *PE*, p. 325. We may add to these images that of the "central man," which Allen says is an ideal man in whom are found "the best attributes of a great many men." Allen correctly sees that Nietzsche was indebted to Emerson's concept of "the central man" for his concept of the "Over-Man." However, he claims that Nietzsche "confessed" this indebtedness. This is questionable. Questionable, too, is the belief that the concept of the "central man" is a Platonic one. For Plato refers to the Idea or form that is the concept of man-in-himself, a unitary, not a synthetic, pure concept. There *is* one Platonic concept of man that is similar to that of Emerson, though by no means identical to it. The just man in Plato's *Republic* is described as one in whom there is a harmony of the appetitive and spirited "parts of the soul" under the governance of reason. Cf. Gay Wilson Allen, *Waldo Emerson*, p. xv. Because Emerson and Nietzsche stress the antagonistic aspects of the self they insist upon the effort of willing required for self-mastery. In terms of Plato's psychology they give priority to the spirited aspect of the self.

91. *SW* 6, *EH* § 2, pp. 350–51.

92. "Manners," *EE*, p. 270.

93. Ibid., pp. 271–72.

94. *Werke* (GOA), XV:85. Cp. Allen, *Waldo Emerson*, p. 470. Allen believes that in *Ecce Homo* Nietzsche is referring to *Daybreak* when he speaks of the *gaya scienza* in Provençal culture. In fact, he is referring to *The Gay Science*.

95. George J. Stack, *Kierkegaard's Existential Ethics*.

96. "Notes," *COL*, p. 345.

97. Cf. Hubbard, *Nietzsche und Emerson*, p. 72. Cp. *SW* 4, *AsZ* § 16, "Of the Higher Men," p. 365.

98. *SW* 6, *A* § 57, pp. 243–44.

99. Thiele is wrong to hold that, in contrast to Nietzsche, Emerson lacked "skeptical probity" (*Friedrich Nietzsche and the Politics of the Soul*, p. 129).

100. "Worship," *COL*, p. 221.

101. "The Preacher," *Lectures and Biographical Sketches;* cited in "Notes," *COL*, p. 390.

102. "The Poet," *PE*, p. 259. Nietzsche reiterates this assertion a number of times and insists that "convictions are prisons." They serve to lull one into self-deception. Only as *means* in the service of "grand passion" are they fertile (*SW* 6:236).

103. *Werke* (GOA) XV:412. Cp. *Werke* XIV:66. In regard to the power possessed by such individuals, Nietzsche observes that "people do not hate a great man's presumptuousness insofar as he feels his strength, but because he wishes to prove it by injuring others, by dominating them. . . . This, as a rule, is even a proof of the absence of a secure sense of power" (*SW* 2, *MAM* § 588, p. 338). The reference to a garden house may have been suggested to him by Emerson himself. For in "Man the Reformer" he writes that "when I go into my garden with a spade, and dig a bed, I feel such an exhilaration and health that I discover that I have been defrauding myself . . . in letting others do for me what I should have done with my own hands" (*Selected Essays*, p. 135).

104. "The Transcendentalist," *PE*, p. 108.

105. *SW* 12:217.

106. *SW* 6, *A* § 3–4, pp. 170–71.

107. Martin Heidegger, *Nietzsche*, 3:227.

108. "Notes," *COL*, p. 358.

109. Alexander Nehamas' elegantly presented argument that Nietzsche created an "ideal character" analogous to a literary character in his image of the beyond-man would probably be applied to Emerson's depiction of sovereign individuals as well. That this character is Nietzsche himself undermines his capacity to admire others (including Emerson) and pulls the teeth of his concern with the possibility of the realization of *Übermenschlichkeit* in *Existenz*. Thus, in his *Nachlass* Nietzsche exclaims: "Goal! *To attain* the beyond-man for a moment. For that I'd suffer everything" (*SW* 10:167). As we've seen in the case of Emerson, because a thinker employs aesthetic images to represent an ideal, this does not mean that the creator of this ideal has abandoned belief in its concrete actualization. Nehamas' claim that Nietzsche was creating a self-portrait (a kind of *imago*) is not supported by the following confession in his notes: "I do not want to live *again*. How have I endured life? By creating. What has made me endure? The vision of the *Übermensch* who *affirms* life. I have tried to affirm it *myself*—ach!" (*SW* 10:137). Cf. Alexander Nehamas, *Nietzsche: Life as Literature*. pp. 165–69, 217–19, 230–34.

110. *The Journals and Miscellaneous Notebooks of Ralph Waldo Emerson*, VIII:228.

Select Bibliography:
Nietzsche and Emerson

Collected Works of Nietzsche

Friedrich Nietzsches Gesammelte Briefe. 5 vols. Leipzig: Insel Verlag, 1908–09.

Friedrich Nietzsche: Sämtliche Briefe. Kritische Studienausgabe. Edited by Giorgio Colli and Mazzino Montinari. 8 vols. Berlin and New York: Walter de Gruyter, 1975.

Friedrich Nietzsche: Sämtliche Werke. Kritische Studienausgabe. Edited by Giorgio Colli and Mazzino Montinari. 15 vols. Berlin and New York: Walter de Gruyter, 1980.

Nietzsche Briefwechsel. Kritische Gesamtausgabe. Edited by Giorgio Colli and Mazzino Montinari. Berlin: Walter de Gruyter, 1975–1992.

Nietzsches Werke. Grossoktavausgabe. 2nd ed. 19 vols. Leipzig: Kroner, 1901–13.

Nietzsches Werke. Kritische Gesamtausgabe. Edited by Giorgio Colli and Mazzino Montinari. 20 vols. (to date). Berlin: Walter de Gruyter, 1967ff.

Historisch-Kritische Gesamtausgabe. 5 vols. Munich: C. H. Beck, 1933–42.

Werke in drei Bänden. Edited by Karl Schlechta. 3 vols. Munich: Carl Hauser, 1964–66.

The Complete Works of Friedrich Nietzsche. Edited by Oscar Levy. 18 vols. 1909–1911. Reprint. New York: Russell and Russell, 1964.

Translations of Nietzsche's Works

Beyond Good and Evil. Translated by Walter Kaufmann. New York: Random House, 1966.

Daybreak. Translated by R. J. Hollingdale. London and New York: Cambridge University Press, 1982.

Ecce Homo. Translated by Clifton Fadiman. In *The Philosophy of Nietzsche*. New York: Modern Library, n.d.

Human, All-Too-Human. Part I. Translated by Helen Zimmern. *The Complete Works of Friedrich Nietzsche*, vol. 6. New York: Russell and Russell, 1964.

Human, All-Too-Human. Part II. Translated by Paul Cohn. *The Complete Works of Friedrich Nietzsche*, vol. 7. New York: Russell and Russell, 1964.

The Birth of Tragedy and *The Genealogy of Morals*. Translated by Francis Golffing. New York: Doubleday, 1956.

The Gay Science. Translated by Walter Kaufmann, New York: Vintage, 1974.

The Will to Power. Translated by Walter Kaufmann and R. J. Hollingdale, New York: Vintage, 1967.

Thus Spoke Zarathustra. Translated by R. J. Hollingdale. New York: Penguin, 1969.

Twilight of the Gods and *The Anti-Christ*. Translated by R. J. Hollingdale. New York: Penguin, 1968.

Untimely Meditations. Translated by R. J. Hollingdale. London and New York: Cambridge University Press, 1983.

Collected Works of Emerson

The Complete Works of Ralph Waldo Emerson. Edited by Edward W. Emerson. 12 vols. Boston, 1903–04.

The Journals of Ralph Waldo Emerson. Edited by Edward W. Emerson and Waldo Emerson Forbes. 10 vols. Boston, 1909–14.

The Journals and Miscellaneous Notebooks of Ralph Waldo Emerson. Edited by William Gilman et al. 14 vols. Cambridge, 1960f.

Additional Works of Emerson

Society and Solitude. Boston, 1889.

Representative Men, Nature, Addresses and Lectures. Boston and New York, 1876.

The Early Lectures of Ralph Waldo Emerson, 1833–1842. Edited by Stephen E. Whicher, Robert E. Spiller, and Wallace E. Williams. 3 vols. Cambridge, 1959.

Select Bibliography: Other Authors

Books

Allen, Gay Wilson. *Waldo Emerson: A Biography*. New York: Viking Press, 1981.

Allison, David, ed. *The New Nietzsche*. Cambridge: MIT Press, 1977.

Andler, Charles. *Nietzsche, sa vie et sa pensée*. 6 vols. Paris: Bossard, 1920–31.

The Annals of America. 20 vols. Chicago: Encyclopaedia Britannica, Inc., 1976.

Baumgarten, Eduard. *Das Vorbild Emersons im Werk und Leben Nietzsches*. Heidelberg: Karl Winter, 1957.

Bernoulli, Carl A., Oehler, Richard, eds. *Nietzsches Briefwechsel mit Franz Overbeck*. Leipzig: Insel, 1916.

Bernstein, John Andrew. *Nietzsche's Moral Philosophy*. Cranbury, N.J.: Associated University Presses, 1987.

Bloom, Harold. *Agon*. Oxford: Oxford University Press, 1982.

Brandes, Georg. *Friedrich Nietzsche*. 1914, Reprint. New York: Haskell House, 1972.

Breazeale, Daniel, trans. and ed. *Philosophy and Truth: Selections from Nietzsche's Notebooks of the Early 1870's*. Atlantic Highlands, N.J.: Humanities Press, 1979.

Buell, Laurence. *Literary Transcendentalism*. Ithaca: Cornell University Press, 1973.

Burroughs, John. *Emerson and His Journals*. Boston: Houghton Mifflin, 1929.

Cavell, Stanley. *Conditions Handsome and Unhandsome: The Constitution of Emersonian Perfectionism*. La Salle: Open Court, 1990.

Cheyfitz, Eric. *The Trans-Parent: Sexual Politics in the Language of Emerson*. Baltimore: Johns Hopkins University Press, 1981.

Chinard, Gilbert. *The Literary Bible of Thomas Jefferson*. Baltimore: Johns Hopkins University Press, 1928.

Derrida, Jacques. *Spurs: Nietzsche's Styles/Éperons: Les Styles de Nietzsche*. Translated by Barbara Harlow. Chicago and London: University of Chicago Press, 1979.

Ellison, Julie. *Emerson's Romantic Style*. Princeton: Princeton University Press, 1984.

Frothingham, Octavius B. *Transcendentalism in New England*. 1876, Reprint. Gloucester, MA : Peter Smith, 1965.

Giamatti, A. Bartlett. *The University and the Public*. New York: Atheneum, 1981.

Heidegger, Martin. *Nietzsche*. Translated by D. F. Krell, J. Stambaugh, and F. A. Capuzzi. 4 vols. San Francisco: Harper and Row, 1979–87.

Hubbard, Stanley. *Nietzsche und Emerson*. Basel: Verlag für Recht und Gesellschaft, 1958.

Hughes, Gertrude R. *Emerson's Demanding Optimism*. Baton Rouge: Louisiana State University Press, 1984.

Jaspers, Karl. *Nietzsche*. Translated by C. F. Walraff and F. J. Schmitz. Tucson: University of Arizona Press, 1965.

Jonas, Hans. *The Phenomenon of Life*. New York: Dell Publishing, 1966.

Kaufmann, Walter. *Nietzsche: Philosopher, Psychologist, Antichrist*. 3rd ed. New York: Vintage, 1968.

Kofman, Sarah. *Nietzsche et la métaphore*. Paris: Payot, 1972.

Konvitz, M. R. ed. *The Recognition of Ralph Waldo Emerson*. Ann Arbor: University of Michigan Press, 1972.

Lampert, Laurence. *Nietzsche's Teaching*. New Haven: Yale University Press, 1986.

Lange, Friedrich A. *History of Materialism*. Translated by Ernest C. Thomas. 3 vols. Boston: Osgood and Co., 1880.

Magnus, Bernd. *Nietzsche's Existential Imperative*. Bloomington: Indiana University Press, 1978.

McGiffert, Arthur C. *A History of Christian Thought*. 2 vols. New York: Charles Scribner's Sons, 1932–33.

Megill, Allan. *Prophets of Extremity: Nietzsche, Heidegger, Foucault, Derrida*. Berkeley: University of California Press, 1985.

Meyer, Richard M. *Nietzsche: seine Leben und seine Werke*. Munich: Beck, 1913.

Michael, John. *Emerson and Skepticism: The Cipher of the World*. Baltimore: Johns Hopkins University Press, 1988.

Nehamas, Alexander. *Nietzsche: Life as Literature*. Cambridge: Harvard University Press, 1985.

Neufeldt, Leonard. *The House of Emerson*. Lincoln, NE: University of Nebraska Press, 1983.

O'Hara, Daniel, ed. *Why Nietzsche Now?* Bloomington: Indiana University Press, 1985.

Packer, B. L. *Emerson's Fall*. New York: Continuum, 1982.

Parrington, Vernon. *Main Currents of American Thought.* 3 vols. New York: Harcourt Brace Jovanovich, 1927.

Paul, Sherman. *Emerson's Angle of Vision.* Cambridge: Harvard University Press, 1952.

Plato. *Gorgias.* Translated by W. Hamilton. Middlesex: Penguin Books, 1971.

Podach, Erich. *Friedrich Nietzsche's Werke der Zusammenbruchs.* Heidelberg: Kampmann, 1961.

Porte, Joel, ed. *Emerson in His Journals.* Cambridge: Harvard University Press, 1982.

Riley, Woodbridge. *American Thought: From Puritanism to Pragmatism and Beyond.* New York: Holt, 1915.

Rittelmeyer, *Friedrich Nietzsche und die Religion.* Ulm: H. Kerler, 1904.

Robinson, David. *Apostle of Culture: Emerson as Preacher and Lecturer.* Philadelphia: University of Pennsylvania Press, 1982.

Salter, William. *Nietzsche the Thinker.* New York: Holt, 1917.

Santayana, George. *Winds of Doctrine.* New York: Charles Scribner's Sons, 1957.

Schacht, Richard. *Nietzsche.* Boston: Routledge, 1983.

Schneider, Herbert W. *A History of American Philosophy.* New York: Columbia University Press, 1946.

Schutte, Ofelia. *Beyond Nihilism: Nietzsche Without Masks.* Chicago: University of Chicago Press, 1984.

Schweitzer, Albert. *Indian Thought and Its Development.* Translated by C. Russell. 1936, Reprint. Gloucester, MA: Peter Smith, 1962.

Simon, Julius. *Ralph Waldo Emerson in Deutschland 1851–1937.* Berlin: Junker und Dünnhaupt, 1937.

Solomon, Robert C. and Higgins, Kathleen M., eds. *Reading Nietzsche.* New York and Oxford: Oxford University Press, 1988.

Soren Kierkegaard's Journals and Papers. Edited and translated by H. V. Hong and E. Hong. 7 vols. Bloomington: Indiana University Press, 1967–78.

Stack, George J. *Kierkegaard's Existential Ethics.* University, AL: University of Alabama Press, 1977.

———. *Lange and Nietzsche.* New York and Berlin: Walter de Gruyter, 1983.

Stambaugh, Joan. *Nietzsche's Thought of Eternal Return.* Baltimore: Johns Hopkins University Press, 1972.

Staten, Henry. *Nietzsche's Voice.* Ithaca: Cornell University Press, 1990.

Thiele, Leslie P. *Friedrich Nietzsche and the Politics of the Soul.* Princeton: Princeton University Press, 1990.

Thurin, Erik. *Emerson as Priest of Pan.* Lawrence, KS: Regents Press of Kansas, 1981.

Vaihinger, Hans. *The Philosophy of 'As-If'.* Translated by C. K. Ogden. London: Routledge, 1924.

Van Veer, David. *Emerson's Epistemology.* Cambridge: Cambridge University Press, 1986.

Wellek, René. *Confrontations: Studies in the Intellectual and Literary Relations between Germany, England, and the United States in the Nineteenth Century.* Princeton: Princeton University Press, 1965.

Whicher, Stephen. *Freedom and Fate: An Inner Life of Ralph Waldo Emerson.* Philadelphia: University of Pennsylvania Press, 1953.

White, Alan. *Within Nietzsche's Labyrinth.* New York and London: Routledge, 1990.

Wilcox, John. *Truth and Value in Nietzsche.* Ann Arbor: University of Michigan Press, 1974.

Yannella, Donald. *Ralph Waldo Emerson.* Boston: Twayne, 1982.

Yoder, R. A. *Emerson and the Orphic Poet in America.* Berkeley and Los Angeles: University of California Press, 1978.

Zaehner, R. C. *Mysticism Sacred and Profane.* New York: Oxford University Press, 1961.

Ziff, Larzer, ed. *Ralph Waldo Emerson: Selected Essays.* New York: Penguin, 1982.

Articles

Cavell, Stanley, "Being Odd/Getting Even," *Salmagundi* 67 (1985): 97–128.

———, "Emerson, Coleridge, Kant," *Post-Analytic Philosophy* (1985): 84–107.

———, "Thinking of Emerson," *New Literary History* 11 (1979): 166–76.

Foot, Philippa, "Nietzsche's Immoralism," *The New York Review of Books* 38 (1991): 18–22.

Foster, Grace R. "The Natural History of the Will," *American Scholar* 15 (1946): 277–87.

Gilman, S. L. "Nietzsches Emerson Lektüre: Eine unbekannte Quelle," *Nietzsche-Studien* 9 (1980): 406–31.

Hummel, Hermann, "Emerson and Nietzsche," *The New England Quarterly* 19 (1946): 63–84.

Rorty, Richard, "Professionalized Philosophy and Transcendentalist Culture," *Georgia Review* 30 (1976): 757–71.

Salaquarda, Jörg, "Der Standpunkt des Ideals bei Lange und Nietzsche," *Studi Tedeschi* 29 (1979): 133–60.

———, "Nietzsche und Lange," *Nietzsche-Studien* 7 (1978): 236–48.

Schottlaender, Rudolf, "Two Dionysians: Emerson and Nietzsche," *South Atlantic Quarterly* 39 (1940): 330–43.

Smith, Henry, "Emerson and the Problem of Vocation," *The New England Quarterly* 12 (1939): 52–67.

Stack, George J. "Eternal Recurrence, Again," *Philosophy Today* 28 (1984): 242–64.

———, "Marx and Nietzsche: A Point of Affinity," *The Modern Schoolman* 9 (1983): 23–39.

—————, "Nietzsche and Boscovich's Theory of Nature," *Pacific Philosophical Quarterly* 62 (1981): 69–87.

—————, "Nietzsche's Antinomianism," *Nietzsche-Studien* 20 (1991): 109–33.

—————, "Nietzsche's Myth of the Will to Power," *Dialogos* 17 (1982): 27–49.

Tuerk, Richard, "Emerson's *Nature*—Miniature Universe," *American Transcendental Quarterly* 1 (1969): 110–13.

Index

A Note About the Author

George J. Stack is Professor of philosophy and chairperson of the Department of Philosophy at SUNY Brockport. He lives in Brockport (a suburb of Rochester, New York). He is the author of several books in philosophy and numerous articles and reviews.